SAS/CONNECT Software
Usage and Reference

Version 6
Second Edition

SAS Institute Inc.
SAS Campus Drive
Cary, NC 27513

The correct bibliographic citation for this manual is as follows: SAS Institute Inc., *SAS/CONNECT® Software: Usage and Reference, Version 6, Second Edition*, Cary, NC: SAS Institute Inc., 1994. 368 pp.

SAS/CONNECT® Software: Usage and Reference, Version 6, Second Edition

Copyright © 1994 by SAS Institute Inc., Cary, NC, USA.

ISBN 1-55544-625-6

All rights reserved. Printed in the United States of America. No part of this publication may be reproduced, stored in a retrieval system, or transmitted, in any form or by any means, electronic, mechanical, photocopying, or otherwise, without the prior written permission of the publisher, SAS Institute Inc.

Restricted Rights Legend. Use, duplication, or disclosure by the U.S. Government is subject to restrictions as set forth in subparagraph (c)(1)(ii) of the Rights in Technical Data and Computer Software clause at DFARS 252.227-7013.

SAS Institute Inc., SAS Campus Drive, Cary, North Carolina 27513.

1st printing, August 1994

The SAS® System is an integrated system of software providing complete control over data access, management, analysis, and presentation. Base SAS software is the foundation of the SAS System. Products within the SAS System include SAS/ACCESS®, SAS/AF®, SAS/ASSIST®, SAS/CALC®, SAS/CONNECT®, SAS/CPE®, SAS/DMI®, SAS/EIS®, SAS/ENGLISH®, SAS/ETS®, SAS/FSP®, SAS/GRAPH®, SAS/IMAGE®, SAS/IML®, SAS/IMS-DL/I®, SAS/INSIGHT®, SAS/LAB®, SAS/NVISION®, SAS/OR®, SAS/PH-Clinical®, SAS/QC®, SAS/REPLAY-CICS®, SAS/SESSION®, SAS/SHARE®, SAS/STAT®, SAS/TOOLKIT®, SAS/TRADER®, SAS/TUTOR®, SAS/DB2™, SAS/GEO,™ SAS/GIS,™ SAS/PH-Kinetics,™ SAS/SHARE*NET,™ SAS/SPECTRAVIEW,™ and SAS/SQL-DS™ software. Other SAS Institute products are SYSTEM 2000® Data Management Software, with basic SYSTEM 2000, CREATE,™ Multi-User,™ QueX,™ Screen Writer,™ and CICS interface software; InfoTap™ software; NeoVisuals® software; JMP®, JMP IN®, JMP Serve®, and JMP *Design*® software; SAS/RTERM® software; and the SAS/C® Compiler and the SAS/CX® Compiler; and Emulus™ software. MultiVendor Architecture™ and MVA™ are trademarks of SAS Institute Inc. SAS Institute also offers SAS Consulting®, SAS Video Productions®, Ambassador Select®, and On-Site Ambassador™ services. *Authorline*®, *Observations*®, *SAS Communications*®, *SAS Training*®, *SAS Views*®, the SASware Ballot®, and *JMPer Cable*® are published by SAS Institute Inc. The SAS Video Productions logo and the Books By Users SAS Institute's Author Service logo are registered service marks and the Helplus logo is a trademark of SAS Institute Inc. All trademarks above are registered trademarks or trademarks of SAS Institute Inc. in the USA and other countries. ® indicates USA registration.

IBM®, DB2®, OS/2®, Presentation Manager®, PS/2®, VM/ESA®, ACF/VTAM,™ and MVS/ESA™ are registered trademarks or trademarks of International Business Machines Corporation. ORACLE® is a registered trademark or trademark of Oracle Corporation.

The Institute is a private company devoted to the support and further development of its software and related services.

Other brand and product names are registered trademarks or trademarks of their respective companies.

Doc P19, 071194

Contents

Reference Aids   ix

Credits   xi

Part 1 · Introduction   1

Chapter 1 · What Is SAS/CONNECT Software?   3

Introduction   3

Using SAS/CONNECT in a Client/Server Environment   3

How SAS/CONNECT Works with the SAS System   8

Where to Go From Here   10

Chapter 2 · Access Methods for SAS/CONNECT Software   11

Introduction   11

Program-to-Program Communications   11

Terminal-Based Communications   12

Summary of Available Connections   13

Part 2 · Using SAS/CONNECT Software   15

Chapter 3 · Ways to Use SAS/CONNECT Software   17

Introduction   18

Using Compute Services with SAS/CONNECT   18

Using Remote Library Services (RLS)   29

Using Data Transfer Services with SAS/CONNECT   40

Combining Compute Services and Data Transfer Services   52

Combining RLS and Data Transfer Services   58

Chapter 4 · Starting and Stopping SAS/CONNECT Software   61

Introduction   61

Using PMENUS to Start and Stop SAS/CONNECT   62

When to Use a Script   64

Basic Script Functions   64

Using a Script to Start and Stop SAS/CONNECT   65

Shortcuts for Starting and Stopping SAS/CONNECT   68

General Script Statement Rules   71

Writing Simple Scripts for Signing On and Signing Off 71

Debugging a Script 78

Sample Scripts 79

SCL Functions Used with SAS/CONNECT 85

Chapter 5 · Using Break Windows 87

Introduction 87

SAS/CONNECT Attention Handler Window 87

Communication Services Break Handler Window 88

When a Host Message Interrupts SAS/CONNECT 90

Chapter 6 · The APPC Access Method 93

Introduction 93

Available Connections 94

System Requirements for CMS 94

System Requirements for MVS 97

System Requirements for OS/2 99

System Requirements for Windows 32s 101

System Requirements for VSE 102

Starting SAS/CONNECT with the APPC Access Method 104

Examples of Signing on Using the APPC Access Method 105

Troubleshooting 110

Chapter 7 · The DECnet Access Method 115

Introduction 115

Available Connections 115

Requirements for OpenVMS 115

Requirements for Windows 3.x 116

Starting SAS/CONNECT with the DECnet Access Method 116

Why Script Files Are Not Needed 117

Using the SAS$CONN.COM Command File for OpenVMS Connections 118

Troubleshooting 118

Chapter 8 · The TCP/IP and TELNET Access Methods 121

Introduction 121

Available Connections for TCP/IP 122

System Requirements for TCP/IP 122

Starting SAS/CONNECT with the TCP/IP Access Method 125

Using Script Files with the TCP/IP Access Method   126

Available Connections for TELNET   126

System Requirements for TELNET   127

Using a Script with the TELNET Access Method   127

Troubleshooting   127

Chapter 9 · The NetBIOS Access Method   131

Introduction   131

Available Connections   131

System Requirements   132

Starting SAS/CONNECT with the NetBIOS Access Method   133

Why Script Files Are Not Needed   133

Environment Variables   134

Troubleshooting   135

Chapter 10 · Using a Spawner Program   137

Introduction   137

Syntax   137

File and Security Options   138

Ending the Spawner Program   140

Chapter 11 · EHLLAPI and 3270 Access Methods   141

Introduction   141

Available Connections   141

Requirements for OS/2   142

Requirements for Windows 32s   142

Requirements for Windows 3.x 142

Starting SAS/CONNECT with the EHLLAPI Access Method   143

Sample Scripts for EHLLAPI   143

Environment Variables for Windows and OS/2   143

Troubleshooting   144

Chapter 12 · Using Protocol Converters and TTY with the ASYNC Access Method   147

Introduction   147

Using a Protocol Converter   148

Using TTY with the ASYNC Access Method   149

The TTY.EXE Program   150

Using Scripts with TTY.EXE 153

Troubleshooting 155

Chapter 13 · General Tips and Troubleshooting 159

Introduction 159

Signing On 159

OS/2 Support 161

SAS/GRAPH Software 162

Miscellaneous Problems 164

Part 3 · SAS/CONNECT Software Syntax and Procedures 171

Chapter 14 · System Options, Statements, Commands, and SCL Functions 173

Introduction 173

System Options 173

Statements and Commands 187

SCL Functions: COMAMID, RLINK, RSESSION, RSTITLE 201

Chapter 15 · The DOWNLOAD Procedure 207

Introduction 207

Syntax for the DOWNLOAD Procedure 208

Syntax for PROC DOWNLOAD 208

Syntax for the WHERE Statement 215

Syntax for the EXCLUDE Statement 216

Syntax for the SELECT Statement 217

Syntax for the TRANTAB Statement 218

Using the MEMTYPE= Option 219

Using the ENTRYTYPE= Option 220

Compiling PROGRAM Entries 223

Transfer Status Windows 223

The BINARY Option 224

PROC DOWNLOAD Output 225

Defining Librefs and Filerefs 226

Non-English Keyboards 226

General Tips for DOWNLOAD 227

Chapter 16 · The UPLOAD Procedure 229

Introduction 229

Syntax for the UPLOAD Procedure 230

Syntax for the PROC UPLOAD Statement 230

Syntax for the WHERE Statement 237

Syntax for the EXCLUDE Statement 238

Syntax for the SELECT Statement 239

Syntax for the TRANTAB Statement 240

Using the MEMTYPE= Option 241

Using the ENTRYTYPE= Option 242

Compiling PROGRAM Entries 245

Transfer Status Windows 245

The BINARY Option 246

PROC UPLOAD Output 247

Defining Librefs and Filerefs 248

Non-English Keyboards 248

General Tips for UPLOAD 249

Chapter 17 · Script Statements 251

Introduction 251

Statement Descriptions 253

Part 4 · Appendices 281

Appendix 1 · Using the Services of SAS/CONNECT and SAS/SHARE Software 283

Introduction 283

Differences in Implementation Between a Single-user Server and a Multi-user Server 283

Appendix 2 · ASCII and EBCDIC Character Set Translation 285

Introduction 285

Translation Tables 285

Appendix 3 · Details for Micro-to-Host Link Releases 289

Introduction 289

Hardware Requirements for the Micro-to-Host Link Connection 290

Software Requirements 290

Required SAS Software 293

Scripts and Script Statements for Micro-to-Host Link Access Methods   295

Checklist for Release 6.04 on PC DOS   297

ASYNC Terminal Emulator Program   298

3270 Keyboard Translation Tables   300

Creating a Keyboard Translation Table   303

Using a Keyboard Translation Table   306

Sample Keyboard Translation Table   306

Micro-to-Host Link Information for the Examples in This Book   312

Break Window for Release 6.04   316

Using Protocol Converters with Micro-to-Host Link Releases   321

System Commands, Options, and Reference Tables for Micro-to-Host Link Releases   322

Troubleshooting Problems in Micro-to-Host Link Releases   331

Glossary   337

Index   355

Reference Aids

Displays

4.1	SAS System `Locals` *Option*	62
4.2	The Signon Window	63
5.1	The SAS/CONNECT Attention Handler Window	88
5.2	The Communication Services Break Handler Window	89
15.1	Transfer Status Window for Downloading a SAS Data Set	224
15.2	Transfer Status Window for Downloading an External File	224
16.1	Transfer Status Window for Uploading a SAS Data Set	246
16.2	Transfer Status Window for Uploading an External File	246
A3.1	The BREAK Window for Release 6.04	317

Figures

1.1	Components of Remote Data Services	4
1.2	Compute Services with RSUBMIT Processing Model	4
1.3	Remote SQL Pass-Through Services	6
1.4	Data Transfer Services Processing Model	7
1.5	RLS Processing Model	8
3.1	Accessing a Remote Data Library	34
3.2	Combined Compute and Data Transfer Services Processing Model	52
3.3	Combined RLS and Data Transfer Services Processing Model	58
17.1	3270 Function Keys and Mnemonics	275
A3.1	U.S. Typewriter Keyboard Layout: Characters	301
A3.2	U.S. Typewriter Keyboard Layout: Scan Codes	301
A3.3	Translation Entry Fields	303
A3.4	A Sample Nonstandard Keyboard: The AZERTY Keyboard	304
A3.5	A Sample Keyboard Translation Table, CUTMODE.XLT	307

Output

15.1	SAS Log Messages from the DOWNLOAD Procedure	225
16.1	SAS Log Messages from the UPLOAD Procedure	247

Tables

2.1	Available Connections	14
14.1	REMOTE= and COMAMID= System Options Local and Remote Hosts	174
15.1	Catalog Entries That Can Be Downloaded	221
16.1	Catalog Entries That Can Be Uploaded	243
17.1	Summary of Script Statements	251
17.2	ASCII Character Mnemonics for ASYNC Connections	272
17.3	Maximum Values for Screen Rows and Columns by 3270 Model Number	277
A2.1	ASCII-to-EBCDIC Translation Table	286
A2.2	EBCDIC-to-ASCII Translation Table	287
A3.1	Summary of Scripts and Options	326
A3.2	Summary of Scripts and Options for Release 6.04 under DOS on the Local Host	330

Credits

Documentation

Design and Production   Design, Production, and Printing Services

Style Programming   Publications Technology Department

Technical Review   Andrea Ball, Bill Brideson, Stephanie Creech, Phillip Anthony Dean, Jr., Cheryl A. Garner, Donald J. Henderson, Glenn Horton, Steve Jenisch, Paul M. Kent, Janice Kolb, Elizabeth C. Langston, Brian R. Perkinson, Joseph G. Slater, Keith Wagner, Jack S. Wallace

Writing and Editing   N. Elizabeth Malcom, Carla Kary Merrill

Software

Many people have contributed to the SAS/CONNECT product and the associated access methods. Developers and testers are listed here.

Compute Services, Data Transfer Services, and Remote Library Services   Bill Brideson, Michael G. Carney, Stephanie Creech, Cheryl A. Garner, Brian R. Perkinson

Communications Access Methods   Daniel C. Berry, Phillip Anthony Dean, Jr., Glenn Horton, Steve Jenisch, Paul M. Kent, David Kolb, Joseph G. Slater

Testing   Andrea Ball, Giselle Cannon, Elizabeth C. Langston, Heesun Park, Stephanie Tysinger

Support Groups

Technical Support   Susan P. Horton, Fran Insley, Janice Kolb, Richard D. Lee

Quality Assurance   Chuck Heatherly, Allen S. Malone, Ruth Meadows

Part 1
Introduction

Chapter 1	What Is SAS/CONNECT® Software?
Chapter 2	Access Methods for SAS/CONNECT® Software

Chapter 1 What Is SAS/CONNECT® Software?

Introduction 3

Using SAS/CONNECT in a Client/Server Environment 3
Compute Services with RSUBMIT in the SAS Client/Server Environment 4
Compute Services with Remote SQL Pass-Through in the Client/Server Environment 5
Data Transfer Services in the SAS Client/Server Environment 6
Remote Library Services in the SAS Client/Server Environment 8

How SAS/CONNECT Works with the SAS System 8
Making a Connection with SAS/CONNECT 9

Where to Go From Here 10

Introduction

SAS/CONNECT software is a cooperative processing product that provides client/server services between a local SAS session and one or more remote SAS sessions. This chapter introduces the general capabilities of SAS/CONNECT.

Using SAS/CONNECT in a Client/Server Environment

The client/server environment of SAS/CONNECT gives you access to the files, hardware resources, and SAS software on various remote hosts to use with a SAS session on the local host. You can connect to multiple remote SAS sessions, process applications, and access data in any of the remote sessions or in your local SAS session. With these capabilities, you use your computing resources to their best advantage by distributing SAS processing to the most appropriate machine.

The client/server capabilities of SAS/CONNECT also enable you to combine data from two seemingly incompatible systems into one data set. For example, you can access data in an ORACLE database on one system and an Rdb/VMS database on another system and combine them on your local host.

SAS/CONNECT provides two sets of services to enable the development of distributed applications:

compute services
> These services give you access to all of the computing resources on your network.

remote data services
> These services give you access to all of your data regardless of where they are stored. As Figure 1.1 illustrates, remote data services can be further divided into *data transfer services* and *remote library services*.

Figure 1.1
Components of Remote Data Services

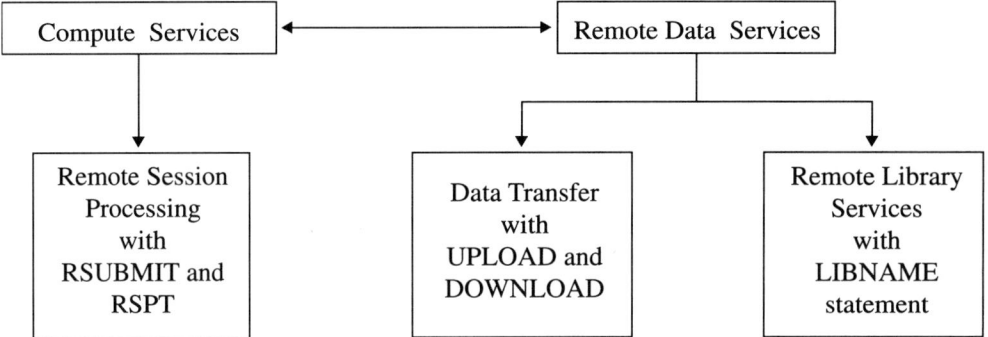

Compute services and remote data service are by no means mutually exclusive. The degree to which each is applied and the most beneficial combination of services are completely determined by the needs and goals of individual applications. Each set of services has a fairly defined set of benefits and drawbacks. By matching these characteristics to the characteristics of your data and your application needs, you can determine how best to combine these services to write the most efficient distributed application. Most often, the best implementation of a distributed application incorporates a combination of these services.

Compute Services with RSUBMIT in the SAS Client/Server Environment

Compute services take advantage of remote computing resources (hardware, software, and data) to execute an application more efficiently by maximizing the use of all computing resources. As Figure 1.2 illustrates, these services enable you to move some or all portions of an application's processing to a remote machine.

Figure 1.2
Compute Services with RSUBMIT Processing Model

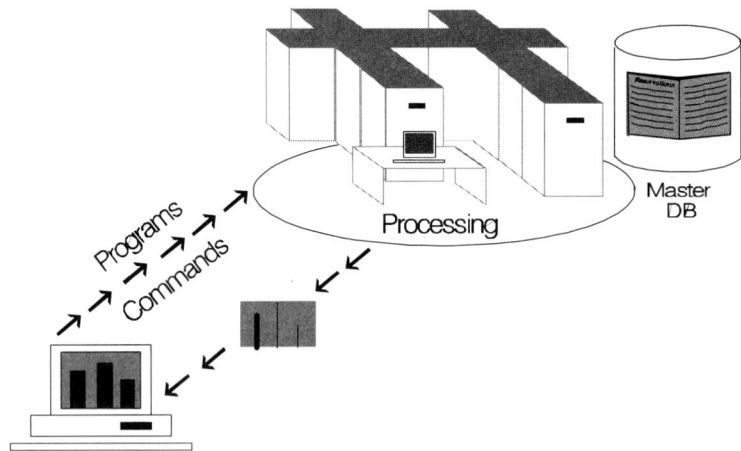

You can:

- take advantage of remote hardware resources
- utilize software available in the remote environment
- interface with existing mainframe and other legacy systems, for example, by building a single SAS program that contains statements that run locally and statements that execute on multiple remote legacy hosts
- execute against the remote copy of the data
- use RSUBMIT to remote-submit macro steps to the remote host and then pass return code information about the remote process to the local SAS session
- execute graphics programs on the remote host and display the graphics locally using the graphics capabilities of the local workstation, plotter, or printer

The results of the remote processing are then returned to the local machine. This is useful when the remote machine has hardware or software resources available to perform the task at hand more efficiently. It can also be preferable if the amount of data to be processed is too large to be moved to the local machine or if the data are updated too frequently for a local static copy to be useful.

Compute Services with Remote SQL Pass-Through in the Client/Server Environment

Remote SQL Pass-Through (RSPT) gives you control of where SQL processing occurs. As Figure 1.3 shows, RSPT allows you to pass SQL statements to a remote SAS SQL processor by passing them through a remote SAS server. You can also use RSPT to pass SQL statements to a remote DBMS by passing them through a remote SAS server and a REMOTE access engine that supports pass-through.

Figure 1.3
Remote SQL
Pass-Through
Services

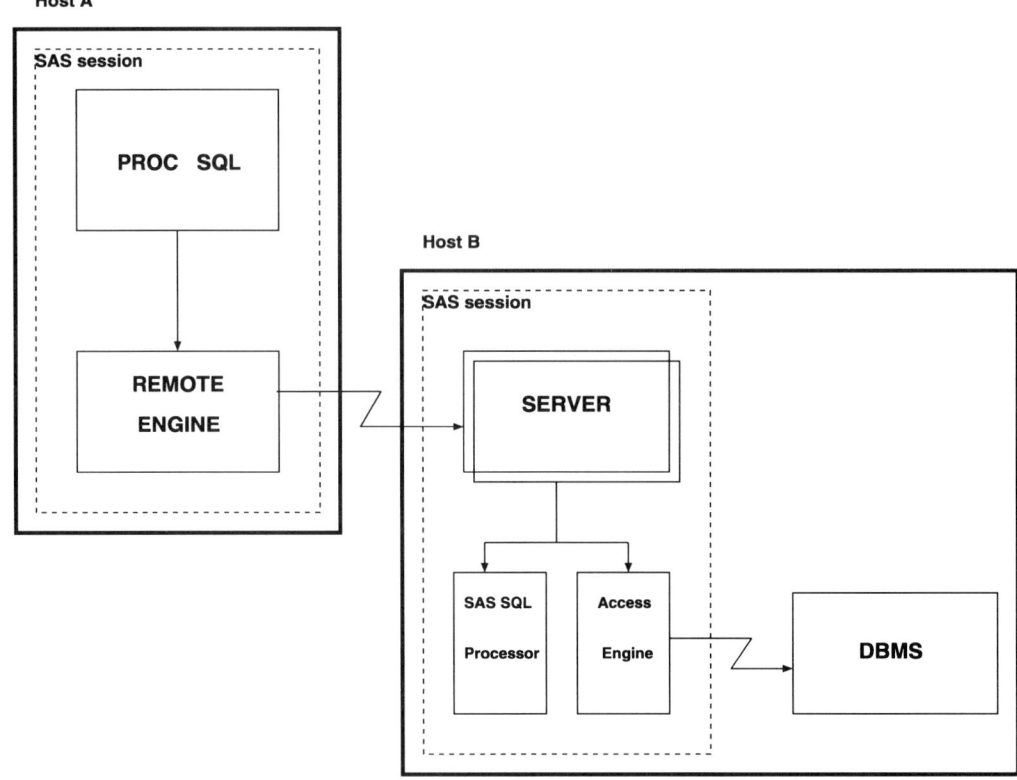

With RSPT you can:

- pass SQL statements to a remote DBMS to select data or execute statements to modify, manipulate, and manage data, including creating DBMS views

- pass SQL statements to SAS SQL to select data or execute statements to modify, manipulate, and manage data, including creating SAS SQL views

You can invoke RSPT through PROC SQL statements passed to the remote server for execution in the server's SAS session, or you can store SQL pass-through statements in local SQL views.

Data Transfer Services in the SAS Client/Server Environment

As Figure 1.4 illustrates, data transfer services provide a method for moving a copy of the data from one machine to another machine. Subsequent local processing takes place against the local copy of the data without generating further network traffic until you decide to update the copy of the data with another transfer.

Figure 1.4
Data Transfer Services Processing Model

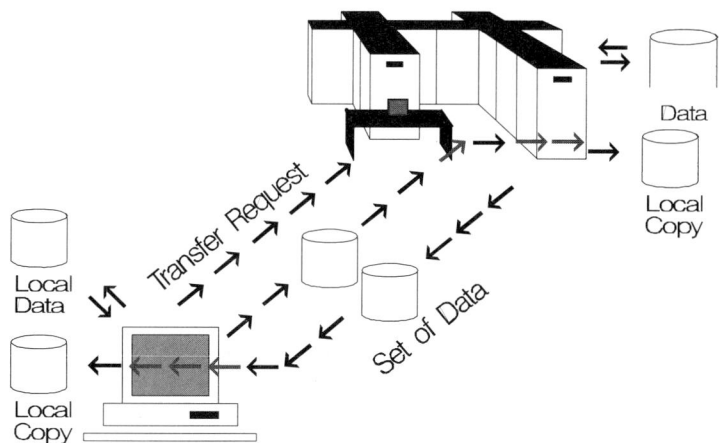

Data are transferred with the UPLOAD and DOWNLOAD procedures. You can transfer SAS data sets, SAS catalogs, and external files in either text or binary format. The file transfer capabilities enable you to:

- automate both data or application distribution and centralized data collection
- increase the robustness of your decision support environment by keeping a local copy of your data, which is insulated from network failure
- transfer multiple SAS files in a single step by using the INLIB= and OUTLIB= options. This capability enables you to transfer an entire library or selected members of a library in a single PROC UPLOAD or PROC DOWNLOAD step.
- specify certain entries in a catalog or certain members in a library that should be uploaded by using the SELECT and EXCLUDE statements
- name a specific translation table to be used during a catalog transfer
- use WHERE processing and SAS data set options when uploading individual SAS data sets
- replicate certain data set attributes when you upload a data set
- back up local files to a remote host
- transfer collections of files, such as a partitioned data set, MACLIB, or directory, between local and remote hosts
- distribute files from one workstation to others by uploading to a remote host and then downloading to other workstations that need the files
- move SAS files between releases of the SAS System as well as across hosts
- transfer catalog entries containing graphics output with a simple one-step process

Remote Library Services in the SAS Client/Server Environment

Remote library services (RLS) use program-to-program communications access methods to access remote data libraries and move the data through the network as the local execution requests it. As Figure 1.5 illustrates, a copy of the data is not written to the local file system, and the data must pass through the network on any subsequent use by the local processing system.

Figure 1.5
RLS Processing Model

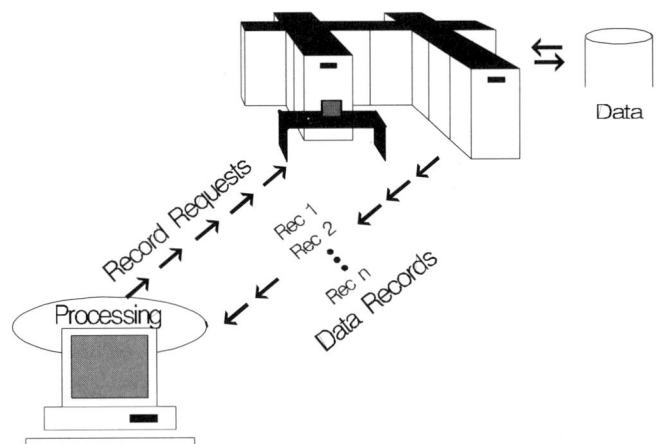

RLS give you:

- transparent access to remote data
- access to current data since no local copy is made
- a reduction of disk space consumption because multiple copies of the data are not created.

Remote library services are enabled in the client/server environment by a *REMOTE engine* that executes in the local or client SAS session and a *server* that executes in the remote or server SAS session. The SAS procedures and DATA steps that execute in the local session pass requests to access remote SAS files to the REMOTE engine. The REMOTE engine communicates the requests for data to the server. The server then administers the requests to SAS files on behalf of the local(client) SAS session.

How SAS/CONNECT Works with the SAS System

SAS/CONNECT connects two SAS sessions together. Each of these sessions is typically running on a different host. Once the connection is made, you have access to the services and resources available to both sessions.

To make the connection, SAS/CONNECT uses a communications access method. There are a number of different access methods supported by SAS/CONNECT. Before you can use SAS/CONNECT, you must configure your hosts for a supported communications access method. This book tells you about the access methods supported and the configuration requirements of SAS/CONNECT for each access method.

You can use SAS/CONNECT in interactive line mode and noninteractive mode, as well as in SAS Display Manager System sessions. Noninteractive mode gives you a way to

- perform daily or nightly automated backups
- initiate transaction processing to a master database at a specified time each day
- centralize and automate data and report distribution to workstations in a network
- centralize and automate data collection from workstations in a network.

Making a Connection with SAS/CONNECT

When you initiate a connection from a local SAS session to a remote host, you invoke the SAS System on the remote host. The terms *remote* and *local* refer to how you interact with a SAS session. These terms are not related to the physical location of the host device. The SAS session in which you issue local commands is the local host. The SAS session to which you direct your remote commands is the remote host. In addition, the term *host* is used to describe any computer and operating system where you can run SAS software.

The remote SAS session is not directly accessible. However, you can think of it as running in a special mode. You can access it only through the SAS/CONNECT link from your local host. All output and log messages produced by the remote session are displayed in the local session.

SAS/CONNECT is easy to use. You can establish connections to multiple remote hosts through a variety of communications methods (described in "Access Methods for SAS/CONNECT Software" on page 11). With a few statements or display manager commands, SAS system options, and the DOWNLOAD and UPLOAD procedures, you can start the connection, communicate with the remote system, and terminate the connection when you are finished.

To initiate and terminate a connection, you invoke the SIGNON and SIGNOFF commands. Depending upon the access method you use, these commands execute a script or connect you directly to the remote host. A *script* is an external file on the local system containing special SAS statements that control the connection. You can use one of the sample scripts provided by SAS Institute, a script furnished by your computing installation, or a script you write on your own.

Four basic actions must occur to start a connection with SAS/CONNECT:

1. Log on to or start your local operating system.
2. Invoke any necessary emulation software.
3. Invoke the local SAS System.
4. Execute the SIGNON command or SIGNON statement.

When you have finished using SAS/CONNECT, you terminate the connection with the SIGNOFF command or SIGNOFF statement.

Where to Go From Here

See "Access Methods for SAS/CONNECT Software" on page 11 for an overview of the communication access methods available with SAS/CONNECT and the platforms they work with. For a summary of information about specific host operating systems and specific access methods, see Table 2.1.

For examples of using SAS/CONNECT with a specific access method, see the chapter for that access method. For general examples illustrating the services of SAS/CONNECT in the client/server environment, see "Ways to Use SAS/CONNECT Software" on page 17.

Chapter 2 Access Methods for SAS/CONNECT® Software

Introduction 11

Program-to-Program Communications 11
Restrictions on Using the SAS X Statement 12

Terminal-Based Communications 12

Summary of Available Connections 13

Introduction

There are two primary types of communication: program-to-program communication and terminal-based communication. This chapter describes these two communication types, highlights the advantages and disadvantages of each, and lists the specific communication or access methods for each type that SAS/CONNECT currently supports. Program-to-program communication methods are required to use RLS with SAS/CONNECT.

    Note: The underlying third-party communications software must be properly installed and configured before SAS/CONNECT can work correctly with it. Most errors generated during SIGNON result from installation or configuration problems with the third-party communications software. These problems must be corrected before SIGNON can be successful.

Program-to-Program Communications

A program-to-program method of communication is designed for the interaction of two processes. This protocol allows much larger packet sizes, transmits data in binary form (and therefore does not require the application to perform any character set encoding), and often performs message notification asynchronously. Program-to-program interfaces may require additional systems software to achieve support on all of the necessary platforms.

    The following connection types are all program-to-program methods of communication.

APPC   is an acronym for Advanced Program-to-Program Communication. This type of connection uses the LU6.2 protocol for distributed processing within an IBM SNA network. The terms APPC and LU6.2 are often used interchangeably.

DECnet   is an acronym for Digital Equipment Corporation's NETworking architecture. SAS Institute uses this term to describe the task-to-task communication interface over a DECnet network.

NetBIOS   is an acronym for Network Basic Input/Output System. It is an operating system interface for application programs running on nodes in a local area network.

TCP/IP   is an acronym for Transmission Control Protocol/Internet Protocol. This is a program-to-program interface that is supported by multiple vendors over multiple vendors' hardware.

Restrictions on Using the SAS X Statement

If you are using an access method that does not require a script file, such as APPC, you should not remote submit the SAS X statement. Access methods that operate without script files are *non-terminal bound* access methods and are not capable of capturing and presenting screen images. When you use the SAS X command, it initiates a subsession of the local operating system, which requires terminal I/O. Terminal I/O expects to be able to send screen images, but non-terminal bound access methods cannot support this I/O.

Terminal-Based Communications

A terminal-based method of communication is designed for displaying data on a terminal and imposes limitations when used for communication between two processes. This protocol limits efficiency because it forces the application to put the data into a screen image even though it is not intended for users to read from the screen. The size of the screen limits the transmission packet size; the application must typically perform character set encoding in order to write data to the screen; and message notification is generally accomplished through polling. Because of the limitations of terminal-based communication methods, these methods cannot support RLS. Terminal-based interfaces are relatively inexpensive and generally available.

The following connection types are all terminal-based methods of communication.

ASYNC
: is an abbreviation for asynchronous. ASYNC is a primitive method of communication that uses phone lines or RS232 type cables as its medium. This is a relatively slow but inexpensive method of communication that requires the application to perform extensive error checking and recovery overhead.

EHLLAPI
: is an acronym for Extended High-Level Language Applications Programming Interface. EHLLAPI is a standard 3270 programming interface that uses SNA's LU2 protocol and is provided by many third party vendors for OS/2, DOS, and Windows workstations. The SAS/CONNECT product first moved to this standard interface with Release 6.06 of the SAS System under OS/2. EHLLAPI, HLLAPI, and 3270 are sometimes used interchangeably.

3270
: refers to the group of non-EHLLAPI vendor proprietary interfaces that use SNA's LU2 protocol. This group includes interfaces such as FORTE, IRMA, and PC3270 that are supported by the micro-to-host link, the precursor to SAS/CONNECT available in Release 6.04 of the SAS System. Most of the vendors providing 3270-type communications have either replaced these interfaces with or added support for the EHLLAPI interface.

TELNET
: is a terminal application interface written to use the TCP/IP protocol. It is less efficient than TCP/IP because it is layered on top of the TELNET terminal protocol. Because TELNET can communicate with an asynchronous interface in the remote environment and can run over an existing TCP/IP network, it is useful with SAS/CONNECT when the remote SAS session does not offer support for the TCP access method.

Summary of Available Connections

Table 2.1 lists all local hosts and all remote hosts available at this time. The contents of the table indicate which communications access methods are available to connect the local and remote hosts. Contact the Technical Support Department at SAS Institute for the most current information on support for additional access methods.

14 *Summary of Available Connections* □ *Chapter 2*

Table 2.1 *Available Connections*

REMOTE HOSTS ▼	RELEASE	LOCAL HOSTS ► MVS	CMS	OpenVMS	UNIX	OS/2	Windows	Windows NT	MS-DOS	VSE
		6.07+	6.07+	6.07+	6.07+	6.08+	6.08+	6.09+	6.04	6.08
MVS	6.07+	APPC TCP/IP	APPC TCP/IP	TCP/IP TELNET	TCP/IP TELNET	Async EHLLAPI APPC TCP/IP TELNET	EHLLAPI TCP/IP* TELNET APPC***	TCP/IP TELNET	Async 3270	APPC
CMS	6.06, 5.18	None	None	TELNET	TELNET	Async EHLLAPI TELNET	EHLLAPI TELNET	TELNET	Async 3270	None
OpenVMS	6.07+	APPC TCP/IP*	APPC TCP/IP*	TCP/IP TELNET DECnet	TCP/IP TELNET	Async EHLLAPI TCP/IP APPC TELNET	EHLLAPI TCP/IP* TELNET APPC***	TCP/IP TELNET	Async 3270	None
UNIX	6.07+	TCP/IP	TCP/IP*	TCP/IP	TCP/IP	Async TCP/IP	DECnet** TCP/IP TELNET	TCP/IP TELNET	Async	None
OS/2	6.08+	None	None	TCP/IP	TCP/IP	APPC TCP/IP	TCP/IP	TCP	None	APPC
Windows NT	6.09+	TCP	TCP	TCP	TCP	TCP Netbios	TCP Netbios APPC***	TCP Netbios	None	None
VSE	6.08	APPC	APPC	None	None	Async EHLLAPI APPC	EHLLAPI APPC***	None	Async 3270	APPC
PRIMOS	6.06, 5.18	None	None	TELNET	TELNET	Async TELNET	TELNET	TELNET	3270	None
AOS/VS	6.06, 5.18	None	None	TELNET	TELNET	Async TELNET	Async	TELNET	Async	None

* TCP/IP for CMS is available only in Release 6.08 and later releases.
** DECnet is available for Windows 3.x but not for Windows 32s.
*** APPC is available for Windows 32s but not for Windows 3.x.
+ This release or a later release of the SAS System for this host.

Part 2
Using SAS/CONNECT® Software

Chapter 3	Ways to Use SAS/CONNECT® Software
Chapter 4	Starting and Stopping SAS/CONNECT® Software
Chapter 5	Using Break Windows
Chapter 6	The APPC Access Method
Chapter 7	The DECnet Access Method
Chapter 8	The TCP/IP and TELNET Access Methods
Chapter 9	The NetBIOS Access Method
Chapter 10	Using a Spawner Program
Chapter 11	EHLLAPI and 3270 Access Methods
Chapter 12	Using Protocol Converters and TTY with the ASYNC Access Method
Chapter 13	General Tips and Troubleshooting

16

Chapter 3 Ways to Use SAS/CONNECT® Software

Introduction 18
About the Examples 18

Using Compute Services with SAS/CONNECT 18
Benefits of Compute Services with RSUBMIT 19
Considerations for Using Compute Services with RSUBMIT 19
Example 1. Compute Services: Saving Remote Processing Results on the Local Host 20
Example 2. Compute Services: Administration Tasks for Remote Data Sets 20
Example 3. Compute Services: Using Remote Applications from a Local Host 21
Example 4. Compute Services: Remote Graphics Processing 22
Compute Services with RSPT 25
Benefits of Using RSPT 26
Connecting to a SAS Server for RSPT 26
Example 5. RSPT Services: Querying a Table in DB2: 27
Example 6. RSPT Services: Subsetting Remote SAS Data 28

Using Remote Library Services (RLS) 29
Benefits of Remote Library Services 30
Considerations for Using Remote Library Services 30
    Types of Data Accessible Through RLS 31
    RLS Restrictions for Short Numerics and Mixed-Type Variables 32
    The Implications of Data Translation for RLS 32
Using WHERE Processing to Reduce Network Traffic 33
Using the TOBSNO= Option to Reduce Network Traffic 33
Connecting to a Server for RLS 34
Example 7. RLS: Accessing Remote Data to Print a List of Reports 35
Example 8. RLS: Accessing Remote Data with the WHERE Statement 36
Example 9. RLS: Updating Remote Data 36
Example 10. RLS: An SCL Program with the WHERE Statement 37
Example 11. RLS: Updating a Remote Data Set by Applying a Local Transaction Data Set 37
Example 12. RLS: Subsetting Remote Data for Local Processing and Display 39

Using Data Transfer Services with SAS/CONNECT 40
Benefits of Data Transfer Services 40
Considerations for Using Data Transfer Services 41
Example 13. Data Transfer Services: Transferring Data with WHERE Statements 42
Example 14. Data Transfer Services: Transferring Specific Member Types with SELECT or EXCLUDE 42
Example 15. Data Transfer Services: Transferring Specific Catalog Entry Types 43
    The Programs 44
Example 16. Data Transfer Services: Transferring Data with Data Set Options and Attributes 45
Example 17. Data Transfer Services: Distributing a .EXE File from the Remote Host to Multiple Local Hosts 45
Example 18. Data Transfer Services: Uploading a Catalog with Graphics Output 47
Example 19. Data Transfer Services: Downloading a Partitioned Data Set from an MVS Host 47
Example 20. Data Transfer Services: Combining Data from Multiple Remote Sessions 49

Combining Compute Services and Data Transfer Services 52
Example 21. Compute Services and Data Transfer Services Combined 53
Example 22. Compute Services and Data Transfer Services Combined 55
Example 23. Compute Services and Data Transfer Services Combined: Macro Capabilities 56

Combining RLS and Data Transfer Services 58
Example 24. RLS and UPLOAD/DOWNLOAD Combined: Distribution of Reports Over a Network 58

Introduction

Once SAS/CONNECT is started, there are many ways to use it in your SAS programming. This chapter describes typical applications, including some that are designed for specific environments.

About the Examples

The examples in this chapter are sample applications that illustrate the services provided by SAS/CONNECT:

- compute services
- remote library services (RLS)
- data transfer services.

The sample applications offer ideas for ways to use these services to your best advantage (either separately or in combination) to achieve optimal development of distributed applications. Both new and experienced SAS/CONNECT users can benefit from the examples in this chapter. To understand the UPLOAD/DOWNLOAD examples, you must be familiar with these procedures (described in "The DOWNLOAD Procedure" on page 207 and "The UPLOAD Procedure" on page 229).

Several of the examples in this chapter employ the concept of a program generator as a solution to a programming task. A *program generator* is a program that writes other programs. For more information about program generators, refer to *SAS Language and Procedures: Usage 2, Version 6, First Edition*.

Using Compute Services with SAS/CONNECT

Compute services give you easy access to many of the remote resources on your network from a single local SAS session. This access results in maximum utilization of all of the computing resources within your organization. Compute services are provided by the RSUBMIT command and Remote SQL Pass-Through (RSPT).

Benefits of Compute Services with RSUBMIT

One or more remote machines on your network may have vector processors or other larger, faster hardware resources that would more efficiently accomplish the CPU intensive portions of your application. Compute services enable you to move any or all segments of an application to a remote machine for execution. The results of the remote execution are returned to the local SAS session for processing, management by the local graphical user interface (GUI), or both.

In addition to CPU resources, a remote machine may have peripherals attached that would otherwise be inaccessible to you on a stand-alone local system. A PC in another part of your organization may have a plotter or printer attached that you need to use. By directing your local SAS session to move its graphics processing to the remote PC and pointing to the PC's output device, you can get a hard copy of your graph from the remote plotter.

Data center rules or data characteristics may mandate a single, centralized copy of the data needed by your application. By moving the processing to the remote system where the data reside, there is no need to transfer or create additional copies of the data. Using only one copy of data can address security needs as well as enable access to data sources that are too large or dynamic to be transferred.

For example, although data links between host systems make file transfers convenient and easy, large files do not move quickly between hosts. Furthermore, it is inefficient to maintain multiple copies of large files when developing and testing programs that are designed to process those files. With SAS/CONNECT you can overcome this limitation by developing programs on one system while running them and keeping the data they use on a different system. (The programs run on the remote host when they are remote-submitted.)

To test your programs, you execute the SAS program on the remote host by remote-submitting it from the local PROGRAM EDITOR window. All processing takes place on the remote host computer where the data reside, but the output appears on your local host. This method requires no file transfer yet permits you to process data stored on one system using programs developed on another system.

Considerations for Using Compute Services with RSUBMIT

Using compute services may introduce some effects that conflict with the goals of your distributed application. The following paragraphs address these side effects and offer alternatives to eliminate or minimize them.

Compute services, by definition, require remote CPU cycles. Because the processing takes place on the remote machine, it requires CPU cycles from that machine. This could be a drawback if the goal is to offload work from the remote system. You can minimize the remote CPU impact by utilizing data transfer services to transfer a copy of the data to the local machine and maintaining the processing on the local CPU or by combining compute services and data transfer services. See "Combining Compute Services and Data Transfer Services" on page 52 for more information.

Compute services also create network traffic in order to return the results of the processing back to the local machine. If the processing needs to be repeated frequently, the best solution is to utilize data transfer services to transfer the necessary data to the local system and maintain the processing in the local environment.

Another effect of using compute services is their demand on remote production data systems as the data are subsetted or pre-processed. You can minimize this effect by careful implementation of your application to eliminate or reduce multiple passes of the data.

Example 1. Compute Services: Saving Remote Processing Results on the Local Host

Purpose

When you use compute services to process data on the remote host, SAS/CONNECT returns output to the local log and listing. You can use the PRINTTO procedure to redirect the output to a file on the local host.

The Program

This example saves data set information for the remote library on the local host.

```
proc printto new print='contents.mvs'; run;

rsubmit;
   /* CONTENTS will produce a list of all */
   /*    data files in the library MVSLIB,*/
   /*    as well as supply variable       */
   /*    information on each data set.    */
 proc contents data=mvslib._all_;
 run;
endrsubmit;

proc printto; run;
```

Example 2. Compute Services: Administration Tasks for Remote Data Sets

Purpose

While working on a local host, you can use compute services to perform administration tasks on remote data sets.

The Program

This example administers password protection to the TASKLIST data set and backs up a data set called CURRENT.

```
rsubmit;
 proc datasets lib=mvslib;
```

```
      /* add an ALTER password to remote data set TASKLIST */
         modify tasklist (alter=sesame) ;
         run;

   /* Maintain a week's worth of backup copies of  */
   /*    data set CURRENT.                         */
         age current backup1 - backup7;
         run;
   quit;
endrsubmit;
```

Example 3. Compute Services: Using Remote Applications from a Local Host

Purpose

Some applications may not be available on every host at your computing site. In addition, applications on a remote host may perform some tasks better than the applications available on your local host. From a local host, you can use compute services to run applications available on a remote host.

The Program

There are two examples. The first example uses an application that is available only on the remote host. The second example uses an application that performs a sorting task more efficiently than the applications available on the local host.

Example 1: SAS/STAT Software

This example assumes SAS/STAT is licensed only on the remote host. The program runs statistical procedures remotely using SAS/STAT.

```
rsubmit;
   /*  The output from GLM is returned to the */
   /*    local SAS listing.                   */
   proc glm data=main.employee outstat=results;
      model sex = income ;
   run;

   /* Use GLM's output data set RESULTS to    */
   /*    create macro variables F_STAT and    */
   /*    PROB--containing the F-statistic     */
   /*    and PROB > F respectively.           */
   data _null_; set results(where=(_type_= 'SS1'));
      call symput('f_stat',f);
      call symput('prob',prob);
   run;

   /* Create macro variables in the local    */
   /*    session which contain the two       */
   /*    statistics of interest.             */
```

```
    %sysrput f_stat=&f_stat;
    %sysrput prob=&prob;
    endrsubmit;
```

Example 2: Sorting
In this example, the remote host has access to a fast sort utility, so the data are sorted on the remote host before they are transferred to the local host.

```
rsubmit;
   /* indicate to the remote host that the HOST sort */
   /*  utility should be used with PROC SORT.        */
   /* Ask SORT to subset out only those observations */
   /* of interest.                                   */
   options sortpgm=host;
   proc sort data=mvslib.inventry out=nostock;
      where status='Out-of-stock';
      by orderdt stockid ;
   run;

   /* output the results; local side will receive */
   /*  the listing from PRINT.                    */
   title 'Inventory that is currently Out of Stock';
   title2 'by Reorder Date';
   proc print data=nostock;
      by orderdt;
   run;
endrsubmit;
```

Example 4. Compute Services: Remote Graphics Processing

Purpose

If you have SAS/GRAPH software installed on both your local host and remote host, you can submit graphics programs from your SAS session on a local host to a remote host SAS session, have the procedure execute on the remote host, and display the graphics output on your local host display (or on a device attached to your local host). The link is especially useful when you want to generate graphics on your local host using a large database on the remote host.

The Program

To display remote host graphics using the link, follow these steps:

1. Use the access method for your hosts to establish the link between your local and remote sessions.

2. Use the RSUBMIT command to submit the following statement from the local host SAS session to the remote host:

    ```
    goptions device=grlink;
    ```

The GRLINK driver is a special driver available with the SAS System. You must always use the GRLINK driver on the remote host when using the link to display remote host graphics on your local host.

If you frequently use the link for remote graphics processing, consider specifying the GRLINK device driver in a script file (if you use one with the SIGNON command). You do this by including the driver specification for the remote host in the TYPE statement that invokes the remote SAS System. In the following example, if you are using TSO through a TCP/IP connection, change the TYPE statement in the script file to the following:

```
type "sas options(remote=tcp device=grlink)";
```

By doing this, every time you use the SIGNON command, you automatically specify the GRLINK driver on the remote host.

3. Submit the following statement to your local host SAS session:

```
goptions device=driver ;
```

where *driver* is the name of the graphics driver for your local host display or attached hardcopy device. For example, if your local host is running OS/2's graphical user interface, Presentation Manager, and you want to display the remote host graph in the local SAS session, specify

```
goptions device=pm;
```

If your local host is a PC with an EGA graphics adapter with at least 128K of memory and you want to display the remote host graph on your local host, specify

```
goptions device=egal;
```

If you have a PostScript printer attached to a PC and you want to output the remote host graph directly to the printer, specify

```
goptions device=ps;
```

To get a complete list of values for the DEVICE= option, run the GDEVICE procedure in your local SAS session.

4. Use the RSUBMIT command to submit your SAS statements, including any LIBNAME statement needed by the remote host. When the SAS/GRAPH procedure runs on the remote host, the output is displayed on your local host or attached device (depending on the driver you specified in your local session). If you did not specify a remote host driver name in step 2, you are prompted by the remote host.

The following example uses compute services to:

❶ Sort data (with PROC SORT)

❷ Summarize the data (with PROC SUMMARY)

❸ Create a vertical bar chart of the data (with PROC GCHART)

```
               rsubmit &rsessid;

❶              proc sort data=master.bgreserv out=tmp;
                  by origin rntltype;
               run;

❷              proc summary data=tmp vardef=n noprint;
                  by origin rntltype;
                  output out=tmprtype;
                run;

               goptions dev=grlink ftitle=centx ftext=simplex htitle=2;

               title 'Rental Types by Franchise';
               pattern value=solid color=blue;

        axis1 label=('Franchise')
        order=('ATLANTA' 'CHICAGO' 'LOS ANGELES' 'NEW YORK' 'TORONTO')
               width=3;
               axis2 label=none width=3;
               axis3 label=none order=0 to 1000 by 100 width=3;
❸              proc gchart data=tmprtype;
                  label rntltype='00'x;
                  label origin='00'x;
                  hbar rntltype / frame
                  sumvar= _freq_
                  maxis=axis2
                  raxis=axis3
                  minor=0
                  nostats
                  group=origin
                  gaxis=axis1
                  discrete;run;quit;

            endrsubmit;
```

5. After you have generated your graphs, you can use the SIGNOFF command to terminate the link between your local host and remote host.

When using the link to display remote host graphs, you can use any graphics procedure on the remote host (including the GREPLAY procedure) and any graphics device driver on the local host.

The GRLINK remote host driver uses the attributes of the driver specified in the local host session when selecting default colors, character sizes, and other attributes. For example, if you specify DEVICE=EGAL in your local session, the GRLINK driver uses the default colors of the EGAL driver, but if you specify the printer driver DEVICE=FX85 in your local session, the GRLINK driver uses only black as a foreground color.

Note the following reminders when using the link for graphics:

☐ Do not specify GOPTIONS NODISPLAY in the program you submit to the remote host. The option is not supported with the GRLINK driver on the remote host.

- Do not specify DEVICE=GRLINK in your local host SAS session. The GRLINK driver can only be specified on the remote host. In your local host SAS session, you can specify only a device driver available with SAS/GRAPH on that host.

- You can use hardware options, such as NOCHARACTERS, only on the local host side. That is, you cannot use hardware options that are not available with your particular local host hardware configuration even though they are supported on the remote host.

- To use the CBACK= or the ROTATE= option, you must specify it in your local host program, not in the program you are submitting to the remote host. If you use the CBACK= or ROTATE= option in the program submitted to the remote host, the option is accepted but has no effect.

- To use the GREPLAY procedure through the link, you must use the NOFS option in the PROC GREPLAY statement.

- Every time you generate graphics output on the local host, it is stored temporarily, while running the same SAS session, in a catalog called GSEG in the WORK library of your local host. Later, displays of the same graphics output can be generated from this catalog. Copy this catalog to a permanent location if you want to retain a copy after termination of your current SAS session.

You can also transfer catalog entries containing graphics output by using the UPLOAD and DOWNLOAD procedures, as described in "Example 18. Data Transfer Services: Uploading a Catalog with Graphics Output" on page 47.

Compute Services with RSPT

The REMOTE engine and the SAS server now support the SQL procedure's Pass-Through Facility. You can pass SQL statements through a multi-user server or through a single-user server in a remote session.

RSPT allows you to create new queries for remote SAS or DBMS data as you need them. Those queries can be stored in PROC SQL views in a local or remote SAS library to be used later in your SAS session or in your SAS applications. This is particularly advantageous if you are not familiar with the syntax for creating SAS/ACCESS views noninteractively.

RSPT also allows you to shift the processing for PROC SQL views from your local SAS session to the server's SAS session. For example, if you specify

```
select emptitle as title, avg(empyears), freq(empnum)
    from sql.employee
    group by title
    order by title;
```

where SQL is the libref for a remote SAS library accessed through RLS, each row of the table EMPLOYEE must be returned to your local SAS session for the summary functions AVG() and FREQ() to be applied to them.

You can reduce the network traffic required by this process by either creating a view in a remote session or using RSPT. To use RSPT, specify

```
select * from connection to remote
    (select emptitle as title, avg(empyears), freq(empnum)
        from sql.employee
        group by title
        order by title);
```

The query is passed through the remote server to the SAS SQL processor, which processes each row of the table and returns only the summary rows to your local SAS session. The shift of data reduction to the server's SAS session reduces network traffic.

Benefits of Using RSPT

Connection to remote SAS data or DBMS data is also provided to some extent by RLS. However, one of the limitations of RLS is that only SAS data sets are supported when the server and user are running on machines with differing internal data representations. This means that you can read and update SAS data views as SAS data sets but you cannot create new PROC SQL or SAS/ACCESS views using RLS. In a cross-machine environment, you have several alternatives for working with views. You can use RSUBMIT to submit PROC SQL statements and create a view in the remote session. You can also use RSPT to create a view either in a remote session or a multi-user server. Only the RSPT alternative allows you to use a multi-user server.

Connecting to a SAS Server for RSPT

The following SQL syntax specifies an RSPT connection to the remote data through a SAS server:

CONNECT TO REMOTE <AS *alias*>
    (SERVER=*serverid* <SAPW=*server-access-password*>
    <DBMS=*dbms-name*> <PT2DBPW=*passthrough-to-DBMS-password*>
    <DBMSARG=(*dbms-argument-1=value* . . . <*dbms-argument-n=value*>)>);

SELECT . . . FROM CONNECTION TO REMOTE | *alias* (*dbms-query*);
EXECUTE (*SQL-statement*) **BY REMOTE** | *alias*;
DISCONNECT FROM REMOTE | *alias*;

For more information about this syntax, see "RSPT Statements" on page 191.

Example 5. RSPT Services: Querying a Table in DB2:

Purpose

This example shows how to query a DB2 table located on a remote host using SQL statements issued from a local host SAS session.

Program

The following sequence of statements would be used in an MVS SAS session to establish a connection to DB2 and query the table SYSIBM.SYSTABLES:

```
connect to db2 (ssid=db2p);

select * from connection to db2
    (select name, creator, colcount
        from sysibm.systables
        where creator='THOMPSON' or creator='JONES');
```

The same connection and query could be performed from an OS/2 SAS session by using RSPT through a SAS server in a remote session under MVS:

```
connect to remote (server=mvs dbms=db2 dbmsarg=(ssid=db2p));

select * from connection to remote
    (select name, creator, colcount
        from sysibm.systables
        where creator='THOMPSON' or creator='JONES');
```

Use the AS alias clause in the CONNECT TO statement to give the connection to the remote DBMS the same name it would have if you connected directly to it. This enables you to use queries without changing the FROM CONNECTION TO clause:

```
connect to remote as db2 (server=mvs dbms=db2 dbmsarg=(ssid=db2p));

select * from connection to db2
    (select name, creator, colcount
        from sysibm.systables
        where creator='THOMPSON' or creator='JONES');
```

Example 6. RSPT Services: Subsetting Remote SAS Data

Purpose

The PROC SQL view SALES93 presents sales data for fiscal year 1993 and was defined on a UNIX workstation as follows:

```
create view servlib.sales93 as
    select sum(amount) as amount
        from sales
        where year=1993;
```

Processing this view using RLS from your local SAS session under Windows is comparatively fast because the view is interpreted in the server's SAS session. The summary function SUM() is applied when the view is interpreted and only the summary row is returned to your local SAS session.

If you wanted to obtain only your own sales data and break down the sales by customer, you could use RLS or RSPT. This example shows you how either of these services could be used and explains why RSPT is a better choice.

RLS Program

You can create a new view in your local SAS library to access the underlying data using RLS from your local SAS session under Windows, as follows:

```
libname mylib 'C:sales';

libname servlib '/dept/sales/revenue' server=servername;

create view mylib.sales93 as
    select customer, sum(amount) as amount
        from servlib.sales
        where year=1993 and salesrep='L. PETERSON'
        group by customer
        order by customer;
```

However, processing this view is expensive because the summary is not performed until the data reach the local SAS session. This means more data are sent across the network. In the following RSPT example, the summary is done before data are transferred, reducing the amount of data that crosses the network.

RSPT Program

The following statements create a new PROC SQL view in a local SAS library that uses RSPT to access the remote SAS data:

```
libname servlib '/dept/sales/revenue' server=servername;

connect to remote (server=servername);
```

```
create view mylib.sales93 as
    select * from connection to remote
        (select customer, sum(amount) as amount
            from servlib.sales
            where year=1993 and salesrep='L. PETERSON'
            group by customer
            order by customer);
```

Note that the LIBREF SERVLIB must be defined for the remote SAS library either in your SAS session or in the server's SAS session. In this example, a LIBNAME statement is executed in the local SAS session to access the library through the server running in the remote session. Alternatively, you could remote submit a LIBNAME statement to define the library.

In attempting to interpret the view in the server's SAS session, the PROC SQL view engine first asks the server to look for a specified libref as the user's libref for a library. If the server finds the specified libref as the user's libref for a library, it translates it to its own libref for that library. If no such libref is found for the user, the SAS SQL processor assumes the specified libref is the server's libref for the library.

You may want to create a view in the remote server, which can be used by many people. By modifying the previous example for all salesreps, the view satisfies the needs of users who are interested in more than one salesrep. The following example creates a view in the server session that summarizes the data by customer for all salesreps, instead of just one:

```
libname servlib '/dept/sales/revenue' server=servername;

connect to remote (server=servername);

execute by remote
    (create view servlib.cust93 as select customer,
        sum(amount) as amount from sales
        where year=1993
        group by customer);
```

Using Remote Library Services (RLS)

Access to data with *remote library services* (RLS) may be through SAS/CONNECT or through SAS/SHARE software. Access, including updating, may be to data stored in SAS data sets, external databases (for example, ORACLE), SAS catalogs, or external files. (For information about the differences between SAS/CONNECT and SAS/SHARE, see "Using the Services of SAS/CONNECT and SAS/SHARE Software" on page 283.)

RLS requires program-to-program communications access methods:

- APPC
- DECNET
- NETBIOS
- TCP/IP.

If the local and remote hosts have different internal data representations, RLS allows you to access SAS data sets, the SAS data sets defined by SAS data views, and external databases defined by access descriptors.

If the local and remote hosts have the same internal data representation, RLS allows you to access SAS data sets, SAS catalogs, SAS data sets defined by SAS data views, and external databases defined by access descriptors.

There are some scenarios for which RLS offers the ideal solution. This section describes some of these scenarios and explains how RLS can fit the needs of your application.

Benefits of Remote Library Services

If you need to maintain a single copy of the data on the remote machine and keep the processing on the local system, then RLS is the superior choice. In general, RLS is the best solution if the amount of data needed by the local processing is small, the remote data are frequently updated, or your data center rules prohibit multiple copies of data.

RLS also provides more transparent data access. This feature eliminates an explicit step of coding an upload or download of the data before processing them. It also permits the GUI of an application to reside on the local system while the data remain in the remote environment (for example, a local FSEDIT session of a remote data set). Applications can be built that provide seemingly identical access to local and remote data, without requiring the end user to know where the data reside.

Using RLS, it is possible to perform updates to data in external databases. RLS enables a single user accessing data stored in an external database to perform updates to that data through the use of the single-user server. This allows you to update remote data in an external database as a result of local processing.

Considerations for Using Remote Library Services

To make the best use of RLS, careful thought must be given to the following:

- the amount of data that will be accessed by your application
- whether you need multi-user or single-user data access
- whether your application will be making multiple passes of the data
- the resulting effects on your network load.

Analyzing these criteria will help you determine when to use RLS and when to use data transfer or compute services. This section describes situations in which RLS may not be the ideal way to access your data and suggests alternative solutions.

Accessing data through remote library services is not efficient for large amounts of data. In this case it is usually better to use compute services to move the processing to the remote system or to use a combination of compute and data transfer services.

Similarly, RLS is not efficient for multiple passes of the data. Although these data move from the remote machine to the local machine, the data are not written to the local disk. If the procedures being run make multiple passes of the data, or the entire procedure must be run more than once against the data, it is better to transfer a copy of the data to the local machine. You incur the network traffic cost once rather than paying the cost on each pass of the data.

Data transfer services may also be a better choice when response time is degraded. This situation can occur if you are accessing remote data that are being simultaneously updated by other users. If delayed response time cannot be tolerated, consider transferring a copy of the data to the local system and removing the live data from your application.

It is very important to remember that the data you access with RLS must still move through the network in order to be processed by the local execution. As a result, you need to program your application to minimize the amount of data being requested by the local processing. The main difference between data transfer services and RLS is that with data transfer services, once the data have moved through the network to the local system, they are written to disk and are available for subsequent local processing. In contrast, RLS moves data through the network to the local system where they are processed by the local execution and then discarded. Subsequent analyses of the same data would require the data to be moved through the network each time the local processing requested them. Therefore, a client/server application should be programmed to optimize the balance between the cost of moving data with RLS, the cost of moving data with data transfer services, the cost of computing on the remote host, and the cost of computing on the local host.

Types of Data Accessible Through RLS

With the current version of RLS, only data stored in SAS data sets or data defined by some type of SAS data view can be accessed across all hosts. Catalog access is not supported if the local and remote platforms have different internal representations of data. This means that while you could use the FSEDIT procedure to update a SAS data set in a remote SAS session, you could not read a SCREEN catalog entry for the procedure from that server. In addition, you could not retrieve a SAS/AF PROGRAM entry or update it with the BUILD procedure. The same holds true for a user-produced format, which is stored in a catalog entry of type FORMAT.

If the local and remote hosts have the same internal representation of data, you can access catalogs with RLS. However, if you attempt to access a SAS catalog when your local and remote SAS sessions are running on machines with different internal representations of data, you receive the following error message:

```
ERROR:  You cannot open <catalog name> through server <rsessid> because
        access to catalogs is not supported when the user machine and
        server machine have different data representations.
```

Data defined by a SAS data view or a SAS/ACCESS access descriptor can be accessed with RLS. The views can be SAS/ACCESS views, DATA step views, or PROC SQL views. Access descriptors are special files produced and used by SAS/ACCESS products to describe data maintained in other vendors' databases such as DB/2 or ORACLE. In both cases, the view or descriptor would be interpreted in the remote session and only the data resulting from the interpretation would move back to the local session for execution. Direct access to either VIEW or ACCESS type files, rather than the data they generate, is not supported.

SAS files of type PROGRAM cannot be accessed cross-machine. These files contain compiled DATA step code, which you cannot execute locally. The DATA step can be executed in the server's execution if referenced by a DATA step view that is interpreted there.

If you attempt to access a SAS utility file of type VIEW, ACCESS, or PROGRAM when your local and remote SAS sessions are running on machines with different internal representations of data, you receive the following error message:

```
ERROR:  You cannot open <utility file name> through server <rsessid>
        because access to utility files is not supported when the user
        machine and server machine have different data representations.
```

RLS Restrictions for Short Numerics and Mixed-Type Variables

SAS data sets that can be accessed with RLS across different host internal data representations should not include two-byte numeric variables. Due to their underlying floating-point representation scheme, most hosts on which the SAS System runs have a minimum numeric variable length of 3. A data set containing a two-byte variable cannot be accessed using RLS from a three-byte host. However, this type of data set could be accessed using the data transfer services of SAS/CONNECT. The UPLOAD and DOWNLOAD procedures automatically add 1 to the length of any numeric variable with a length less than 8 before transferring it to the target host.

With clever programming in the DATA step, it is possible to store numeric values in character variables and character values in numeric variables. These programming techniques must not be used in any data set that will be accessed with RLS. RLS performs character translation on character variables and numeric translation on numeric variables. As a result, the value the programmer expected will not be preserved. There are no means to detect such usage. Therefore, no message is issued.

The Implications of Data Translation for RLS

When accessing data with RLS, translation occurs on numeric variables only if the local machine and the remote machine represent floating point numbers differently. Translation occurs on character variables only if their character representations differ. Values are translated directly from the source representation to the target representation; they do not pass through transport format. Translation occurs when data flow from the remote to the local session and when data flow from the local to the remote session. Therefore, when the local and remote machines have different internal representations of data, the data that flow from a remote to a local session and are then sent back to the remote session undergo two translations.

Especially with numeric variables, translation from one representation to another may alter the value of the variable. The common type of alteration is loss of precision. This occurs when the source representation uses more bits to represent the mantissa than the target representation. There is no warning produced about loss of precision during translation.

The data transfer services of UPLOAD and DOWNLOAD preserve precision by adding 1 to the length of any numeric variable with a length less than 8 before transferring it to the target host.

A rare type of value distortion is loss of magnitude. This occurs when the source representation has a greater exponent range than the target representation and a value with a magnitude lying in the excess range of the source representation is translated. Of course the magnitude of this type of distortion is potentially very great, as is the percentage change. The following warning is produced when this type of alteration occurs:

```
WARNING: The magnitude of at least one numeric value was
         decreased to the maximum the target representation
         allows, due to representation conversion.
```

Refer to the description of numeric precision in *SAS Language: Reference, Version 6, First Edition* for a detailed discussion about the numeric representation of SAS variables.

Using WHERE Processing to Reduce Network Traffic

When using RLS, one of the best ways to reduce the amount of data that needs to move through the network to the local process is to use WHERE statement processing whenever possible. When WHERE statements are used, the WHERE clause is passed to the remote environment, interpreted, and only the data meeting the selection criteria are transferred to the local environment for processing. If the data you are accessing are stored in an external database, the WHERE statement is passed to the database and evaluated, if possible. If the database cannot complete the evaluation, the server completes it before returning any of the data to the REMOTE engine in the local session. The examples show how to use WHERE statements.

Using the TOBSNO= Option to Reduce Network Traffic

You can control the number of observations that are transmitted in each exchange with a SAS server using multi-observation buffering. By default, the server does multi-observation buffering when a file has been opened with an access pattern and mode of output or sequential input. *Open mode* refers to the way that a particular file is opened: input, output, or update. *Access pattern* refers to the way that a particular file is being accessed: sequential, random, BY-group rewind, or two-pass sequential.

The TOBSNO= data set option specifies the number of observations to be transmitted in each multi-observation exchange with a SAS server. However, the ability of the server to do multi-observation buffering and the benefit of using it are dependent on the open mode and access pattern for the file being requested.

If a file is opened in UPDATE mode, only one observation is returned per exchange with the server.

If the open mode is anything other than UPDATE, and TOBSNO= is set, the specified number of observations is transmitted in each exchange with the server. Because the SAS/CONNECT server access is single-user and typically sequential, it can be beneficial to use the TOBSNO= option.

If this option is omitted, its value is calculated based on the observation length and the server's default transmission buffer size of 32K.

The TOBSNO= option is valid only for data sets opened for input or output and accessed through a SAS server using the REMOTE engine. If this option is specified for a data set opened for update or accessed using another engine, it is ignored.

The following typically use sequential access:

- PROC COPY
- the DATA step SET statement without POINT= or KEY=.

The following typically use non-sequential access:

- PROC FSEDIT
- PROC FSBROWSE.

Connecting to a Server for RLS

To access a server, you submit a LIBNAME statement to your local SAS session to define a remote SAS data library. The location of the remote SAS data library is determined by the value of the SERVER= option in the LIBNAME statement. Figure 3.1 shows how the LIBNAME statement is used to access a remote data library.

Figure 3.1
Accessing a Remote Data Library

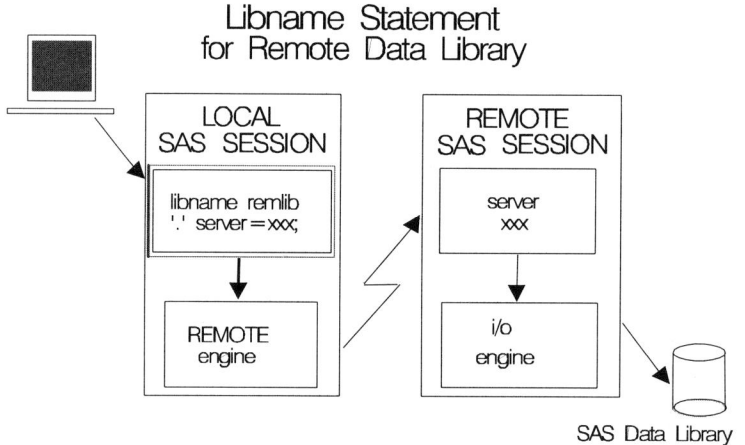

The LIBNAME syntax is:

LIBNAME *libref* REMOTE <*'SAS-data-library'* | SLIBREF=>
    SERVER=<*rsessid\servername*>
    <*engine/host-options*>;

A single-user server is initialized in the remote SAS environment when a LIBNAME statement that references a SAS data library in the remote environment is executed by the local SAS session. No action is needed in the remote environment to initialize the server. All actions are controlled from the local SAS session. To start the server:

1. Sign on to create the remote session.

2. Specify the remote session id in the SERVER= option of the LIBNAME statement.

To access a multi-user server, it must already be created and running. You specify the name of the server in the SERVER= option of the LIBNAME statement. The value of the SERVER= option is first checked to see if it matches the remote session id of one of the current SAS/CONNECT conversations. If it fails to match any of the current remote session ids, it is assumed to identify a multi-user server. Therefore, if you are accessing both a single-user server and a multi-user server from your local SAS session, you must use unique values for the SERVER= option. The use of the single-user server takes precedence over the use of the multi-user server. In addition, because you control the name of the single-user server, conflicts for data access cannot occur.

Once you have a libref defined to a server, you should avoid clearing and reassigning the libref multiple times. Repeating this sequence is inefficient because, as the last libref associated with a server is cleared, the local session disconnects from the server. When the same libref is reissued, the local session must again connect to the server. To avoid this overhead, clear the defined librefs once you have completed any processing that accesses data defined by these librefs.

A server does not terminate when the last LIBNAME statement is cleared. A multi-user server remains active, awaiting connections from users until it is stopped by a PROC OPERATE (refer to documentation for SAS/SHARE for more information about multi-user servers). A single-user server remains active, awaiting new connections from a local session until you sign off. The remote session also remains active for subsequent remote submits. To terminate both the remote single-user server as well as the remote SAS session, you must issue the SIGNOFF command at the completion of all remote processing.

Example 7. RLS: Accessing Remote Data to Print a List of Reports

Purpose

The following example uses RLS to access a small portion of the data that exist in a remote SAS data set in order to print a list of the reports that are being requested by the local workstation. This is a good use of RLS, provided the REPORTS.REQUEST data set has a small number of observations.

The Program

```
signon rempc;
/* define remote library to local session */
libname reports REMOTE 'd:\prod\reports' server=rempc;
data _null_;
   set reports.request;
   if (copy = "Y") then do;
      put "Report " rptname " has been requested";
   end;
```

❶

❶ The value for SERVER is the same as the remote session id used with the signon statement: `rempc`.

Example 8. RLS: Accessing Remote Data with the WHERE Statement

Purpose

WHERE statement processing is used to modify the previous example in order to reduce the amount of data that is being requested and the impact on network traffic. The WHERE statement moves to local processing only those observations for which a report is being requested. This move is more efficient than moving every observation to local processing and checking the COPY variable for a Y value.

The Program

```
signon rempc;
/* define remote library to local session */
libname reports REMOTE 'd:\prod\reports' server=rempc;
/* use WHERE statement to filter unneeded observations */
data _null_;
   set reports.request;
   where copy = "Y";
      put "Report " rptname " has been requested";
   end;
```

Example 9. RLS: Updating Remote Data

Purpose

This simple example enables you to take advantage of the mainframe's superior data handling and security features while you work in a user-friendly GUI environment. In this example, RLS is used to update remote data. This application of RLS eliminates the need to transfer a disk copy of the data to the local system before processing the data. It also involves low volume, transaction processing.

The Program

```
/* define remote human resources library to local SAS  */
/* session                                             */
libname rlib REMOTE 'hrs.emp.data' server=mvs-serverid;

/* execute local fsedit to update employee data set    */
/* that exists on MVS.                                 */
proc fsedit data=rlib.employee;
   run;
```

Note: This example can be modified to access a single-user server by first issuing a SIGNON command and then using the remote session id for the value of the SERVER=

option in the LIBNAME statement.

Example 10. RLS: An SCL Program with the WHERE Statement

Purpose

This example is an excerpt from an SCL program that uses RLS to query a remote reservation data base. Reservations are selected based on the value stored in the *resnum* variable. The use of the WHERE clause in this example is important because the WHERE clause is applied in the remote session before any data are transferred. As a result, only the observations meeting the criteria are moved to the local session. This example is a good use of RLS because (like the previous example) it involves transaction-type processing and enables the local GUI to be used for data entry on the selected observations in the database.

If you were to use the SCL LOCATEC function, on the other hand, every observation would be transferred to the local session and compared against the specified criteria. The response time in this case would be poor, at best. These alternative programming choices emphasize the importance of being aware of the amount of data that local processing is requesting and minimizing this amount when using RLS.

The Program

```
signon mvs;
/* define remote library to local SAS session     */
libname master REMOTE "hq.prod.data" server=mvs;

/* open remote Headquarters data base */
rdsid = open("master.reserv", 'u');
/* build and apply where clause to speed up retrieval */
wherecls = "resnum=" || "'" || resnum || "'";
rc = where(rdsid, wherecls);
call set(rdsid);
rc = fetchobs(rdsid, 1);
```

Example 11. RLS: Updating a Remote Data Set by Applying a Local Transaction Data Set

Purpose

In cases where data must be kept current and the number of updates you need to perform is small, RLS can be used efficiently between a local and a remote host. RLS enables you to perform a local update to a remote data set.

The Program

This example creates a data set remotely by remotely submitting a DATA step. Next, it creates a local transaction data set. Using RLS, it assigns a local LIBNAME to the remote library. Finally, the program modifies the remote data set with the local transations.

```
        signon;
        rsubmit;

❶       data sasuser.sbudget;
           length category $ 9;
           input category $ balance;
           format balance dollar10.2;
           datalines;
        utilities   500
        mortgage    8000
        telephone   1000
        food        3000;
        run;

        endrsubmit;

❷       data bills;
           length category $ 9;
           input category $ billamt;
           datalines;
        utilities   45.83
        mortgage    649.95
        food        68.21;
        run;

❸       libname rlslib slibref=sasuser server=&rsession;

❹       data rlslib.sbudget;
           modify rlslib.sbudget bills;
           by category;
           balance=balance-billamt;
        run;

❺       data _null_;
           set rlslib.sbudget;
           put 'Balance for ' category @25 'is: ' balance;
        run;

❻       signoff;
```

❶ Create the master data set, SBUDGET, in the SASUSER library of the remote session.

❷ Create a local or work transaction data set for updating the remote SBUDGET data set.

❸ Assign a local library to the SASUSER library in the remote session.

❹ Apply the transaction data set to the remote SBUDGET data set.

❺ Review the results; all items except TELEPHONE will be updated.

❻ Sign off from the remote host. The libref RLSLIB is deassigned as part of the sign-off processing.

Example 12. RLS: Subsetting Remote Data for Local Processing and Display

Purpose

If the amount of data needed for a processing job is small, RLS is an efficient way to gather current data on a remote host for local processing and display. This program subsets the data on the remote host so only the data you need are transferred. This method saves computing resources on the remote machine and diminishes network traffic while giving you access to the most current data.

The Program

In this example, a large reservations database exists on a remote UNIX platform. Several local procedures need to be run against a small subset of the data contained in the master reservations database. This situation is ideal for RLS.

The LIBNAME statement is issued in the local SAS session to define the remote library containing the RESERVC data set. PROC SORT sorts the remote data set, writing the subsetted data to the local disk.

The WHERE= and KEEP= options are specified in the PROC SORT statement to reduce the amount of data that moves through the network to local processing. Only the data meeting the WHERE and KEEP criteria are moved across the network to the local session.

PROC SORT creates the subsetted data set on the local machine, allowing all subsequent processing to run on the local machine without further remote CPU consumption. PROC SUMMARY and PROC REPORT summarize and format the local data so that they can be displayed to the user using the NOTEPAD command.

```
       init:
    submit continue;
```

❶
```
    libname remote '/u/user1/reservations' server=srv1;
```

❷
```
    proc sort data=remote.reservc(keep=company origin where=(origin='ATLANTA'))
       out=tmp;
      by company;
    run;
```

❸
```
    proc summary data=tmp vardef=n noprint;
      by company;
      output out=tmp2;
    run;
```

❹
```
    proc printto new print=work.view.report.source;run;
    proc report ls=74 ps=85 split="/" HEADLINE HEADSKIP CENTER NOWD;
    column ("Totals" "" "" "" company _freq_);
    define company / group format=$40. width=40 spacing=2 left "Company";
    define _freq_ / sum width = 14 spacing=2 right "# Reservations";
```

```
            rbreak after /ol dul skip summarize color=cyan;run;
            proc  printto print=print;run;
       endsubmit;

❺      call execcmdi('notepad work.view.report.source; color back blue;');

       _status_ = 'H';
       return;

       main:
       return;

       term:
       return;
```

❶ Submit local LIBNAME to define the remote library.

❷ PROC SORT runs locally, but accesses the remote data set RESERVC. A subset of RESERVC is written to the local data set TMP. The WHERE= and KEEP= options minimize the amount of data that must move across the network.

❸ Summarize the local data set.

❹ Create a report using this local, summary data set.

❺ Display the report.

Using Data Transfer Services with SAS/CONNECT

For many applications, *data transfer services* offer the maximum benefit. SAS/CONNECT provides these services with the UPLOAD and DOWNLOAD procedures. This section describes scenarios that are well-suited to a data transfer solution.

Benefits of Data Transfer Services

A major benefit of data transfer services is to offload work from a remote system to one or more local machines and boost response time for production systems running in the remote environment. Once the data are downloaded to the local machine, all subsequent data access and processing is done by the local processor. By moving a copy or subset of the original data to the local machine, production applications can be run on the local machine without further remote CPU consumption or impact on remote production data systems.

Moving a copy of the data to your local system adds robustness to your decision support environment. In the case of a network failure that would temporarily eliminate access to the remote data, you can continue working with your local copy of the data.

You can transfer only the data that you need by using WHERE processing, data set options, or both to dynamically subset the data as they are being transferred to the local machine. This reduces network traffic and gives you exactly the data you need on the local system.

Data transfer services not only facilitate moving data from a larger source to a requesting local workstation, but also support the model of a centralized control point, such as a mainframe, initiating communication to a network of workstations. This model enables centralized distribution of data and applications. Automated jobs can be run during non-peak hours to distribute data and applications to multiple machines that have need of the data and applications for the next day's work. Similarly, jobs can be set up to query a network of workstations for the purpose of gathering data and storing it in a centralized repository.

Another reason to use data transfer services is for backup purposes. Data and applications can be copied from a local system with small memory resources to a remote system with more memory resources, providing a backup in case of loss on the local system.

Application developers can also make use of data transfer services. Many applications are developed to run on a remote host and take advantage of its compute services. Data transfer services reduce the workload on your remote host during development of these applications because you can use the local host as a program development tool. You can perform program editing, testing, and debugging with the local host's resources instead of the remote host's resources.

The development environments at many computing installations often have a higher number of users working on one system than on other systems. On the system with the heaviest load, response time, execution queues, and other performance factors are degraded because so many people are running applications concurrently. With data transfer services, you avoid contention for heavily used host resources by creating and testing SAS programs on a less busy system (your *local* system) and then remote-submitting the fully developed and tested program to the heavily loaded system (your *remote* system). Each time you execute a program in a local host SAS session for testing purposes, you avoid adding to the load on the remote host computer. This method can result in significant savings of remote host resources and convenience for you.

For example, suppose you are developing a SAS program to be run as a production program on the remote host. Your program analyzes data in a SAS data set on the remote host system and creates several reports from the analysis information. To run many tests of the program before it is perfected and avoid the delays involved in working on the remote host, create and store the SAS program on your local host. Test the program by downloading the SAS data set analyzed by the program, or test the program with data stored in the local host. Once the program is complete and correct, upload the program file to the remote host.

Considerations for Using Data Transfer Services

Depending on the goals of your application, data transfer services may have side effects that conflict with your needs. This section addresses these side effects and offers alternatives to eliminate or minimize them.

Transferring a copy of the data to another file system creates multiple copies of the data. If the remote data are updated frequently, it may not be possible to keep a local copy of the data current enough to be useful. In addition, security restrictions at your site may prohibit multiple copies of the data. In this case, consider using compute services if the amount of data involved is large. If the amount of data is small to medium, RLS allows the processing to take place on the local system and the data to come from a remote source as the execution requests it. Both of these alternatives eliminate the need for multiple copies of data.

Keep in mind that data transfer services are less transparent than RLS. Transferring the data is an explicit step that must be done prior to initiating any local processing. If the volume of data to be accessed is not large and your application requires more transparent access, use RLS.

There may also be situations in which a combination of services is the best choice. For examples of combined services, see "Combining Compute Services and Data Transfer Services" on page 52 and "Combining RLS and Data Transfer Services" on page 58.

To understand the examples in this section, you must be familiar with the syntax for the UPLOAD and DOWNLOAD procedures (described in "The UPLOAD Procedure" on page 229 and "The DOWNLOAD Procedure" on page 207). (For details that apply to micro-to-host link releases, see "Details for Micro-to-Host Link Releases" on page 289.)

Example 13. Data Transfer Services: Transferring Data with WHERE Statements

Purpose

The UPLOAD and DOWNLOAD procedures process WHERE statements and the WHERE= data set option when you transfer a single SAS data set. The transferred data set contains only the observations that meet the WHERE condition.

The Program

The following example illustrates using a WHERE statement with the UPLOAD procedure.

```
proc upload data=labeled out=new;
   where lname < 'K';
run;
```

Example 14. Data Transfer Services: Transferring Specific Member Types with SELECT or EXCLUDE

Purpose

If you include the INLIB= and OUTLIB= options in the PROC UPLOAD or PROC DOWNLOAD statements, you can specify which member types to transfer by using the MEMTYPE= option in one of the following statements:

- PROC UPLOAD
- PROC DOWNLOAD
- SELECT
- EXCLUDE.

Valid values of the MEMTYPE= option are DATA, CATALOG (or CAT), and ALL. If you use this option in the EXCLUDE statement, you can specify only one value. If you use this option in the PROC UPLOAD or PROC DOWNLOAD statement, you can specify a list of MEMTYPE values enclosed in parentheses.

The Programs

Example 1: MEMTYPE= in the PROC UPLOAD Statement
This example uploads all catalogs and data sets that are in the THIS library on the local host and stores them in the THAT library on the remote host.

```
proc upload inlib=this outlib=that memtype=(data catalog);
```

Example 2: MEMTYPE= in the EXCLUDE Statement
This sample program uploads all catalogs and data sets except the data sets named Z4, Z5, Z6, and Z7 that are in the WORK library on the local host and stores them in the WORK library on the remote host:

```
proc upload inlib=work outlib=work mt=all;
   exclude z4-z7 / memtype=data;
run;
```

Example 3: MEMTYPE= in the SELECT Statement
This example downloads the catalogs named NAMES and JUNK and the data set named MEDIA in the WORK data library on the remote host and stores them in the LOCAL library on the local host:

```
proc download inlib=work outlib=local;
   select names junk media(data) / memtype=cat;
run;
```

Example 15. Data Transfer Services: Transferring Specific Catalog Entry Types

Purpose

When you include the INCAT= and OUTCAT= options in the PROC UPLOAD or PROC DOWNLOAD statement, you can specify which entry types to transfer by using the ENTRYTYPE= option in one of the following statements:

- PROC UPLOAD
- PROC DOWNLOAD
- SELECT
- EXCLUDE.

The ENTRYTYPE= option is required only if you use a SELECT or EXCLUDE statement. If you omit the entry type and also omit the SELECT and EXCLUDE statements, all catalog entries are transferred.

The Programs

Example 1: Using the ENTRYTYPE= Option in the PROC UPLOAD Statement

This example uploads all LIST catalog entries from the CAT catalog of the WORK library on the local host and stores them in the UPCAT catalog of the WORK library on the remote host:

```
proc upload incat=work.cat outcat=work.upcat et=list;
run;
```

Example 2: Using the ENTRYTYPE= Option in the EXCLUDE Statement for DOWNLOAD

This example downloads all catalog entries except the formats named XYZ and GRADES that are in the REMOTE.FORMATS catalog on the remote host and stores them in the LOCAL.OUTFMT catalog on the local host:

```
proc download incat=remote.formats outcat=local.outfmt;
   exclude xyz grades / entrytype=format;
run;
```

Example 3: Using the ENTRYTYPE= Option in the SELECT Statement for UPLOAD

If the USER= SAS system option is set to WORK, this example uploads the format catalog entries named XYZ and ABC, the informat catalog entry named GRADES, and the CBT entries named A and B that are in the WORK.FORMATS catalog on the local host and stores them in the WORK.OUTFMT catalog on the remote host:

```
proc upload incat=formats outcat=outfmt;
   select xyz.format grades abc (et=format) / et=infmt;
   select a b /et=cbt;
run;
```

Example 4: Using the ENTRYTYPE= Option in Two SELECT Statements

This example maintains the original ordering and grouping when transferring catalog entries containing graphics output. Assume that you have a catalog named FINANCE that has two entries containing graphics output, INCOME and EXPENSE. You want to download the two catalog entries containing graphics output in the order they are stored on the remote host; that is, you want INCOME to appear before EXPENSE, not alphabetically as the DOWNLOAD procedure would normally transfer them. In addition, you have some catalog entries that are grouped by the name GROUP1 and you want to preserve the grouping when the entries are downloaded. Remote submit the following program to transfer these entries in the order you specify in the first SELECT statement and in the group you specify in the second SELECT statement:

```
proc download incat=rhost.finance outcat=lhost.finance et=grseg;
   select income expense;
   select group1;
run;
```

Example 16. Data Transfer Services: Transferring Data with Data Set Options and Attributes

Purpose

PROC UPLOAD and PROC DOWNLOAD permit you to specify SAS data set options in the DATA= and OUT= options. Note that SAS data set options are not supported with the INLIB= and OUTLIB= options, even when you upload only data sets. The data set options must be associated with a specific SAS data set, so they must be used in the DATA= or OUT= options. There are additional restrictions described in "The DOWNLOAD Procedure" on page 207 and "The UPLOAD Procedure" on page 229.

The sample program illustrates using the DATA= option and the INDEX=NO option. It also shows the use of the DROP= SAS data set option. Note that because no OUT= option is specified, the transferred data set inherits the characteristics of the input data set except the index (since the INDEX=NO option is specified).

The Program

```
proc download data=idx(drop=sex) index=no;
run;
```

Example 17. Data Transfer Services: Distributing a .EXE File from the Remote Host to Multiple Local Hosts

Purpose

Access to remote host files through SAS/CONNECT makes it easy to distribute information to large numbers of local host users. Rather than distributing files on diskettes, one central file on the remote host can be copied by each local host with SAS/CONNECT.

For example, suppose you update an executable on your PC and would like to distribute the update to other PCs in your organization. You decide that the most efficient way to update all PCs is to upload PROGRAM.EXE to the remote host and notify each person who uses this software on their workstations that the file is available and should be downloaded. This method allows all users on the local host quick access to the updated software and eliminates passing a diskette from user to user.

Note: A SAS/CONNECT application like this one, in which an external nontext file is uploaded and then downloaded, requires the BINARY option. The BINARY option is used in the DOWNLOAD and UPLOAD procedures. The BINARY option transfers files without any character conversion (for example EBCDIC to ASCII) or insertion of record delimiters.

The Programs

Example 1: UPLOAD

The PROGRAM.EXE module must first be uploaded to an external file on the remote host. You start SAS/CONNECT and remote submit these statements:

```
filename rfile 'remote-host-file';

proc upload infile='a:\program.exe'
            outfile=rfile binary;
   run;
```

This example uses a SAS FILENAME statement to identify the target file on the remote host.

Notice that the INFILE= and OUTFILE= options are used rather than DATA= and OUT= in the PROC UPLOAD statement. This is because the file being uploaded is an external file, not a SAS data set.

Execute the PROC UPLOAD program with an RSUBMIT command. As the program executes, messages are displayed in the LOG window tracking the procedure's status. When the step completes successfully, the following message is displayed:

```
NOTE: Remote submit complete.
```

Example 2: DOWNLOAD

With the PROGRAM.EXE module available on the remote host, each user on the local host at the installation can acquire the update module by downloading it from the remote host.

The process for downloading the PROGRAM.EXE module is like the process for uploading except that you invoke the DOWNLOAD procedure and the target file is on the local host, not the remote host. For example, to copy the PROGRAM.EXE module to your \SAS\SASEXE directory, use this PROC DOWNLOAD step:

```
filename rfile 'remote-host-file';

proc download infile=rfile
              outfile='program.exe' binary;
   run;
```

This example uses a SAS FILENAME statement to identify the target file on the remote host.

The INFILE= and OUTFILE= options are used rather than the DATA= and OUT= options in the PROC DOWNLOAD statement.

Execute the PROC DOWNLOAD step with the RSUBMIT command. As the file downloads, messages are displayed in the LOG window tracking the status of the transfer. When the step completes successfully, the following message is displayed:

```
NOTE: Remote submit complete.
```

Example 18. Data Transfer Services: Uploading a Catalog with Graphics Output

Purpose

You can use the UPLOAD and DOWNLOAD procedures to transfer catalog entries containing graphics output. By default, the catalog entries are transferred individually and are re-created in the destination catalog in alphabetical order. You can alter the order or grouping of the catalog entries in the destination catalog, however, by using SELECT statements in the UPLOAD and DOWNLOAD procedures.

The Program

Assume that you have a catalog named FINANCE that has two entries containing graphics output, INCOME and EXPENSE. You want to download the two catalog entries containing graphics output in the order they are stored on the remote host. For example, you want INCOME to appear before EXPENSE, not alphabetically as the DOWNLOAD procedure would transfer them by default. In addition, you have some catalog entries that are grouped by the name GROUP1 and you want to preserve the grouping when the entries are downloaded. This program preserves the order and grouping through the use of SELECT statements.

```
proc upload incat=rhost.finance
    outcat=rhost.finance et=grseg;
    select (income expense);
    select group1;
run;
```

Example 19. Data Transfer Services: Downloading a Partitioned Data Set from an MVS Host

Purpose

This example shows users with an MVS host how to download all members of a partitioned data set. Suppose you need to download a collection of SAS programs from an MVS host to your local host. The SAS programs are members of one partitioned data set called MYHOST.SAS.PROGRAMS. You know you can copy the programs to the local host with SAS/CONNECT software and the DOWNLOAD procedure, but you do not want to type and remote submit a PROC step for each of the members.

The Program

You can use the SOURCE procedure, a SAS utility procedure under MVS, to build PROC DOWNLOAD steps automatically. The program that follows, DOWNLINK.SAS, is a program generator that uses PROC SOURCE for this purpose.

❶
```
filename inpds 'myhost.sas.programs' shr;
```
❷
```
filename gen 'programs.allsas' lrecl=80 blksize=6160
      disp=(new,catlg) space=(trk,(10,1)) volser=abc123;
```

❸
```
proc source nodata noprint indd=inpds outdd=gen;
     before 'proc download infile=inpds(xxxxxxxx)' 28 noblank;
     before "                 outfile='xxxxxxxx.sas';" 24 noblank;
     before 'run;';
run;
```

❹
```
%include gen;
```

❶ The first FILENAME statement defines the fileref INPDS for the MYHOST.SAS.PROGRAMS partitioned data set, which contains the SAS programs to be downloaded to the local host.

❷ The second FILENAME statement defines the fileref GEN and creates the data set PROGRAMS.ALLSAS, which is the target file for the program that PROC SOURCE generates.

❸ The PROC SOURCE step collects the names of the members in the partitioned data set MYHOST.SAS.PROGRAMS. These member names are inserted in a series of PROC DOWNLOAD statements by the BEFORE statements of the SOURCE procedure. The generated statements are written to the PROGRAMS.ALLSAS file referenced by OUTDD=GEN in the PROC SOURCE statement.

❹ The %INCLUDE statement calls the newly generated PROC DOWNLOAD program, and the steps execute.

Here is a GEN program created by the DOWNLINK.SAS program:

```
proc download infile=inpds(APPEND)
              outfile='APPEND.sas';
run;
proc download infile=inpds(OTREPORT)
              outfile='OTREPORT.sas';
run;
proc download infile=inpds(QUARTRPT)
              outfile='QUARTRPT.sas';
run;
proc download infile=inpds(TIMERPT)
              outfile='TIMERPT.sas';
run;
proc download infile=inpds(UPDATES)
              outfile='UPDATES.sas';
run;
```

Using the DOWNLINK.SAS Program

The DOWNLINK.SAS program is an external file stored on your local host. Follow these steps to use the DOWNLINK.SAS program:

1. Start SAS/CONNECT software.

2. Issue an INCLUDE command to bring the DOWNLINK.SAS program into the PROGRAM EDITOR window (assume that \PGMS is the directory), for example,

   ```
   include '\ pgms\ downlink.sas'
   ```

3. PROC SOURCE is a remote host SAS procedure, so you must execute the DOWNLINK.SAS program with the RSUBMIT command. The GEN program generated by DOWNLINK.SAS is created and executed on the remote host.

As the programs execute, messages are displayed in the LOG window tracking their status. When both programs complete successfully, the following message is displayed:

```
NOTE: Remote submit complete.
```

Example 20. Data Transfer Services: Combining Data from Multiple Remote Sessions

Purpose

Using SAS/CONNECT to establish links to multiple remote hosts, you can access data on several hosts, draw that data together on the local host, and analyze the combined data. For example, if you have data stored under MVS in a DB2 database and related data in an ORACLE database under VMS, you can use SAS/CONNECT in combination with SAS/ACCESS to combine that data on your local host. This example uses salary and employee data gathered from two remote hosts to illustrate the process.

The Program

This example signs on to two remote hosts, downloads data from both hosts, and performs analyses on the local host. Note that this example uses the SIGNON and RSUBMIT statements. Therefore, it can be run from a line-mode session as well as from a display manager session.

```
        /* establish link to MVS */
❶   options remote=a comamid=ehllapi;
    filename rlink 'MVS-script-file';
    signon a;


        /* download DB2 data using SAS/ACCESS view */
❷   rsubmit a;
❸      libname db 'SAS-library-with-DB2-descriptor' disp=shr;
❹   proc download data=db.employee out=db2dat;
        run;
❺   endrsubmit;
```

```
            /* establish link to VMS */
❻ options remote=internet address comamid=tcp;
    filename rlink 'VMS-script-file ';
    signon internet address;

        /* download ORACLE data using SAS/ACCESS view */
❷ rsubmit internet address;
❸     libname oracle 'SAS-library-with-ORACLE-descriptor ';
❹ proc download data=oracle.employee out=oracdat;

    run;
❺ endrsubmit;

        /* sign off both links */
❼ signoff internet address;
❽ filename rlink 'MVS-script-file ';
    signoff a;

        /* join data into SAS view */
❾ proc sql;
    create view joindat as
            select * from db2dat, oracdat
            where oracdat.emp=db2dat.emp;

        /* create summary table */
❿ proc tabulate data=joindat format=dollar14.2;
    class workdept sex;
    var salary;
    table workdept*(mean sum) all,
            salary*sex;
    title1 'Worldwide Inc. Salary Analysis by Departments';
    title2 'Data Extracted from Corporate DB2 Database';
    run;

        /* display graphics */
⓫ proc gchart data=joindat;
    vbar workdept/type=sum
                sumvar=salary
                subgroup=sex
                ascending
                autoref
                width=6
                ctext=cyan;
    pattern1 v=s c=cyan;
    pattern2 v=s c=magenta;
    format salary dollar14.;
    title1 h=5.5pct f=duplex c=white
            'Worldwide Inc. Salary Analysis';
    title2 h=4.75pct f=duplex c=white
            'Data Extracted from Corporate DB2 Database';
    run;
    quit;
```

Ways to Use SAS/CONNECT Software □ *Using Data Transfer Services with SAS/CONNECT* **51**

❶ To sign on to a remote host, you need to provide several items of information:

- the remote-session id, which is specified in a REMOTE= system option or as an option in the SIGNON statement.

- the communications access method, which is specified with the COMAMID= system option in an OPTIONS statement.

- the script file to use when signing on to the remote host. This script file is usually associated with the fileref RLINK. Using this fileref is the easiest method for accessing the script file.

When you have provided all of the necessary information, you can submit the SIGNON statement. It is not necessary to specify the remote-session id in the SIGNON statement, but it makes the program easier to read. If you omit the remote-session id, the RSUBMIT statement submits the statements to the remote session identified most recently in a SIGNON or RSUBMIT statement or command or in a REMOTE= system option.

❷ Once you have established links to two or more sessions, you can remote submit statements to any of the remote hosts by simply identifying in the RSUBMIT statement which host should process the statements. When the remote-session id has been established by a previous statement or option, you are not required to specify the remote-session id in the REMOTE statement. This example includes the remote-session id in the RSUBMIT statements, even when the remote-session id is not required, to clarify which host is processing each set of statements.

❸ Associate a libref with the library containing the SAS/ACCESS view of the database on the remote host.

❹ The SAS/ACCESS view can then be downloaded to the local host. Note that when you download a view of a database, a temporary SAS data set is materialized from the view and downloaded to the local host. In this example, the output data set on the local host is a temporary SAS data set.

❺ The ENDRSUBMIT statement ends the block of statements submitted to the remote host named in the previous RSUBMIT statement.

❻ To establish a second remote session, reset the REMOTE= and COMAMID= options to values appropriate for the second host. You also need to reset the fileref RLINK to associate it with the script file for the second remote host.

❼ When you are finished with a remote host, you can terminate the link with the SIGNOFF statement. When you submit the SIGNOFF statement, it is recommended that you identify which remote session should be signed off, either by including the remote session id in the SIGNOFF statement or by using the REMOTE= system option. You also need to be sure that the fileref RLINK is associated with the script for the remote host that you want to sign off from. In this example, RLINK is associated with the VMS script in the most recent FILENAME statement, so you can sign off from VMS without reissuing that FILENAME statement.

❽ These FILENAME and SIGNOFF statements set up the script file and then sign off from MVS.

❾ On the local host, you can now use the SQL procedure to join into a single view the two SAS data sets created when you downloaded the views from the remote host.

⑩ To analyze the joined data, simply use the name of the view on the local host in a PROC TABULATE step.

⑪ If you have SAS/GRAPH on your local host, you can also use graphics procedures to analyze the view created from the two remote databases.

Combining Compute Services and Data Transfer Services

Your application will benefit from combining these services if you need information from data stored on a remote system and you do not want to move a copy of the data to the local system. Reasons for not moving a copy of the data could include:

□ the amount of data is too large

□ the data are frequently updated

□ you want to avoid data duplication.

Regardless of the motivation for reducing the amount of data that is transferred, incorporating compute services will achieve your goal. As Figure 3.2 illustrates, compute services enable you to format and pre-process data into a subsetted or summarized form on the remote system prior to transferring the subsequent smaller amount of data to the local platform. This balances the use of CPU cycles between the local and remote systems and minimizes the amount of data contributing to network traffic.

Figure 3.2
Combined Compute and Data Transfer Services Processing Model

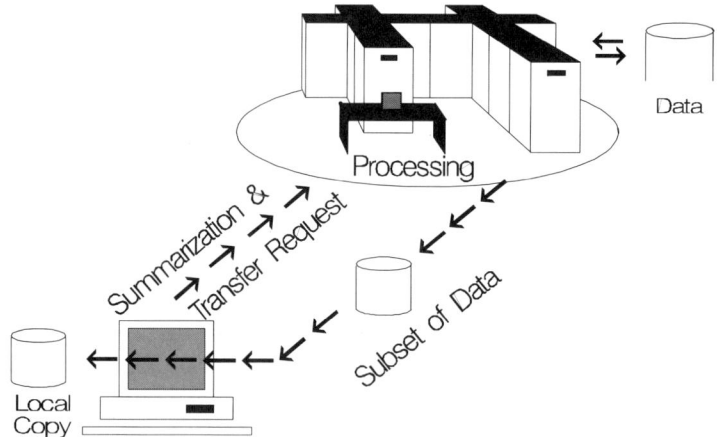

Example 21. Compute Services and Data Transfer Services Combined

Purpose

The SAS/CONNECT statements SIGNON, SIGNOFF, RSUBMIT, and ENDRSUBMIT enable you to submit statements to a remote host from a line-mode session on the local host. You can include these statements in a SAS program and do both local and remote processing within a single SAS program. This program can be run in an interactive line-mode SAS session, in a noninteractive SAS session, or by including the program in a session running the SAS Display Manager System on your local host. In each case, the program executes statements on both the local host and the remote host.

The Program

For example, suppose that you want to perform some processing on a remote host, download the resulting SAS data set, create a permanent data set on the local host, and print a report on the local host.

The following example illustrates how to put all of these tasks into a single program.

```
          /* prepare to sign on */
❶  filename rlink 'script-file-name ';
❷  options comamid=communications-access-method  remote=remote-session-id ;
❸  libname lhost 'local-SAS-data-library ';

          /* sign on and download data set */
❹  signon remote-session-id ;
❺  rsubmit remote-session-id ;
❻     libname rhost 'remote-SAS-data-library ';
   proc sort data=rhost.master out=rhost.sales
             where gross > 5000;
             by lname dept;
      run;
❼  proc download data=rhost.sales out=lhost.sales;

      run;
❽  endrsubmit;

          /* print data set in local session */
❾  proc print data=lhost.sales;
      run;
```

❶ Associate the script file that you use to sign on with the fileref RLINK.

❷ Specify the COMAMID= and the REMOTE= system options in an OPTIONS statement. These two system options define to the local session what type of link you want to establish to which remote host.

❸ Define a libref for the SAS data library on the local session where the downloaded data set should be stored.

❹ Sign on to the remote host.

It is not necessary to include *remote-session-id* when you have defined the REMOTE= system option in a previous OPTIONS statement.

❺ After the link is established, the RSUBMIT statement sends statements to the remote session for processing until an ENDRSUBMIT statement is encountered. Although it is not necessary to include *remote-session-id*, using *remote-session-id* in the RSUBMIT statement clarifies which remote session should process a group of statements when more than one link is active. If you omit *remote-session-id*, the RSUBMIT statement submits the statements to the remote session identified most recently in a SIGNON or RSUBMIT statement or a REMOTE= system option.

❻ Define the libref for the SAS data library on the remote host.

❼ The PROC DOWNLOAD step transfers the data from the library on the remote host (RHOST) to the library on the local host (LHOST).

❽ The ENDRSUBMIT statement signals the end of the block of statements to be submitted to the remote session. Statements following the ENDRSUBMIT statement are processed by the local session.

❾ The PROC PRINT step executes in the local session and reads the SAS data set that was downloaded in the PROC DOWNLOAD step.

Running the Program
You have several options for running this program:

- Type and submit each line in a line-mode SAS session. All of the statements between the RSUBMIT and ENDRSUBMIT statements are sent to the remote host for processing. All other statements are processed on the local host.
  Note: When statements are submitted to the remote host, several statements may be grouped into a single packet of data sent to the remote host. Therefore, a line that is remote-submitted is not necessarily processed immediately after you enter it on the local host.

- Build a file containing all of these statements and use a %INCLUDE statement to include the file in a line-mode session. The file is processed immediately.

- Build a file containing all of these statements and run a noninteractive SAS job to process the statements as follows:

    ```
    sas file-containing-program
    ```

    If you use this method, the script used to sign on and sign off can also log on to and log off from the remote host by including the userid and password for the remote host. (Note that including the userid and password in your script might pose security problems at your site. Check with your SAS Software Representative before creating this kind of script.) Refer to "Starting and Stopping SAS/CONNECT Software" on page 61 for more information about automatic log-on scripts.

- Build a file containing all of these statements and use an INCLUDE command to include the file in a display manager session. You must submit the included statements from display manager.

Example 22. Compute Services and Data Transfer Services Combined

Purpose

In cases where the same remote data set needs to be manipulated by multiple local hosts, data transfer services can be used to distribute the subset of data needed by each local host. Each local host receives only the data it needs and uses its compute services to process that data in the local GUI.

With this method, local hosts do not have to continually access the data set on the remote machine. Instead, the remote machine queries each local host for the data it needs and then transfers that data to the local host. In addition, compute services are used at the local host, which can be more efficient in many cases.

The Program

This SCL program fragment distributes a reservations data set from a remote host at a central office to local hosts at a number of franchise offices. The program enables distribution of reservations to a franchise office by using a WHERE statement to select the desired reservations. The actual application that contains this program is implemented using the macro facility and a control data set to provide remote session ids for each franchise. The macro makes it easy to distribute reservations to any number of franchises as well as to add or delete franchises as needed. This example represents one iteration of the macro.

```
    INIT:

    submit continue;
    signon atlanta;

    rsubmit;
        libname mres "d:\counter";
        libname backup "d:\counter\backup";

    rsubmit;
❶       proc upload data=hq.reserv
            out=update status=no;
            where origin="Atlanta";
        run;

❷       proc sort data=update;
            by resnum;
        run;

❸       proc copy in=mres out=backup;
            select reserv;
        run;
```

56 *Combining Compute Services and Data Transfer Services* □ *Chapter 3*

```
❹          data mres.reserv;
               update mres.reserv update;
               by resnum;
           run;
        endrsubmit;
        signoff;
        endsubmit;
```

❶ Upload all reservations for a particular location.

❷ Sort uploaded data sets for merging.

❸ Backup existing data set.

❹ Merge new and existing data sets.

Example 23. Compute Services and Data Transfer Services Combined: Macro Capabilities

Purpose

SAS/CONNECT is fully functional from within the macro facility. Both the UPLOAD and the DOWNLOAD procedures can update the macro variable SYSINFO and set it to a nonzero value when the procedure terminates due to errors. You can also use the %SYSRPUT macro statement on the remote host to send the value of the SYSINFO macro variable back to the local SAS session. Thus, you can submit a job to the remote host and test whether a PROC UPLOAD or DOWNLOAD step has successfully completed before beginning another step on either the remote host or the local host.

The Program

For example, suppose that you have a transaction file on your local host and you want to upload it to the remote host and then use it to update a master file. You can test the results of the PROC UPLOAD step on the remote host by checking the value of the SYSINFO macro variable. If the transaction file was successfully uploaded, the master file is updated with the new information. If the upload was not successful, you receive a message explaining the problem. You can use the %SYSRPUT macro statement to send the return code from the remote host back to the local session. Your SAS session on the local host can test the results of the upload and, if it is successful, use the DATASETS procedure to archive the transaction data set.

```
❶     libname trans 'local-SAS-data-library';
❷     rsubmit;
❸        proc upload data=trans.current out=current;
          run;
❹        %sysrput retcode=&sysinfo;
          %macro updatem;
```

```
❺          %if &sysinfo=0 %then %do;
               libname perm 'remote-SAS-data-library';
               data perm.employee;
                  update perm.employee current;
                  by empid;
               run;
            %end;
❻          %else %put UPLOAD of CURRENT failed. Master file was not updated.;
         %mend updatem;
❼       %updatem
      endrsubmit;

❽    %macro chkcode;
❾       %if &retcode=0 %then %do;
❿          proc datasets lib=trans;
               copy out=backup;
            run;
         %end;
      %mend chkcode;
⓫    %chkcode
```

❶ Associate a libref with the SAS data library containing the transaction data set on the local host.

❷ Use the RSUBMIT statement to upload the data set and process the UPDATEM macro on the remote host.

❸ Because you specify a single-level name for the OUT= argument, the PROC UPLOAD step creates a temporary copy of the transaction data set on the remote host.

❹ If the PROC UPLOAD step successfully completes, the SYSINFO macro variable is set to 0. The %SYSRPUT macro statement creates the RETCODE macro variable on the local host and puts the value stored in the SYSINFO macro variable into RETCODE. The RETCODE macro variable can be tested by statements processed by the local host to determine if the PROC UPLOAD step was successful.

❺ This step tests the SYSINFO macro variable on the remote host. If the PROC UPLOAD step is successful, the transaction data set is used to update the master data set.

❻ If the SYSINFO macro variable is not set to 0, the PROC UPLOAD step has failed. In this case, the remote host sends messages to the SAS log, which appear in the local SAS session, notifying you that the step has failed.

❼ This macro statement executes the UPDATEM macro on the remote host.

❽ The CHKCODE macro is executed on the local host because it follows the ENDRSUBMIT statement.

❾ This statement tests the value of the RETCODE macro variable created by the %SYSRPUT macro statement on the remote host to see if the PROC UPLOAD step was successful.

❿ When the transaction data set has been successfully uploaded and added to the master data set, the transaction file can be archived on the local host by using the COPY statement in the DATASETS procedure.

⓫ This macro statement executes the CHKCODE macro on the local host.

Combining RLS and Data Transfer Services

When the amount of information needed from a remote host is small, (for example, the value of one variable for no more than a dozen records), RLS can be used to move the data to a local host. As Figure 3.3 illustrates, once at the local host, the data can be used in a larger processing task and the results (for example, reports) can be transferred with UPLOAD across the network as required.

Figure 3.3
Combined RLS and Data Transfer Services Processing Model

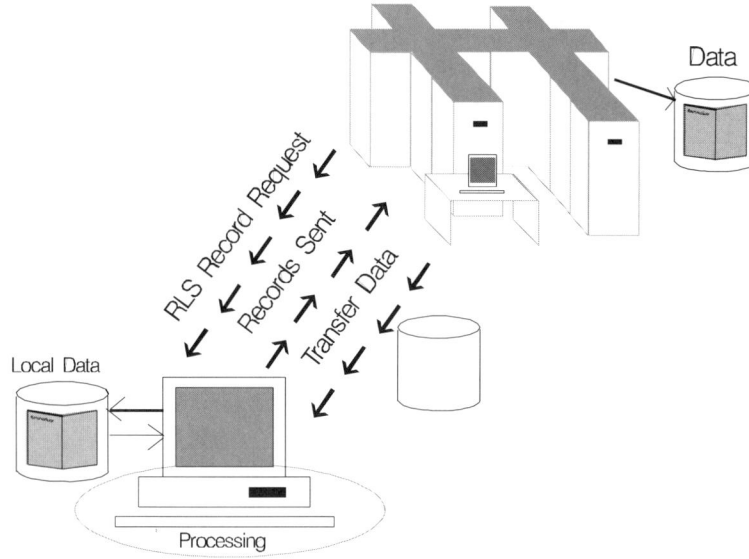

Example 24. RLS and UPLOAD/DOWNLOAD Combined: Distribution of Reports Over a Network

Purpose

The following program enables distribution of production reports from a company's headquarters location to each of its franchise offices based on the information contained in the control data set maintained by each of the franchise offices. This application was implemented with the macro facility to enable the mainframe to initiate a conversation with each of the franchise workstations and transfer a set of reports to the franchise based on selection criteria.

The Program

```
/*--------------------------------*/
/* Name: DISTRPT.PROGRAM          */
/*                                */
/* This program distributes reports */
/* to the franchise offices.      */
/*                                */
/*--------------------------------*/

length rc 8;

INIT:

submit continue;
/* set up distribution macro */
```
❶ ```
%macro distrib;
```

❷ ```
%let francity=Atlanta NYC LA Dallas Chicago;
   %let franhost=mvsatl unixnyc unixla vaxdal hqvax;
```

❸ ```
%let j=1;
   %do %while(%scan(&francity,&j) ne);
     %let nextfran=%scan(&francity,&j);
     %let nextrem=%scan(&franhost,&j);

         ...

     %let j=%eval(&j+1);
   %end;

options remote=&nextrem;
```
❹ ```
signon;
```
❺ ```
x "alloc fi(xferrpt)
   da('sascgg.sugi18.xferrpt') shr";
```
❻ ```
rsubmit;
   filename frptlib "d:\counter\reports\prod";
endrsubmit;
/* use SAS/CONNECT server */
```
❼ ```
libname rpt REMOTE "d:\counter\reports"
           server=&nextrem;
```
❽ ```
data _null_;
   set rpt.preport end=finish;
   file xferrpt;
   if _n_ = 1 then
      put "rsubmit;";

     /* transfer desired reports named by */
     /* name variable in preport data set */
```

60 *Combining RLS and Data Transfer Services* □ *Chapter 3*

```
❾      if (copy = "Y") then do;
           put "proc upload
                   infile='sascgg.sugi18."name"'";
           put "outfile=frptlib("name")
                   status=no;run;";
       end;
       if finish then
          put "endrsubmit;";
    run;
    /* upload desired reports */
❿   %include xferrpt;

    signoff;
    %end;

    /* do until */
    %end;
    %mend;

    /* invoke macro to distribute reports */
⓫   %distrib;
    endsubmit;

    _status_ = 'H';

    return;

    MAIN:
    return;
    TERM:
    return;
```

❶ Begin the distribution macro definition.

❷ Initialize the list of remote franchise offices (**francity**) and their node names (**franhost**) to be used as the REMOTE= value.

❸ Scan to the next office and node name to be processed.

❹ Specify the remote office nodename as the REMOTE= value and sign on to the remote franchise.

❺ Allocate an MVS file that will contain generated UPLOAD statements.

❻ Remote submit a fileref to define the PC library to which reports will be uploaded.

❼ Connect to single-user server to access the library that contains the report-selection data set.

❽ Execute the DATA step to evaluate report-selection data (**RPT.PREPORT**) and create upload statements to transfer reports (**XFERRPT**).

❾ If the selection criterion is yes, create the appropriate PROC UPLOAD statement for the particular report.

❿ Include the generated SAS job in the local MVS SAS session for execution.

⓫ Invoke the macro.

Chapter 4 Starting and Stopping SAS/CONNECT® Software

Introduction 61

Using PMENUS to Start and Stop SAS/CONNECT 62
Starting SAS/CONNECT with the Signon Option 62
Stopping SAS/CONNECT with the Signoff Option 63

When to Use a Script 64

Basic Script Functions 64

Using a Script to Start and Stop SAS/CONNECT 65
Starting SAS/CONNECT with an Automatic Logon Script 66
Starting SAS/CONNECT with a Manual Logon Script 67
Stopping SAS/CONNECT with an Automatic Logoff Script 68
Stopping SAS/CONNECT with a Manual Logoff Script 68

Shortcuts for Starting and Stopping SAS/CONNECT 68
Starting Multiple SAS/CONNECT Sessions 69

General Script Statement Rules 71
Syntax 71

Writing Simple Scripts for Signing On and Signing Off 71
Script for EHLLAPI Connections 72
Script for TCP/IP Connections 75

Debugging a Script 78
Statements Useful for Debugging 79

Sample Scripts 79
Automatic Logon 79
Manual Logon 82

SCL Functions Used with SAS/CONNECT 85
Locating and Storing Sample Script Files with SCL Functions 85

Introduction

This chapter describes starting and stopping SAS/CONNECT from the pull-down menu user interface. This chapter also provides information for using, writing, and modifying scripts for starting and stopping SAS/CONNECT.

Some SAS/CONNECT access methods such as NETBIOS, DECnet, and (in most cases) APPC, have no need of a script to start and stop a link. Other access methods do use scripts. Whether you are a systems programmer responsible for supporting SAS/CONNECT users or a user who needs to write your own script, the information in this chapter can get you started. In addition to explaining how to use a script to start SAS/CONNECT, this chapter describes the basic functions of a script and presents rules for script statements. Sections on debugging and locating scripts are also included. For complete descriptions of each script statement used in the examples, see "Script Statements" on page 251.

There are four SCL functions that you can use to gather and store connection information about a SAS/CONNECT session. This chapter provides an example of using

SCL functions. They are also described in "System Options, Statements, Commands, and SCL Functions" on page 173.

Using PMENUS to Start and Stop SAS/CONNECT

The SAS System provides a menu bar that you can use to issue commands and perform other operations during a SAS session. This menuing system is called the *PMENU facility*. This section describes how to use the **Signon** and **Signoff** pull-down menu options to start and stop a SAS/CONNECT conversation.

You can also submit statements instead of using pull-down menus to start and stop SAS/CONNECT conversations. The remaining chapters of this book describe how to submit statements for starting and stopping, should you prefer to use that method.

Starting SAS/CONNECT with the Signon Option

To start a SAS/CONNECT session:

1. In the SAS: PROGRAM EDITOR window, select **Locals** from the menu bar. The **Locals** pull-down menu appears, as shown in Display 4.1.

Display 4.1
SAS System Locals Option

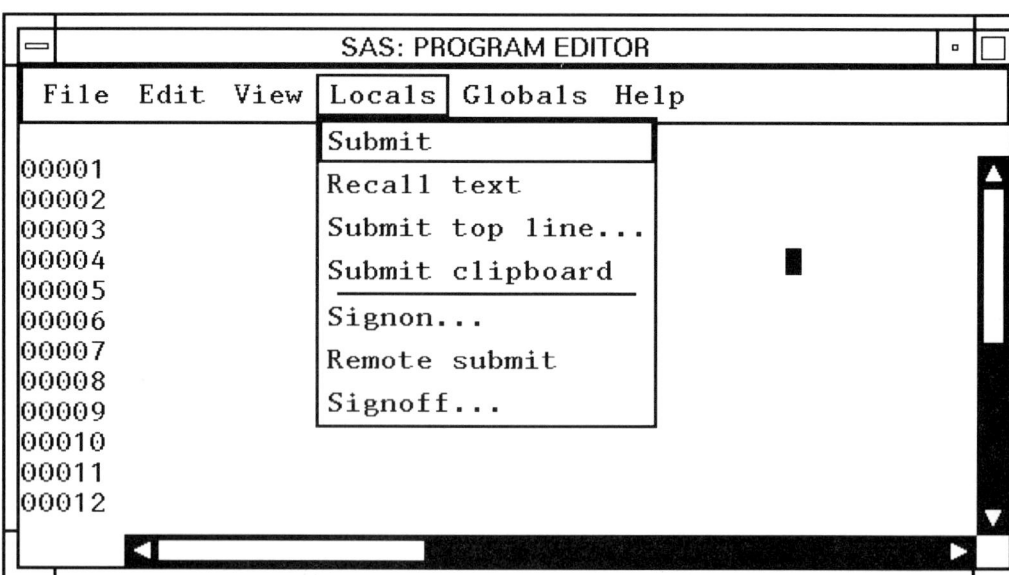

2. Select **Signon** from the **Locals** pull-down menu. The Signon window appears, as shown in Display 4.2.

Display 4.2
The Signon Window

```
┌──────────────────────── Signon... ─────────────────────────┐
│                                                            │
│  Enter script file name: [                              ]  │
│                                                            │
│  Enter remote= value:    [      ]                          │
│                                                            │
│  Enter communications                                      │
│  access method id value: [      ]                          │
│                                                            │
│  NOTE: Leave a field blank to use the current setting.     │
│                                                            │
│              [  OK  ]              [ Cancel ]              │
└────────────────────────────────────────────────────────────┘
```

3. Fill in the entry fields in the Signon window using these guidelines:

   Enter script file name:
   If your access method does not require a script file, leave this field blank. If your access method requires a script file, type the full path and name of the script file. For example, if you are connecting to a remote MVS host using the TCP/IP access method, you would type:

   pathname/tcptso.scr

   For more information about the names and locations of scripts used with a particular access method, see the chapter for that access method.

   Enter remote= value:
   Type the value specified for your access method. For example, use the host internet address for the TCP/IP access method. For more information about the REMOTE= value used for a particular access method, see the chapter for that access method.

   Enter communications access method id value:
   Type the value for the COMAMID= option. For example, with the TCP/IP access method, type

   TCP

   For more information about the COMAMID= value used for a particular host and access method, see "COMAMID= System Option" on page 174.

4. Select [OK] to sign on, or select [Cancel] to return to the PROGRAM EDITOR window without signing on.

Stopping SAS/CONNECT with the Signoff Option

To stop a SAS/CONNECT conversation by signing off, select `Signoff` from the `Locals` pull-down menu shown in Display 4.1.

After you sign on to a SAS/CONNECT session, the values you typed in the Signon window remain in effect during your current SAS session. If you sign off and later during that session want to sign on again, you can leave the fields blank. Simply select [OK] to sign on to the same host with the same access method used previously.

Once you end your SAS session, the values in the Signon window are deleted and you must type them again to sign on during a new SAS session.

When to Use a Script

How do you know if you need to write or modify a script? Some SAS/CONNECT access methods, such as NETBIOS, DECnet, and (in most cases) APPC, have no need of a script to start and stop a link. Other access methods do require one. The chapters in this book that describe specific access methods tell you if a script is necessary and provide examples. They also tell you the names of the sample scripts supplied with SAS/CONNECT. Your site may also have sample scripts available from your system administrator.

If the available sample scripts are not suited to your purposes, you can write your own script. If you do need to write or modify a script, review the examples in this chapter and see "Script Statements" on page 251 for descriptions of the script statements used in the examples.

Basic Script Functions

A script is a SAS program stored in a file on the local host. However, the programming statements in a script are not the usual SAS programming statements. Instead, scripts use a specialized set of SAS statements called *script statements.* Scripts are executed to initiate or terminate SAS/CONNECT conversations. Scripts that initiate the link are executed by submitting the SIGNON statement, and scripts that terminate the link are executed by submitting the SIGNOFF statement. In most cases, the same script is used to sign on and sign off.

A script can be a simple, short program or a long, complex program depending on what you want the script to do. All scripts must do at least three things:

- invoke the SAS System on the remote host (with the SAS command).
- set the appropriate communications options for the remote SAS session in the SAS command. On the remote host, the script sets the COMAMID= and DMR system options.
- determine when the remote SAS session is ready for communications with the local SAS session. In most cases, the script waits for messages from the remote SAS session.

Most scripts also perform a number of other optional functions, including the following:

- issue the remote host's logon command and prompt the user for a userid and password
- issue informative messages to the user about whether or not script execution is proceeding successfully
- combine both sign-on and sign-off functions
- conditionally execute labeled portions of the script so that one script can accommodate multiple types of connections (for example, ASYNC and 3270)
- issue remote host commands, such as commands setting session features or defining remote host files
- define any response expected from the remote host
- conditionally execute script subroutines to handle successful operations and error conditions
- set all communications parameters for ASYNC connections.

The sample scripts from SAS Institute perform all of these functions. By studying their contents, you can see how to use script statements to do these things.

Note that scripts that log on to the remote host include information specific to the computing installation and may need minor modifications to work with your logon sequence.

Using a Script to Start and Stop SAS/CONNECT

This section shows you how to start and stop SAS/CONNECT from a SAS Display Manager System session using the sample scripts supplied by SAS Institute. You find these scripts in the following directories where the SAS System is installed: *

Windows	*sasroot*\CONNECT\SASLINK
OS/2	*sasroot*\CONNECT\SASLINK
MVS	*prefix*.CTMISC
CMS	RLINKSCR MACLIB
VSE	plib library under psub sublibrary
VMS	SAS$ROOT:[TOOLS]
UNIX	*sasroot*/misc/connect

All sample scripts start and stop SAS/CONNECT. An automatic logon script prompts you for ID and password input to log on to a remote host. You must log on to the remote system before running a manual logon script.

For easy association of a script with its intended remote system, the naming conventions for most of the sample scripts are based on the access method and the name of the remote operating system. Most access methods use automatic logon scripts. Only EHLLAPI and ASYNC give you the choice of manually logging on to the remote host. For these access methods, the naming convention is based on the type of script and the name of the remote system. For example, TCPTSO.SCR is the script for a TCP access method and a TSO remote host, and TELVMS.SCR is the script for a TELNET access method and a VMS remote host.

If you are an experienced user and you already know how to start and stop the link, you can skip the step-by-step instructions and see "Shortcuts for Starting and Stopping SAS/CONNECT" on page 68 and "Starting Multiple SAS/CONNECT Sessions" on page 69.

---

* The term *sasroot* is not actually part of the pathname; it represents the name of the directory where the SAS System is installed at your site.

Starting SAS/CONNECT with an Automatic Logon Script

Automatic logon sample scripts must be modified with installation-specific information before you can use one to start the link.

1. Log on to or start your local system. If you need a terminal emulator, invoke it on your local system.

2. Invoke the SAS System in the local session. Enter

   ```
   sas
   ```

3. Type an OPTIONS statement in the PROGRAM EDITOR window of the local SAS session. The OPTIONS statement must specify the COMAMID= system option and the REMOTE= system option. For example, use an OPTIONS statement like the following:

   ```
   options comamid=communications-method remote=remote-session-id ;
   ```

   See "System Options, Statements, Commands, and SCL Functions" on page 173 for more information about specifying values for these options.
   Use the SUBMIT command, statement, or function key to execute the OPTIONS statement.

4. Execute the SIGNON command or type the SIGNON statement in the local SAS session.
   You can also use the PMENU facility to select the SIGNON command. The PMENU facility provides pull-down menus with items you can select to control your SAS session. To use the PMENU facility, issue the PMENU command to replace the command line with an action bar. See "Access Methods for SAS/CONNECT Software" on page 11 for instructions for using pull-down menu options to sign on and sign off a SAS/CONNECT conversation.
   Specify the appropriate sample script for your remote operating system:

   ```
   signon 'external-file-name-of-script'
   ```

   After the SIGNON command executes successfully, a message in the LOG window indicates that the link is established.

You are now ready to use SAS/CONNECT. You can remote submit SAS programs to execute on the host, access a single-user server with RLS, and upload and download SAS data sets, catalogs, and external files.

Starting SAS/CONNECT with a Manual Logon Script

This section applies to manual logon with EHLLAPI or RAYSNC for OS/2 or EHLLAPI for Windows.

To use one of the manual logon sample scripts to start the link:

1. Log on to or start your local system. If you need a terminal emulator, invoke it on the local system.

2. Log on to the remote computer with the normal logon procedure for that system.

3. Return to the local session after you log on to the remote system.

4. Invoke the SAS System in the local session. Enter

   ```
   sas
   ```

5. Type an OPTIONS statement in the PROGRAM EDITOR window of the local SAS session. The OPTIONS statement must specify the COMAMID= system option and the REMOTE= system option. For example, use an OPTIONS statement like the following:

   ```
   options comamid=communications-method remote=remote-session-id ;
   ```

   where *communications-method* can be EHLLAPI, RASYNC, or TCP for OS/2, or EHLLAPI for Windows, and *remote-session-id* is the name (short or long) of the session established with your emulation software of the COM port being used for ASYNC communications.

   Use the SUBMIT command, statement, or function key to execute the OPTIONS statement.

6. Issue the SIGNON command or type the SIGNON statement in the PROGRAM EDITOR window of the local SAS session.

   Specify the appropriate sample script for your remote operating system:

   ```
   signon 'external-file-name-of-script '
   ```

   After SIGNON is successful, a message in the LOG window indicates that the link is established.

   You can also use the PMENU facility to sign on, as described in "Using PMENUS to Start and Stop SAS/CONNECT" on page 62.

You are now ready to use SAS/CONNECT. You can remote submit SAS programs to execute on the remote system, access a single-user server with RLS, and upload and download SAS data sets, catalogs, and external files.

Stopping SAS/CONNECT with an Automatic Logoff Script

If you use an automatic logoff script to stop the link, issue the SIGNOFF command or type the SIGNOFF statement in the local SAS session:

    signoff 'external-file-name-of-script'

After the SIGNOFF command executes successfully, a message in the LOG window indicates that the link is terminated.

The sample scripts for automatic log on also log off from your remote system session.

Stopping SAS/CONNECT with a Manual Logoff Script

This section applies only to EHLLAPI or RAYSNC for OS/2 and EHLLAPI for Windows. When you are ready to terminate the link, use the SIGNOFF command or SIGNOFF statement. The SIGNOFF command executes a script containing statements that terminate the link. The sample scripts from SAS Institute are designed for both the SIGNON and SIGNOFF commands so you only need one script, not two.

If you use a manual logoff script to stop the link:

1. Issue the SIGNOFF command or type the SIGNOFF statement in the local SAS session:

        signoff 'external-file-name-of-script'

    You can also signoff with the PMENU facility, described in "Using PMENUS to Start and Stop SAS/CONNECT" on page 62. After the SIGNOFF command executes successfully, a message in the LOG window indicates that the link is terminated.

2. Log off the remote system. The sample scripts for manual remote system log off do not automatically log off from your remote system session. You must log off manually. After the link successfully terminates, return to your remote session and log off the remote system.

Shortcuts for Starting and Stopping SAS/CONNECT

You can simplify the process of starting and stopping the link by following these recommendations:

- Review the contents of your SAS autoexec file. The *autoexec file* is a file of SAS statements that may be executed automatically when you begin a local session. The autoexec file should include a FILENAME statement that defines the fileref RLINK. Be sure that it gives the correct file specification for the script you use to start SAS/CONNECT.

    By assigning the fileref RLINK to your script, you can start the link without specifying the script's name with the SIGNON command and stop it without specifying the script name with the SIGNOFF command. This is because RLINK is the default fileref for script files.

- Also check your autoexec file for an OPTIONS statement. If there is an OPTIONS statement, be sure that it specifies the COMAMID= system option and the REMOTE= system option and that they are set correctly. If there is no OPTIONS statement, you should add one, specifying the COMAMID= and REMOTE= system options. For example, under OS/2 your OPTIONS statement might include these values:

    ```
    options comamid=tcp remote=internet-address;
    ```

    By including an OPTIONS statement with the REMOTE= and COMAMID= system options in the autoexec file, you avoid having to execute an OPTIONS statement in each SAS session using SAS/CONNECT.

Modifying your autoexec file as recommended eliminates a step in the process of starting the link, and you can use the short form of the SIGNON and SIGNOFF commands. For example, to start the link with an automatic logon script:

1. Log on to or start your local system.
2. Invoke the SAS System in the local session.
3. Issue the SIGNON command or submit the SIGNON statement.

    ```
    signon
    ```

If you use the shortcuts, you only need to issue the SIGNOFF command or submit the SIGNOFF statement to stop the link:

```
signoff
```

To start the link with a manual logon script, perform these steps:

1. Log on to or start your local system. If you need a terminal emulator, invoke it on the local system.
2. Log on to the remote system.
3. Return to the local session.
4. Invoke the SAS System in the local session.
5. Issue the SIGNON command or submit the SIGNON statement.

    ```
    signon
    ```

Starting Multiple SAS/CONNECT Sessions

An easy way to start up multiple SAS/CONNECT sessions is by using your autoexec file to invoke multiple sessions when you start a local SAS session.

For example, if you wanted to connect to a TSO host through the APPC access method and a VMS host through the TCP/IP access method, your autoexec file could contain the following:

```
   /* Start a TSO session */
filename rlink 'TSO-script-file ';
options comamid=appc remote=LUNAME of APPC/MVS;
signon;


   /* Start a VMS session */
filename rlink 'VMS-script-file ';
options comamid=tcp remote=internet-address;
signon;
```

After your autoexec processing is complete, you can direct statements to either remote host from a single SUBMIT block in your local SAS session. You do this by preceding each section of statements with an RSUBMIT statement that specifies the remote host's session id. You end the block with an ENDRSUBMIT statement. For example, to remote-submit to the TSO host:

```
rsubmit LUNAME of APPC/MVS;

   statements...

endrsubmt;
```

and remote-submit to the VMS host by entering:

```
rsubmit internet-address;

   statements...

endrsubmt;
```

Issue the SIGNOFF command or submit the SIGNOFF statement when you are finished. Note that you must have the appropriate script file to sign off from each host. A simple, direct method for ensuring that you are using the correct script file when signing off of multiple remote sessions is to define the RLINK fileref before each signoff as in the following example.

Submit these statements to the local host:

```
filename rlink 'TSO-script-file ';
signoff LUNAME of APPC/MVS;
filename rlink 'VMS-script-file ';
signoff internet-address;
```

For more information about SIGNON, SIGNOFF, and RSUBMIT, see "System Options, Statements, Commands, and SCL Functions" on page 173.

General Script Statement Rules

To write a script, you need to read about the specific information for each statement in the script. This section contains general rules applying to some or all script statements. Each statement description in "Script Statements" on page 251 indicates the applicable access method. In addition, Table 17.1 shows the access method for which each script statement is effective. A script statement that is not valid for your access method is ignored.

Syntax

- Like other SAS statements, all script statements must end with a semicolon.

- Script statements have a free format, which means that there are no spacing or indention requirements. A statement can be split across several lines, or one line can contain one or more statements. Statement keywords can be in uppercase, lowercase, or mixed case.

- Text strings enclosed in quotes are case sensitive. For example, if your script defines a text string in a WAITFOR statement, be sure that the uppercase and lowercase letters in the text string match the text string from the remote host exactly.

- Any script statement can include a label specification. The label must be a valid SAS name, with a maximum of eight characters. The first character must be a letter or underscore. A label must be followed immediately by a colon (:) and must be defined only once in the script.

- Some script statements specify a time in seconds. The form of the time specification is

  n SECONDS

  where *n* can be any number, including decimal fractions. SECOND is an alias for SECONDS. For example, all of the following time specifications are valid:

  0 SECONDS

  0.25 SECONDS

  1 SECOND

  3.14 SECONDS.

- If a script statement specifies a quoted string, such as a remote host command, you can use either single or double quotes. Follow the same rules you use for embedded quotes in SAS statements to embed quotes in script statements.

Writing Simple Scripts for Signing On and Signing Off

This section illustrates how to write two simple scripts. The first one signs on and off over an EHLLAPI 3270 connection to CMS as the remote host. This script assumes that the user has already logged on to CMS and simply wants to establish a link with SAS/CONNECT. The second is for signing on and off over a TCP/IP connection. This script uses UNIX as the remote host. The techniques used in these scripts are basic to writing scripts. For examples of more complicated scripts, refer to the sample scripts listed at the end of the chapter.

When you are writing scripts or modifying existing ones, the WAITFOR and TYPE statements require special attention to detail. To ensure that the script recognizes the expected prompt for each stage of signing on, you must be careful to specify the exact sequence of prompts and responses for the remote host. The simplest method for determining these is to go to the remote host and manually go through the process that you want to capture in the WAITFOR and TYPE statements. For each display on the remote host, choose a word from that display for the WAITFOR statement. Whatever information you type to respond to a display should be specified in the TYPE statement. Be sure to note all carriage returns or other special keys.

If TSO is the remote host and you need to use a TYPE statement greater than 80 characters in a signon script, divide the TYPE statement into two or more TYPE statements. To divide the TYPE statement, insert a hyphen (-) at the division point. The remote TSO host interprets the hyphen as the continuation of the TYPE statement from the previous line. For example, to divide the following TYPE statement:

```
type "sas options ('dmr comamid=pclink')" enter;
```

change it to:

```
type "sas options ('dmr comamid=-" enter;
type "pclink')" enter;
```

Remember not to add any spaces around the hyphen.

Script for EHLLAPI Connections

This script signs on and off using the EHLLAPI access method. In this sample script, the remote host is a CMS system, but the process for other remote systems is very similar.

```
/* trace on; */
/* echo on;  */
/*--------------------------------------------------------------------
   Copyright (C) 1990 by SAS Institute Inc., Cary NC
   name:     cms.scr
   purpose:  SAS/CONNECT SIGNON/SIGNOFF script for connecting to
             a CMS host using the EHLLAPI or RASYNC access methods
             from a local OS/2 system or the EHLLAPI access method
             from a local WINDOWS 3.0 system.
   notes:    1. The communication parameters may need to be changed
                for your site.
   assumes:  1. This script assumes the remote session is already
                logged on.
             2. The command to execute SAS in your remote (CMS)
                environment is "sas".  If this is incorrect for your
                site, change the contents of the line that contains ...
                type "sas ...
   support:  SAS Institute staff
   --------------------------------------------------------------------*/

log "NOTE: Script file 'cms.scr' entered.";
```

❶ `if signoff then goto signoff;`
   `if fullscreen then goto on32;`

   `/*---- RASYNC SIGNON FROM A LOCAL OS/2 SYSTEM ----------------------*/`

   `log 'NOTE: Signing on async device.';`

   `baud 1200;`
   `parity none;`
   `stopbits 1;`
   `databits 8;`

   `type cr;`
   `waitfor 'dc1', 10 seconds: noinit;`
   `type 'set autoread on' cr;`
   `waitfor dc1, 20 seconds: timeout;`
   `type 'terminal linesize off' cr;`
   `waitfor dc1, 20 seconds: timeout;`
   `type 'set blip off' cr;`
   `waitfor dc1, 20 seconds: timeout;`
   `log 'NOTE: Starting remote SAS now.';`
   `/* noterminal suppressses prompts from remote SAS session.    */`
   `/* no$syntaxcheck prevents remote side from going into syntax */`
   `/* checking mode when a syntax error is encountered.          */`
   `type 'sas (dmr comamid=rasync noterminal no$syntaxcheck)' cr;`
   `waitfor 'PACKET': onok, 60 seconds: nosas;`

   `/*---- EHLLAPI SIGNON ------------------------------------------*/`

   `on32:`
❷ `log 'NOTE: Signing on fullscreen device.';`

   `type clear;`
❸ `waitfor 'VM READ', 'RUNNING', 20 seconds: noinit;`

   `log 'NOTE: Starting remote SAS now.';`

   `/* noterminal suppressses prompts from remote SAS session.    */`
   `/* no$syntaxcheck prevents remote side from going into syntax */`
   `/* checking mode when a syntax error is encountered.          */`

❹ `type 'sas (dmr comamid=pclink noterminal no$syntaxcheck)' enter;`
   `goto continue;`
   `continue:`
❺ `waitfor 'IN PROGRESS', 60 seconds: nosas;`

   `onok:`
   `log 'NOTE: SAS/CONNECT conversation established.';`
❻ `stop;`

   `/*---- RASYNC SIGNOFF ------------------------------------------*/`

   `/*---- EHLLAPI SIGNOFF -----------------------------------------*/`

❼ ```
   signoff:
     log 'NOTE: SAS/CONNECT conversation terminated.';
     log 'NOTE: Remote session left logged on.';
     stop;

   /*----- SUBROUTINES ---*/

   /*----- ERROR HANDLING --*/
```
❽ ```
   noinit:
     snapshot;
     log 'ERROR: Did not get remote prompt.  Remote session not active.';
     log 'NOTE: You must log on to the remote session before signing on';
     log '      using this script file.';
     abort;
```
❾ ```
   nosas:
     snapshot;
     log 'ERROR: Did not get SAS software startup messages.';
     abort;

   timeout:
     log 'ERROR: Timeout waiting for remote session response.';
     abort;
```

❶ The IF/THEN statement can detect whether the script was called by the SIGNON command or statement, or the SIGNOFF command or statement. When you are signing off, the IF/THEN statement directs script processing to the statement labeled SIGNOFF. See step 7.

❷ The LOG statement issues the message enclosed in quotation marks in the log file or LOG window of the local SAS session. Although it is not necessary to include LOG statements in your script file, the LOG statements keep the user informed of the progress of the connection.

❸ The WAITFOR statement defines what prompt is expected from the remote host, in this case either VM READ or RUNNING, and specifies that if that prompt is not received within 20 seconds, the script processing should branch to the statement label named at the end of the WAITFOR statement.

❹ This TYPE statement invokes the SAS System on the remote host. The DMR system option is necessary to invoke a special processing mode for SAS/CONNECT. The COMAMID= system option specifies the access method used to establish the connection.

❺ The phrase **IN PROGRESS** is displayed when a SAS session is started on the remote host with the DMR system option and COMAMID=PCLINK. The WAITFOR statement looks for this phrase to be issued by the remote host to know that the connection has been established. If the **IN PROGRESS** response is received within 60 seconds, processing continues with the next LOG statement. If the **IN PROGRESS** response does not occur within 60 seconds, the script assumes that the SAS session has not started and processing branches to the statement labeled NOSAS.
```

Starting and Stopping SAS/CONNECT Software □ *Writing Simple Scripts for Signing On and Signing Off* **75**

❻ When the connection has been successfully established, you must stop the rest of the script processing. Without this STOP statement, processing continues through the remaining statements in the script.

❼ These statements are executed when the script is invoked to terminate the link. The first IF statement (see step 1) sends processing to this section of the script when the script is invoked by a SIGNOFF command or statement. Note that this section simply issues a LOG statement to notify the user that the link is terminated and stops the link. No other processing occurs during signoff in this script.

❽ These statements are processed only if the prompt expected in the first WAITFOR statement is not received. The SNAPSHOT statement captures any messages from the remote host; the subsequent statements issue messages to the local SAS log and then abnormally end the script processing as well as the SIGNON.

❾ These statements are processed only if the response expected in step 5 is not received. This section issues messages to the local SAS log and then abnormally ends the script processing as well as the SIGNON.

Script for TCP/IP Connections

```
/* trace on; */
/* echo  on; */
/*-------------------------------------------------------------------*/
/*--            Copyright (C) 1990 by SAS Institute Inc., Cary NC  --*/
/*--                                                               --*/
/*-- name:      tcpunix.scr                                        --*/
/*--                                                               --*/
/*-- purpose:   SAS/CONNECT SIGNON/SIGNOFF script for connecting   --*/
/*--            to any UNIX host via the TCP access method         --*/
/*--                                                               --*/
/*-- notes:  1. This script may need modifications that account    --*/
/*--            for the local flavour of your UNIX environment.    --*/
/*--            The logon procedure should mimic the events that   --*/
/*--            you go through when "telnet"-ing to the same       --*/
/*--            UNIX host.                                         --*/
/*--                                                               --*/
/*--         2. You must have specified OPTIONS COMAMID=TCP        --*/
/*--            in the local SAS session before using the signon   --*/
/*--            command.                                           --*/
/*--                                                               --*/
/*-- assumes: 1. The command to execute SAS in your remote (UNIX)  --*/
/*--             environment is "sas". If this is incorrect        --*/
/*--             for your site, change the contents of the line    --*/
/*--             that contains:                                    --*/
/*--                type 'sas ...                                   --*/
/*--                                                               --*/
/*-- support:   SAS Institute staff                                --*/
/*--                                                               --*/
/*-------------------------------------------------------------------*/
```

```
❶   log "NOTE: Script file 'tcpunix.scr' entered.";

        if not tcp then goto notcp;
❷   if signoff then goto signoff;

        /* --------------- TCP SIGNON ------------------------------------*/

❸   waitfor 'login:' , 120 seconds: noinit;



    /*----------------UNIX LOGON--------------------------------------*/
    /*-- for some reason, it needs a LF to turn the line around    --*/
    /*-- after the login name has been typed. (A CR will not do)   --*/
    /*---------------------------------------------------------------*/

❹   input 'Userid?';
❺   waitfor 'Password', 30 seconds : nolog;
        input nodisplay 'Password?';
        type LF;

    unx_log:
❻   waitfor '$'
                , '>'               /*-- another common prompt character --*/
                , '%'               /*-- another common prompt character --*/
                , '}'               /*-- another common prompt character --*/
                , 'Login incorrect'    : nouser
                , 'Enter terminal type' : unx_term
                , 30 seconds           : timeout
                ;


    log 'NOTE: Logged onto UNIX... Starting remote SAS now.';

    /* noterminal suppressses prompts from remote SAS session.    */
    /* no$syntaxcheck prevents remote side from going into syntax */
    /* checking mode when a syntax error is encountered.          */

❼   type 'sas -dmr -comamid tcp -device grlink -noterminal -no$syntaxcheck' LF;
❽   waitfor 'SESSION ESTABLISHED', 90 seconds : nosas;

❾   log 'NOTE: SAS/CONNECT conversation established.';
        stop;


    /*---------------- TCP SIGNOFF -----------------------------------*/
    signoff:
❿   waitfor '$'
                , '>'               /*-- another common prompt character --*/
                , '%'               /*-- another common prompt character --*/
                , '}'               /*-- another common prompt character --*/
                , 30 seconds
                ;
```

```
            type    'logout' LF;
            log 'NOTE: SAS/CONNECT conversation terminated.';
            stop;




   /*-------------- SUBROUTINES -----------------------------------*/

   unx_term:
   /*-------------------------------------------------------------*/
   /*-- some unixen want the terminal-type.                    --*/
   /*-- so tell them we are the most basic of terminals.       --*/
   /*-------------------------------------------------------------*/
            type 'tty' LF;
            goto unx_log;



   /*-------------- ERROR ROUTINES --------------------------------*/
```
⓫
```
   timeout:
        log 'ERROR: Timeout waiting for remote session response.';
        abort;

   nouser:
        log 'ERROR: Unrecognized userid or password.';
        abort;

   notcp:
        log 'ERROR: Incorrect communications access method.';
        log 'NOTE: You must set "OPTIONS COMAMID=TCP;" before using this';
        log '      script file.';
        abort;

   noinit:
        log 'ERROR: Did not understand remote session banner.';

   nolog:
        log 'ERROR: Did not receive userid or password prompt.';
        abort;

   nosas:
        log 'ERROR: Did not get SAS software startup messages.';
        abort;
```

❶ The LOG statement sends the message enclosed in quotation marks to the log file or LOG window of the local SAS session. Although it is not necessary to include LOG statements in your script file, the LOG statements keep the user informed on the progress of the connection.

❷ The IF/THEN statement can detect whether the script was called by the SIGNON command or statement or the SIGNOFF command or statement. When you are signing off, the IF/THEN statement directs script processing to the statement labeled SIGNOFF. See step 10.

❸ The WAITFOR statement waits for the remote host's login prompt and specifies that if that prompt is not received within 120 seconds, the script processing should branch to the statement labeled NOINIT.

❹ The INPUT statement displays a window with the text **Userid** to allow the user to enter a remote host logon userid. The TYPE statement sends a line feed to the remote host to enter the userid to the remote host.

❺ This WAITFOR statement waits for the remote host's password prompt and branches to the NOLOG label if it is not received within 30 seconds. The INPUT statement following the WAITFOR statement displays a window for the user to enter a password.

❻ The WAITFOR statement waits for one of several common UNIX prompts and branches to various error handles if a prompt is not seen. Verify that the WAITFOR statement in the script looks for the correct prompt for your site.

❼ This TYPE statement invokes the SAS System on the remote host. The DMR option is necessary to invoke a special processing mode for SAS/CONNECT. The COMAMID= option specifies the access method used to make the connection.

❽ The phrase **SESSION ESTABLISHED** is displayed when a SAS session is started on the remote host with the DMR and COMAMID=TCP options. The WAITFOR statement looks for the words **SESSION ESTABLISHED** to be issued by the remote host to know that the connection has been established. If the **SESSION ESTABLISHED** response is received within 90 seconds, processing continues with the next LOG statement. If the **SESSION ESTABLISHED** response does not occur within 90 seconds, the script assumes that the remote SAS session has not started and processing branches to the statement labeled NOSAS.

❾ When the connection has been successfully established, you must stop the rest of the script processing. Without this STOP statement, processing continues through the remaining statements in the script.

❿ This section of code is executed when the script is invoked to terminate the link. The first IF statement (see step 2) sends processing to this section of the script when the script is invoked by a SIGNOFF command or statement. Note that this section waits for a remote host prompt before typing **LOGOUT** in order to log off the remote host. The script then issues a LOG statement to notify the user that the link is terminated and stops the link.

⓫ These statements are processed only if the prompts expected in the previous steps are not received. This section of the script issues messages to the local SAS log and then abnormally ends the script processing as well as the SIGNON.

Debugging a Script

When writing scripts, you can take advantage of programming techniques to simplify debugging a new or modified script. These techniques are outlined in this section.

Statements Useful for Debugging

- For ASYNC, TELNET, and TCP connections, the ECHO statement causes remote host messages to be displayed while a WAITFOR statement executes. This enables you to monitor activity on the remote host during the WAITFOR pause.

- For 3270 connections, the SNAPSHOT statement sends all messages on the current 3270 display to the local LOG window or file so you can see if any error messages or conditions occurred in the remote session.

- The TRACE statement enables you to specify that some or all script statements be displayed as the script executes. This capability can help you isolate the source of a script problem. The TRACE statement can be used with any type of connection.

Sample Scripts

This section shows two sample logon scripts: one is automatic, the other is manual. When an automatic logon script runs, you are prompted for your userid and password; the script then signs on to the remote host. With a manual logon script, you must first log on to the remote host, then run the manual script to sign on.

Automatic Logon

Connections with the TCP/IP access method can only be made through an automatic logon script. This example is a SAS/CONNECT signon/signoff script for connecting to a VMS host through the TCP access method.

```
/* trace on; */
/* echo on;  */
/*-------------------------------------------------------------*/
/*--            Copyright (C) 1990 by SAS Institute Inc., Cary NC  --*/
/*--                                                               --*/
/*-- name:     tcpvms.scr                                          --*/
/*--                                                               --*/
/*-- purpose:  SAS/CONNECT SIGNON/SIGNOFF script for connecting    --*/
/*--           to any VMS host via the TCP access method.          --*/
/*--                                                               --*/
/*-- notes:    1. This script may need modifications that account --*/
/*--              for the local flavour of your VMS environment.  --*/
/*--              The logon procedure should mimic the events that --*/
/*--              you go through when "telnet"-ing to the same    --*/
/*--              VMS host.                                        --*/
/*--                                                               --*/
/*--           2. You must have specified OPTIONS COMAMID=TCP     --*/
/*--              in the local SAS session before using the signon --*/
/*--              command.                                         --*/
/*--                                                               --*/
```

```
/*-- assumes: 1. The command to execute SAS in your remote (VMS) --*/
/*--             environment is "sas". If this is incorrect for  --*/
/*--             your site, change the contents of the line that --*/
/*--             contains:                                        --*/
/*--                type "sas ...                                 --*/
/*--                                                              --*/
/*--          2. The remote (VMS) system prompt is a "$".         --*/
/*--                                                              --*/
/*-- support:    SAS Institute staff                              --*/
/*--                                                              --*/
/*--------------------------------------------------------------------*/
```

❶ log "NOTE: Script file 'tcpvms.scr' entered.";

❷ if not tcp then goto notcp;
❸ if signoff then goto signoff;

```
/*------------------------VMS LOGON-----------------------------*/
```

❹ waitfor 'Username:', 120 seconds : noinit;
❺ input 'Userid?';
   type CR;
   waitfor 'Password:', 60 seconds : nopass;
   input nodisplay 'Password?';
   type CR;

   waitfor '$',
           'authorization failure' : nouser,
           120 seconds   : nostrt;

strt_sas:
❻ log 'NOTE: Logged on to VMS.... Starting remote SAS now.';

   /* noterminal suppressses prompts from remote SAS session.   */
   /* no$syntaxcheck prevents remote side from going into syntax */
   /* checking mode when a syntax error is encountered.   */

❼ type 'SAS/DMR/COMAMID=TCP/DEVICE=GRLINK/NOTERMINAL/NO$SYNTAXCHECK' CR;
❽ waitfor 'SESSION ESTABLISHED', 120 seconds : nosas;

   log 'NOTE: SAS/CONNECT conversation established';
   stop;

```
/*------------------------VMS LOGOFF----------------------------*/
```
❾ signoff:
    type 'logout' CR;
    waitfor 'logged out at' , 120 seconds : noterm;

    log 'NOTE: SAS/CONNECT conversation terminated.';
    stop;

```
/*-------------- ERROR ROUTINES --------------------------------*/
```

❿
```
notcp:
   log 'ERROR: Incorrect communications access method.';
   log 'NOTE: You must set "OPTIONS COMAMID=TCP;" before using this';
   log '     script file.';
   abort;

nouser:
   log 'ERROR: Invalid USERNAME/PASSWORD combination.';
   abort;

noinit:
   log 'ERROR: Did not understand remote session banner.';
   abort;

nopass:
   log 'ERROR: Did not get password prompt.';
   abort;

nostrt:
   snapshot;
   log 'ERROR: Did not get VMS startup messages after logon.';
   abort;

nosas:
   snapshot;
   log 'ERROR: Did not get SAS software startup messages.';
   abort;

noterm:
   snapshot;
   log 'WARNING: Did not get messages confirming logoff.';
   abort;
```

❶ For both signon and signoff, this note identifying the script being processed is written to the LOG window of the local SAS session.

❷ If you have not set your COMAMID= system option to TCP, processing is directed to step 10 and aborted.

❸ If the script is being executed because you are signing off, processing is directed to step 9.

❹ The WAITFOR statement defines what prompt is expected from the remote host. When the prompt is received, processing goes to step 5. If the expected prompt is not returned within 120 seconds, an error message is written to the SAS log and the script aborts.

❺ These statements control logon to the remote host. This section combines TYPE and WAITFOR statements to send characters to the remote host and pause until the expected response is received. The INPUT statement prompts the user for a value, which is passed on to the remote host.

❻ If logon is successful, the message is written to the local host log.

❼ The TYPE statement invokes the SAS System on the remote host. The DMR system option is necessary to invoke a special processing mode for SAS/CONNECT. The

COMAMID= system option specifies the access method used to establish the connection. The DEVICE= option specifies the GRLINK graphics device driver in case you'll be doing remote graphics processing.

❽ The WAITFOR statement looks for the message **SESSION ESTABLISHED** which is displayed when a SAS session starts on the remote host. If the message is found within 120 seconds, signon is successful. The message is written to the log. If 120 seconds pass before signon is complete, the error message is written to the log and processing aborts.

❾ This portion of the script performs sign-off processing. The script issues the LOGOUT command and waits for confirmation that you are logged off. If no confirmation is received in 20 seconds, then the warning message is written to the log and the script stops.

❿ Processing is directed here if the expected responses are not received.

Manual Logon

Before executing this script, you should have already logged on to the remote system; this script signs on to the remote TSO host.

```
/* trace on; */
/* echo on;  */
/*-----------------------------------------------------------------
    Copyright (C) 1990 by SAS Institute Inc., Cary NC
    name:      tso.scr
    purpose:   SAS/CONNECT SIGNON/SIGNOFF script for connecting to a
               MVS/TSO host using either the EHLLAPI or RASYNC access
               method from a local OS/2 system or the EHLLAPI access
               method from a local WINDOWS 3.0 system
    notes:     1. The communication parameters may need to be changed
                  for your site.
    assumes:   1. This script assumes the remote session is already
                  logged on.
               2. The command to execute SAS in your remote (MVS/TSO)
                  environment is "sas". If this is incorrect for your
                  site, change the contents of the line that contains ...
                  type "sas ...

    support:   SAS Institute staff
  -----------------------------------------------------------------*/
```

❶ log "NOTE: Script file 'tso.scr' entered.";

❷ if signoff then goto signoff;
   if fullscreen then goto on32;

```
          /*---- RASYNC SIGNON FROM A LOCAL OS/2 SYSTEM----------------------*/

             log 'NOTE: Signing on async device.';

❸   baud 1200;
       parity none;
       stopbits 1;
       databits 8;

❹   type cr;
       waitfor 'READY', 10 seconds: noinit;
       waitfor 1 second;
       log 'NOTE: Starting remote SAS now.';
       /* noterminal suppressses prompts from remote SAS session.    */
       /* no$syntaxcheck prevents remote side from going into syntax */
       /* checking mode when a syntax error is encountered.          */
       type "sas options('dmr,comamid=rasync,noterminal,no$syntaxcheck')" cr;
       waitfor 'PACKET': onok, 60 seconds: nosas;

     /*---- EHLLAPI SIGNON ----------------------------------------*/

❺     on32:
         log 'NOTE: Signing on fullscreen device.';

         waitfor 'READY', 0 seconds: noinit;
         log 'NOTE: Starting remote SAS now.';
         /* noterminal suppressses prompts from remote SAS session.    */
         /* no$syntaxcheck prevents remote side from going into syntax */
         /* checking mode when a syntax error is encountered.          */
         type "sas options('dmr,comamid=pclink,noterminal,no$syntaxcheck')" enter;
         goto continue;
❻     continue:
         waitfor 'IN PROGRESS', 20 seconds: waitsas;

❼     onok:
         log 'NOTE: SAS/CONNECT conversation established.';
         stop;

     /*---- RASYNC SIGNOFF ----------------------------------------*/

     /*---- EHLLAPI SIGNOFF ----------------------------------------*/

❽     signoff:
         log 'NOTE: SAS/CONNECT conversation terminated.';
         log 'NOTE: Remote session left logged on.';
         stop;

     /*----- SUBROUTINES ------------------------------------------*/

❾     waitsas:
         log 'NOTE: Waiting for startup screen...';
         type EREOF enter;
         goto continue;
```

```
                  /*----- ERROR HANDLING -------------------------------------------*/
❿ noinit:
     snapshot;
     log 'ERROR: Did not get remote prompt.  Remote session not active.';
     log 'NOTE: You must log on to the remote session before signing on';
     log '     using this script file.';
     abort;

⓫   nosas:
     snapshot;
     log 'ERROR: Did not get SAS software startup messages.';
     abort;
```

❶ LOG statements write messages to the local host's SAS log providing information about the progress of the signon.

❷ The IF statement tests for a limited set of conditions and then directs processing to the appropriate statement label. For example, if the SIGNOFF command or statement invokes this script, processing jumps to the SIGNOFF label. See step 8 in this list. The FULLSCREEN condition indicates that the link to the remote host is using the EHLLAPI access method.

❸ For connections that do not meet the condition of the previous IF statement, that is, asynchronous connections, the script sets the necessary communications parameters. These, like other portions of the script, may be modified to better suit your use of SAS/CONNECT.

❹ The WAITFOR and TYPE statements start the SAS session via the asynchronous connection.

❺ These statements write the message to the local host's log. The WAITFOR statement looks for the remote host READY prompt and processing goes to step 10 if no prompt is received. When the READY prompt is received, the TYPE statement invokes the SAS System on the remote host. The DMR system option is necessary to invoke a special processing mode for SAS/CONNECT. The COMAMID= system option specifies the access method used to establish the connection. The DEVICE= option specifies the GRLINK graphics device driver in case you'll be doing remote graphics processing.

❻ The WAITFOR statement looks for the message IN PROGRESS, which is displayed when a SAS session starts on the remote host. If the message is not found, processing goes to the WAITSAS label in step 9.

❼ This LOG statement prints a message to the log to indicate that you have successfully established a link.

❽ These statements are executed when step 2 directs processing here. The two notes are written to the local log, and the link is terminated.

❾ Processing continues from step 6. The note is written to the local log, and processing returns to step 6.

❿ Processing continues from step 4 if the READY prompt is not received. The SNAPSHOT statement captures messages displayed on the remote host and writes them to the local host's log. The log messages can help you determine what has occurred on the remote host to interrupt the signon. You can save or print the local log to have a record of these messages. The error and note messages are written to the local log, and the script aborts.

⓫ Processing continues from step 4 if the second WAITFOR statement does not receive the string in less than 60 seconds. The SNAPSHOT statement captures messages displayed on the remote host and writes them to the local host's log. The log messages can help you determine what has occurred on the remote host to interrupt the signon. You can save or print the local log to have a record of these messages. The error message is written to the local log, and the script aborts.

SCL Functions Used with SAS/CONNECT

The Screen Control Language (SCL) of SAS/AF and SAS/FSP software provides four functions that can be used with SAS/CONNECT. For more information on how to use these functions, see "SCL Functions: COMAMID, RLINK, RSESSION, RSTITLE" on page 201.

The COMAMID function returns a string containing all communications access methods (comamids) that are valid for the operating system where the SCL code executes. This is useful for providing a list of comamids for users.

The RLINK function determines whether a conversation has been established between the current SAS session and a remote session.

The RSTITLE function saves the remote session id and its corresponding description for an existing connection. This information can then be retrieved with the RSESSION function and used to build a list of connections. SAS/ASSIST software uses these descriptions to build a list of connections you can select when submitting to a remote host.

The RSESSION function returns the name and description of the specified remote session. You must have previously specified the description and saved it using the RSTITLE function.

Locating and Storing Sample Script Files with SCL Functions

The SAS system option SASSCRIPT= defines the location of the SAS/CONNECT script files. The value of the SASSCRIPT= SAS system option is a logical name or one or more aggregate storage locations (such as directories or partitioned data sets). When you set the SASSCRIPT= system option, it generates another SAS system option, SASFRSCR, which is set to the value of a fileref that is used to build a list of scripts for SCL applications. When you establish a link while using SAS/ASSIST, this product uses the information provided by the SASFRSCR option to provide a list of available scripts. You can also build a similar menu of script files for user-written applications by accessing the SASFRSCR SAS system option from an SCL program.

The following an SCL program obtains the value of the SASFRSCR system option and uses it to create a list of scripts. Refer to *SAS Screen Control Language: Reference, Version 6, First Edition* for information on the SCL functions used in this example.

```
INIT;
return;

MAIN:
     /* Get internally-assigned fileref */
   fileref=optgetc('sasfrscr');
```

```
      /* Open the directory (aggregate storage location) */
   dirid=dopen(fileref);

      /* Get the number of files */
   numfiles=dnum(dirid);

      /* Define a custom selection list the length of the      */
      /* number of files and allowing users to make one choice. */
   call setrow(numfiles,1);
return;

TERM:
    /* Close the directory  */
   rc=dclose(dirid);
return;

GETROW:
       /* Display the list of file names  */
   filename=dread(dirid,_currow_);
return;

PUTROW:
      /* Get directory path name.  */
   fullname=pathname(fileref);

      /* Concatename file name user selects with directory pathname.  */
   name=fullname ||'/'|| filename;
   /* other SCL statements to use complete file name stored in name */
return;
```

Chapter 5 Using Break Windows

Introduction 87

SAS/CONNECT Attention Handler Window 87

Communication Services Break Handler Window 88

When a Host Message Interrupts SAS/CONNECT 90
Reading the Host Message 90
Responding to the Message 90
Continuing SAS/CONNECT Processing 90
Example 91

Introduction

This chapter discusses ways to handle problems that occur when you use SAS/CONNECT. Problems can arise from errors you make, from host conditions, from hardware failures, and so on.

Break windows appear when you encounter problems such as errors or system interruptions. To solve such problems successfully, all users need to be familiar with break windows and their uses. Other problems can be solved through programming techniques, keyboard sequences, or circumventions. In addition to the information in this chapter, "General Tips and Troubleshooting" on page 159 can help you solve problems, and "Starting and Stopping SAS/CONNECT Software" on page 61 contains information about debugging scripts. (For information specific to micro-to-host link releases, see "Details for Micro-to-Host Link Releases" on page 289.)

The SAS System provides two break windows to enable you to handle system interruptions and error conditions while using SAS/CONNECT:

- Communication Services Break Handler window
- SAS/CONNECT Attention Handler window.

These break windows also enable you to interrupt processing if you need to. You may see either of these break windows depending on the program statements that are executing.

The Communication Services Break Handler window contains selections for actions you can take in response to a problem or an interruption. Invoking the SAS/CONNECT Attention Handler window is one of the actions you can select. Typically, you select the Attention Handler window to cancel statements that you have submitted to the remote host.

SAS/CONNECT Attention Handler Window

If you need to interrupt processing of statements submitted to the remote host, issue a break signal:

OS/2	CTRL-C or CTRL-BREAK
Windows	CTRL-BREAK
UNIX	CTRL-C (This key combination can be reset with the UNIX STTY command. During a SAS session in DMS mode under The X Window

(UNIX continued)

System, you can select an interrupt button in the SAS Session Manager window to issue a break signal.)

MVS	ATTN key
CMS	PA1
VAX	CTRL-C
VSE	ATTN key

After you issue a break signal, the SAS/CONNECT Attention Handler window appears, with the selections shown in Display 5.1.

Note: With the APPC access method, the SAS/CONNECT Attention Handler window will not be displayed if a CTRL-BREAK sequence is issued during a remote submit. Instead, the Global Handler window will be displayed with a prompt for terminating the SAS session.

Display 5.1
The SAS/CONNECT Attention Handler Window

The following selections are available in the Attention Handler window:

a   aborts the statements that are currently being processed on the remote host but keeps the link open. This option is useful if you want to terminate a very large file transfer or if you want to interrupt a remote SAS job that is generating many error messages.

c   continues the remote job. Select this option if you decide that you do not want to interrupt the remote job.

Communication Services Break Handler Window

If the application detects an error condition and you are running one of the terminal-based access methods, the Communication Services Break Handler window appears with one or more of the selections shown in Display 5.2. This window also appears if you issue a break signal while any communications access method is executing.

For example, if you are running the EHLLAPI access method and you specify a LIBNAME or FILENAME statement for a file that does not exist on a remote host, you are notified of this problem by the Communication Services Break Handler window.

Display 5.2
The Communication Services Break Handler Window

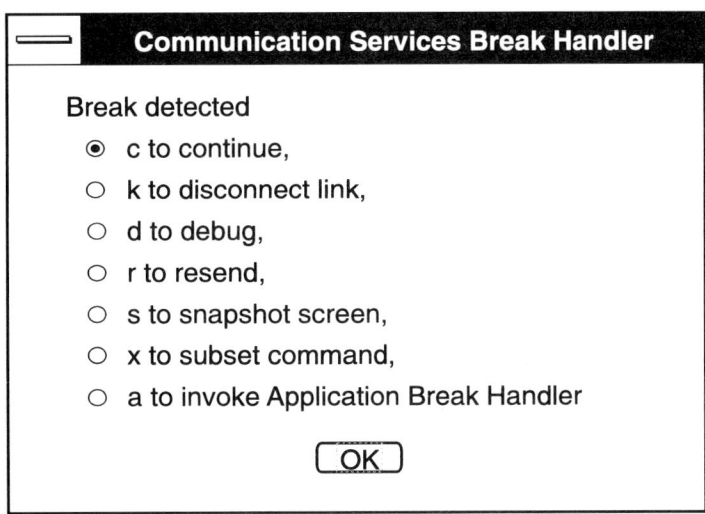

When the Communication Services Break Handler window appears, you can control what happens next by selecting specific actions from a menu. The selection items in this window differ across access methods, but the functions provided are the same for all access methods. These functions are:

☐ Invoke the Application Break Handler window.

☐ Continue processing of the command or program running when the break signal was issued or the host message interrupted.

☐ Disconnect the link and abort processing of the RSUBMIT, SIGNON, or SIGNOFF command.

☐ Resend the last information transmitted over the link. Information travels over the link in units called *packets*. Occasionally, a packet is lost or garbled, and link processing stalls. When this happens, use the R command to resend the previous packet and resume processing.

☐ Snap (copy) a message from a remote host to the local LOG window. Blank lines in the remote host screen are not copied. This command is applicable only for EHLLAPI connections. In situations where a message from the remote host causes an interruption, use this funciton to snap the message from the remote host into the LOG window where you can read it.
  This item appears only in the window for EHLLAPI connections.

☐ Send the specified string to the remote host for execution as though the string had been input (typed) from a terminal. After the string executes, SAS/CONNECT prompts you for another break window command; in most cases, you can respond to the second prompt for a break window command by selecting the function that continues processing.
  This function is applicable when a remote host message interrupts processing. You can use this function to respond to the remote host message so processing can resume.
  This function is a choice only in the window for TCP, TELNET, EHLLAPI, and ASYNC connections.

☐ Enter the subset mode of the local host.

When a Host Message Interrupts SAS/CONNECT

As stated earlier, messages from the host will interrupt link processing. The interruption continues until the host message is resolved. Therefore, you must respond to host messages so that processing can resume.

There are several ways to handle host interruptions, but all of them involve

- reading the host message
- responding to the message
- continuing SAS/CONNECT processing.

Reading the Host Message

If you have a TELNET, TCP, or ASYNC connection, messages from the remote host are written to the SAS LOG window. To read them, go to the LOG window.

If you have a 3270 connection, a message sent by the host is not automatically displayed in the LOG window of your local host. You may snap the message to your log by issuing the S command from the Communication Services Break Handler window (which appears when a message is detected), or you can hot-key to the 3270 session and read the message.

Responding to the Message

Once you have seen the message from the remote host, you must respond to the message before link processing can resume.

For TELNET, TCP, or ASYNC connections, many of the messages from the remote host require no response. If you have a TELNET, TCP, or ASYNC connection and the Communication Services Break Handler window has appeared, you can use the break window T command to respond to the host or switch to a TTY program connection.

If you have a 3270 connection, switch to the 3270 session with which your local host is connected and respond to the message in that session. For example, if you are running OS/2 on the local host, invoke the Task Manager, select the 3270 Terminal Emulation task, switch to the session to which you are linked, and respond to the message. In many cases, the only response necessary is to press the PA2 or ENTER key to clear the display.

Continuing SAS/CONNECT Processing

After you respond successfully to the host message, you can continue processing in one of the following ways:

- If you have a TELNET, TCP, or ASYNC connection, the Communication Services Break Handler window reappears after you type your response to the remote host. Select C to continue the link processing.

- If you have a 3270 connection, return to your local SAS session and select C to continue the link processing. For example, if you are running OS/2 on the local host, respond to the remote host's message in the 3270 session, reinvoke the Task Manager, and return to the SAS session under OS/2. Select C to continue the link processing.

Example

Suppose you write a program to execute on the remote host, but you misspell the name of a SAS data library referenced in a LIBNAME statement in the program. Without realizing your error, you issue the RSUBMIT command to execute your program. The remote host cannot find the library referenced in the program and issues an error message.

If you have an ASYNC connection, the message is displayed in the LOG window of the local SAS session. You can simply correct the error and submit the statements to the remote host again. If you have an EHLLAPI connection, the host message brings up the Communication Services Break Handler window automatically.

To respond:

1. Use the S command in the break window to view the message from the remote host. The S command takes a snapshot and displays it in the LOG window. You can print the saved snapshot if you want to save it for later examination. Alternatively, you can read the message when you switch to the remote host session to respond to the message. In this example, the remote host tells you that the library you named in the LIBNAME statement does not exist and asks if you want to create it.

2. Switch to the remote host session to respond to the message. For this example, type YES or NO and press ENTER. For many kinds of messages that you receive from the remote host, you can respond by simply pressing ENTER.

3. Switch back to the local SAS session and select C from the break window. The remote host resumes processing.

Chapter 6 The APPC Access Method

Introduction 93

Available Connections 94

System Requirements for CMS 94
Configuring CMS Userids for APPC 95
    Communications Directory Files 95
    $SERVER$ NAMES Directory 96
    Tailoring the PROFILE EXEC File 97

System Requirements for MVS 97
SAS System Options for MVS 98

System Requirements for OS/2 99
Environment Variables for OS/2 99

System Requirements for Windows 32s 101
Environment Variables for Windows 32s 101

System Requirements for VSE 102
SAS System Options for VSE 104

Starting SAS/CONNECT with the APPC Access Method 104
Using Script Files to Start SAS/CONNECT with APPC 105

Examples of Signing on Using the APPC Access Method 105
CMS to MVS 105
Windows 32s to MVS 106
MVS to CMS 107
MVS to OS/2 107
OS/2 to OS/2 108
OS/2 to MVS 108
OS/2 to TSO under MVS 109
OS/2 to VSE 109

Troubleshooting 110
Messages 110
References 114

Introduction

Advanced Program-to-Program Communication (APPC) is IBM's strategic enterprise connectivity solution. Based on Systems Network Architecture (SNA) logical unit type 6.2 (LU 6.2), APPC is the foundation for distributed processing within an SNA network. The APPC access method works over a variety of connections, such as channel-to-channel, SDLC, token ring, Ethernet, and X.25 links. You do not need to know the connection used at your site to use the APPC access method.

This chapter describes the hosts and systems software supported by SAS/CONNECT for this access method. This information is based on the support available at the time this book was written. Contact the Technical Support Division at SAS Institute for the most current information on additional supported hosts or systems software.

Available Connections

You can use SAS/CONNECT in a peer-to-peer configuration between the following hosts:

- CMS
- MVS
- OS/2
- VSE
- Windows (Windows 32s can be used as a local host in an APPC connection).

Note: Check with your SAS Software Representative to be sure that the APPC access method has been configured at your site as described in the installation instructions for the SAS System.

System Requirements for CMS

To use the APPC access method, your site must meet the following requirements:

- You must have the APPC access method installed for SAS/CONNECT.
- You must have VM/SP Release 6 or VM/ESA.
- To communicate with other CMS systems, you must have the Transparent Services Access Facility (TSAF). TSAF provides interprocessor communication services for up to eight VM/SP systems located within a single TSAF collection.
- To communicate with other systems outside of the TSAF collection that are connected by an SNA network, you must have Advanced Communication Facility/Virtual Telecommunications Access Method (ACF/VTAM), Group Control System (GCS), and APPC/VM VTAM Support (AVS) installed.

APPC protocol requires that SNA session limits be raised above zero between two logical units wishing to support user communications. The protocol command that manages those limits is Change Number Of Sessions (CNOS). Unlike the APPC implementation in other environments, IBM's APPC/VM does not support a programmatic interface to this command; instead, the operator must manually enter control information at an AVS console. Therefore, for your site to run SAS/CONNECT from a local CMS machine to either an MVS, OS/2, VSE, or another CMS machine within the TSAF collection, your systems personnel must establish procedures to issue CNOS commands to AVS to set session limits between the AVS outbound gateway and the appropriate remote system logical unit partner. These commands must be reissued any time a remote system logical unit experiences an outage and has to be restarted (including any time a remote OS/2 host is rebooted). If the commands are not reissued, communication between two partner logical units cannot proceed. If you do not have authority to issue CNOS commands, ask your systems personnel to reissue the commands.

If you experience problems establishing a connection from CMS to either CMS, MVS, VSE, or OS/2, check with your Systems Administrator to ensure that the gateway is correctly defined and activated and that the CNOS command has been correctly issued. Refer to the SAS System Installation Instructions for more details about the CNOS command.

Configuring CMS Userids for APPC

To use SAS/CONNECT with CMS, you need to set up a communications directory file if CMS is used as the local host and a $SERVER$ NAMES directory if CMS is used as the remote host. In addition, you may need to edit the PROFILE EXEC file for the userid on the remote CMS host. The next sections describe how to do these tasks.

Communications Directory Files

To establish a SAS/CONNECT conversation from a CMS system as the local host, you must use the communications directory entry set up in a file on the local CMS session as the REMOTE= value. This communications directory file can reside at the system level or the user level or both. By default, the system-wide communications directory file is named SCOMDIR NAMES, and the default user communications directory file is UCOMDIR NAMES. The format of a CMS communications directory entry is as follows:

```
:NICK.luname   :LUNAME.gateway targetlu
               :TPN.SASRMT
               :MODENAME.modename
               :SECURITY.level
               :USERID.user1
               :PASSWORD.user1pw
```

where:

NICK.*luname*
: specifies the eight-character symbolic destination name of the resource.
  Note: Due to restrictions on non-VM systems, a CMS user cannot take advantage of the aliasing support implicit in the CMS communication directory structure when accessing a non-VM system. Instead, the NICK value in the communications directory must be identical to the *targetlu* value in the :LUNAME definition.

LUNAME.*gateway targetlu*
: is a combination of two eight-character names. The first part of the name is the defined gateway name for connections outside of the TSAF collection, and the rest of the LUNAME is the name of the partner logical unit.

TPN.SASRMT
: indicates the transaction program name as it is known to the target LU. For SAS/CONNECT this will always be SASRMT.

MODENAME.*modename*
: specifies the mode name of the SNA session connecting the gateway to the target LU.

SECURITY.*level*
: specifies the security type of the conversation. If the target LU is configured to validate security, set level to PGM and define a userid and password. Otherwise, set level to NONE.

USERID.*user1*
: indicates the access security userid that is presented to the target logical unit for verification.

PASSWORD.*user1pw*
: indicates the access security password presented to the target LU.

Note: You can omit specifying the USERID and PASSWORD parameters if you have added a fully qualified APPCPASS statement to your CP directory. The APPCPASS statement may be a more secure method of presenting userid and password information to a target LU than using the USERID and PASSWORD parameters here. Refer to VM/ESA Connectivity Planning, Administration and Operation (SC24-5448) for more details on the APPCPASS directory statement.

The following example enables a VM-to-VM connection. In this example, the NICK value (**CONNVM**) is different from the *targetlu* value (**N01SASPG**).

```
:NICK.CONNVM    :LUNAME.N01SASOG N01SASPG
                :TPN.SASRMT
                :MODENAME.MSASIND
                :SECURITY.PGM
                :USERID.USER1
                :PASSWORD.XXXX
```

This example enables a VM-to-MVS connection. In this example, the NICK value (**N01TGT62**) is identical to the *targetlu* value (**N01TGT62**).

```
:NICK.N01TGT62  :LUNAME.N01SASOG N01TGT62
                :TPN.SASRMT
                :MODENAME.MSASIND
                :SECURITY.PGM
                :USERID.USER2
                :PASSWORD.XXXX
```

$SERVER$ NAMES Directory

To establish a SAS/CONNECT conversation to a remote CMS system, you must set up the $SERVER$ NAMES directory in the remote CMS environment. This directory defines the EXEC to be run when the connection is made to the remote CMS system. The format of a CMS $SERVER$ NAMES directory entry is shown here:

```
:NICK.SASRMT    :LIST.userid1 . . . useridn|.*
                :MODULE.execname
```

A description of the directory entry follows:

NICK.SASRMT   specifies the eight-character symbolic destination name of the resource. For SAS/CONNECT, the program is always SASRMT.

LIST.*userid1* . . . *useridn*   enables you to limit the users that are allowed to connect to this system. Specifying LIST.* lets all users connect.

MODULE.*execname*   specifies the EXEC to be executed when a connection is made to the remote CMS system. This replaces the script file used to signon and signoff. The main function of this EXEC is to invoke the remote SAS session with the desired SAS options.

A sample $SERVER$ NAMES file follows:

```
$SERVER$ NAMES
:NICK.SASRMT   :LIST.*
               :MODULE.RMTBOOT
```

The RMTBOOT EXEC specified in the previous example might be structured as follows:

```
/*   This is the BOOTSTRAP EXEC */
/*   for the remote CMS host */
say 'Remote Bootstrap in Progress'
say 'Invoking the SAS System      '
'EXEC SAS (COMAMID=APPC DMR REMOTE=N01SASPG)'
queue 'CP logoff'
exit
```

Note: The SAS system options included in this example (COMAMID, DMR, and REMOTE) are required to invoke SAS/CONNECT on the remote host.

Tailoring the PROFILE EXEC File

You must also ensure that the appropriate CMS SET commands are specified in the remote CMS virtual machine to allow the virtual machine to function as a remote host. The easiest way to ensure that these commands always get issued is to edit the PROFILE EXEC file on the remote CMS userid and add the following logic:

```
/*   Make sure that we are set up to accept */
/*   connections if we get autologged       */
if substr(diagrc(24,-1),11,1) = '2' then do
   'SET SERVER ON'
   'SET FULLSCREEN OFF'
   'SET AUTOREAD OFF'
end
```

Since this logic is part of the PROFILE EXEC, these CMS commands are issued at logon if the CMS userid is being autologged through a SAS/CONNECT signon.

System Requirements for MVS

To use the APPC access method, your site must meet the following requirements:

- You must have the APPC access method installed for SAS/CONNECT.
- You must have Version 3, Release 2 or later of VTAM.

In addition, you can use MVS as the remote host only under these conditions:

- If the MVS remote host has Version 4, Release 2 or later of MVS/ESA, with APPC/MVS configured, you can connect from a local MVS, CMS, VSE, OS/2, or Windows 32s host.

☐ If the MVS remote host does not have Version 4, Release 2 or later of MVS/ESA, with APPC/MVS configured, you can use a script to connect from a local OS/2 session to the remote MVS session.

SAS System Options for MVS

To use the APPC access method, you must have certain MVS-specific SAS system options defined at the time that you invoke the SAS System. In most cases, your SAS Software Representative defines these options in the configuration file for your site, so you should not have to specify these options.

APPCSEC=*userid.password*
: specifies the userid and password to pass to the remote host. Use this option in an OPTIONS statement under MVS when you establish a link to a remote CMS, MVS, VSE, or OS/2 (when OS/2 is password protected) host. Both the userid and the password can contain alphanumeric characters and the special characters @, #, and $. If the remote host is case sensitive for the userid and password, specify the value in the appropriate case and enclose it in quotation marks.

    The userid is optional and is usually omitted when both the MVS and CMS hosts have the same userid. In this case, the MVS session derives the userid from the appropriate Accessor Environment Element (ACEE). If this option is used when connecting to an OS/2 host, you must have userid and password profiles previously defined on the OS/2 host. Unlike most other SAS system options for APPC, this option will probably not be set up by your SAS Software Representative.

LUPOOL= USER
LUPOOL=ALL
: specifies when an LU should be acquired from a pool. Setting this option to USER enables pool use for local MVS SAS sessions. Setting this option to ALL enables pool use for both local and remote MVS SAS sessions. USER is the default value.

LU62MODE=*name*
: specifies the communications mode to use. SASAPPC is the default mode name. The mode name, whether you specify it with the LU62MODE option or allow it to default to SASAPPC, must be defined in both the local and the remote environments. For MVS, this is done with a MODEENT macro.

The following options are used together to produce an LU name. The LUPREFIX, LUFIRST, and LULAST options describe the pool of LUs from which an LU is dynamically selected. These options are used only when pool use is enabled. (Setting LUPOOL=USER enables LU pool use only for local sessions under MVS; setting LUPOOL=ALL enables pool use for both local and remote sessions under MVS.) These options may be used to specify an actual LU name or an ACBNAME chosen by your systems administrator to eliminate dependency between the SAS configuration and naming changes in your network. In either case, ask your SAS Software Representative or systems personnel to provide you with the values for the following options:

LUPREFIX=*name*
: specifies the LU (ACBNAME) prefix to use to create a pool of LUs.

LUFIRST=*suffix*
: specifies the numeric LU (ACBNAME) suffix of the first LU in the pool.

LULAST=*suffix*
    specifies the numeric LU (ACBNAME) suffix of the last LU in the pool. The size of a pool is determined as follows:

    pool-depth= LULAST - LUFIRST + 1

    If an LU is not acquired after cycling through the pool, the signon fails.

    Note: SAS/CONNECT does not support communication through the transaction program (TP) scheduler's LU using the APPC/MVS subsystem communication interfaces. Therefore, you must specify the LUPOOL= option. This release uses APPC/MVS subsystem services simply to invoke the remote SAS session. SAS/CONNECT opens a separate access method control block (ACB) and performs subsequent communication through the standard APPC/VTAM interface.

    Note: With batch jobs under MVS, SAS/CONNECT always returns a system condition code of 0. To determine if the SAS/CONNECT job was successful, use the SAS/CONNECT %SYSRPUT statement to check the SYSRC automatic macro variable.

System Requirements for OS/2

To use the APPC access method, your site must have the following:

- Release 2.x or later of OS/2.
- the APPC access method installed and configured for SAS/CONNECT. Sample configuration files are included in *sasroot*\CONNECT\SASMISC. Refer to the README.OS2 file in this directory for more information.
- One of the following packages:
    - Extended Services 1.0 or later
    - IBM's CM/2, Version 1.0 or later
    - any OS/2 2.0 emulation program that supports IBM's APPC standard.

Environment Variables for OS/2

Under OS/2, you can set the value of environment variables in either of the following ways:

- execute this statement from the SAS PROGRAM EDITOR window:

    ```
    options set=variable-name variable-value;
    ```

    Enclose *variable-value* in quotation marks if it contains special characters.

- add this line to the SAS configuration file.

    ```
    -set variable-name variable-value
    ```

In most cases, your SAS Software Representative defines the environment variables in the configuration file for your site; however, you can specify them using either of the two methods described above. The recommended method of defining environment variables is by using the SET command in the SAS configuration file. Use **PROC OPTIONS** to verify the values are correctly set.

The following environment variables can be specified:

APPC_LUNAME

specifies the name of the logical unit (LU) to use. A SAS/CONNECT conversation via APPC exists between a local LU and a remote LU. An OS/2 workstation might have multiple dependent LUs defined, via Communications Manager, to support multiple concurrent remote sessions established by this workstation. This variable may be used to override the default LU that was configured with Communications Manager.

APPC_LU62MODE

specifies the communications mode to use. The default mode name is SASAPPC. The mode name, whether you specify it with the APPC_LU62MODE variable or allow it to default to SASAPPC, must be defined in both the local and the remote environments. For OS/2, this is done with Communications Manager. Do not specify a null or blank value for this variable.

APPC_SECURE

specifies a userid.password string, _PROMPT_, _UPM_, or _NONE_. You can specify a userid and password in the form

```
userid.password
```

but keep in mind that this undermines security by putting the userid and password as readable values in the SAS configuration file. If you specify _PROMPT_, the user is prompted for a userid and password for the remote host. You must specify either the *userid.password* string or _PROMPT_ to signon to CMS, VSE, and APPC/MVS. The default is _NONE_.

If you are connecting to an OS/2 session, you can omit this parameter (which causes the value to default to _NONE_) unless you have established user profiles on the OS/2 host with Communications Manager or with User Profile Management.

If _UPM_ is specified, the User Profile Management login userid and password are utilized.

APPC_SURROGATE_LUNAME

specifies which LU to use for a SAS/CONNECT remote session on MVS. If this variable is not defined, the MVS remote session dynamically selects an LU from the pool of LUs defined on MVS for this purpose. Using this variable can decrease the amount of configuration needed for the OS/2 workstation.

Note: The value of this variable is not the same as the value specified for the REMOTE= option.

Refer to the sample files in *sasroot*\CONNECT\SASMISC for examples that illustrate these variables.

System Requirements for Windows 32s

To use the APPC access method, your site must have one of the following packages installed:

- Microsoft SNA Server, Version 2.0 or later
  Installation of the SNA Server for Windows 32s requires the following procedures:

  1. Install SNA Server(s). An SNA Server must execute under the Windows NT operating system. It functions as the gateway to an SNA network.

     All local and remote logical unit pairings are defined at the SNA Server, along with the session properties (MODEs) that will be used for each pair. If you will be connecting to a remote MVS LU, then you may want to configure the local LU as having an "implicit incoming remote LU". With this configuration, MVS surrogate LUs do not have to be defined to the SNA Server. Otherwise, all MVS surrogate LUs must be defined to the SNA Server.

  2. Install SNA Server client(s). To use Windows 32s as an SNA Server client, install the Windows version 3.x client software under the Windows 32s operating system. The SAS System uses Universal Thunking techniques to access the Windows 3.x 16-bit DLLs while executing under Windows 32s.

     The only configuration item that is necessary on a Windows 32s SNA Server client is specification of the domain in which an SNA Server resides. This specification allows data to be routed to the SNA Server over a local area network (LAN). To allow the Windows 32s client machine to connect automatically to an SNA Server when booted, add WNAP.EXE to the LOAD= command line under the [WINDOWS] section within the WIN.INI file.

  3. Apply patch 34 to every Windows NT SNA Server that is running Version 2.0.

     Refer to the documentation for Microsoft SNA Server for more information and configuration specifications.

- any program that supports Microsoft's APPC WOSA standard.

  Sample configuration files are included in the installation diskettes in *sasroot*\CONNECT\SASMISC. Refer to the README.WNS file in this directory for details.

Environment Variables for Windows 32s

Under Windows 32s, you can set the value of environment variables in either of the following ways:

- execute the following statement from the SAS PROGRAM EDITOR window:

  ```
  options set=variable-name variable-value;
  ```

  and enclose *variable-value* in quotation marks if it contains special characters.

- add the following line to the SAS configuration file:

  ```
  -set variable-name variable-value
  ```

In most cases, your SAS Software Representative defines the environment variables in the configuration file for your site. However, you can specify them using either of the two methods described above. The recommended method of defining environment variables is by using the SET command in the SAS configuration file. Use PROC OPTIONS to verify that the values are set correctly.

The following environment variables can be specified:

APPC_LUNAME
: specifies the name of the local logical unit (LU) to use. This variable is required unless a default local APPC LU has been defined to the SNA Server.

APPC_LU62MODE
: specifies the communications mode to use. The default name is SASAPPC. The mode name, whether you specify it with the APPC_LU62MODE variable or allow it to default to SASAPPC, must be defined in both the local and the remote environments. Mode characteristics can be configured as part of the Microsoft SNA Server product.

APPC_SECURE
: specifies a *userid.password string*, _PROMPT_, or _NONE_. You can specify:

    ```
    userid.password
    ```

    but keep in mind that this undermines security by putting the userid and password as readable values in the SAS configuration file. If you specify _PROMPT_, the user is prompted for a userid and password for the remote host. You must specify either the *userid.password* string or _PROMPT_ to sign on to CMS, VSE, and APPC/MVS. The default is _NONE_.

    If you are connecting to an OS/2 session, you can omit this parameter (which causes the value to default to _NONE_) unless you have established a user profile on the OS/2 host with Communications Manager or with User Profile Management.

APPC_SURROGATE_LUNAME
: specifies which LU to use for a SAS/CONNECT remote session under MVS. If this variable is not defined, the MVS remote session dynamically selects an LU from the pool of LUs defined under MVS for this purpose.

APPC_PARTNER_COUNT
: specifies the number of simultaneous partners that this local session will have at any one time. This estimate permits better allocation of memory for resources for internal control block usage.

System Requirements for VSE

The APPC access method requires:

- VTAM, Version 3, Release 2 or later

The APPC access method executes as a separate VTAM application. Therefore, it must be defined to VTAM. The following example APPL definition uses SASAPPC as both the application name and ACBNAME (ACBNAME must match the APPCAPPL= option of the SAS System). This example allows for 32,767 sessions (16,384 contention winners, 16,383 contention losers) per LU/MODE pair. Actually, only 1 contention winner and 1 contention loser session per LU/MODE pair is needed for SAS/CONNECT without RLS. With RLS session usage varies. This example also specifies:

- one automatic session startup
- no draining of allocation requests
- session deactivation responsibility which is that of the initiating remote LU that sent the initial CNOS request
- parallel sessions
- support for FMH5s containing access security information.

Example

```
SASAPPC  APPL  AUTH=(ACQ,NOCNM),
    ACBNAME=SASAPPC,APPC=YES,AUTOSES=1,DSESLIM=32767,
    DDRAINL=NALLOW,DMINWNL=16384,DMINWNR=16383,
    DRESPL=NALLOW,PARSESS=YES,SECACPT=CONV,
    MODETAB=SASAPPC
```

Note: This new definition must be cataloged in source format in the VSE librarian sublibrary that contains the VTAM configuration definitions (usually PRD2.CONFIG).

The following LOGMODE entries must also be added to your logmode table. The first entry is a reserved mode name that is used by VTAM for control operator functions. The second entry in this example (SASAPPC) is the mode that defines the session parameters that exist between VSE and its partner LUs). This mode name must match the value specified in the APPCLOGM= SAS system option.

```
SNASVCMG  MODEENT  LOGMODE=SNASVCMG,
    TYPE=X'00',
    FMPROF=X'13',
    TSPROF=X'07',
    PRIPROT=X'B0',
    SECPROT=X'B0',
    COMPROT=X'50B3',
    PSERVIC=X'060200000000000000000300'
SASAPPC  MODEENT  LOGMODE=SASAPPC,
    TYPE=X'00',
    FMPROF=X'13',
    TSPROF=X'07',
    PRIPROT=X'B0',
    SECPROT=X'B0',
    COMPROT=X'50B3',
    PSERVIC=X'060200000000000000100F00'
```

Note: After adding these new entries to the logmode table, the table must then be reassembled and linkedited so that it resides in the VSE librarian sublibrary that contains the VTAM configuration definitions (usually PRD2.CONFIG).

SAS System Options for VSE

This section lists all of the SAS system options that are specific to VSE or require additional explanation for use with VSE.

APPCAPPL=*APPC-application-id*
> specifies the APPC VTAM application id. This option triggers VTAM initialization for the APPC access method. Therefore, do not specify this option unless you are planning to use the APPC access method so that you will not incur any additional resource overhead. This option is required for both client and server usage.
>
> Default: blank
>
> Valid as part of: SAS System initialization

APPCLOGM=*APPC-logmode*
> specifies the APPC VTAM LOGMODE entry to be used with the APPC access method. This option is required only when VSE is executing as the client.
>
> Default: SASAPPC
>
> Valid as part of: SAS System initialization, user invocation, OPTIONS statement

APPCSEC=*security-presentation-enablement*
> specifies the conversation-level security that should be enabled when the SNA LU Type 6.2 (APPC) transaction program is initiated. The following is a description of the values that are valid for this option:
>
> _NONE_
> > disables security presentation to the remote host.
>
> _PROMPT_
> > specifies that the user should be prompted for the security information (userid and password) that is presented to the remote host.
>
> *userid.password*
> > specifies the userid and password that must be presented to the remote host for security.
> > **Note:** If the userid or password contains numeric or special characters, enclose *userid.password* in quotation marks.
>
> Default: _NONE_
>
> Valid as part of: SAS System initialization, user invocation, OPTIONS statement

Starting SAS/CONNECT with the APPC Access Method

To use the APPC access method with SAS/CONNECT, you must specify the following SAS system options before you sign on:

- COMAMID=APPC
- REMOTE=*remote-session-id*.

The values for the REMOTE= option vary depending on your host:

- When the remote host is running MVS/ESA, specify the logical unit name that is configured to APPC/MVS scheduler for the REMOTE= value.

- If the remote host is running MVS but not MVS/ESA and the local host is OS/2, specify the 3270 EHLLAPI short or long session id of the remote 3270 session. (You defined the short and long session id with the emulation program that you are using.)

- When the remote host is running CMS, specify the name of the AVS gateway for the REMOTE= value.

- When the remote host is running OS/2, specify the name of the control point or other OS/2 locally defined logical unit.

- When the remote host is running VSE, specify the VTAM APPL ID that has been set up for APPC LU6.2 communications.

Ask your SAS Software Representative to provide these names.

Using Script Files to Start SAS/CONNECT with APPC

If you are connecting from OS/2 to a release of MVS that is earlier than Version 4, Release 2 of MVS/ESA, you must use a script file to establish the connection. The sample script file is located in *sasroot*\CONNECT\SASLINK\APPCTSO.SCR. This script requires that you have a TSO userid to enable you to log on to MVS.

For all other connections using the APPC access method, you do not need to use a script file because APPC has the ability to interface with the APPC/MVS subsystem to initiate a remote session, assuming a correct definition. If you have defined the RLINK fileref prior to establishing a connection, when you sign on, SAS/CONNECT processes and loads the script file identified by the RLINK fileref. The access method attempts to use the script file, leading to undesirable results. If you have defined the RLINK fileref and do not want to free it, use the NOSCRIPT option in the SIGNON and SIGNOFF commands or statements, as shown here:

```
signon noscript;
signoff noscript;
```

Examples of Signing on Using the APPC Access Method

This section provides examples of how to use APPC between CMS, MVS, VSE, and OS/2.

CMS to MVS

The following example illustrates how to establish a connection between a CMS local host and a remote host running MVS/ESA with APPC/MVS subsystem support correctly defined. The configuration file on the remote MVS host should be set up by your SAS Software Representative and should contain the following options:

DMR
COMAMID=APPC
REMOTE=*LUname-of-APPC/MVS-scheduler*
LUPREFIX=*prefix*
LUFIRST=*begin-suffix*
LULAST=*end-suffix*
LU62MODE=*mode-name*
LUPOOL=ALL
NOTERMINAL
NO$SYNTAXCHECK

The *LUname-of-APPC/MVS-scheduler* must be set up in a CMS communications directory. In most cases, your SAS Software Representative sets up this name at the time the APPC access method is installed for SAS/CONNECT. If you need to create your own communications directory, see "Communications Directory Files" on page 95.

Submit the following statements to the local CMS host:

```
options comamid=appc remote=luname-of-APPC/MVS;
signon;
```

Windows 32s to MVS

The following example illustrates how to establish a connection between Windows 32s as the local host and a remote host running MVS/ESA with APPC/MVS subsystem support correctly defined. The configuration file on the MVS host should be set up by your SAS Software Representative and should contain the following options:

DMR
COMAMID=APPC
REMOTE=*LUuname-of-APPC/MVS scheduler*
LUPREFIX=*prefix*
LUFIRST=*begin-suffix*
LULAST=*end-suffix*
LU62MODE=*mode-name*
LUPOOL=ALL
NOTERMINAL
NO$SYNTAXCHECK

The configuration file on the local Windows 32s host should be set up by your SAS Software Representative and should contain the following option statements:

SET APPC_LU62MODE *mode_name*
SET APPC_LUNAME *local LU defined on the NT server*

With Microsoft's SNA Server, all definitions (logical units and modes) are located on the Windows NT SNA Server gateway.

Submit the following statements to the local host:

```
options comamid=appc remote=luname of APPC/MVS;
options set=appc_secure userid.password;
signon;
```

MVS to CMS

The following example illustrates how to establish a connection between an MVS local host and a CMS remote host. Verify that the configuration file or the SASBOOT EXEC file on the remote CMS host contains the following options:

DMR
COMAMID=APPC
REMOTE=*name-of-AVS-private-gateway*

Submit the following statements to the MVS host:

```
options comamid=appc remote=name-of-AVS-private-gateway appcsec=userid.password;
signon;
```

Note: The REMOTE= value on both the MVS and CMS hosts is the name of the AVS private gateway logical unit.

If you need to modify or create your own RMTBOOT EXEC, see "$SERVER$ NAMES Directory" on page 96.

MVS to OS/2

The following example illustrates how to establish a connection between MVS as the local host and OS/2 as the remote host. The configuration file on the OS/2 host should contain the following options:

-DMR
-COMAMID APPC
-REMOTE *name-of-locally-defined-OS/2-LU*
-NOTERMINAL
-NO$SYNTAXCHECK

Submit the following statements to the MVS host:

```
options comamid=appc remote=name-of-locally-defined-lu;
signon;
```

Note: The REMOTE= value on both the MVS and OS/2 hosts is the name of the OS/2 control-point logical unit.

OS/2 to OS/2

The following example illustrates how to establish a connection between two OS/2 hosts. The configuration file on the remote host should contain the following options:

-DMR
-REMOTE *name-of-control-point-LU-for-remote-PC*
-COMAMID APPC
-NOTERMINAL
-NO$SYNTAXCHECK

> **Note:** This example assumes default values for the OS/2 environment variables. Submit the following statements to the local host:
>
> ```
> options comamid=appc remote=name-of-control-point-LU-for-remote-PC;
> signon;
> ```

> **Note:** The REMOTE= value on both hosts is the name of the remote OS/2 control-point logical unit.

OS/2 to MVS

The following example illustrates how to establish a connection between an OS/2 local host and a remote host running MVS/ESA with APPC/MVS subsystem support correctly defined. The configuration file on the remote MVS host should be set up by your SAS Software Representative and should contain the following options:

DMR
COMAMID=APPC
REMOTE=*LUname-of-APPC/MVS-scheduler*
LUPREFIX=*prefix*
LUFIRST=*begin-suffix*
LULAST=*end-suffix*
LU62MODE=*mode-name*
LUPOOL=ALL
NOTERMINAL
NO$SYNTAXCHECK

> Submit the following statements to the local OS/2 host:
>
> ```
> options comamid=appc remote=luname-of-APPC/MVS;
> set=appc_secure userid.password;
> signon;
> ```

OS/2 to TSO under MVS

If you do not have APPC/MVS or if for other reasons you need to connect to TSO instead of APPC/MVS, you must use a script with the SAS/CONNECT session. A sample script is located in *sasroot*\CONNECT\SASLINK\APPCTSO.SCR. The following example illustrates how to establish a connection between an OS/2 local host and TSO under MVS. The configuration file on the remote host should contain the following options:

DMR
REMOTE=*session-id*
LUPREFIX=*prefix*
LUFIRST=*begin-suffix*
LULAST=*end-suffix*
LU62MODE=*mode-name*
LUPOOL=ALL|LUNAME=*reserved-LUname*
COMAMID=APPC
NOTERMINAL
NO$SYNTAXCHECK

Submit the following statements to the OS/2 host:

```
options comamid=appc remote=session-id;
filename rlink sasroot\CONNECT\SASLINK\appctso.scr;
signon;
```

If you have customized your script file, assign the RLINK fileref to your custom script instead of APPCTSO.SCR.

Note: The REMOTE= value on both the MVS and OS/2 hosts is the short or long session id of the remote session.

OS/2 to VSE

The following example illustrates how to establish a connection between OS/2 as the local host and VSE as the remote host. Before connecting to VSE, the SAS Multiuser program must already be executing on the target VSE machine. To connect to VSE you must specify a valid SAS Multiuser userid and password. Userid and password combinations are controlled by the SAS Multiuser security table. Within this security table you may also specify a unique user configuration file that will take effect when a particular remote APPC user connects to VSE. By default, the following options automatically take effect when a remote APPC user connects to VSE:

```
dmr
comamid=appc
noterminal
no$syntaxcheck
```

Submit the following statements to the local OS/2 host:

```
options comamid=appc remote=VSE-VTAM-APPL-id;
signon;
```

Note: Since SAS Multiuser access security is required, set OS/2 environment variable APPC_SECURE appropriately.

Troubleshooting

Until the configuration is properly specified, it can be difficult to establish communications within an SNA network, especially for a host subarea peripheral node. To simplify troubleshooting, SAS/CONNECT uses a convention for error handling that passes information to you to help you debug your configuration. The information SAS/CONNECT passes to you includes operation codes, return codes, and sense data, framed within the context of the function the software is trying to perform. SAS/CONNECT does not attempt to interpret this information. Use this information to work with network systems and SAS support personnel at your site to resolve the problem.

Messages

Each message follows this format:

```
ERROR: APPC communication failure: transaction program = program-name
       opcode = operation-code prc = primary-rc src = secondary-rc
```
where:

- opcode   is the failing verb operation code.
- prc   is the primary return code.
- src   is the secondary return code. When an allocation error occurs (`prc=0003`), the `src` field contains the necessary SNA sense data. Refer to the sources listed in "References" at the end of this chapter for explanations of sense data.

For more information on all of these fields, refer to the sources listed in "References" at the end of this chapter.

Note: Most failures are caused by configuration or network setup errors or they occur because the application you are attempting to communicate with is not currently running or has rejected your connection request.

The following messages document some common failures:

```
ERROR: APPC communication failure: transaction program = SASRMT
       (or SASVQEL)
       opcode = 1A00 prc = F012 src = 00000000.
```
A CONVERT request (`opcode = 1A00`) has failed for reason COMMUNICATION_SUBSYTEM_NOT_LOADED (`prc = F012`). Communications Manager must be started on the local workstation before any services can be utilized.

```
ERROR: APPC communication failure: transaction program = SASRMT
       (or SASVQEL)
       opcode = 0100 prc = 0001 src = 00000018.
```
An ALLOCATE request (`opcode = 0100`) has failed with a PARAMETER_CHECK (`prc = 0001`) because of an UNKNOWN PARTNER LU condition (`src = 00000018`). The user-supplied partner LU alias (the REMOTE= value) is not defined to the local node or to the designated network node directory server. Check the DEFINE_PARTNER_LU definition in the NDF file.

ERROR: APPC communication failure: transaction program = SASRMT
      (or SASVQEL)
      opcode = 0100 prc = 0003 src = 08570003.
   An ALLOCATE request (opcode = 0100) has failed with an ALLOCATION_ERROR
   (prc = 0003). The src in this case has been overridden by sense code 08570003
   indicating the SSCP-SLU session is inactive. An attempt to communicate with a
   VTAM-owned logical unit has failed because the application does not have an active
   control session with VTAM (the host APPL/ACB is not OPEN). Ask your systems
   administrator why the partner LU (REMOTE= value) is not active.

ERROR: APPC communication failure: transaction program = SASRMT
      (or SASVQEL)
      opcode = 0100 prc = 0003 src = 081C0103.
   An ALLOCATE request (opcode = 0100) has failed with an ALLOCATION_ERROR
   (prc = 0003). The src in this case has been overridden by sense code 081C0103
   indicating that the function cannot be executed because the receiver has an error
   condition. The last four digits, 0103, indicate the remote node is not responding to
   polling requests, perhaps because it is turned off or because the hardware is not
   functioning correctly.

ERROR: APPC communication failure: transaction program = SASRMT
      (or SASVQEL)
      opcode = 0D00 prc = 0003 src = 080F6051.
   A RECEIVE_AND_POST (opcode = 0D00) request has failed with an
   ALLOCATION_ERROR (prc = 0003). The src in this case has been overridden by
   sense code 080F6051 indicating that the receiver does not accept the Access Security
   Information field. For example, the supplied userid/password combination may be
   invalid or one or both of the fields may have been omitted and the remote partner
   requires them. Check to see if your system is case sensitive; if so, use the appropriate
   case and enclose the userid and password in quotation marks.

ERROR: APPC communication failure: transaction program = SASRMT
      opcode = 0D00 prc = 0003 src = 10086021.
   A RECEIVE_AND_POST (opcode = 0D00) request has failed with an
   ALLOCATION_ERROR (prc = 0003). The src in this case has been overridden by
   sense code 10086021 indicating that the transaction program name specified by the
   FMH-5 Attach command was not recognized by the receiver. This may occur if the
   SASRMT transaction program is not properly defined at the remote system, or there
   was a failure in the initialization of the environment within which to run the transaction
   program. It might also occur because you failed to supply an uppercase userid when you
   tried to perform a SAS/CONNECT signon to a CMS host.

ERROR: APPC communication failure: transaction program = SASRMT
      opcode = 0100 prc = 0003 src = 08970015.
   An ALLOCATE request (opcode = 0100) has failed with an ALLOCATION_ERROR
   (prc = 0003). The src in this case has been overridden by sense code 08970015
   indicating that a session initiation request has been received for an independent LU that
   has not been defined to the destination VTAM. If *appc.luname* is not specified,
   SAS/CONNECT uses CP_ALIAS by default. To avoid this problem, use the
   APPC_LUNAME environment variable to specify a local LU alias that is also defined
   to the destination VTAM.

ERROR: APPC communication failure: transaction program = SASRMT
      opcode = 0100 prc = 0003 src = 00821002.
   An ALLOCATE request (opcode = 0100) has failed with an ALLOCATION_ERROR
   (prc = 0003). The src in this case has been overridden by sense code 00821002

indicating that the mode name specified to present session parameters to the remote LU is not defined to the remote LU. The OS/2 to MVS connection communications mode defaults to SASAPPC. To circumvent, use the APPC_LU62MODE environment variable to specify a correctly defined mode name known to both the local and remote LUs.

```
ERROR: APPC communication failure: transaction program = SASRMT
       opcode = 0100 prc = 0003 src = 08970015.
ERROR: Remote SIGNON cancelled.
```
Occurs when OS/2 is the local host. Use the APPC_LUNAME environment variable to specify the local LU alias.

```
ERROR: APPC communication failure: transaction program = SASVQEL
       opcode = 0D00 prc = 0003 src = 084C0000
ERROR: Remote SIGNON cancelled.
```
Occurs when SIGNON is attempted between two OS/2 hosts. To circumvent the problem, verify that the SASVTP62 transaction program has been correctly configured to Extended Services. The parameter TP_OPERATION should be specified as QUEUED_OPERATOR_PRELOADED and *not* as NONQUEUED_AM_STARTED. If you do use NONQUEUED_AM_STARTED, the Extended Services Attach Manager attempts to load the FILESPEC'd program, which is a placeholder and will not be found.

```
ERROR: APPC communication failure: transaction program = SASRMT
(or SASVQEL)
       opcode = 1A00 prc = 0001 src = 00000406
```
A CONVERT request has failed with a parameter check (`prc=0001`) because a conversion error occurred (`src=00000406`). This failure typically occurs when an invalid character is present in a user-supplied string, such as APPC_USER or APPC_SECURE. Verify that the values you have specified contain only uppercase letters A through Z, lowercase letters a through z, numerics through 9, and special characters $, #, and @.

```
ERROR: APPC communication failure: transaction program = SASRMT
(or SASVQEL)
       opcode = 1A00 prc = F012 src = 00000000
```
Communications Manager must be started on the local workstation before any services can be utilized. If Communications Manager has not been started, this error occurs.

```
ERROR: APPC transaction program failure: rc=00040008 sense=10086021
```
The COMAMID option is spelled incorrectly in the SASBOOT utility of the remote CMS system.

```
ERROR: APPC transaction program failure: rc=00040008 sense=10086021
ERROR: Remote SIGNON to XXXX cancelled.
```
The sense data (`10086021`) indicate that the necessary transaction program configuration has not occurred in the CMS environment. There needs to be a $SERVER NAMES file present that maps the SASRMT transaction program to the BOOT EXEC that initiates the SAS System.

```
ERROR: Target application partner could not be located.
ERROR: Remote SIGNON to xxxxxxxx cancelled.
```
SIGNON has failed from CMS to MVS. Check the UCOMDIR NAMES file for misspellings or an incorrect password.

```
ERROR: VTAM Communications Failure: ACB initialization error. Verify
       pooling options (LUPOOL, LUPREFIX, LUFIRST, LULAST) or that
       the target ACD is not already in use.
IEF170I SAS ABEND 0999.
```
    Occurs when issuing a SIGNON to the SAS System on a remote MVS host if the SRBEXIT parameter of the MVS LU APPL definition is set to YES.

    SRBEXIT=YES uses SRB-enablement. This is a privileged and optimized method by which VTAM can deliver asynchronous event notification to an application. To do this, the VTAM application must be running in supervisor state or authorized through APF (Authorized Program Facility). This mode is generally reserved for operating system services. SAS is not an application of this class and does not support SRBEXIT enablement. By setting SRBEXIT=NO or deleting the parameter so that it defaults to NO, VTAM is informed that SAS is a problem-state program with no special privilege authorization.

```
ERROR: VTAM Communications Failure: ACB initialization error when
       using the APPC access method and SAS/CONNECT software.
```
    Occurs if all of the available LUs are defined to APPC/MVS using LUADD ACBNAME. To avoid this problem verify that all LUs are *not* defined to APPC/MVS.

```
ERROR: VTAM Communications Failure: ACB initialization error. Verify
       LU options.
ERROR: The target ACB is not already in use.
```
    Occurs in SAS/CONNECT conversations between two MVS hosts if the LU_NAME parameter is defined in the local session instead of using LU pools.

Communication partner has terminated the conversation.

    When signing on to a remote APPC/MVS system, you can avoid this error by adding REMOTE=*ACBname* to the SAS configuration file on the MVS host, where *ACBname* is the LU defined to the APPC/MVS scheduler.

USER1701 ABEND

    Occurs under MVS when an ACB associated with a pool of LUs fails to open. Many events can cause this ABEND. Follow these guidelines to resolve the problem:

- Verify that all required zaps and maintenance are applied.
- Check pool definitions: LUFIRST, LULAST, LUPREFIX and refer to the installation and administration documentation for the SAS System under MVS, Release 6.08 and later.
- Verify that the REMOTE= value is the logical unit defined to the APPC/MVS scheduler through APPCPM*xx* in SYS1.PARMLIB.
- Verify that the REMOTE= logical unit defined to APPC/MVS is defined to the SAS System through your MVS SAS configuration file.
- Query VTAM to verify that the logical units are active.

If you cannot resolve a problem from the explanations given here and by using the cited resources, call SAS Technical Support for assistance. You will probably be asked to generate traces that document the problem, so be sure that you or your site support personnel are familiar with the tracing services available through OS/2 Extended Services and VTAM.

References

You may find the following IBM publications helpful in debugging your configuration. Refer to *IBM System/370 Bibliography* (GC20-0001) for current information on the IBM publication numbers.

- *SNA Technical Overview*
- *SNA Formats*
- *VTAM Programming for LU6.2*
- *VM/ESA Connectivity Planning, Administration and Operation.*

For more information on Communications Manager and OS/2 APPC services, refer to these publications from IBM:

- *Extended Services for OS/2 Communications Manager User's Guide*
- *Extended Services for OS/2 Communications Manager Configuration Guide*
- *Extended Services for OS/2 Problem Determination Guide for the Service Coordinator*
- *Extended Services for OS/2 Programming Services and Advanced Problem Determination for Communications*
- *Extended Services for OS/2 Communications Manager System Management Programming Reference*
- *Extended Services for OS/2 APPC Programming Reference.*

Chapter **7** The DECnet Access Method

Introduction 115

Available Connections 115

Requirements for OpenVMS 115

Requirements for Windows 3.x 116

Starting SAS/CONNECT with the DECnet Access Method 116
REMOTE= Option for OpenVMS-to-OpenVMS Connection 116
REMOTE= Option for Windows-to-OpenVMS Connection 117

Why Script Files Are Not Needed 117

Using the SAS$CONN.COM Command File for OpenVMS Connections 118

Troubleshooting 118

Introduction

DECnet is Digital Equipment Corporation's proprietary networking software. Many other manufacturers support the DECnet protocol. DECnet connectivity may be achieved over Ethernet or token ring links, or with point-to-point connections such as satellite links, leased lines, or asynchronous links. You do not need to be aware of the link used at your site to use the DECnet access method.

This chapter describes the hosts and systems software supported by SAS/CONNECT for this access method. This information is based on the support available at the time this book was written. Contact the Technical Support Division at SAS Institute for the most current information on additional supported hosts or systems software.

This chapter describes the system requirements for using the DECnet access method. The SAS Software Representative at your site can help you determine if your site meets these requirements.

Available Connections

You can use SAS/CONNECT in a peer-to-peer configuration between two OpenVMS hosts. In addition you can use Windows 3.x as a local host in a DECnet connection to an OpenVMS host.

Check with your SAS Software Representative to be sure that the DECnet access method has been installed at your site.

Requirements for OpenVMS

You must have DECnet installed at your site, and you must have TMPMBX and NETMBX privileges to use the DECnet access method. In addition, you may need to ask your SAS Software Representative to provide you the node names that can be used with the REMOTE= value.

Requirements for Windows 3.x

You must have Windows Version 3.1 or later and Digital Equipment Corporation's PATHWORKS for MS-DOS Version 4.0 or later. PATHWORKS must be installed and selected in the Windows setup as the current network on any Windows node that will be used as a local host.

Starting SAS/CONNECT with the DECnet Access Method

To use the DECnet access method with SAS/CONNECT, specify the following SAS system options before you sign on:

- COMAMID=DECNET
- REMOTE=*host-id*

The REMOTE= value for the DECnet access method represents the Access Control Information (ACI) for the remote host. If proxy access is enabled on the DECnet network, you only need to specify the remote nodename; otherwise, you must include username and password information in the ACI. Using proxy access provides more security for your system. The complete form of the ACI is:

nodename"username password"::

In most cases, you need to create a nickname for the ACI to use this information as the value for the REMOTE= option because the value can be no more than eight characters. Creating a nickname is described in the next section.

If you want to be prompted for either the username or the password to be supplied to the remote host, specify a question mark (?) in place of either the username or password or both:

nodename"? ?"::

REMOTE= Option for OpenVMS-to-OpenVMS Connection

On the local OpenVMS host, you can specify a REMOTE= value that is a nickname for the Access Control Information (ACI) of the remote host if you have previously defined any of the forms listed below to be equivalent to *nodename"username password"*:

- an OpenVMS logical name, as illustrated here:

```
$ define mynode "node""username password""::"
$ sas/comamid=decnet/remote=mynode
1? signon;
```

- a SAS macro variable, as illustrated here:

```
$ sas/comamid=decnet
1? %let mynode=node"username password" ::;
2? options remote=mynode;
3? signon;
```

- a DCL symbol, as illustrated here:

```
$ mynode := "node""username password""::"
$ sas/comamid=decnet/remote=mynode
1? signon;
```

Note: The colons (::) are optional, but the quotation marks must be used as shown. If a question mark (?) is used in place of either the username or the password, you will be prompted for the information.

If you have defined all three of these, the order of precedence from highest to lowest is logical name, macro variable, DCL symbol. None of these nicknames can be the same as the node name.

REMOTE= Option for Windows-to-OpenVMS Connection

On the local Windows 3.x host, you can specify a REMOTE= value that is a nickname for the Access Control Information (ACI) of the remote OpenVMS host if you have previously defined a SAS macro variable to be equivalent to the *node"username password"* as illustrated here:

```
c:\> d:\sas\sas comamid decnet
1? %let mynode=node"username password";
2? options remote=mynode;
3? signon;
```

Note: A question mark (?) can be used in place of either the username or the password if you want to be prompted for the information.

You can also use a DOS environment variable as follows:

```
c:\> SET  mynode=node"username password"
c:\> d:\sas\sas comamid decnet
1? options remote=mynode;
2? signon;
```

Why Script Files Are Not Needed

The DECnet access method does not use a script file to sign on or sign off. Although it does not cause errors if you specify a script file when you are using the DECnet access method, you do waste processing time. If you have defined the RLINK fileref prior to establishing a connection, when you sign on, SAS/CONNECT processes and loads the script file identified by the RLINK fileref. The DECnet access method then ignores the script. If you have defined the RLINK fileref and do not want to free it, you can avoid wasting processing time by using the NOSCRIPT option in the SIGNON and SIGNOFF commands or statements:

```
signon noscript;
signoff noscript;
```

You do not need a script file because DECnet automatically creates its remote partner by connecting to an object. For OpenVMS, DECnet connects to the SAS$CONN object, which creates a remote process and runs the SAS$CONN.COM command file to invoke the SAS session on the remote host. This process replaces the need for a script file. SAS/CONNECT includes a default SAS$CONN.COM file in the SAS$ROOT:[TOOLS] directory.

Using the SAS$CONN.COM Command File for OpenVMS Connections

For OpenVMS connections, you must associate a command file with the SAS$CONN object name. There are two methods for doing this:

- put the command file SAS$CONN.COM in the user's default login directory. The advantage of this method is that each user can tailor the command file. However, you have many copies of the command file on the system.

- use NCP (Network Control Program) to tell DECnet where the command file is. Normally a systems administrator runs NCP, which needs to be done only once before using the connection. The advantage of this method is that you only need one copy of the file on the system. However, if SAS$CONN is a known object, the system uses the declared file and ignores any tailored copy of SAS$CONN.COM in a user's login directory.

A sample SAS$CONN.COM command file for OpenVMS follows:

```
set def disk:[user.directory]
sas/dmr/comamid=decnet
```

The first line sets the default directory to the directory where you want to run the SAS System; the second line invokes the remote SAS session.

Troubleshooting

Various errors may occur when you initially try to establish a connection over a network with the DECnet access method. Many of these problems are related to the network. SAS/CONNECT indicates when errors of this nature occur by presenting a general message with the specific return code for the error. The form of the message is:

```
ERROR: Network request failed (rc 0xnn)
```

where *nn* is a non-zero return code that indicates the specific problem. The following list explains the most common failures in establishing DECnet communications.

ERROR: Network request failed (rc 0x03)...
The SAS$CONN file is not defined on the remote host. This file is necessary to invoke the remote SAS session. Ensure that the file exists and is properly defined to NCP or that it exists in the remote login directory.

ERROR: Network request failed (rc 0x10)...
The hostname you specified as the REMOTE= value is invalid. Check with your systems personnel for valid names at your site.

ERROR: Network request failed (rc 0x13)...
Permission to access the remote host was denied. Verify that you specified a valid userid and password for the remote system.

ERROR: Network request failed (rc 0x50)...
ERROR: Network request failed (rc 0x51)...
Your network is down or can't be reached. Check with your systems personnel.

ERROR: Network request failed (rc 0x64)...
ERROR: Network request failed (rc 0x65)...
Your remote host is down or can't be reached. Check with your systems personnel.

ERROR: Network request failed (rc 0x24) - no privilege for attempted operation.
Permission to perform the requested operation was denied. Verify that you have the privileges assigned correctly on your system.

ERROR: Network request failed (rc 0xF4) - network partner exited.
When trying to establish a conversation to a remote VMS system, this message appears if the remote SAS System cannot create a work directory.

To resolve this error, change the SET DEF DISK statement in the SAS$CONN.COM file to a valid directory. This statement can be removed completely and the remote SAS System will create a WORK directory under the directory it is being executed from. This statement should only be used if the user needs the work directory created in a different location.

ERROR: Network request failed.
ERROR: Remote SIGNON to nodename cancelled.
This error occurs if the remote node is busy or the login command files are long. In either case, the remote node does not respond in time and the local node times out.

To increase the time needed before a connection request times out on the local node, increase the NCP parameter EXECUTOR OUTGOING TIMER. To increase the time needed before a connection request times out on the remote node, increase the NCP parameter EXECUTOR INCOMING TIMER.

For Windows, this error message is:

```
ERROR: Network request failed (rc 0x3C) - Error number 0x3C00 occurred.
ERROR: Remote SIGNON to nodename cancelled.
```

For VMS, this error message is:

```
ERROR: Network request failed (rc 0xF4) - network partner exited.
ERROR: Remote SIGNON to nodename cancelled.
```

If you cannot resolve a problem from the explanations given here, contact SAS Technical Support for assistance.

Chapter 8 The TCP/IP and TELNET Access Methods

Introduction 121

Available Connections for TCP/IP 122

System Requirements for TCP/IP 122
TCP/IP with MVS 122
TCP/IP with CMS 123
TCP/IP with OpenVMS on VAX 123
TCP/IP with OpenVMS on AXP 124
TCP/IP with OS/2 124
TCP/IP with Windows 32s 124
TCP/IP with Windows 3.x 124
TCP/IP with Windows NT 125

Starting SAS/CONNECT with the TCP/IP Access Method 125
Specifying the UNIX Domain Under CMS 125

Using Script Files with the TCP/IP Access Method 126

Available Connections for TELNET 126

System Requirements for TELNET 127

Using a Script with the TELNET Access Method 127

Troubleshooting 127

Introduction

Many hosts support the Transmission Control Protocol/Internet Protocol (TCP/IP). From host to host, TCP/IP configurations vary depending on which release of the SAS System is running and what level of TCP/IP support is available on the host. Hosts running Release 6.07 and later releases of the SAS System provide full TCP support and require a supported TCP/IP product on both the local and the remote host.

Connections to hosts running releases earlier than Release 6.07 of the SAS System use the TELNET access method. The TELNET access method is also useful when the remote node does not have a supported TCP/IP package. For the TELNET access method, a supported TCP/IP package must be installed on the local node. The remote node does not have to run a supported TCP/IP product, but must run some TCP/IP product to make the node accessible via TELNET.

This chapter describes the hosts and systems software supported by SAS/CONNECT for this access method. This information is based on the support available at the time this book was written. Contact the Technical Support Division at SAS Institute for the most current information about additional supported hosts or systems software.

This chapter begins with a description of fully-supported TCP/IP connections between hosts. A description of TELNET connections follows the TCP/IP description.

The TCP and TELNET access methods use line-mode TELNET protocol to establish and terminate a link with the remote system. This requires a login script on the local system. Once the connection is made to the remote node, the TCP/IP protocol is used for most subsequent communication. You cannot sign on if you are using TELNET in full-screen mode. You must use line mode.

Available Connections for TCP/IP

You can use the TCP/IP access method in a peer-to-peer configuration between any of the following hosts:

- CMS
- MVS
- OS/2
- OpenVMS
- UNIX
- Windows
  You can use Windows 32s or Windows 3.x as a local host in a TCP/IP connection.
- Windows NT
  If you are using Windows NT as a remote host, you must have the spawner program running on the Windows NT node to which you connect. See "Using a Spawner Program" on page 137 for more information about the spawner.

System Requirements for TCP/IP

The following sections describe the system requirements for using the TCP/IP access method. The SAS Software Representative at your site can help you determine if your site meets these requirements.

TCP/IP with MVS

SAS/CONNECT requires the following levels of system software to support the TCP/IP access method when running Releases 6.07 or 6.08 without any maintenance:

- IBM MVS TCP/IP Release 2.1 or later
- IBM MVS TCP/IP Version 2 Pascal API subroutine module
- IBM VS Pascal Release 2 Run-Time Library.

  Note: The Run-Time Library requires an ETC HOSTS host file and services file. SAS/CONNECT requires the following levels of systems software to support the TCP/IP access method when running SAS Release 6.08 TS405 and higher:

- IBM TCP/IP, Release 2.0 or later, or SAS/C Transient Library, Release 5.50 or later. (The SAS/C Transient Library is provided with the SAS/CONNECT product.)
- Interlink's SNSTCP (This requires a PTF from Interlink. If you have difficulty identifying the PTF with Interlink, contact SAS Technical Support.)

Note: If you are not using a name server, you must have the ETC HOSTS file and services file.

Check with your SAS Software Representative to ensure that these requirements are met by your site.

TCP/IP with CMS

To use the TCP/IP access method with CMS, your system must be running:

- IBM's VM TCP/IP Version 2 or later.

Note: If you do not use a name server at your site, define a configuration file with a file identifier of ETC HOSTS conforming to the format of an /etc/hosts file under the UNIX operating system.

You will also need a services file. These files may be provided by your systems personnel on a globally available minidisk.

TCP/IP with OpenVMS on VAX

To use the TCP/IP access method with OpenVMS on a VAX system, you must have Version 5.3 or higher of OpenVMS and one of the following packages:

- DEC TCP/IP Services for OpenVMS, Version 2.0

- Version 1.3a of VMS/ULTRIX Connection with the latest patch kit from Digital Equipment Corporation's Customer Support Center or a higher version of VMS/ULTRIX Connection

- Wollongong's PathWay Runtime Release 1.1

- TGV's MultiNet Software with UCX compatibility

- any package that provides an interface compatible with DEC TCP/IP Services for OpenVMS, formerly known as UCX.

Alternatively, you could have Version 5.1 or higher of OpenVMS and

- WIN/TCP Software, Version 5.2, by the Wollongong Group, Inc.

One of these software packages must be installed on any OpenVMS node used as a local or remote host. If only one of these packages is installed, SAS/CONNECT detects which package is available and uses it.

If more than one package is installed on the same node, SAS/CONNECT will use the DEC TCP/IP Services for OpenVMS or VMS/ULTRIX Connection package (the first is simply a newer version of the second package) unless you specify to use a Wollongong package (PathWay Runtime is a newer version of WIN/TCP). If you have both types of packages, you can force SAS/CONNECT to use the Wollongong version (PathWay Runtime or WIN/TCP) by defining the SAS$TCP_TYPE logical name as shown here:

```
DEFINE SAS$TCP_TYPE "W"
```

TCP/IP with OpenVMS on AXP

To use the TCP/IP access method with OpenVMS on an AXP system, your system must be running Release 6.09 SAS/CONNECT and one of the following:

- DEC TCP/IP Services for OpenVMS, Version 3.0
- TGV's MultiNet Software, Release 3.2, Rev. D
- any package that provides an interface compatible with DEC TCP/IP Services for OpenVMS.

TCP/IP with OS/2

To use the TCP/IP access method with OS/2, your system must be running one of the following:

- Novell's LAN Workplace for OS/2 Version 3.0 or later. This package allows you to use OS/2 only as a local host.
- IBM's TCP/IP Version 1.2.1 or later
- FTP Software PC/TCP for OS/2 Version 1.3 or later

Note: If you use the Installation and Configuration Automation Tool (ICAT) to configure IBM TCP/IP Version 1.2.1 for OS/2, you must provide the hostname under the "Configure Services" option.

If you omit the hostname, when you attempt to sign on with SAS/CONNECT, you receive the following error:

```
ERROR: Access method initialization failed.
```

TCP/IP with Windows 32s

To use TCP/IP with Windows 32s, your system must be running:

- any TCP/IP package that provides a Winsock Version 1.1 API.

SAS/CONNECT does not support Version 1.0 of the WINSOCK.DLL module. However, it does support Version 1.1 and above.

TCP/IP with Windows 3.x

To use the TCP/IP access method with Windows 3.x, your system must be running one of the following:

- Novell's LAN Workplace for DOS, Version 4.0 or later.
- Microsoft's LAN Manager, Version 2.1 or later.
- Digital Equipment Corporation's PATHWORKS for DOS (TCP/IP), Version 2.0.

- any vendor package that provides a Winsock Version 1.1 API. SAS/CONNECT does not support Version 1.0 of the WINSOCK.DLL module. However, it does support Version 1.1 and above.

   Note: Windows 3.x can only be used as the local host in a TCP/IP connection.

TCP/IP with Windows NT

To use the TCP/IP access method with Windows NT, your system must be running Release 6.09 SAS/CONNECT (or later) and the following:

- Microsoft's TCP/IP System Driver, which is provided with Windows NT.

Starting SAS/CONNECT with the TCP/IP Access Method

To use the TCP/IP access method with SAS/CONNECT, specify a script file to be used when you sign on and sign off. Also, specify the following SAS system options before you sign on:

- COMAMID=TCP
- REMOTE=*internet-address*

   Note: The value of the REMOTE= option must be a valid SAS name. If you have an Internet address that exceeds eight characters or does not conform to SAS naming conventions in any other way, assign the address to a macro variable and specify the macro variable for the REMOTE= value, as illustrated here:

   ```
   %let mynode=internet-address ;
   options remote=mynode;
   ```

Do not choose a macro name that is also a valid hostname on your network. The SAS System first attempts to reach a network host of the REMOTE= option value (in this example, `mynode`).

Specifying the UNIX Domain Under CMS

Under CMS, you can define a macro variable that can be used as the REMOTE= value to specify a fully-qualified host name when signing onto a remote UNIX host. However, there are two alternative methods you can use to make this easier:

- You can specify the fully-qualified domain name in an ETC RESOLV file on your CMS A disk. The file should consist of a line similar to the following:

   ```
   domain unx.xyz.com
   ```

- You can specify the following CMS GLOBALV statement:

   ```
   GLOBALV SELECT UNNAMED SET LOCALDOMAIN unx.xyz.com
   ```

In either case, *unx.xyz.com* should be the fully-qualified domain name of your UNIX host and then you only have to specify the node name as the REMOTE= value.

Using Script Files with the TCP/IP Access Method

To use one of the sample script files supplied with SAS/CONNECT for the TCP/IP access method, assign the RLINK fileref to one of the following script files, depending on what remote host you are connecting to:

Remote Host	Assign RLINK fileref to:
CMS	tcpcms.scr
OS/2	tcpos2.scr
MVS	tcptso.scr
UNIX	tcpunix.scr
OpenVMS	tcpvms.scr
Windows NT	tcpwnt.scr

Check with your SAS Software Representative to find where the script files are located on your local hosts. These sample script files are included with SAS/CONNECT and should be installed at the time that the product is installed.

Note: If you are connecting to OS/2 as the remote host, your script must invoke the SASDMR program in the TYPE statement that starts the remote SAS session. You use the same SAS system options with the SASDMR program as you would in the SAS command. The SASDMR command invokes a special version of the SAS program that redirects the output from the remote SAS session back to the local SAS session.

Available Connections for TELNET

You can use TELNET between any of the following hosts:

- VMS
- UNIX
- OS/2
- Windows (3.x and 32s)
- Windows NT.

System Requirements for TELNET

Using the TELNET or TCP access method, you can connect to any supported platform that is on the TCP/IP network and is running a SAS release that has the corresponding access method support with SAS/CONNECT properly licensed. With the TCP access method, one of the supported TCP/IP products must be installed on any node, local or remote, that you want to use with SAS/CONNECT. For the TELNET access method, a supported TCP/IP package must be installed on the local node. The remote node does not have to run a supported TCP/IP product, but must run some TCP/IP product to make the node accessible through TELNET.

For those cases where your local node has a supported TCP/IP package but your remote node does not, you can use TELNET to establish a connection. (See "System Requirements for TCP/IP" on page 122 for a list of the supported TCP/IP packages for your local host.)

When using the TELNET access method, specify TELNET for the local COMAMID value and RAYSNC for the remote COMAMID value.

Note: SAS/CONNECT requires TELNET to operate in a line-by-line mode. Full-screen mode is not supported.

Using a Script with the TELNET Access Method

To use one of the sample script files supplied with SAS/CONNECT for the TELNET access method, assign the RLINK filref to one of the following script files based on the remote host you are connecting to:

- `telaos.scr` (AOS/VS remote host)
- `telcms.scr` (CMS remote host)
- `telprim.scr` (PRIME remote host)
- `teltso.scr` (TSO remote host)
- `telvms.scr` (VMS remote host).

The automatic logon sample scripts must be modified to add information that is specific to your site. Do not attempt to start the link with an automatic logon script until the necessary modifications have been made. (Your SAS Software Representative or Consultant may have altered these scripts as needed.) If someone has altered an automatic logon sample script for users at your installation, you need to load a copy of the modified file on your local host. For UNIX hosts, copy the file to the *sasroot*/`misc`/`connect` directory, and make sure it replaces the unmodified version.

Troubleshooting

- For TELNET, the WAITFOR statement in the script should look for all possibilities. The number of seconds specified to wait if no condition is met should be less than the amount of time allowed by the connection itself before it drops because there is no activity. If the WAITFOR statement is not set properly, the following message will appear during an asynchronous SIGNON:

```
ERROR: Read Error
```

- For TELNET, if the SIGNON command appears to hang during a SIGNON, change the EOPCHAR in the SIGNON script to LF. The default EOPCHAR is CR and is not recognized by some remote systems.

- For TCP/IP, SAS/CONNECT may be unable to connect to the TCP socket. The following system message appears:

  ```
  connection refused
  ```

  The connection may fail at SIGNON for the following reasons:

  - The remote side is not listening.
  - The packet sequence is out of order, which can indicate that the routers are not working properly.
  - The maximum number of connections has been reached.
  - There is a flow problem, which indicates that too many packets are being sent to the remote side at once.

  On MVS, use the NETSTAT utility to show active sockets and to show who is waiting on a socket.

- When signing on using TCP/IP and LAN Workplace for OS/2, the following error can occur:

  ```
  ERROR:  Supporting Access Method Initialization Failed.
  ```

- A SIGNON from SAS for Windows, Release 6.08 may fail with the following message in a File Error dialog box:

  ```
  Cannot find WSOCKETS.DLL
  ```

  There are two reasons for this failure. The first and most common reason is that the DOS PATH statement does not contain the directory where the Microsoft LAN Manager V2.1+ TCP/IP product is installed.

  The second common reason for failure is that the WSOCKETS.DLL module is not in the C:LANMAN.DOSNETPROG subdirectory (assuming C:LANMAN.DOS is the parent directory where the Microsoft LAN Manager V2.1+ is installed). This file must be present for the SIGNON to be successful.

- A SIGNON from SAS for Windows, Release 6.08 may fail with the following message in a File Error dialog box:

  ```
  Cannot find WLIBSOCK.DLL
  ```

  This failure often occurs if WLIBSOCK.DLL is not located in a subdirectory of the Novell LAN Workplace directory defined by the EXCELAN environment variable. For the Novell LAN Workplace for DOS, Release V4.0 the subdirectory is BIN40. For the Novell LAN Workplace for DOS, Release V4.1, the subdirectory is BIN.

- With SAS for Windows, Release 6.08 and the Novell LAN Workplace for DOS, the following error is generated during a TCP SIGNON if the EXCELAN environment variable is not found:

  ```
  Cannot find WSOCKETS.DLL
  ```

This variable should be set in the AUTOEXEC.BAT file. To verify that it has been set, type **SET** at your DOS prompt. EXCELAN should be one of the variables listed and should point to your XLN directory if you are running Novell's LAN Workplace for MS-DOS V4.0, or to the NET directory if you are running Novell's LAN Workplace for MS-DOS V4.1. XLN and NET are the default directory names and may have been changed during the installation of the software. An example of the SET statement is:

```
SET EXCELAN=C:NET
```

This environment variable is required by SAS/CONNECT to be set for all release levels of Novell's LAN Workplace for DOS.

Chapter 9 The NetBIOS Access Method

Introduction 131

Available Connections 131

System Requirements 132
Requirements for OS/2 132
Requirements for Windows 132
Requirements for Windows NT 133

Starting SAS/CONNECT with the NetBIOS Access Method 133

Why Script Files Are Not Needed 133

Environment Variables 134

Troubleshooting 135

Introduction

The Network Basic Input/Output System (NetBIOS) is an operating system interface for applications programs running on nodes in a local area network. NetBIOS provides peer-to-peer communications between the supported hosts.

This chapter describes the hosts and systems software supported by SAS/CONNECT for this access method. This information is based on the support available at the time this book was written. Contact the Technical Support Division at SAS Institute for the most current information on additional supported hosts or systems software.

Note: There are two methods of interfacing with NetBIOS under OS/2. The NetBIOS access method uses the IBM NetBIOS 3.0 API, and the MNetBIOS access method uses the LAN Manager 1.0 Submit API. Reference to the NetBIOS access method could mean either NetBIOS or MNetBIOS with respect to OS/2.

Available Connections

If you have the NetBIOS access method installed, you can use SAS/CONNECT in a peer-to-peer configuration between either of the following hosts:

- OS/2
- Windows NT
- Windows. (You can use Windows 32s or Windows 3.*x* as a local host in a NETBIOS connection.)

Check with your SAS Software Representative to be sure that the NetBIOS access method has been installed on your PC. If you are using OS/2 or Windows NT as a remote host, you must have a spawner program running on the OS/2 or Windows NT node to which you connect. The spawner program supplied with SAS/CONNECT is described in "Using a Spawner Program" on page 137.

System Requirements

The following sections describe the system requirements for using the NetBIOS access method. The SAS Software Representative at your site can help you determine if your site meets these requirements.

Requirements for OS/2

Under OS/2 Version 2.0 or later, SAS/CONNECT provides access methods to support both the IBM NetBIOS 3.0 Interface and the LAN Manager 1.0 Submit Interface.

The following products are supported for the IBM NetBIOS 3.0 Interface:

- IBM's NTS/2, Version 1.0 or higher
- IBM's LAN Enabler, Version 2.0 or higher
- IBM's LAN Server, Version 2.0 or higher.

The following products are supported for the LAN Manager 1.0 Submit Interface:

- Novell's Netware Requestor for OS/2 2.0
- IBM's LAN Enabler, Version 2.0 or higher
- IBM's LAN Server, Version 2.0 or higher.

Note: Be sure to use the same vendor or compatible vendors on both sides of the connection. Microsoft and IBM NetBIOS are compatible but neither is compatible with Novell.

Sample configuration files are included on the installation diskettes in *sasroot*\CONNECT\SASMISC. Refer to the README.OS2 file in this directory for more information.

Requirements for Windows

Under both Windows Version 3.x and Windows 32s, SAS/CONNECT supports the NetBIOS software that is loaded into DOS.

Two possible packages are:

- LAN Support Program from IBM
- Netware Requestor from Novell.

Note: Be sure to use the same vendor or compatible vendors on both sides of the connection. Microsoft and IBM NetBIOS are compatible with each other, but neither one is compatible with Novell.

Sample configuration files are included on the installation diskettes in *sasroot*\CONNECT\SASMISC. For Windows 3.*x*, refer to the README.WIN file in this directory for more information. For Windows 32s, refer to the README.WNS file in this directory for more information.

Requirements for Windows NT

Under Windows NT, SAS/CONNECT supports the IBM-compatible NetBIOS that is included with Windows NT.

Starting SAS/CONNECT with the NetBIOS Access Method

To use the NetBIOS access method with SAS/CONNECT, specify the following SAS system options before you sign on:

- COMAMID=NETBIOS or COMAMID=MNETBIOS.

  - For Windows 3.1 or Windows NT, always use COMAMID=NETBIOS.
  - For OS/2 and the IBM NetBIOS 3.0 Interface, use COMAMID=NETBIOS.
  - For OS/2 and the LAN Manager 1.0 Submit Interface, use COMAMID=MNETBIOS.

- REMOTE=*network-name*. The REMOTE= value for the NetBIOS access method is the *network-name* that you specify for the NETNAME argument to the spawner program on the remote PC. See "Using a Spawner Program" on page 137 for more information on the spawner program.

You may need to specify some other setup options with the SET= SAS system option (see "Environment Variables" on page 134).

Why Script Files Are Not Needed

The NetBIOS access method does not use a script file to sign on or sign off. You do not need a script file because the NetBIOS access method connects to the spawner program running on the remote node. The spawner program then invokes the remote SAS session. This process replaces the need for a script file. However, you must have the spawner program running on the remote host (see "Using a Spawner Program" on page 137 for more information about spawner programs).

Although it does not cause errors if you specify a script file when you are using the NetBIOS access method, you do waste processing time. If you have defined the RLINK fileref prior to establishing a connection, when you sign on, SAS/CONNECT processes and loads the script file identified by the RLINK fileref. The NetBIOS access method then ignores the script. If you have defined the RLINK fileref and do not want to free it, you can avoid wasting processing time by using the NOSCRIPT option in the SIGNON and SIGNOFF commands or statements, as shown in the following statements:

```
signon noscript;
signoff noscript;
```

Environment Variables

SAS/CONNECT provides several environment variables to fine-tune your connections over NetBIOS. You may need to work with some of these variables if you are experiencing problems.

Under OS/2, Windows 3.*x*, Windows 32s, and Windows NT, you can set the value of these variables in either of the following ways:

- execute this statement from the SAS PROGRAM EDITOR window:

    ```
    options set=variable-name variable-value;
    ```

    Enclose *variable-value* in quotation marks if it contains special characters.

- add this line to the SAS configuration file.

    ```
    -set variable-name variable-value
    ```

Use PROC OPTIONS to verify the values are correctly set.

For both of the formats listed above, *variable-name* and *variable-value* can be any of the following:

VQMLINKS *number-of-links*
: specifies the number of links that can be active at the same time. Each time you sign on to a remote host, you initiate one link. If you want to sign on to more than one remote host during a single SAS session, set VQMLINKS to the number of links that will be active at the same time. There is no limit on the number of links you can specify, but use the smallest number possible to conserve NetBIOS session resources. The number you specify for this option must be the same or less than the maximum number of sessions that are configured for NetBIOS when it is installed. If you specify 0, VQMLINKS defaults to the number of sessions configured for a single NetBIOS user.

    For use with SAS/CONNECT, set both VQMLINKS and VQMCONVS to 1. Specify a higher value if you are running both SAS/CONNECT and SAS/SHARE in a single SAS session.

VQMCONVS *number-of-conversations*
: specifies the number of conversations that can occur simultaneously. For SAS/CONNECT, each time you sign on to a remote host, you initiate one conversation; therefore, set this value to the same number as VQMLINKS. There is no limit on the number of conversations you can specify, but use the smallest number possible to conserve NetBIOS command resources. The number you specify for this option must be the same or less than the number of commands that are configured for NetBIOS. If you specify 0, VQMCONVS defaults to the number of commands configured for a single NetBIOS user.

    For use with SAS/CONNECT, set both VQMLINKS and VQMCONVS to 1. Specify a higher value if you are running both SAS/CONNECT and SAS/SHARE in a single SAS session.

VQADAPTR *adapter-number*
: specifies which network adapter, and therefore which network, to use when establishing the link. This option is not needed if you are connected to only one network. Use this option only when COMAMID=NETBIOS. If COMAMID=MNETBIOS, refer to the VQNETNAME environment variable.

Note that if both the local and remote host are connected to multiple networks, both hosts must specify the same network to establish a connection. For example, if your node has network connections for a token-ring network and an Ethernet network and you want to connect to another node on the Ethernet network, you must set VQADAPTR to the correct adapter number for that network. This doesn't necessarily mean that the value of VQADAPTR is the same on both hosts. One host may have adapter 0 set to Ethernet while the other host has adapter 1 set to Ethernet. In this case, VQADAPTR has to be 0 for the one host and 1 for the other host.

Check with your SAS Software Representative or your PC installation staff if you need help determining which adapter to use for each network.

VQNETNAME

Specifies which network in the NetBIOS driver table should be used. Currently, Netware Requestor for OS/2 does not allow the access method to specify the network name but instead always uses the first network driver in the table.

Troubleshooting

Various errors may occur when you initially try to establish a connection over a network with the NetBIOS access method. Many of these problems are related to the network. SAS/CONNECT attempts to present an error message that indicates the cause of the error. The following list explains the most common problems in establishing NetBIOS communications.

ERROR: Network Request Failed rc=38. Requested resource(s) not available.

There are not enough system resources available to satisfy either the VQMLINKS= or VQMCONVS= request. This error can be caused by either of the following situations:

- The default value of either VQMLINKS= or VQMCONVS= requests more resources than are available. The default value for both options is 0, which normally implies 16 NetBIOS sessions and 16 commands with most implementations.

- You have specified a value for either VQMLINKS= or VQMCONVS= and there are not enough resources to satisfy the request.

To correct this error, specify a new value for either VQMLINKS= or VQMCONVS= on either the local or remote session, as appropriate.

ERROR: Network Request Failed rc=22. Too many commands outstanding.

The number of simultaneous conversations requested is greater than the allocated commands allow and the request has failed. You are using too many resources.

To correct this problem, either increase the number of conversations allowed or decrease the number of simultaneous conversations. To increase the number of conversations allowed, increase the value of the VQMCONVS= option on either the local or remote session, as appropriate, provided sufficient system resources are available. In general, one conversation is required for each concurrent SAS/CONNECT session as well as each remote libname.

ERROR: Network request failed (rc 0x14) - Cannot find name called.
The SAS/CONNECT spawner program cannot be found. Verify the following:

- you have the proper network selected
- you have specified the correct name for the spawner program
- the spawner program is started.

ERROR: Network request failed (rc 0xA7) - Unknown NETBIOS return code.
NETBIOS is not set up to run in the Windows environment.

ERROR: File not found loading \sas\core\sasexe\sasvnnet.dll;
    File contributing to error: ACSNETB
ERROR: File not found loading \sas\core\sasexe\sasvnmne.dll;
    File contributing to error: NETAPI
The NETBIOS or MNETBIOS access method was loaded but the supporting vendor software was not found. You must specify the correct path location in the LIBPATH statement for one of the following:

- ACSNETB.DLL, for IBM NetBIOS 3.0 compatible interfaces
- NETAPI.DLL, for LAN Manager 1.0 NetBIOS Submit compatible interfaces.

ERROR: Network request failed (rc 0x05) - Command timed out.
During a NETBIOS SIGNON, SASDMR.EXE could not be executed from the directory the spawner program is executing from. To resolve this problem, add the SAS 6.08 or later directory to the OS/2 PATH= statement in the OS/2 CONFIG.SYS file.

To test and verify that SASDMR.EXE is functional, execute the spawner program and then terminate it with a CONTROL-C. From the directory that you are in after terminating the spawner, type **SASDMR** and press Enter. A SAS.DMR icon should appear in the Minimized Window Viewer - Icon View. Once SASDMR can successfully be executed from this directory, the SIGNON will be successful.

Chapter 10 Using a Spawner Program

Introduction 137

Syntax 137

File and Security Options 138
Specifying the File for the Spawner to Run 138
Securing Access 139

Ending the Spawner Program 140

Introduction

A spawner program listens for incoming requests to connect the requesting program to a program on the spawner machine. To use OS/2 as a remote host with the NETBIOS access method or Windows NT as a remote host with the NETBIOS or TCP/IP access methods, you must run the spawner program provided with SAS/CONNECT on the node that serves as the remote host. Once this program is started, users can connect to the OS/2 or Windows NT node using the NETBIOS access method by setting the REMOTE= option to the NETNAME value defined with the spawner program. Users can connect to the NT node using the TCP/IP access method by setting the REMOTE= option to the internet address defined for the remote NT node.

This chapter explains how to start the spawner program and describes the options that enable you to customize and secure your environment.

Note: The spawner program is stored on the remote host in the *sasroot*\CONNECT\SASEXE directory.

Syntax

The syntax for the spawner program is:

SPAWNER -COMAMID *access-method-id* -NETNAME *network-name*
    <-ADAPTER *n*> <-DRIVER *device-driver*> <-HELP>
    <*file-and-security-options*>

-COMAMID *access-method-id*
    specifies the access method to use. Valid values for -COMAMID depend upon the operating system of the node executing the spawner program. You can use NETBIOS or MNETBIOS when running on an OS/2 node, and you can use NETBIOS or TCP when running on a Windows NT node. In either case, you can specify multiple -COMAMID options and values if multiple connections will be made to this node with more than one type of access method.

-NETNAME *network-name*
    provides a network name that the network running NETBIOS can use to access the spawner program. This name is the value that the user specifies for the REMOTE= option on the local host. The name must be eight or fewer characters. The -NETNAME option applies only to the NETBIOS access method.

Optional arguments include the following:

-ADAPTER *n* specifies which adapter number the spawner should use when communicating through the IBM NETBIOS API. The default is adapter 0. This option is useful if you are running NETBIOS and you want to use an adapter other than adapter 0.

-DRIVER *device-driver* specifies the name of the device driver that the spawner should use when communicating through the OS/2 MNETBIOS access method. The default is to use the first driver listed in the name table. This option is only needed if you have more than one NETBIOS network device driver installed on the node running the spawner.
 Note: The Novell requestor for OS/2 does not support the -DRIVER option.

file-and-security-options are described in the following sections.

-HELP prints a list of valid parameters.

You can shorten option names by specifying only the first letter (or any number of leading letters) when you invoke the spawner. For example, the following command brings up a spawner and listens for a REMOTE= value of SASDMR.

```
spawner -n sasdmr
```

File and Security Options

This section describes how to control the way a spawner invokes the SAS System and restrict the user ids that can connect to the spawner.

Specifying the File for the Spawner to Run

The spawner program listens for incoming connection requests and upon receipt of such a request, executes a file that invokes the SAS System. The default file is SAS.EXE in the directory from which the spawner is invoked. If you wish to execute SAS from a different path or execute other statements before invoking SAS, use one or both of the following options when you start the spawner program:

-FILENAME specifies the name of a batch (.BAT) file for Windows NT, or a command (.CMD) file for OS/2, that the spawner executes to invoke the remote SAS session.
 With Windows NT, this option is only used when you specify NETBIOS as the -COMAMID value when you invoke the spawner.
 Your batch file must contain the following two lines:

```
cd \msas_wnt
sas.exe -nologo $SASDMR MSGQUEUE %1 %2 %3 %4 %5 %6 %7 %8 %9
```

The first line changes to the directory where the SAS executable is stored. The second line invokes SAS. Add options as needed to this SAS invocation.

With OS/2, you can use a REXX command file that contains statements in the following format:

```
/* Invoke remote SAS session */
parse arg parameters
'drive:path\file-name.ext  SAS-options ' parameters
```

The first line must be a comment line to indicate to the OS/2 command processor that this is a REXX file. Type the second line as shown because you *must* parse the arguments passed to the REXX file and pass them on to your SAS session. On the third line, specify the location of the file to be invoked. Also include any SAS options on this line inside the quotation marks. You do not need to specify the DMR option or the COMAMID= value; these options are set automatically.

Note: The last word on the second and third lines, **parameters**, can be any term, but it must be the same term on both lines.

-USERCMDS   causes the spawner to ask the SAS/CONNECT user for the name of the file to invoke to run the remote SAS session. The spawner program presents an interactive prompt to the local SAS session. If the user enters only a return, the program uses the file specified by the -FILENAME option. If the -FILENAME option was not specified, the program uses the default filename, SAS.EXE.

If the user supplies the name of an OS/2 command file, the file must be a REXX file that follows the guidelines described for the -FILENAME option.

Securing Access

You may want to restrict connection to the spawner to a specified group of users. Use the option described here and set up the ACI.DAT file, also described in this section.

-PROTECTION tells the spawner to restrict access to the remote machine by using username and password protection. The spawner program presents an interactive prompt to the local SAS session to ask for the username and password. You must have already specified permissible usernames and passwords in the ACI.DAT file. This file is described below. By default, protection is disabled.

To limit access to the remote host, you must define a file called ACI.DAT in the directory from which you invoke the spawner program. In this file, specify usernames, passwords and, optionally, the name of a file to run to start the remote SAS session when that user establishes a connection. The format for each entry is shown here.

```
username password  NETBIOS filename.ext
```

Put each user's entry on a separate line. If you are running OS/2 and you specify a file, it must be a REXX command file that follows the guidelines described for the -FILENAME option in the previous section. If you are running on Windows NT, it must be a batch (.BAT) command file. If you include the name of a file that is to be executed when a specific user establishes a connection, precede the filename with the NETBIOS keyword. Usernames and passwords are restricted to 8 characters and filenames are restricted to 32 characters.

Ending the Spawner Program

To end the spawner program, type CTRL-C or double-click on the top left corner of the Windows NT or OS/2 window running the program.

Chapter 11 EHLLAPI and 3270 Access Methods

Introduction 141

Available Connections 141

Requirements for OS/2 142

Requirements for Windows 32s 142

Requirements for Windows 3.x 142

Starting SAS/CONNECT with the EHLLAPI Access Method 143

Sample Scripts for EHLLAPI 143

Environment Variables for Windows and OS/2 143

Troubleshooting 144

Introduction

The EHLLAPI access method provides terminal-based communication from a PC to another host. EHLLAPI support is included in 3270 terminal emulation software. The EHLLAPI access method works over a variety of connections such as COAX, synchronous, and token ring. You do not need to know the connection used at your site to use the EHLLAPI access method.

This chapter describes the hosts and systems software supported by SAS/CONNECT for this access method. This information is based on the hosts and systems software available for this access method at the time this book was written. Contact the Technical Support Division at SAS Institute for the most current information on additional supported hosts or systems software.

This chapter also describes the system requirements for using the EHLLAPI access method. The SAS Software Representative at your site can help you determine if your site meets these requirements.

Available Connections

The EHLLAPI access method permits you to connect from OS/2, Windows 32s, or Windows 3.x to:

- CMS
- MVS
- VSE.

The PC must always be the local host with this access method.

Requirements for OS/2

Your site must have Release 1.3 or later of OS/2 and one of the following:

- IBM's CM/2, Version 1.0 or higher (with correction patch XR06055)
- Extended Services 1.0 or later
- any OS/2 2.0 or later emulation program that supports the EHLLAPI standard.

Sample configuration files are included on the installation diskettes in *sasroot*\CONNECT\SASMISC. Refer to the README.OS2 file in this directory for details.

Requirements for Windows 32s

For the EHLLAPI access method, use the same software emulation packages that are supported for the Windows 3.x environment. The SAS System uses Universal Thunking techniques to obtain access to those 16-bit DLLs. The supported emulation packages are:

- EXTRA for Windows, Version 3.3 or later, from Attachmate
- IRMA WorkStation for Windows, Version 1.0 or later, from Digital Communications Associates
- Personal Communications/3270, Version 2.0 or later, from IBM
- Rumba, Version 3.1 or later, from Wall Data Incorporated
- any emulation program that supports the EHLLAPI standard.

Sample configuration files are included on the installation diskettes in *sasroot*\CONNECT\SASMISC. Refer to the README.WNS file in this directory for details.

Requirements for Windows 3.*x*

To use the EHLLAPI access method, your site must have one of the following:

- EXTRA for Windows, Version 3.3 or later, from Attachmate
- IRMA WorkStation for Windows, Version 1.0 or later, from Digital Communications Associates
- Personal Communications/3270, Version 2.0 or later, from IBM
- Rumba, Version 3.1 or later, from Wall Data Incorporated
- any emulation program that supports the EHLLAPI standard

Personal Communications/3270, Version 2 must have the corrective service diskette for R200, PTF Number IP00841 applied in order to work with SAS/CONNECT. After application of the diskette, Personal Communications/3270 will be updated to Version 2.00 CSD 2. You can verify this update by selecting **About** from the Personal Communications/3270 help screen.

Note: Be sure that the directory that contains the EHLLAPI DLL library for the emulator you use is defined in the DOS PATH command before invoking your Windows session. Only one 3270 emulation package should be listed in the DOS PATH command.

Sample configuration files are included on the installation diskettes in *sasroot*\CONNECT\SASMISC. Refer to the README.WIN file in this directory for details.

Starting SAS/CONNECT with the EHLLAPI Access Method

To use the EHLLAPI access method with SAS/CONNECT, specify the following SAS system options before you sign on:

- COMAMID=EHLLAPI
- REMOTE=*remote-session-id*. The remote session id can be either the short or long session id of the remote session. You specify these names when you configure the emulation package to communicate between the PC and the remote host.

In addition, you need to specify a script file to be used when you sign on and sign off. Instructions for using a script with SIGNON and SIGNOFF are given in "Starting and Stopping SAS/CONNECT Software" on page 61.

The scripts provided with SAS/CONNECT are described below in "Sample Scripts for EHLLAPI".

Sample Scripts for EHLLAPI

To use one of the sample script files supplied with SAS/CONNECT for the EHLLAPI access method, assign the RLINK fileref to one of the following script files, depending on what remote host you are connecting to:

CMS.SCR or LOGCMS.SCR	if the remote host is running CMS.
TSO.SCR or LOGTSO.SCR	if the remote host is running MVS.
VSE.SCR or VSECICS.SCR	if the remote host is running VSE.

For OS/2 and Windows, these script files are usually located in the *sasroot*\CONNECT\SASLINK directory.

Environment Variables for Windows and OS/2

Several 3270 vendors for Windows 3.x and Windows 32s have selected different DLL names for their EHLLAPI support.

To compensate for the different names without adding redundant access methods, SAS/CONNECT dynamically loads the EHLLAPI DLL library support installed by the vendor by looking in the DOS PATH or OS/2 LIBPATH paths for the appropriate DLL files.

SAS/CONNECT first checks the SET variable VQDLLNAME for a DLL library name. If the VQDLLNAME variable specifies a name, that DLL is loaded from one of the paths in the PATH or LIBPATH commands. You can use the SET= option to specify the location of the library, as follows:

```
options set=vqdllname 'filename-of-DLL-library';
```

Note: You can omit the .DLL extension on the filename for the VQDLLNAME variable. Do not specify a disk drive or pathname. The DLL location must be found by using the DOS PATH or OS2 LIBPATH paths.

Currently for OS/2, the only valid value for the VQDLLNAME variable is ACS3EHAP. If you do not specify the VQDLLNAME variable, SAS/CONNECT searches the LIBPATH paths to locate the ACS3EHAP module for the IBM Communications Manager.

For Windows, if you do not specify the VQDLLNAME variable, SAS/CONNECT searches for DLL names in the following order and uses the first valid DLL name it finds:

ACS3EHAP   This file exists if you have Irma Workstation for Windows 3.1 or Attachmate installed.

PCSHLL   This file exists if you have IBM PC/3270 for Windows 3.1 installed.

EEHLLAPI   This file exists if you have Rumba software installed.

For example, if you are running Rumba software and you have not specified the VQDLLNAME variable, then Windows 3.x searches first for the ACS3EHAP file, then the PCSHLL DLL files in the DOS PATH, and finally the EEHLLAPI.DLL file, which it finds because Rumba is installed.

Note: Make sure only one 3270 emulation directory is in the PATH at a time if multiple 3270 emulators are installed. Only one such emulator can be used at a time.

Troubleshooting

If you encounter difficulties in establishing a conversation, SAS/CONNECT provides the following messages to help you troubleshoot the problem.

ERROR: No available HLLAPI session.
    The wrong REMOTE= value has been specified. The REMOTE= value should match the remote host session name.

NOTE: (11320k) badly formatted SAS remote screen
WARNING: - message received from Host
ERROR: user-requested abort encountered.
    SASHOST ENDED DUE TO ERROR.
    The **NOTE** and **WARNING** messages appear on the PC. The **ERROR** message appears on the remote host. These messages occur after the SIGNON command if the 3174 controller does not have the file transfer aid byte set correctly. Option 125 (file transfer aid) must have digit 6 set to 1 to allow packets to be sent to complete the SIGNON. This problem also occurs with other controllers. The option will typically be identified on other controllers by a name similar to *file transfer aid*.

Bad 3270 status. Please reset keyboard.
    A problem exists in either the software you are using, other than SAS/CONNECT, or in VTAM. Add a WAITFOR statement that waits for at least 1 second before issuing the TYPE statement that caused the message to occur.

ERROR: Failed to load the HLLAPI DLL module.
During SIGNON with Windows, the module may not load because:

- The PATH of the emulator was not specified in the PATH statement in the AUTOEXEC.BAT file. Type the PATH command from a DOS prompt to determine if the emulator is listed. Only one 3270 emulation package should be listed in the PATH and, it should be listed first, if possible.

- The HLLAPI interface was not loaded with the emulation package. Check the documentation of your package to see what steps are necessary to load the HLLAPI interface.

- The HLLAPI module name (.DLL) is named something other than ACS3HAP.DLL, PCSHLL.DLL, or EHLLAPI.DLL (for Windows). See "Environment Variables for Windows and OS/2" on page 143 for more information about using the SET=VQDLLNAME with other emulators.

Chapter 12 Using Protocol Converters and TTY with the ASYNC Access Method

Introduction 147

Using a Protocol Converter 148
Preparing to Use a Protocol Converter 148
Steps for Using a Protocol Converter 149

Using TTY with the ASYNC Access Method 149

The TTY.EXE Program 150
Setting Communications Parameters 151
TTY Functions 151
Preparing to Use the TTY Program 152
Starting TTY with SAS/CONNECT 152
Ending a TTY Session 153

Using Scripts with TTY.EXE 153
Sample Script Connecting to VSE with a Protocol Converter 153

Troubleshooting 155
ASYNC Port Fails 156
Problems with the ASYNC Connection 156
Script SIGNON Fails 158

Introduction

Protocol converters simulate a 3270-type terminal on a variety of asynchronous terminal types. Most protocol converters perform data conversion that enables an asynchronous terminal to operate like a full-screen 3270-type terminal. SAS/CONNECT does not use the full-screen capabilities of the protocol converter. As a result, when you use a protocol converter with SAS/CONNECT, it must operate in *transparent mode.* Transparent mode enables the remote host to send ASCII data directly to the local host without performing the normal data conversion for 3270-type appearance.

SAS/CONNECT supports the ASYNC access method for OS/2, but not for Windows. The Windows environment does not allow applications to share the communications port. SAS/CONNECT has to be able to share the communications port with an asynchronous emulation package in order to establish a conversation.

SAS/CONNECT under OS/2 supports two protocol converters:

- IBM 7171

- Commtex Cx-80.

This chapter describes the requirements for each protocol converter and explains how to prepare for and use a protocol converter with SAS/CONNECT.

SAS/CONNECT includes a simple terminal emulation program, called TTY, that provides the requisite terminal emulation. You must use this program to access the remote host when using a protocol converter. This chapter explains how to use TTY.

In addition to the TTY program, SAS/CONNECT includes two sample command files that facilitate use of TTY with protocol converters:

- TTY7171.CMD
- TTYCTEX.CMD

These command files start TTY with appropriate communications parameters and use a keyboard translation table that simplifies using the protocol converter with SAS/CONNECT.

Using a Protocol Converter

This section describes how to use SAS/CONNECT with OS/2 to MVS, CMS, or VSE through two protocol converters:

- IBM 7171
- Commtex Cx-80.

   Note: You cannot use a protocol converter to connect to Release 5.16 under VSE.

Preparing to Use a Protocol Converter

Before using SAS/CONNECT with a protocol converter, complete the following steps:

1. Determine the full pathname of the script that you must use to sign on through your protocol converter. SAS Institute supplies sample scripts, which are usually located in the *sasroot*\CONNECT\SASLINK directory.
      Your site may also have a customized script; see your SAS Software Consultant for the correct pathname. *

2. Determine the full pathname of the sample TTY command file (usually *sasroot*\CONNECT\SASTTY\TTY.CMD) and the keyboard translation tables used for your protocol converter. The following files are typically stored in the directory, *sasroot*\CONNECT\SASTTY:

   TTY7171.XLT   translation table for using TTY with the IBM 7171

   TTYCTEX.XLT   translation table for using TTY with the Commtex Cx-80.

3. To use the TTY program, make sure a statement that defines the correct device driver is included in the CONFIG.SYS file when you boot OS/2. Specify the following DEVICE statement.

```
device=c:\os2\com.sys    /* OS/2 2.0 */
device=c:\os2\com0n.sys  /* OS/2 1.3 */
```

---

*   If necessary, you can write your own script following the example shown in "Using Scripts with TTY.EXE" on page 153.

This device driver must be installed before you can use the MODE command to set communications parameters for a serial port. Sample MODE command parameters are included in the TTY.CMD file for your protocol converter.

Use the sample TTY.CMD file to customize a file for your site, then move the customized TTY.CMD file to a location in your path to execute it.

Steps for Using a Protocol Converter

Use SAS/CONNECT with the IBM 7171 or the Commtex Cx-80 protocol converter by following these steps.

1. From an OS/2 command prompt, invoke the TTY command file and specify either 7171 or CTEX in the TTY command. For example, if you are using an IBM 7171 protocol converter and you have the *sasroot* directory in your command path, you could invoke the TTY program as follows:

    ```
    tty 7171
    ```

2. Log on to the remote host.

3. Suspend (do not terminate) the session on the remote host by pressing ALT-Q. Do not enter either C or Q in response to the prompt. Suspending TTY returns you to the OS/2 session.

4. Invoke the SAS System under OS/2 and locally submit the following SAS statement:

    ```
    options comamid=rasync remote=com-port-id ;
    ```

    A link established through a protocol converter is an asynchronous connection so you must use COMAMID=RASYNC on the local side.

5. Submit the following SIGNON statement to sign on to the SAS System on the remote host, where *protocol-converter-script*.SCR is the pathname of the script file for your protocol converter:

    ```
    signon 'protocol-converter-script.scr';
    ```

6. When the link is established, this message appears in the LOG window:

    ```
    Remote signon complete
    ```

Using TTY with the ASYNC Access Method

Execution of the ASYNC access method depends on the TTY.EXE program and cannot be used in conjunction with any other ASYNC terminal emulation package for OS/2. This is because the OS/2 environment does not directly support COM port sharing; however, OS/2 does allow the port to be opened with a shared mode. Therefore, the TTY program was coded such that it opens the COM port with a shared mode and then synchronizes subsequent use of the port with SAS by suspending the COM port for SAS to use without dropping the line.

Normally, you invoke TTY from a command prompt, log on to the desired remote host, press ALT-Q to suspend the TTY program, and then execute a SAS/CONNECT signon command from your SAS session on OS/2.

You can set the baud rate, parity, stop bits, and so on one of two ways:

□   Use the MODE command.

□   Set the parameters in the SAS/CONNECT script file. All or none of the parameters should be specified in the script file.

If the SAS/CONNECT break window appears, TTY can also be used to interact with the remote session by typing C for CONTINUE from the OS/2 command prompt where you invoked TTY. When you are ready for SAS/CONNECT to continue the conversation with the remote session, again press ALT-Q in TTY and type C in the SAS/CONNECT break window to continue.

The RASYNC access method can only be used from OS/2 2.0 for a serial port that is being controlled by the basic COM.SYS driver. It cannot be used for SAS/CONNECT under OS/2 using the OS/2 Extended Services ACDI support for serial ports.

Basic serial port support is automatically installed when OS/2 2.0 is installed. Make sure the following statement is in your config.sys file for OS/2:

```
DEVICE=C:\OS2\COM.SYS
```

ASYNC support uses the facilities of the OS/2 DosOpen API and therefore supports serial ports COM1, COM2 and COM3. Use one of the following statements to indicate which serial port is desired (where *x* is 1, 2 or 3):

```
options remote=comx;
signon comx;
```

Note: The RASYNC access method is not a part of the SAS System for Windows because the Windows environment does not allow a serial port to be opened in a shared mode. Since the port cannot be opened in a shared mode, it is not possible for TTY to suspend the port for use by SAS without dropping the line.

The TTY.EXE Program

TTY.EXE is stored on your local host in the file *sasroot*\CONNECT\SASEXE\TTY.EXE. The *sasroot* directory contains a .CMD file that simplifies invoking the TTY program. To invoke the TTY program, issue the following command from the local host:

```
tty
```

When you invoke the TTY program, you can specify the following options. Note that the -C option and the -E option have default values when you do not specify the option. The other options have no default values.

-B *rate*   sets the baud rate. Valid values for *rate* are 110, 150, 300, 600, 1200, 2400, 4800, 9600, and 19200.

-C *com-port*   sets the communications port. Valid values for *com-port* are COM1, COM2, and COM3. If you omit this option, the default value is COM1.

-D *data-bits*   sets the number of data bits. Valid values for *data-bits* are 7 and 8.

-E *setting* sets echoplex. Valid values for *setting* are ON and OFF. If you omit this option, the default value is ON.

-H *method* sets the handshaking method. Valid values for *method* are HARDWARE, NONE, and SOFTWARE (for XON/XOFF).

-P *type* sets the parity. Valid values for *type* are EVEN, MARK, NONE, ODD, and SPACE.

-S *stop-bits* sets the number of stop bits. Valid values for *stop-bits* are 1 and 2.

-X *file-spec* names the keyboard translation table to be used with protocol converters.

Setting Communications Parameters

You can set the baud rate, parity, data bits, stop bits, and handshaking that the TTY program uses in two ways:

□ Specify the communications parameters by using the options described in the previous section when you invoke the TTY program. In this case, you must also specify the communications parameters in the script that you use to sign on.

□ Issue an OS/2 MODE command to set the communications parameters before you invoke the TTY program. When you invoke TTY, do not specify any options in the command. The script that you use to sign on should omit the statements to set communications parameters (or should specify the same settings for the communications parameters as were specified in the MODE command).

TTY Functions

You can use the following key combinations to initiate functions while the TTY program is running:

ALT-B signals a 220-millisecond break to the host.

ALT-C clears the display.

ALT-E toggles echoplex on and off.

ALT-F opens and closes an OS/2 file that records all TTY activity.

ALT-H displays help for the TTY program.

ALT-Q suspends or quits the TTY program. If you press this combination without selecting either C or Q, the Data Terminal Ready (DTR) signal is kept enabled (held high) so that you do not drop the host connection. Keeping the DTR signal high enables you to run SAS/CONNECT.

ALT-R issues prompts enabling you to change communications parameters. Note that when you exit the TTY program (with ALT-Q), the communications port, baud, parity, data bits, and stop bits are reset to the status they had before you invoked the TTY program. Therefore, once you have set communications parameters using one of the methods described earlier in "Setting Communications Parameters", you cannot change these communications parameters for SAS/CONNECT by using ALT-R.

Preparing to Use the TTY Program

Before you begin using the TTY program,

1. Make sure the CONFIG.SYS file includes the following statement, where *n* is 1 if you have a PC AT and 2 if you have a PS/2:

    ```
    device=c:\os2\com.sys    /* OS/2 2.0 */
    device=c:\os2\com0n.sys  /* OS/2 1.3 */
    ```

    When invoking TTY, the following message occurs if the user's OS/2 CONFIG.SYS file does not contain a device statement loading the COM01.SYS or COM02.SYS driver:

    ```
    DOS open of com port failed, rc=110
    ```

2. To simplify invoking TTY, be sure you have a .CMD file in your working directory or the *sasroot* directory named TTY.CMD. Include in the command file the complete pathname of the TTY command with all the options set as you want to use them. For example, the following statement runs TTY using COM1, 9600 baud, no parity, 8 data bits, and 1 stop bit.

    ```
    sasroot\connect\sasexe\tty
    -b 9600 -p none -d 8 -s 1
    ```

    Although this step is not required, it simplifies the process of using TTY. If you do not have a .CMD file, you must specify this information each time you invoke TTY.

Starting TTY with SAS/CONNECT

The following steps describe how to use the TTY program to establish a link with an ASYNC connection:

1. Open an OS/2 command prompt session.
2. Be sure the directory containing the .CMD file described earlier in step 2 in "Preparing to Use the TTY Program" is in your command path.
3. Invoke the TTY.CMD file.
4. If you are using a manual log-on script, log on to the remote host; otherwise, skip to the next step.
5. Suspend TTY by pressing ALT-Q. Do not enter either C or Q at the prompt that requests you to continue or quit.
6. Return to the Window List by pressing ALT-ESC.
7. Return to your SAS session on OS/2 or invoke one if you do not currently have a session open.
8. Sign on to the link using the appropriate script file. Specify the communications port where TTY is invoked as the value of the REMOTE= system option and COMAMID=RASYNC. The link is now established.

Do not attempt to use TTY for other functions when a SAS/CONNECT link is established.

Ending a TTY Session

When you have finished using the link and want to end the TTY session, use these steps.

1. Sign off from the link.
2. Switch to the OS/2 command prompt where you invoked TTY.
3. If you used a manual log-on script, type C to continue and press ENTER. Log off from the remote host and then press ALT-Q. If you used an automatic log-on script, skip to the next step.
4. Type Q to quit, and press ENTER. The TTY session ends, and you are returned to the OS/2 command prompt.

Using Scripts with TTY.EXE

The scripts provided with SAS/CONNECT for use with protocol converters are:

CMS7171.SCR or CMSCTEX.SCR
    to connect to CMS from OS/2

TSO7171.SCR or TSOCTEX.SCR
    to connect to MVS from OS/2

VSE.SCR
    to connect to VSE from OS/2 using 7171

VSECICS.SCR
    to connect directly to a CICS session from OS/2 using 7171

Scripts are located in the *sasroot*\CONNECT\SASLINK directory for OS/2.
To use your script successfully, verify that the asynchronous communications parameters (baud rate, data bits, handshaking, parity, and stop bits) are set correctly for your computing installation. See "Setting Communications Parameters" on page 151 for information on how to set these parameters. If you do not know what the settings should be, ask your SAS Software Representative or Consultant.

Sample Script Connecting to VSE with a Protocol Converter

The following script is available with SAS/CONNECT under OS/2. It is located in *sasroot*\CONNECT\SASLINK\VSECICS.SCR. Protocol converters are also supported under MVS and CMS.

You can use this script to establish connections or you can create your own script using this one as a model. Note that you must include the DMR and COMAMID= options in the TYPE statement that invokes the SAS System under VSE.

```
/* trace on;  */
/* echo on;   */
/*------------------------------------------------------------------------
      Copyright (C) 1992 by SAS Institute Inc., Cary NC
      name:       vsecics.scr
      purpose:    SAS/CONNECT SIGNON/SIGNOFF script for connecting
                  to a VSE host via CICS using either the EHLLAPI
                  or RASYNC access methods from a local OS/2 system
                  or the EHLLAPI access method from a local WINDOWS
                  3.0 system.
      notes:      1. The communication parameters may need to be changed
                     for your site.
      assumes:    1. This script assumes the  SAS/VSE host supervisor is
                     already up and running and CICS is ready to accept
                     the SAS transaction.
                  2. The command to invoke the SAS CICS transaction
                     is "sasc".  If this is incorrect for your site,
                     change the contents of the lines that contain...
                     type "sasc ...
      support:    SAS Institute Staff
-------------------------------------------------------------------------*/

   log "NOTE: Script file 'vsecics.scr' entered.";

   if signoff then goto signoff;

/*------------------------------------------------------------------------
   The emulation session should already be connected to CICS.  CICS
   should be ready to accept the SAS transaction.
-------------------------------------------------------------------------*/

   if fullscreen then goto on32;

/*--- RASYNC SIGNON FROM A LOCAL OS/2 SYSTEM ----------------------------*/

   log 'NOTE: Signing on to VSE via an IBM 7171 protocol converter';

   baud 9600;
   parity none;
   databits 8;
   stopbits 1;
   handshaking none;

   maxi 220;
   maxo 220;
```

```
    /*-----------------------------------------------------------------------
        Invoke the SAS CICS transaction to start a remote VSE SAS session.
        Note: The 7171 protocol converter does not support extended data
        stream (non-queriable device).
        The SAS CICS transaction, 'sasc', may be different at your site.
    ------------------------------------------------------------------------*/
        log "NOTE: Starting remote SAS now.";

        /* noterminal suppressses prompts from remote SAS session.   */
        /* no$syntaxcheck prevents remote side from going into syntax */
        /* checking mode when a syntax error is encountered.          */
        type "sasc 'dmr comamid=rsas7171 noterminal no$syntaxcheck'" ENTER;

    /*------------------ logon to SAS Multiuser system ----------------------*/
        waitfor 'Enter your SAS userid:', 5 seconds: nouserid;
        input 'Enter SAS userid:';
        type ENTER;
        waitfor 'Enter password', 5 seconds: nopasswd;
        input nodisplay 'Enter password:';
        type ENTER;

        waitfor 'PACKET': onok, 120 seconds: nosas;


    /*------------------------- signoff -------------------------------------*/
    signoff:
        log 'NOTE: SAS/CONNECT conversation terminated.';
        stop;

    /*--------------------- ERROR HANDLING ----------------------------------*/
    nouserid:
    nopasswd:
        log 'ERROR: Did not get userid or password prompt.';
        log '       Snapshot of emulation session follows:';
        snapshot;
        abort;

    nosas:
        log 'ERROR: Did not get SAS Multiuser startup messages.';
        log '       Snapshot of emulation session follows:';
        snapshot;
        abort;
```

Troubleshooting

If you are having trouble establishing a link through a protocol converter or with the ASYNC access method, this section provides some suggestions for determining possible causes for the problem.

ASYNC Port Fails

If you do not get a response from your ASYNC port when executing TTY it may be because the OS/2 MODE command parameters are not properly supported. Follow these guidelines:

OS/2 2.0   If you use values other than OFF for the parameters, the modem, cable, and network must each support all of the following OS/2 MODE command parameters:

TXDMA	OCTS
RXDMA	DTR
IDSR	RTS.
ODSR	

The cable must be a seven pin cable to support these parameters. If either the modem, cable, or network does not support all of the parameters, TTY will not work unless you specify OFF for all of the parameters except DTR. For example,

```
mode com#: baud, parity, databits, stopbits, TXDMA=OFF, RXDMA=OFF,
          IDSR=OFF, ODSR=OFF, OCTS=OFF, DTR=ON, RTS=OFF
```

OS/2 1.3   If you use values other than OFF for the parameters, the modem, cable, and network must each support all of the following OS/2 MODE command parameters:

XON	OCTS
IDSR	DTR
ODSR	RTS

The cable must be a seven pin cable to support these parameters. If either the modem, cable, or network does not support all of the parameters, TTY will not work unless you specify OFF for all of the parameters except DTR. For example,

```
mode com#: baud, parity, databits, stopbits, XON=OFF,
          IDSR=OFF, ODSR=OFF, OCTS=OFF, DTR=ON, RTS=OFF
```

Note: Your configuration may have worked previously for TTY with DOS because DOS does not require all of the parameters that OS/2 requires.

Problems with the ASYNC Connection

- If you have an ASYNC connection and you get an error message during script execution that indicates that input data have been lost, the problem may be that the local host is not waiting long enough before responding to input from the remote host. As a result, the local host may try to send data to the remote host before the remote host has finished its previous message. The LINEWAIT statement or the DELAY statement may resolve this problem. The LINEWAIT statement specifies the time the local host waits after receiving input from the remote host. The DELAY statement sets the length of the pause between each character transmitted.

- The MAXI and MAXO parameters are valid only for the TELNET and ASYNC methods. They are not valid for the TCP access method.

    When signing on using the TCP access method, the following errors occur if the MAXI and MAXO parameters are implemented in the signon script:

    ```
    ERROR:  Script parameter MAXI not valid for access method.
    ERROR:  Script parameter MAXO not valid for access method.
    ```

- If you have an ASYNC connection and receive the following message, the error may be due to line noise:

    ```
    Communications receive error.
    D packet not received. Sending T packet.
    ```

    Try increasing the value set by the RETRY statement or decreasing the values set by the MAXI and MAXO statements.

- Handshaking should be used for everything or for nothing. If handshaking is not specified correctly, the following symptoms may occur:

hung connection

garbage characters (inbound)

break (inbound)

repeated text (inbound).

- If you receive the following message:

    ```
    ERROR: COM port already in use
    ```

    - Verify that you pressed ALT-Q for TTY to suspend the COM port. TTY and SAS/CONNECT cannot use the COM port at the same time. TTY and SAS/CONNECT synchronize use of the COM port when the SAS/CONNECT break window is active or TTY has been suspended with ALT-Q.
    - Check whether another application or ACDI is using the COM port.

- The specifications for communications parameters must be consistent between TTY and the SIGNON script. If the communication parameters specified in the SIGNON script are different from those being used by TTY, the following error message appears during an asynchronous SIGNON:

    ```
    ERROR:  Read Error
    ```

- The WAITFOR statement in the script should look for all possibilities. The number of seconds specified to wait if no condition is met should be less than the amount of time allowed by the connection itself before it drops because there is no activity.

    If the WAITFOR statement is not set properly, the following message appears during an asynchronous SIGNON:

    ```
    ERROR:  Read Error
    ```

Script SIGNON Fails

If the script fails to sign on to the connection, note any messages from the remote host that appear in the SAS log. These messages may explain why the link could not be established. In addition, if you want to view messages from the remote host you can switch to the TTY session that you are using to access the protocol converter, type C to continue the TTY session, and ask the protocol converter to reshow the last 3270 screen.

If the host SAS session is still active, you can end it by typing $ABORT on the host display.

If you are having trouble debugging your script, remove the comment marks (/* */) from the TRACE and ECHO statements at the beginning of the script. When the TRACE and ECHO features are enabled, you receive information that shows when the script fails and what statements are sent to the host.

Chapter 13 General Tips and Troubleshooting

Introduction 159

Signing On 159
Packet-Failure Message 159
Absence of SAS Software Start-up Messages 160
Host-Not-Active Message 160
Requested-Link-Not-Found Message 161

OS/2 Support 161
Alarm While Signing On 162
Local Area Networks 162
Configuration for Token Ring Networks 162

SAS/GRAPH Software 162
IBM 3274 Controller 163
Graphics Adapter 163
Requirements for the GRLINK Device Driver 163
Rotating Graphics 164
Changing Background Color 164

Miscellaneous Problems 164
DOWNLOAD and UPLOAD Procedures 164
Preserving Numeric Precision on Different Hosts 167
Remote Submit Events 167

Introduction

This chapter answers questions you may have about using SAS/CONNECT. The questions are grouped to help you find the ones most pertinent to your use of SAS/CONNECT. You may find it helpful to scan all of the questions in the sections that are relevant to your tasks to become familiar with some of the more common questions.

Signing On

Packet-Failure Message

Problem

You are signing on to a 3270 connection through an IBM 3174 control unit, and you receive the following message:

```
Received host T packet reason ?
M outbound packet failure
```

Explanation

The File Transfer Aid option (option 125) of the 3174 control unit must have digit 6 set to 1. Refer to pages 316 through 317 of IBM's *3174 Subsystem Control Unit Customizing Guide* (order number GA23-0214) for information on setting this option.

Absence of SAS Software Start-up Messages

Problem

While signing on to a remote session, you receive the following message:

```
ERROR: Did not get SAS software startup messages
```

Explanation

This message occurs if the command to invoke the SAS System on the remote host is not correct in the script file used for signing on. Check your script file and make sure that the TYPE statement that invokes the SAS System on the remote host uses the correct SAS command for your site. At some sites, the command to invoke the SAS System is not the default command name, SAS.

Host-Not-Active Message

Problem

While signing on to a remote session, you receive the following message:

```
ERROR: Did not get Host prompt. Host not active.
```

Explanation

If you are signing on to a 3270 connection, one of the following actions may overcome the problem:

- If you are using OS/2, Windows 3.*x*, or Windows 32s on the local host, switch to your remote host session and check for any terminal error messages that may appear there. Respond to these messages and switch back to the local SAS session.

- Make sure you are at the remote prompt before attempting to sign on. For example, if the remote host is running TSO, you must not be in an ISPF session. SAS/CONNECT expects the TSO READY prompt.

- Check the script you used to sign on to ensure that the character string in the WAITFOR statement that tests for the remote system prompt exactly matches a character string that normally appears on the remote screen. The WAITFOR statement is case sensitive.

- If you do not find any errors after checking the previous items in this list, modify the script file at the location where the error message appears in the file. Add a SNAPSHOT statement before the LOG statement that produces the error message. The SNAPSHOT statement sends a copy of the remote screen to the LOG window or file on the local host. You can examine the SAS log on the local host to see what is displayed by the remote host at the time that the WAITFOR statement executes.

If you are signing on to an ASYNC, TELNET, or TCP connection, one of the following actions may overcome the problem:

- For ASYNC connections, make sure that you are at the remote prompt before attempting to sign on.
- Check the script you used to sign on to ensure that the character string in the WAITFOR statement that tests for the remote system prompt exactly matches a character string that normally appears on the remote system. The WAITFOR statement is case sensitive.
- Check the value of the REMOTE= option on the local host to be sure it specifies the correct COM port or IP address.
- For ASYNC connections, verify that you have set the communications parameters (baud, parity, data bits, stop bits, and handshaking) for your connection in the script file or in a MODE command on the local host.
- If you do not find any errors after checking the previous items in this list, modify the script file by adding a TRACE ON statement and an ECHO ON statement at the beginning of the script file. These statements send a copy of the remote screen to the LOG window or to a file on the local host. You can examine the SAS log on the local host to see what is displayed by the remote host at the time the WAITFOR statement executes.

Requested-Link-Not-Found Message

Problem

While signing on to a remote session from a local MVS host, you receive the following message:

```
ERROR: XMS Communication Failure:  requested-link XVT not found.
```

Explanation

This error occurs if the COMAMID= value is not submitted on the local MVS host when a SIGNON is initiated from MVS. To resolve this error, submit the COMAMID= option before attempting the SIGNON.

OS/2 Support

Users of SAS/CONNECT on OS/2 may have questions about communications packages, the alarm that sounds when signing on, hardware and software requirements, and local area networks. These topics are covered in the following sections.

Alarm While Signing On

Question

Can you turn off the alarm that sounds when you are establishing a link with a 3270 connection?

Answer

Yes. Refer to the documentation for your communications package.

Local Area Networks

Question

For 3270 connections, does SAS/CONNECT work with local area networks?

Answer

If the 3270 network software is functional with your remote host, SAS/CONNECT should work through the network. SAS/CONNECT communicates using the HLLAPI interface, which handles 3270 communications with the network.

Configuration for Token Ring Networks

Question

For 3270 connections, what configuration is required for SAS/CONNECT to support a token ring network?

Answer

SAS/CONNECT does not require any special configuration. The token ring network configuration requires a 3174 control unit or a $37x\,5$ control unit directly on the token ring network to be able to emulate a 3270-type terminal with OS/2 over a token ring network.

SAS/GRAPH Software

When SAS/CONNECT and SAS/GRAPH are used together, questions may develop concerning the transfer of catalog entries containing graphics output, the effect of an IBM 3274 control unit on the graphics display, requirements for the GRLINK driver, insufficient memory messages, the need for a graphics adapter, and options for displaying graphs on the local host. These issues are addressed in the following sections.

IBM 3274 Controller

Question

Does the IBM 3274 control unit have to be customized for graphics in order to use the GRLINK device driver?

Answer

No; no special hardware or configuration is needed because SAS/CONNECT passes data using packets. The IBM 3274 control unit has no effect on remote processing of graphics. You also do not need 3270 emulation software with graphics capabilites. You do need SAS/GRAPH on both your remote host and your local host for remote graphics processing. SAS/GRAPH simply uses the graphics capabilities of the PC to display the graphics created by the remote host.

Graphics Adapter

Question

Is it possible to transfer graphics catalogs and is a graphics adapter required?

Answer

Yes, you can transfer graphics catalogs using one of the following methods:

- using the INCAT and OUTCAT options with the DOWNLOAD and UPLOAD procedures, described in "The DOWNLOAD Procedure" on page 207 and "The UPLOAD Procedure" on page 229.

- using the GRLINK facility, described in the example in "Example 4. Compute Services: Remote Graphics Processing" on page 22. If you choose the GRLINK facility, locally submit the following statement to transfer the catalog entries without viewing any graphs:

    ```
    goptions nodisplay;
    ```

    Whichever method you use, a graphics adapter is not required.

Requirements for the GRLINK Device Driver

Question

Do you need SAS/GRAPH on a remote host in order to use the GRLINK device driver?

Answer

Yes, SAS/GRAPH is required on both the local host and the remote host.

Rotating Graphics

Question

How can you rotate a graph when you display it on the local host or attached hard-copy device?

Answer

GOPTIONS ROTATE should be specified in the local session to rotate the graph. Do not specify GOPTIONS ROTATE in the remote session.

Changing Background Color

Question

How do you change the background color for a graph that you create on the remote host and display on the local host?

Answer

Specify the following statement in the local SAS session before remote-submitting the graphics step:

```
goptions cback=color ;
```

Miscellaneous Problems

Other miscellaneous questions may develop as you use SAS/CONNECT. The following sections address some of those questions.

DOWNLOAD and UPLOAD Procedures

Problem

When you try to use the UPLOAD or DOWNLOAD procedures, you receive one of the following error messages:

```
ERROR: Procedure DOWNLOAD not found.

ERROR: Procedure UPLOAD not found.
```

Explanation

These procedures are processed by the remote host, not the local host. Therefore, you must remote-submit the procedure. The message occurs when you submit the statements to the local host.

Problem

During a PROC DOWNLOAD or PROC UPLOAD step, you receive the following error message:

```
ERROR 200-322: The symbol is not recognized.
```

Explanation

This problem occurs if the remote file being referenced by the INFILE or OUTFILE option begins with a special character and is specified as FILEREF(*filename*), for example:

```
PROC UPLOAD INFILE=pcflref OUTFILE=hstflref($filname); run;
```

To avoid the problem, put single quotes (') around the filename, as shown in the following example:

```
PROC UPLOAD INFILE=pcflref OUTFILE=hstflref('$filname'); run;
```

Problem

You transfer a *variable* block binary file with a record length (LRECL) greater than 256 bytes and SAS/CONNECT segments the file into multiple 256-byte records. For example, downloading a binary file with a LRECL of 1024 would result in four 256-byte records.

Explanation

The data are not lost when the file is segmented by SAS/CONNECT. Using the LRECL option in the remote or local FILENAME statement does *not* avoid this problem. To avoid the problem, follow these steps:

1. Define the MVS FILENAME statement using RECFM=U parameter.

   ```
   FILENAME VFILE 'VARIABLE.BLOCK.FILE' RECFM=U;
   ```

2. Use the DOWNLOAD procedure with the BINARY option to transfer the file. Information displayed in the local LOG windows regarding the transfer shows how many bytes were transferred, for example:

   ```
   NOTE: 1231 bytes were transferred at 1231 bytes/second.
   ```

   In this example, 1231 bytes were transferred.

3. On the local side, use the RECFM= and LRECL= options in the INFILE statement, which points to the transferred file, where RECFM is set to S370VB and LRECL is set to the number of bytes transferred.

Problem

You transfer a *fixed* block binary file with a record length (LRECL) greater than 256 bytes and SAS/CONNECT segments the file into multiple 256-byte records. For example, downloading a binary file with a LRECL of 1024 would result in four 256-byte records.

Explanation

The data are not lost when the file is segmented by SAS/CONNECT. Using the LRECL option in the remote or local FILENAME statement does *not* avoid this problem. To avoid the problem, follow these steps:

1. Use the DOWNLOAD procedure with the BINARY option to transfer the file.
2. The INFILE statement used to read in the transferred file *must* contain the options RECFM=F and LRECL=*xxxx*, where LRECL is equal to the LRECL parameter on the remote system.

Problem

When you use DOWNLOAD on a print file, the EBCDIC carriage-control character `'F1'x` is not downloaded.

Explanation

To avoid the problem, change the SAS System option FILECC to NOFILECC. The NOFILECC option indicates that data in column 1 of a printer file should be treated as data and not carriage control. For the SAS System Releases 6.07 and 6.08, the default setting is NOFILECC. Earlier releases use FILECC as the default setting, and you must change it to NOFILECC to DOWNLOAD `'F1'x` successfully. In addition, the DCB characteristics of the print file must include a RECFM of FBA or VBA.

Problem

The DOWNLOAD procedure does not translate the carriage-control character `F1` that was present in the external file you downloaded.

Explanation

The MVS carriage control character `'F1'x` should be translated to ASCII `'31'x`, but instead it is translated to ASCII `'20'x`.

ASCII `'31'x` is 1. It is not possible to DOWNLOAD an external file and convert the MVS carriage-control character `'F1'x` to the ASCII carriage-control character `'0D'x`. The MVS EBCDIC value would have to be `'0D'x` to convert to ASCII `'0D'x`. If `'31'x` is missing, refer to the previous problem in this section.

Preserving Numeric Precision on Different Hosts

Question

What does it mean when I get the following message during a data set transfer?

```
WARNING: The length of one or more variables has been promoted to
         preserve precision.
```

Answer

The SAS System stores all numeric values using floating-point representation. Different hosts have different floating-point representations. For example, 370 floating-point format provides 1 sign bit, 7 exponent bits, and 56 fraction bits to store an 8-byte floating-point number. In contrast, the PC floating-point format provides 1 sign bit, 11 exponent bits, and 52 fraction bits to store the same 8-byte floating-point number. Any time data are transferred from one host to a different host, they are stored differently. In an effort to preserve precision across hosts, the data transfer services (UPLOAD and DOWNLOAD procedures) of SAS/CONNECT increase the length by 1 byte of any variable that has been explicitly assigned a length less than 8 bytes. The warning message appears in the local SAS log to inform you when one or more variables in the newly created data set have longer lengths (increased by 1 byte) than in the original data set.

For more information about numeric precision, refer to the section "Numeric Values" in Chapter 3, "Components of the SAS Language," in *SAS Language: Reference, Version 6, First Edition*.

Remote Submit Events

Problem

The first time you remote submit a PROC statement, you receive the following message:

```
ERROR 2-12: Invalid option.
```

Explanation

The remote AUTOEXEC.SAS file contains an OPTIONS statement that has not been closed by a semicolon (;). To avoid this problem, add the semicolon (;) to the OPTIONS statement in the remote AUTOEXEC.SAS file.

Problem

After signing on with the NOTERMINAL option specified for the remote host, a requestor window appears when a LIBNAME statement is remote-submitted using the WAIT= option.

Explanation

To prevent this window from appearing, specify the NOFILEPROMPT SAS System option on the remote host.

Problem

After you start a SAS/CONNECT conversation with the NOTERMINAL option, any remote-submitted statements that follow a syntax error are only parsed and not processed.

Explanation

When a SAS/CONNECT conversation is started with the NOTERMINAL option, the internal option $SYNTAXCHECK is automatically set. If you remote-submit a statement that follows a syntax error, the statement is parsed but not processed. In the following example,

```
data a; do i=1 to 10;outpt;end;run;
data b; x=1;run;
```

data set A will not be created because of the syntax error caused by `outpt`. Data set B will not be created because the SAS System is in syntax check mode from the previous `outpt` syntax error. The DATA step will only be parsed.

To avoid this problem, add the NO$SYNTAXCHECK option to the remote SAS System invocation options in the script file.

Problem

You cannot remote-submit code that uses square brackets because the keyboard on your local host does not support these characters.

Explanation

The less than symbol (<) and greater than symbol (>) can be used in place of square brackets. Use < for the left square bracket ([) and > for the right square bracket (]).

In OpenVMS, for example, square brackets are typically used to delineate the directory name in a path name. However, you can use < and > as equivalent delimiters. For example:

```
libname sales 'disk:<sales.years.1991>';
```

Problem

After remote-submitting a full-screen procedure, you receive the following message:

```
ERROR: No terminal connected to the SAS session.
```

Explanation

SAS/CONNECT does not support remote submission of full-screen procedures.

Problem

When remote-submitting a JCL batch job under MVS SAS 6.08, you receive the following message:

```
JOB OPTIONS(JOB01501) SUBMITTED ***.
```

Explanation

A break window appears on the local host display explaining that a message was received from the remote host. Press Enter on the remote host side and select **CONTINUE** from the local break window.

When remote submitting a JCL batch job to Release 6.07 of SAS under MVS, the message does not appear on the remote side; therefore, the break window does not appear. A beep sounds, but the remote submit continues uninterrupted.

The following is an example of a remote submission of a JCL batch job:

```
DM 'RSUBMIT'; X 'SUBMIT JOBS.CNTL(OPTIONS)'; ENDRSUBMIT;
```

Note: If remote submit is not used and the JCL batch job is submitted from Release 6.07 or 6.08 of SAS under MVS, the message *does* appear. ENTER must be pressed to continue SAS System processing.

To avoid receiving the above message and the interaction required to clear it, you can direct your JCL to the internal reader. The FILENAME statement can be used in place of the TSO ALLOCATE or JCL DD statements. A sample SAS program using the FILENAME statement to write to an internal reader is:

```
rsubmit;

  /* filename to point to JCL code  */
  filename injcl '.misc.jcl' disp=shr;

  /* filename to internal reader  */
  filename outrdr sysout=a pgm=intrdr recfm=fb lrecl=80;

  /* data step to submit job to batch queue  */
  data _null_;
    infile injcl(myjcl);
    file outrdr noprint notitles;
    input;
    put _infile_;
  run;
endrsubmit;
```

Part 3
SAS/CONNECT® Software Syntax and Procedures

Chapter 14	System Options, Statements, Commands, and SCL Functions
Chapter 15	The DOWNLOAD Procedure
Chapter 16	The UPLOAD Procedure
Chapter 17	Script Statements

Chapter 14 System Options, Statements, Commands, and SCL Functions

Introduction 173

System Options 173

Statements and Commands 187
   With Script Files 189
   In the SAS Autoexec File 190
   With the DOWNLOAD and UPLOAD Procedures 191

SCL Functions: COMAMID, RLINK, RSESSION, RSTITLE 201

Introduction

This chapter describes all SAS system options, statements, commands, and SCL functions used with SAS/CONNECT. Some of the SAS features described are used only with SAS/CONNECT. Other features are used in standard SAS programming as well as with SAS/CONNECT.

The sections in this chapter provide the syntax and a description of each feature. The heading for each feature provides the following information:

- purpose
- environment in which you use the system option, statement, command, or SCL function.

All features are listed alphabetically in a section.

System Options

To use SAS/CONNECT, you need to specify several SAS system options. Some options are used in your local SAS session. Other options are specified when you invoke the SAS System on the remote host. This section describes the COMAMID=, DMR, and REMOTE= system options.

COMAMID= System Option

Identifies communications access method

Local and remote

Syntax

COMAMID=*access-method-id*

Description

The COMAMID= system option specifies a communications access method to be used by SAS/CONNECT when connecting to remote hosts. To establish the link between two hosts running the SAS System, use the COMAMID= system option on both hosts. Specify the COMAMID= system option in an OPTIONS statement before you sign on to the link. On the remote host, include the COMAMID= system option in the script TYPE statement that invokes the remote SAS session.

On the local host, you must specify both a COMAMID= system option and a REMOTE= system option. Use Table 14.1 to select the appropriate values for the COMAMID= and REMOTE= system options for both hosts. (For micro-to-host link values, see "Details for Micro-to-Host Link Releases" on page 289.)

Note: You may need to customize some scripts for your site. The table notes indicate modifications that are necessary, but your site may require more.

Table 14.1   REMOTE= and COMAMID= System Options Local and Remote Hosts

If your local host is ...	and your remote host is ...	then use this COMAMID= value on the local host ...[1]	use this REMOTE= value on the local host ...[1]	and use this supplied script.[2]
MVS	MVS	APPC	*luname-of-APPC/MVS*	none, in most cases[3]
		TCP	*internet-address*	tcptso.scr
	CMS	APPC	*name-of-AVS-gateway*	none
		TCP	*internet-address*	tcpcms.scr
	OpenVMS	TCP	*internet-address*	tcpvms.scr

(continued)

Table 14.1 (continued)

If your local host is ...	and your remote host is ...	then use this COMAMID= value on the local host ...[1]	use this REMOTE= value on the local host ...[1]	and use this supplied script.[2]
	UNIX	TCP	*internet-address*	tcpunix.scr
	OS/2	APPC	*name-of-control-point-lu*	none
		TCP	*internet-address*	tcpos2.scr
	Windows NT	TCP	*internet-address*	tcpwnt.scr
	VSE	APPC	*VTAM APPLID*	none
CMS	MVS	APPC	*luname-of-APPC/MVS*	none, in most cases[3]
		TCP	*internet-address*	tcptso.scr
	CMS	APPC	*name-of-AVS-gateway*	none
		TCP	*internet-address*	tcpcms.scr
	OS/2	APPC	*name-of-control-point-lu*	none
		TCP	*internet-address*	tcpos2.scr
	OpenVMS	TCP	*internet-address*	tcpvms.scr
	UNIX	TCP	*internet-address*	tcpunix.scr
	Windows NT	TCP	*internet-address*	tcpwnt.scr
	VSE	APPC	*VTAM APPLID*	none

(continued)

COMAMID= System Option *continued*

Table 14.1 (continued)

If your local host is ...	and your remote host is ...	then use this COMAMID= value on the local host ...[1]	use this REMOTE= value on the local host ...[1]	and use this supplied script.[2]
OpenVMS	MVS	TCP	*internet-address*	tcptso.scr
		TELNET	*internet address*	teltso.scr
	CMS	TCP	*internet-address*	tcpcms.scr
		TELNET	*internet address*	telcms.scr
	OpenVMS	TCP	*internet-address*	tcpvms.scr
		TELNET	*internet-address*	telvms.scr
		DECNET	*host-id*	none
	UNIX	TCP	*internet-address*	tcpunix.scr
	OS/2	TCP	*internet-address*	tcpos2.scr
	Windows NT	TCP	*internet-address*	tcpwnt.scr
	Primos	TELNET	*internet-address*	telprim.scr
	AOS/VS	TELNET	*internet-address*	telaos.scr
UNIX	MVS	TCP	*internet-address*	tcptso.scr
		TELNET	*internet address*	teltso.scr

(continued)

Table 14.1 (continued)

If your local host is ...	and your remote host is ...	then use this COMAMID= value on the local host ...[1]	use this REMOTE= value on the local host ...[1]	and use this supplied script.[2]
	CMS	TCP	*internet-address*	tcpcms.scr
		TELNET	*internet address*	telcms.scr
	OpenVMS	TCP	*internet-address*	tcpvms.scr
		TELNET	*internet address*	telvms.scr
	UNIX	TCP	*internet-address*	tcpunix.scr
	OS/2	TCP	*internet-address*	tcpos2.scr
	Windows NT	TCP	*internet-address*	tcpwnt.scr
	Primos	TELNET	*internet-address*	telprim.scr
	AOS/VS	TELNET	*internet-address*	telaos.scr
OS/2 (except with Release 6.06)	MVS	APPC	*luname-of-APPC/MVS*[3]	none, in most cases[3]
		EHLLAPI	*name-of-remote-session*	tso.scr or logtso.scr
		TCP	*internet-address*	tcptso.scr
		TELNET	*internet-address*	teltso.scr
		RASYNC	COM*n*	tso.scr, logtso.scr, tso7171.scr, or tsoctex.scr

(continued)

COMAMID= System Option *continued*

Table 14.1 (continued)

If your local host is ...	and your remote host is ...	then use this COMAMID= value on the local host ...[1]	use this REMOTE= value on the local host ...[1]	and use this supplied script.[2]
	CMS	APPC	*name-of-AVS-gateway*	none
		EHLLAPI	*name-of-remote-session*	cms.scr or logcms.scr
		TCP	*internet-address*	tcpcms.scr
		TELNET	*internet-address*	telcms.scr
		RASYNC	COM*n*	cms.scr, logcms.scr, cms7171.scr, or cmsctex.scr
	OpenVMS	TCP	*internet-address*	tcpvms.scr
		TELNET	*internet-address*	telvms.scr
		RASYNC	COM*n*	vms.scr or logvms.scr
	UNIX	TCP	*internet-address*	tcpunix.scr
		RASYNC	COM*n*	unix.scr or logunix.scr
	OS/2	APPC	*name-of-control-point-lu* (for the remote PC)	none
		TCP	*internet-address*	tcpos2.scr

(continued)

Table 14.1 (continued)

If your local host is ...	and your remote host is ...	then use this COMAMID= value on the local host ...[1]	use this REMOTE= value on the local host ...[1]	and use this supplied script.[2]
		NETBIOS	*network-name*	none
	Windows NT	TCP	*internet-address*	tcpwnt.scr
		Release 6.09 NETBIOS	*network-name*	
	VSE	EHLLAPI	*name-of-remote-session*	vse.scr or vsecics.scr
		APPC	*VTAM APPLID*	none
		RASYNC	COM*n*	vse.scr
	Primos	TELNET	*internet-address*	telprim.scr
		RASYNC	COM*n*	prim.scr or logprim.scr
	AOS/VS	TELNET	*internet-address*	telaos.scr
		RASYNC	COM*n*	aos.scr or logaos.scr
OS/2 (with Release 6.06)	MVS	EHLLAPI	*name-of-remote-session*	tso.scr or
		RASYNC	COM*n*	tso.scr, logtso.scr, tso7171.scr, or tsoctex.scr
	CMS	EHLLAPI	*name-of-remote-session*	cms.scr or

(continued)

COMAMID= System Option *continued*

Table 14.1 (continued)

If your local host is ...	and your remote host is ...	then use this COMAMID= value on the local host ...[1]	use this REMOTE= value on the local host ...[1]	and use this supplied script.[2]
		RASYNC	COM*n*	cms.scr, logcms.scr, cms7171.scr, or cmsctex.scr
	OpenVMS	RASYNC	COM*n*	vms.scr or logvms.scr
	UNIX	RASYNC	COM*n*	unix.scr or logunix.scr
	VSE	EHLLAPI	*name-of-remote-session*	vse.scr or vsecics.scr
		RASYNC	COM*n*	vse.scr
	Primos	RASYNC	COM*n*	prim.scr or logprim.scr
	AOS/VS	RASYNC	COM*n*	aos.scr or logaos.scr
Windows	MVS	EHLLAPI	*name-of-remote-session*	tso.scr or logtso.scr
		TCP	*internet-address*	tcptso.scr
		TELNET	*internet-address*	teltso.scr
		APPC[4]	*LUNAME of APPC/MVS*	none

(continued)

Table 14.1 (continued)

If your local host is ...	and your remote host is ...	then use this COMAMID= value on the local host ...[1]	use this REMOTE= value on the local host ...[1]	and use this supplied script.[2]
	CMS	EHLLAPI	*name-of-remote-session*	cms.scr or logcms.scr
		TCP	*internet-address*	tcpcms.scr
		TELNET	*internet-address*	telcms.scr
		APPC[4]	*name of AVS gateway*	none
	OpenVMS	TCP	*internet-address*	tcpvms.scr
		TELNET	*internet-address*	telvms.scr
		DECNET[5]	*host-id*	none
	UNIX	TCP	*internet-address*	tcpunix.scr
	OS/2	TCP	*internet-address*	tcpos2.scr
		NETBIOS	*network-name*	none
		APPC[4]	*name of control point LU* (for the remote PC)	none
	Windows NT	TCP	*internet-address*	tcpwnt.scr
		NETBIOS	*network-name*	none

(continued)

COMAMID= System Option *continued*

Table 14.1 (continued)

If your local host is ...	and your remote host is ...	then use this COMAMID= value on the local host ...[1]	use this REMOTE= value on the local host ...[1]	and use this supplied script.[2]
	VSE	EHLLAPI	*name-of-remote-session*	vse.scr
		APPC[4]	*VTAM APPLID*	none
	Primos	TELNET	*internet-address*	telprim.scr
	AOS/VS	TELNET	*internet-address*	telaos.scr
Windows NT	MVS	TCP	*internet-address*	tcptso.scr
		TELNET	*internet-address*	teltso.scr
	CMS	TCP	*internet-address*	tcpcms.scr
		TELNET	*internet-address*	telcms.scr
	OpenVMS	TCP	*internet-address*	tcpvms.scr
		TELNET	*internet-address*	telvms.scr
	UNIX	TCP	*internet-address*	tcpunix.scr
	OS/2	TCP	*internet-address*	tcpos2.scr
		NETBIOS	*network-name*	none
	Windows NT	TCP	*internet-address*	tcpwnt.scr
		NETBIOS	*network-name*	none

(continued)

Table 14.1 (continued)

If your local host is ...	and your remote host is ...	then use this COMAMID= value on the local host ...[1]	use this REMOTE= value on the local host ...[1]	and use this supplied script.[2]
	Primos	TELNET	*internet-address*	telprim.scr
	AOS/VS	TELNET	*internet-address*	telaos.scr
VSE	MVS	APPC	*LUNAME of APPC/MVS*	none
	CMS	APPC	*name of AVS gateway*	none
	OS/2	APPC	*name of control point LU* (for the remote PC)	none
	VSE	APPC	*VTAM APPLID*	none

Table Notes

1. Submit these options in the OPTIONS statement on the local host.
2. Use a FILENAME statement to associate this script with the RLINK fileref or another fileref that you will use in the SIGNON and SIGNOFF commands.
3. You need to use a script with APPC only when you are running a version of MVS/ESA earlier than Version 4, Release 2 on MVS as the remote host. In this case use the APPCTSO.SCR script. In addition, if you are using a script, the value of the REMOTE= option on the local host is the *session id*, not the *luname-of-APPC/MVS*.
4. APPC is available with Windows 32s only.
5. DECNET is available with Windows 3.*x* only.

Specifying the COMAMID= System Option on the Local Host

Typically, you set up the SAS autoexec file on the local host so that the COMAMID= system option executes automatically. To accomplish this, include an OPTIONS statement in the autoexec file that sets the value of the COMAMID= system option for the local host each time the local SAS System is invoked.

If you do not include an OPTIONS statement specifying the COMAMID= system option in your SAS autoexec file, you can use one of these methods to specify the system option on the local host:

☐ Type and submit the OPTIONS statement before executing a SIGNON command.

☐ If you are using pull-down menus in the SAS Display Manager System, complete the COMAMID field in the dialog box that appears after you select the SIGNON item from the pull-down menu.

☐ Include the COMAMID= system option in the SAS command that starts the SAS session on the local host.

☐ Include the COMAMID= system option in the SAS configuration file that is processed when you start the SAS session on the local host. See the SAS documentation for your local host for more information on the configuration file.

Specifying the COMAMID= System Option on the Remote Host

For the remote host, you can specify the COMAMID= system option in the TYPE statement that contains the SAS command in the script you use to sign on. Alternatively, you can specify the COMAMID= system option in the configuration file that is processed when you invoke the SAS System on the remote host. If you fail to specify the COMAMID= option in one of these places, an error message is issued and the link terminates.

DMR System Option

Invokes a remote version of the display manager for use with SAS/CONNECT

Remote

Syntax

DMR

Description

The DMR system option must be specified either in the remote CONFIG.SAS file or on the SAS command line to invoke a remote SAS display manager session on the remote host.

The remote display manager session receives input from the local SAS session and sends log and output lines to the local session's LOG and OUTPUT windows or files.

REMOTE= System Option

Identifies which remote session to connect to

Local

Syntax

REMOTE=*remote-session-id*

Description

Use the REMOTE= system option to identify which remote session to use with SAS/CONNECT. There is no default value for the REMOTE= system option; you must supply one.

When you are signing on, the REMOTE= system option is used in combination with the COMAMID= system option. Valid combinations of values for these system options are shown in Table 14.1.

You can also use the REMOTE= system option to identify the session to which statements should be remote-submitted when you have multiple links established.

SIGNON Example

This example shows the OPTIONS statement you use on the local host and the TYPE script statement that invokes the SAS System on the remote host. (For additional examples, refer to the chapters for each access method.)

Suppose you use Communications Manager to communicate with a CMS remote host and you have named this session MYCMS. Specify the COMAMID= and REMOTE= system options in the local SAS session OPTIONS statement as follows:

```
options comamid=ehllapi remote=mycms;
```

The TYPE statement in the script that invokes the SAS session on the CMS host looks like this:

```
type "sas (dmr comamid=pclink noterminal no$syntaxcheck)" enter;
```

Note: You can omit the REMOTE= system option and specify the remote-session id in the SIGNON command if you have assigned the fileref RLINK to the script file that is used to sign on.

Examples for Remote-Submitting

Suppose that you have signed on to both a VMS host with TCP/IP, using REMOTE=*internet-address*, and an MVS host with EHLLAPI, using REMOTE=A. You can remote-submit statements to either of these hosts by specifying the remote-session id

REMOTE= System Option *continued*

when you issue the RSUBMIT statement or command. This example submits statements to both hosts:

```
options remote=a;
rsubmit;
    statements for MVS remote host a
endrsubmit;
options remote=internet-address;
rsubmit;
    statements for VMS remote host internet-address
endrsubmit;
```

Note: You can omit using the REMOTE= system option and simply include the remote-session id in the RSUBMIT statement as follows:

```
rsubmit a;
    statements for MVS remote host a
endrsubmit;
rsubmit internet-address;
    statements for VMS remote host internet-address
endrsubmit;
```

TRANTAB= System Option

Specifies the translation tables to be used by various parts of the SAS System

Local

Syntax

TRANTAB=(*catalog-entries*)

Description

Use this system option to specify a translation table (other than the default shipped from SAS Institute) for your entire SAS session or job, including all file transfers you do. Tables are specified in a parenthetical list that has eight positions. The position in which a table appears in the list determines the type of translation table being specified. Individual entries in the list are separated by commas. See the list of positions and types that follows:

Position	Type of Translation Table
first	local-to-transport-format
second	transport-to-local-format
third	lowercase-to-uppercase

Position	Type of Translation Table
fourth	uppercase-to-lowercase
fifth	character classification
sixth	scanner translation
seventh	delta characters
eighth	scanner character classification

The SAS System tries to locate the catalog entires containing the translation tables first in SASUSER.PROFILE and then in SASUSER.HOST.

▶ *Caution* . . . . *Changing Translation Tables*
Do not change translation tables unless you are familiar with their purpose. Translation tables are used internally by the SAS supervisor to implement National Language Support (NLS). If you are unfamiliar with the purpose of translation tables, do not change the specifications without proper technical advice. ▲

To change one table, specify null entries for the other tables. For example, to change the lowercase-to-uppercase table, which is third in the list, specify the following:

```
options trantab = ( , , new-uppercase-table);
```

The other tables remain unchanged. The output from PROC OPTIONS reflects the last specification for the TRANTAB option and not the composite specification. For example:

```
options trantab = ( , , new-uppercase-table);
options trantab = ( , , , new-lowercase-table);
```

PROC OPTIONS shows that the value for TRANTAB is (, , , *new-lowercase-table*), but both the *new-uppercase* and *new-lowercase* tables are in effect.

For more information about the TRANTAB procedure, see SAS Technical Report P-222, *Changes and Enhancements to Base SAS Software, Release 6.07* and SAS Technical Report P-197, *The TRANTAB Procedure, Release 6.06*.

Statements and Commands

The following section describes the statements and commands you can use with SAS/CONNECT. The FILENAME statement is not limited to use with SAS/CONNECT, but it is included here to describe how it can best be used with the link.

ENDRSUBMIT Statement

Indicates the end of a group of statements that should be submitted to the remote host for processing

Local

Syntax

ENDRSUBMIT<CANCEL>;

Description

The ENDRSUBMIT statement signals the end of a group of statements that begins with either of these statements:

```
dm 'rsubmit';   /* all releases */

rsubmit;        /* Release 6.06 or later */
```

The remote host processes the statements between either of these statements and ENDRSUBMIT.

You do not need to use the ENDRSUBMIT statement with the RSUBMIT command, only with the RSUBMIT statement or the DM RSUBMIT statement.

The CANCEL option terminates the block of statements without executing the statements. This option is useful in a line-mode session if you see an error in a previously entered statement and you want to cancel the step.

The ENDRSUBMIT statement can be used in any kind of SAS session on the local host, but it is particularly useful for running SAS/CONNECT from an interactive line-mode session or a noninteractive job. The RSUBMIT and ENDRSUBMIT statements enable you to include statements that should be processed by the local host in the same file as statements to be processed by a remote host. The statements for the remote host are enclosed between the RSUBMIT and ENDRSUBMIT statements. All of the other statements in the program are processed by the local host when you execute the program. The following template can be used to build a file that includes statements for both the remote and local hosts in the same program:

```
statements for local host
rsubmit;
   statements for remote host
endrsubmit;
more statements for local host
```

For an example of remote submitting by using the RSUBMIT and ENDRSUBMIT statements, refer to the example of a line-mode session in the description of the SIGNON statement later in this chapter.

FILENAME Statement

Associates a SAS fileref with an external file

Local and remote

Syntax

FILENAME *fileref* '*filespec*' <*host-options*>;

Description

The FILENAME statement associates a SAS *fileref*, a file reference name, with a *filespec*, a host-dependent external file name. Filerefs are a shorthand method for specifying a file in SAS statements and commands. Once you define a fileref for a file, you can use the fileref, rather than the longer file specification, to reference the file throughout a SAS session or program. The FILENAME statement and filerefs are useful in many SAS programs, not just with SAS/CONNECT.

In the FILENAME statement, *fileref* specifies the fileref to be associated with the external file; *filespec* specifies the name of the external file. The fileref must conform to the rules for SAS names. The form of the filespec differs from system to system. On some systems you must include a fully-qualified filename. Other systems may permit partial pathnames.

Note that a fileref remains associated with an external file for the duration of the SAS session only. The association is not permanent. Also, a fileref must be defined before a SAS statement or command using the fileref can execute. Therefore, the FILENAME statement must execute before the statement or command using the fileref.

With Script Files

A common use of the FILENAME statement with SAS/CONNECT is to define filerefs for script files. * A script's fileref can then be specified in SIGNON and SIGNOFF commands to identify the script to start or terminate the link.

You can define a default fileref for a script with the FILENAME statement. The default script fileref is RLINK. If you define RLINK as the fileref for your script, you do not need to specify any fileref or filespec in SIGNON and SIGNOFF commands or statements; you simply use the command or statement. When SAS executes a SIGNON or SIGNOFF command without a fileref or filespec, SAS automatically searches for a file defined with RLINK as the fileref. If RLINK has been defined, SAS executes the corresponding script.

---

* You can also use the FILENAME statement to specify an alternate 3270 keyboard translation table. Keyboard translation tables are discussed in "ASCII and EBCDIC Character Set Translation" on page 285.

FILENAME Statement *continued*

Examples

Suppose your SAS Software Representative writes a script and copies it to a directory on your local system. If you want to define the default fileref RLINK for your script, use the following FILENAME statement:

```
filename rlink 'external-file-name';
```

Because you defined RLINK as the script's fileref, you can use the shortest form of the SIGNON and SIGNOFF commands or statements. For example, to start the link, enter

```
signon
```

To terminate the link, enter

```
signoff
```

If you use one script to start the link and a different script to terminate the link, define a unique fileref for each script. For example, you can use the following FILENAME statements:

```
filename rlink 'start-link-script-file';
filename endit 'end-link-script-file';
```

Subsequently, to start the link, enter the following command or statement, which uses the default fileref RLINK for the signon script.

```
signon
```

To terminate the link, enter

```
signoff endit
```

In the SAS Autoexec File

You can make starting and ending SAS/CONNECT even easier by adding the FILENAME statement defining the script's fileref to an autoexec file.* An *autoexec file* is a file of SAS statements and commands that you can set up to execute automatically each time you invoke the SAS System. Its purpose is to automate the execution of statements, commands, and entire programs that you use routinely in SAS processing. If you use an autoexec file that contains a FILENAME statement defining your script's fileref, you do not have to type and execute the FILENAME statement each time you want to invoke the link.

Refer to the SAS documentation for your environment for more information on setting up an autoexec file.

---

* This method is discussed in "Starting and Stopping SAS/CONNECT Software" on page 61.

With the DOWNLOAD and UPLOAD Procedures

You can also use the FILENAME statement with the DOWNLOAD and UPLOAD procedures when copying external files. You can submit the FILENAME statement to define the fileref for the external file on the local host; you remote-submit the FILENAME statement to define the fileref for the external file on the remote host.

Example

Suppose you want to download an external file from the remote host to a directory-based local system. You can submit the following FILENAME statement to assign the fileref on the local host:

```
filename lhost 'local-file-name';
```

Then remote-submit these statements to assign the fileref on the remote host and perform the download:

```
filename rhost 'remote-file-name';

proc download infile=rhost outfile=lhost;
run;
```

See "Ways to Use SAS/CONNECT Software" on page 17 for more examples of the FILENAME statement and the DOWNLOAD and UPLOAD procedures.

RSPT Statements

Statements used for Remote SQL Pass-Through

Local

Syntax

The SQL procedure Pass-Through facility consists of three statements and a FROM-clause component. The SQL syntax for these statements is:

CONNECT TO *dbms-name* <AS *alias*>
   <(*dbms-argument-1=value...<dbms-argument-n=value*>)>;

SELECT ... FROM CONNECTION TO *dbms-name* | *alias* (*dbms-query*);
EXECUTE (*SQL-statement*) **BY** *dbms-name* | *alias*;
DISCONNECT FROM *dbms-name* | *alias*;

For RSPT, use the SQL syntax as follows:

CONNECT TO REMOTE <AS *alias*>
   (SERVER=*serverid* <SAPW=*server-access-password*>
   <DBMS=*dbms-name*> <PT2DBPW=*passthrough-to-DBMS-password*>
   <DBMSARG=(*dbms-argument-1=value ... <dbms-argument-n=value*>)>);

RSPT Statements *continued*

SELECT . . . FROM CONNECTION TO REMOTE | *alias* (*dbms-query*);
EXECUTE (*SQL-statement*) BY REMOTE | *alias*;
DISCONNECT FROM REMOTE | *alias*;

Description

CONNECT TO REMOTE <AS *alias*>
  establishes a connection to a remote DBMS or to remote SAS data through a SAS server. This statement is required (RSPT does not support implicit connection). You can connect more than once to the same server specifying different DBMS= values. You can also connect to more than one server at a time.

SERVER= *serverid*
  specifies the name of the remote SAS server. If the server is a multi-user server, *serverid* is the name specified for the ID= option in the PROC SERVER statement. If the server is a single-user server running in a SAS/CONNECT remote session, *serverid* is the name of the SAS/CONNECT remote session. In either case, *serverid* is the same name specified for the SERVER= option in a LIBNAME statement.

SAPW=*server-access-password*
  is the password for controlling user access to a multi-user server specified for the UAPW= option in the PROC SERVER statement. If UAPW= is specified when the server is started, you must specify SAPW= in a CONNECT TO REMOTE statement that specifies that server.

DBMS=*dbms-name*
  is the name of the remote DBMS you want to connect to. This is the same name you would specify in a CONNECT TO statement if you were connecting directly to the DBMS. This option is used if you want to connect to a remote DBMS instead of the remote SAS SQL processor.

PT2DBPW=*passthrough-to-DBMS-password*
  is the password for controlling pass-through access to remote DBMS databases specified for the PT2DBPW= option in the PROC SERVER statement. If PT2DBPW= is specified when the server is started, you must specify PT2DBPPW= in a CONNECT TO REMOTE statement that specifies that server and specifies DBMS=.

DBMSARG=(*dbms-argument-1*=*value*. . .<*dbms-argument-n*=*value*>)
  are the arguments required by the remote DBMS to establish the connection. These are the same arguments you would specify in a CONNECT TO statement if you were connecting directly to the DBMS.

FROM CONNECTION TO REMOTE | *alias* (*dbms-query*)
  specifies the connection to the remote SAS SQL processor or the remote DBMS as the source of data for the SELECT statement and the recipient of the *dbms-query*. For remote SAS data accessed through the PROC SQL view engine, *dbms-query* is any valid PROC SQL SELECT statement. For a remote DBMS, *dbms-query* is the same SQL query you would specify if you were connected directly to the DBMS

EXECUTE (*SQL-statement*) **BY** REMOTE | *alias*
  specifies an SQL statement to be executed by the SAS SQL processor or by the remote DBMS in the server's SAS session. For remote SAS data accessed through the PROC SQL view engine, *SQL-statement* is any valid PROC SQL statement except SELECT.

For a remote DBMS accessed through a single-user server in a SAS/CONNECT session, *SQL-statement* is the same SQL statement you would specify if you were connected directly to the DBMS. For a remote DBMS, this statement may not be used if the DBMS is accessed through a remote multi-user server.

DISCONNECT FROM REMOTE | *alias*;
   ends the connection to the remote DBMS or to the SAS SQL processor in the server's SAS session.

RSUBMIT Command and Statement

Submits statements typed on the local host to the remote host for processing

Local

Syntax

RSUBMIT <*remote-session-id*>

Description

The RSUBMIT command and the RSUBMIT statement cause SAS programming statements in the local SAS PROGRAM EDITOR window to execute on a remote SAS System. The primary difference between the command and the statement is that the command can be used only from a display manager session or within the DM statement. The RSUBMIT statement can be used in any kind of SAS session on the local host.

The *remote-session-id* option indicates the name of the session where you want to submit the statements when you have multiple SAS/CONNECT sessions active. If you have only one active session, *remote-session-id* is not needed. When you have multiple remote sessions active and you omit this option, the statements are remote-submitted to the current remote session. The current remote session is the one specified in the most recently successful REMOTE= system option, SIGNON command or statement, or RSUBMIT command or statement.

The RSUBMIT command differs from the standard SUBMIT command because statements execute on the remote host. Even though the statements execute in the remote environment, all responses and output are displayed in your local SAS log and output listing as they would be if you executed the program in the local SAS System.

Execute the RSUBMIT command from the command line of the local PROGRAM EDITOR window. Or you can embed the RSUBMIT command within a DM statement, which treats commands as if they were issued from a display manager command line. You can also use the KEYS window to assign the RSUBMIT command to a key. See "KEYS" in Chapter 17, "SAS Display Manager Windows," in *SAS Language: Reference Version 6, First Edition* or Chapter 9, "Starting and Running SAS Programs," in the *SAS Language Guide for Personal Computers, Release 6.03 Edition* for details on the KEYS window. The

RSUBMIT Command and Statement *continued*

RSUBMIT command can be used to execute most kinds of SAS programs on the remote host.*

The RSUBMIT statement is particularly useful for running SAS/CONNECT from an interactive line-mode session or a noninteractive job. The RSUBMIT and ENDRSUBMIT statements enable you to include statements that should be processed by the local host in the same file as statements to be processed by the remote host. The statements for the remote host are enclosed between the RSUBMIT and ENDRSUBMIT statements. All of the other statements in the program are processed by the local host when you execute the program. The following template can be used to build a file that includes statements for both the remote and local hosts in the same program:

```
statements for local host
rsubmit;
   statements for remote host
endrsubmit;
```

Note: The DOWNLOAD and UPLOAD procedures must be executed with the RSUBMIT command or statement; you cannot execute them with the SUBMIT command.

Example

Suppose you want to use the remote system to execute a SAS program that calculates summary statistics from variables in a very large SAS data set and then download the summary statistics to your local session. You enter the following program in the PROGRAM EDITOR window of your local session:

```
libname remtdata 'external-file-name';


proc summary data=remtdata.clinic;
   class diagnose;
   var age income visits;
   output out=sumstat n= mean= mage mincome mvisits;
run;

proc download data=sumstat out=summary;
run;
```

To execute the program on the remote system, enter **rsubmit** on the command line of the PROGRAM EDITOR window. Alternatively, you can press the RSUBMIT function key.

---

* You should not remote-submit windowing procedures (such as SAS/FSP or SAS/AF procedures) or Version 5 full-screen procedures (such as the Version 5 DATASETS procedure).

SIGNOFF Command and Statement

Terminates the link between SAS sessions

Local

Syntax

SIGNOFF <*option*>

Description

The SIGNOFF command and the SIGNOFF statement terminate a link between a local SAS session and a remote SAS session and execute a script if you are using an access method that requires a script file. Issue the SIGNOFF command from the command line of any local SAS display manager window or from a DM statement. You can also issue a SIGNOFF statement from the local SAS session, which is especially useful for interactive line-mode sessions or noninteractive jobs.

The primary difference between the command and the statement is that the command can be used only from the command line of a display manager session or within the DM statement. The SIGNOFF statement can be used in any kind of SAS session on the local host.

You can specify one of these options in a SIGNOFF command or statement:

fileref
: is a fileref associated with the script that terminates the link. The fileref must be defined by a previously executed FILENAME statement.

    At many computing installations, you use the same script to start and terminate a link. If you use one script to do both, you need to assign only one fileref.

    If the fileref you define for the script is the default fileref RLINK, omit this specification in the SIGNOFF command.

'*filespec*'
: is the name of the script you want to execute. Use the filespec in the SIGNOFF command when no fileref has been defined for the script you want to execute. The filespec can be either a fully qualified filename or the name of a file in the current working directory. Do not specify both a fileref and a filespec.

NOSCRIPT
: specifies that no script should be used to sign off. This is useful if you do not need any additional script functionality as you sign off from the link. When you use NOSCRIPT, the SIGNOFF command executes faster and requires less memory, but no special functions, such as logging off the remote host or error processing, are performed.

remote-session-id
: is the name of the session that you want to end. If you omit this option, the current remote session is ended. The current remote session is the one specified in the most recently successful REMOTE= system option, SIGNON command or statement, or RSUBMIT command or statement.

    When you specify *remote-session-id*, the script associated with the default fileref RLINK is executed. In this case, you must have a valid script file associated with the fileref RLINK.

SIGNOFF Command and Statement *continued*

When the SIGNOFF command executes, the usual SAS log messages for the remote SAS System appear in the LOG window on your local host. When the link has been terminated, the following message is displayed:

```
NOTE: REMOTE SIGNOFF TO remote-session-id COMPLETE.
```

Examples

Suppose you assign the fileref RLINK to your script with the following FILENAME statement, where *external-file-name* is the name of your script:

```
filename rlink 'external-file-name';
```

Then you can use the short form of the SIGNOFF command or statement to terminate the link:

```
signoff;
```

If you have multiple remote sessions executing, you can specify which session to sign off by using the remote-session id. Remember that you must have the signoff script assigned to the fileref RLINK:

```
signoff a;
```

Suppose that you assign some other fileref to the script:

```
filename endit 'external-file-name';
```

Then you must specify the fileref in the SIGNOFF command or statement because it is not the default script fileref:

```
signoff endit;
```

When you are using a fileref other than RLINK for the signoff script and you have multiple remote sessions executing, use the REMOTE= system option to specify which session should be ended. Submit this statement before using the SIGNOFF command illustrated in the previous example:

```
options remote=a;
```

If you are using RLINK or any other fileref in the SIGNOFF statement, remember that you can define the script's fileref in a FILENAME statement in the SAS autoexec file. Then you do not have to type and execute the FILENAME statement before you use the SIGNOFF command.

If you do not assign any fileref to the script, you must specify the filespec in the SIGNOFF command. For example, you can use the following command:

```
signoff 'external-file-name';
```

If you do not want to perform any special processing when you sign off, you can omit the script used for signing off, as in this example:

```
signoff noscript;
```

SIGNON Command and Statement

Initiates a link between a local SAS session and a remote SAS session

Local

Syntax

SIGNON <*option*>

Description

The SIGNON command and SIGNON statement initiate a link between a local SAS session and a remote SAS session and execute a script file if you are using an access method that requires a script file. Issue the SIGNON command from the command line of any local SAS display manager window. You can also issue a SIGNON statement from the local SAS session, which is especially useful for interactive line-mode sessions or noninteractive jobs.

The primary difference between the command and the statement is that the command can be used only from the command line of a display manager session or within the DM statement. The SIGNON statement can be used in any kind of SAS session on the local host.

You can specify one of these options in a SIGNON command:

fileref
> is a fileref associated with the script that starts the link. The fileref must be defined by a previously executed FILENAME statement.
>
> If the fileref you define for the script is the default fileref RLINK, omit this specification in the SIGNON command.

'filespec'
> is the name of the script you want to execute. Use the filespec in the SIGNON command when no fileref has been defined for the script you want to execute. The filespec can be either a fully qualified filename or the name of a file in the current working directory. Do not specify both a fileref and a filespec.

NOSCRIPT
> specifies that no script should be used to sign on. This is useful if you have already invoked the SAS session on the remote host and you do not need any additional script functionality. When you use NOSCRIPT, the SIGNON command executes faster and requires less memory, but it does not invoke a SAS session on the remote host or perform any special processing such as error processing or logging on to the remote host.

remote-session-id
> is the name of the session that you want to begin. If you omit this option, you must use the REMOTE= system option before issuing the SIGNON command. Whether you use *remote-session-id* in the SIGNON command or in the REMOTE= system option,

SIGNON Command and Statement *continued*

subsequent RSUBMIT, SIGNON, or SIGNOFF commands or statements that omit *remote-session-id* default to this session id.

When you specify *remote-session-id*, the script associated with the default fileref RLINK is executed. In this case, you must have a valid script file associated with the fileref RLINK.

TBUFSIZE=*value*
specifies the buffer size that SAS/CONNECT should use for transmitting data. TBUFSIZE should only be specified with program-to-program communications access methods, such as APPC, DECnet, NETBIOS and TCP/IP. The default buffer size is 32K. Specify a value greater than or equal to 1024. For example, to get a buffer size of 16K, specify `TBUFSIZE=16384`.

The packet sizes of terminal-based access methods are limited by the screen size and cannot be overridden. Because the default value is the maximum buffer size allowed, the TBUFSIZE option is ignored if it is specified with terminal-based access methods such as ASYNC, EHLLAPI, 3270, and TELNET.

When the SIGNON command executes, the usual SAS log messages for the remote SAS System display in your local LOG window. When the link has been successfully established, the following message is displayed:

```
NOTE: REMOTE SIGNON TO remote-session-id  COMPLETE.
```

Examples of the SIGNON Command and SIGNON Statement

These examples use the SIGNON statement, which requires a semicolon (;). The SIGNON command does not use the semicolon.

Suppose you specify the name of the session in an OPTIONS statement:

```
options remote=a;
```

You then assign the fileref RLINK to your script with the following FILENAME statement, where *external-file-name* is your script:

```
filename rlink 'external-file-name';
```

Now you can use the short form of the SIGNON command or statement to initiate a link:

```
signon;
```

If you assign the fileref RLINK to your script, you can specify the remote-session id in the SIGNON statement without having to issue an OPTIONS statement:

```
signon a;
```

You can assign some other fileref to the script, as in the following example:

```
filename startup 'external-file-name';
```

In this case, you must specify the fileref in the SIGNON command or statement. Since you can use only one option in the SIGNON command or statement, you must execute an OPTIONS statement to identify the remote-session id:

```
options remote=a;
```

You can now issue this SIGNON command or statement:

```
signon startup;
```

If you are using RLINK or any other fileref in the SIGNON command or statement, remember that you can define the script's fileref in a FILENAME statement in the SAS autoexec file. Then you do not have to type and execute the FILENAME statement before you use the SIGNON command.

If you do not assign a fileref to the script, you must execute an OPTIONS statement that specifies the remote-session id in the REMOTE= system option before specifying the filespec in the SIGNON command. For example, first execute this statement:

```
options remote=a;
```

Then you can use the following command:

```
signon 'external-file-name'
```

The SIGNON statement is particularly useful for running SAS/CONNECT from an interactive line-mode session or a noninteractive job. For line-mode and noninteractive sessions, use the SIGNON statement in combination with the SIGNOFF, RSUBMIT, and ENDRSUBMIT statements.

Example of SIGNON, RSUBMIT, ENDRSUBMIT, and SIGNOFF Statements

Suppose you want to use two remote hosts to execute SAS programs and download data to a local host. In this example, the fileref RLINK is assigned to the script filename used to initiate and terminate the link to the VMS host and then reassigned to the script filename used to initiate and terminate the link to the MVS host. The local host is a UNIX system, so the remote-session ids are the names of the host machines at the site. In this example, the two remote hosts are named TSO and VAX.

The following program can be submitted on a local UNIX host from a display manager, interactive, or noninteractive line-mode session:

```
   /* set communications access method */
options comamid=tcp;

   /* initiates link to a VMS remote host */
filename rlink 'VMS-external-file-name';
signon vax;

   /* initiates link to an MVS remote host */
filename rlink 'MVS-external-file-name';
signon tso;
```

SIGNON Command and Statement *continued*

```
        /* submit statements to a VMS remote host */
rsubmit vax;
    statements to be processed by the VMS remote host
endrsubmit;

        /* submit statements to an MVS remote host */
rsubmit tso;
    statements to be processed by the MVS remote host
endrsubmit;

    /* terminates both links */
signoff tso;
filename rlink 'VMS-external-file-name';
signoff vax;
```

The statements enclosed by the RSUBMIT and ENDRSUBMIT statements are processed by the remote host. The remaining statements are processed by the local host.

%SYSRPUT Statement

Assigns a value on the remote host to a macro variable on the local host

Remote

Syntax

%SYSRPUT *macro-variable=value*;

Description

The %SYSRPUT statement is a macro statement submitted to the remote host to assign a value available on the remote host to a macro variable that can be accessed on the local host. *Value* can be a macro variable reference or a character string. The %SYSRPUT macro statement is similar to the %LET macro statement because it is used to assign a value to a macro variable; however, the %SYSRPUT statement assigns a value to a variable on the local host, not on the remote host where the statement is processed. The %SYSRPUT statement places the macro variable into the current referencing environment of the local host.

Examples

This example illustrates how to download a file and return information about the success of the step from a noninteractive job. When remote processing is completed, the job then checks the value of the return code stored in RETCODE. Processing continues on the local host if the remote processing is successful.

The %SYSRPUT statement is useful for capturing the value returned in the SYSINFO macro variable and passing that value to the local host. The SYSINFO macro variable contains return-code information provided by SAS procedures. In the following example, the %SYSRPUT statement follows a PROC DOWNLOAD step, so the value returned by SYSINFO indicates the success of the PROC DOWNLOAD step:

```
rsubmit;
   %macro download;
      proc download data=remote.mydata out=local.mydata;
      run;
      %sysrput retcode=&sysinfo;
   %mend download;
   %download
endrsubmit;

%macro checkit;
   %if &retcode = 0 %then %do;
      further processing on local host
   %end;
%mend checkit;
%checkit
```

A SAS/CONNECT batch (noninteractive) job always returns a system condition code of 0. To determine the success or failure of the SAS/CONNECT noninteractive job, use the %SYSRPUT macro statement to check the value of the automatic macro variable SYSERR. For more information on the SYSERR macro variable, refer to *SAS Guide to Macro Processing, Version 6, Second Edition.*

This example shows how to determine what remote system the SAS/CONNECT conversation is attached to.

Remote submit the following statement:

```
%sysrput rhost=&sysscp;
```

To copy the value of RHOST into a local variable for further manipulation, use the following statement:

```
newvar="&rhost";
```

Double quotes (") must be used.

SCL Functions: COMAMID, RLINK, RSESSION, RSTITLE

The Screen Control Language (SCL) of SAS/AF and SAS/FSP provides four functions that can be used with SAS/CONNECT. This section describes these functions.

COMAMID SCL Function

Returns a string containing all of the comamids valid for the operating system where the SCL code executes

Local and remote

Syntax

cval=**COMAMID()**;

Description

The COMAMID function returns a string containing all of the communications access methods (comamids) that are valid for the operating system where the SCL code executes. Each value is separated by a blank. This function is useful for providing a list of comamids for users. The list is displayed as determined by the developer. The function merely returns a string of values.

Example

The following program fragment gets the string of comamids that are valid for the operating system under which this SCL program is executed. Once that string is returned, one way to display the values would be in a listbox. Although this example does not include it, you would specify that the listbox be filled with the text string **cval**.

```
comlist = makelist();
   str = comamid();
   do i = 1 to 10;
      com = scan(str,i,' ');
      if com ^= ' ' then
         comlist = insertc(comlist,com,i);
   end;
```

RLINK SCL Function

Determines whether a link was established between a local and a remote SAS session

Local and remote

Syntax

rc=**RLINK**(*remote-session-id*);

Description

The RLINK function verifies whether a link was established between the local SAS session and a remote SAS session. *Remote-session-id* is the name of the remote session (specified by the REMOTE= value) that is being tested.

Example

The following statements test whether a link was established between the local SAS session and the remote SAS session with the identifier REMSESS.

```
rc=rlink('REMSESS');
if (rc=0) then
   _msg_='No link exists.';
else
   _msg_='A link exists.';
```

RSESSION SCL Function

Returns the name, description, and SAS System version of a remote session

Local and remote

Syntax

cval=**RSESSION**(*n*);

Description

The RSESSION function returns the session identifier and corresponding description for a remote session. You must have previously defined the description using the RSTITLE function.

cval
    is the character string containing the following information:

    characters 1 through 8
        the session identifier (REMOTE= value)

    characters 9 through 40
        the description

n
    is the number of the remote session for which to get session information. If no remote link exists, the returned value is blank. If a link exists but no description was specified, characters 9 through 40 in the returned value are blanks.

RSESSION SCL Function *continued*

Example

This example loops through four sessions and gets the remote session/description, which is returned using the RSESSION function. The program puts the descriptions in separate arrays for later use (for example, to display a choice of remote sessions to upload to).

```
do i = 1 to 4;
    word = rsession(i);
    if word ^= ' ' then do;
        remote = substr(word,1,8);
        desc = (substr(word,9,20));
        if rlink(remote) then do;
            if desc =' ' then desc = remote;
            cnt = cnt + 1;
            entrys{cnt} = remote;
            comam{cnt} = desc;
        end;
    end;
end;
```

RSTITLE SCL Function

Defines a description for an existing connection to a remote session

Local and remote

Syntax

sysrc=**RSTITLE**(*session-id,description*);

Description

The RSTITLE function saves the session identifier and description for an existing connection to a remote session. This information can be retrieved using the RSESSION function to build a list of connections. The list can then be used to select a connection when submitting statements to a remote host.

The value of *sysrc* is 0 if the description was saved or nonzero if the operation failed.

The value of *session-id* is the name of the remote session (specified by the REMOTE= value). The string can be up to eight characters long.

The value of *description* is a description to associate with the remote session. The string can be up to 40 characters long.

Example

The following statements define the description **MVS Payroll Data** for the remote session with the identifier **A**:

```
session='A';
descrip='MVS Payroll Data';
rc=rstitle(session,descrip);
```

Chapter 15 The DOWNLOAD Procedure

Introduction 207

Syntax for the DOWNLOAD Procedure 208

Syntax for PROC DOWNLOAD 208
PROC DOWNLOAD Statement Options 209
Default Naming Conventions for Downloaded Data Sets 212
Data Set Options and Attributes for the DOWNLOAD Statement 214

Syntax for the WHERE Statement 215

Syntax for the EXCLUDE Statement 216
    Members of a SAS Data Library 216
    Entries in a SAS Catalog 216

Syntax for the SELECT Statement 217
    Members of a SAS Data Library 217
    Entries in a SAS Catalog 217

Syntax for the TRANTAB Statement 218
Requirements for the TRANTAB Statement 218
Options for the TRANTAB Statement 219

Using the MEMTYPE= Option 219

Using the ENTRYTYPE= Option 220
Rules for Specifying Entry Types 220
Valid Entry Types 221

Compiling PROGRAM Entries 223

Transfer Status Windows 223

The BINARY Option 224
Example of the BINARY Option 225

PROC DOWNLOAD Output 225

Defining Librefs and Filerefs 226

Non-English Keyboards 226

General Tips for DOWNLOAD 227

Introduction

Once you have started SAS/CONNECT, you can transfer files between your remote session and your local session. The DOWNLOAD procedure copies a file stored on the remote host to your local host.
    With SAS/CONNECT PROC DOWNLOAD you can:

- transfer multiple SAS files in a single step by using the INLIB= and OUTLIB= options. This capability enables you to transfer an entire library or selected members of a library in a single PROC DOWNLOAD step.

- specify certain entries in a catalog or certain members in a library that should be downloaded by using the SELECT and EXCLUDE statements.
- specify a specific translation table that should be used when downloading a SAS catalog.
- use WHERE processing and SAS data set options when downloading individual SAS data sets.
- replicate certain data set attributes when you download a data set.

This chapter describes the syntax and specifications for the DOWNLOAD procedure. For examples that use this syntax, see "Ways to Use SAS/CONNECT Software" on page 17.

Syntax for the DOWNLOAD Procedure

The DOWNLOAD procedure is controlled by the following statements:

PROC DOWNLOAD <*data-set-option(s)*>
  <*catalog-option(s)*>
  <*library-option(s)*>
  <*external-file-option(s)*>
  <STATUS=NO>;
WHERE *where-expression-1* <*logical-operator where-expression-n*>;
EXCLUDE *list* </MEMTYPE=*mtype* | ENTRYTYPE=*etype*>;
SELECT </MEMTYPE=*mtype* | ENTRYTYPE=*etype*>;
TRANTAB NAME=*translation-table-name*
  <TYPE=(*etype-list*)>
  <OPT=DISP SRC (DISP SRC)>;

The following sections give the syntax for these statements.

Syntax for PROC DOWNLOAD

PROC DOWNLOAD <*data-set-option(s)*>
  <*catalog-option(s)*>
  <*library-option(s)*>
  <*external-file-option(s)*>
  <STATUS=NO>;

- *data-set-options* can be one or more of the following:

  DATA=*remote-SAS-data-set* OUT=*local-SAS-data-set*
  INDEX=NO

- *catalog-options* can be one or more of the following:

  ENTRYTYPE=*etype*
  INCAT=*remote-SAS-catalog* OUTCAT=*local-SAS-catalog*

□ *library-options* are the following:

INDEX=NO
INLIB=*remote-SAS-library* OUTLIB=*local-SAS-library*
MEMTYPE=(*mtype-list*)
INDEX=NO

□ *external-file-options* are the following:

BINARY
INFILE=*remote-file-identifier* OUTFILE=*local-file-identifier*

PROC DOWNLOAD Statement Options

The following options can be used with the PROC DOWNLOAD statement:

BINARY
    specifies that you want to download a binary image (an exact copy) of an external remote host file. Use this option only for downloading external files.
    The BINARY option prevents record delimiters from being inserted at each host record. In addition, if the remote host uses a different method of data representation, the BINARY option prevents any data translation such as conversion from EBCDIC to ASCII. See "The BINARY Option" on page 224 for more information.

DATA=*remote-SAS-data-set*
    names a SAS data set you want to download from the remote host to your local host. If the data set is a permanent SAS data set, you must define a libref before the PROC DOWNLOAD statement and specify the data set's two-level name.
    If you specify the name of a data view in the DATA= option, the materialized data are downloaded to the local host, not the view definition.
    If you do not use the DATA=, INCAT=, or INFILE= option, the last SAS data set created on the remote host during your SAS session is downloaded.
    If you use the DATA= option, you must either use the OUT= option or omit all other options.

ENTRYTYPE=*etype*
ETYPE=*etype*
ET=*etype*
    specifies a catalog entry type to be downloaded. You can use this option only when you specify the INCAT= and OUTCAT= options. See "Using the ENTRYTYPE= Option" on page 220 for more information.

INCAT=*remote-SAS-catalog*
    names a SAS catalog you want to download from the remote host to your local host. If the catalog is stored in a permanent SAS data library, you must define a libref before the PROC DOWNLOAD statement and specify the catalog's two-level name. To download all of the catalogs in a SAS data library, specify

    INCAT=*libref*._ALL_

    If you specify this form for the INCAT= value, you must specify the same form for the OUTCAT= value.

You can transfer catalogs with entries containing graphics output as well as other catalog entries. Table 15.1 summarizes the catalog entries that can be transferred between different releases of the SAS System.

If you use the INCAT= option, you must also use the OUTCAT= option.

IN=*remote-SAS-library*
INLIB=*remote-SAS-library*
INDD=*remote-SAS-library*
: names a SAS data library you want to download from the remote host to your local host. All three forms of this option are equivalent. This option must be used with the OUTLIB= option (in any of its forms). Before using this option, you must define the libref used for *remote-SAS-library*.

The INLIB= option must be used with the OUTLIB= option, but you can use any form of the INLIB= option with any form of the OUTLIB= option. The following examples illustrate some valid pairs of these options:

INLIB= OUTLIB=
INLIB= OUT=
IN= OUT=
IN= OUTDD=
INDD= OUTDD=
INDD= OUTLIB=

INDEX=NO
: specifies that when you download a SAS data set that has an index, the index is not re-created on the local host. You can specify this option with the DATA= option (if you omit the OUT= option) or with the INLIB= and OUTLIB= options. Note that the index is re-created by default when you download a single data set and omit the OUT= option or when you download a SAS data library.

If you specify the OUT= option with the DATA= option, the index is not re-created. To create an index for the output data set, use the INDEX= data set option in the data set name you specify in the OUT= option to define the index. The INDEX= data set option is described in Chapter 8, "SAS Data Set Options," in SAS Technical Report P-222.

INFILE=*remote-file-identifier*
: specifies the external file you want to download from the remote host to the local host; *remote-file-identifier* can be one of the following:

  fileref
  : is used if you have defined a fileref on the remote host that is associated with a single file. You must define the fileref before the PROC DOWNLOAD statement.

  fileref(member)
  : is used if you have defined a fileref on the remote host that is associated with an aggregate storage location, such as a directory, a partitioned data set, or a MACLIB; *member* then specifies the particular file in that aggregate storage location. You must define the fileref before the PROC DOWNLOAD statement. Refer to the SAS documentation for your remote host for more information on this use of filerefs.

  '*external-file-name*'
  : is used to define explicitly the file to be downloaded.

If you use the INFILE= option, you must also use the OUTFILE= option.

MEMTYPE=(*mtype-list*)
MT=(*mtype-list*)
MTYPE=(*mtype-list*)
> specifies one or more member types to be downloaded. You can specify this option only with the INLIB= and OUTLIB= options. See "Using the MEMTYPE= Option" on page 219 for more information.

OUT=*local-SAS-data-set*
> names the local host SAS data set to which you want the downloaded data set written. If you want to create a permanent SAS data set, you must define the libref before the PROC DOWNLOAD statement and specify a two-level SAS data set name.
>
> The OUT= option is a valid form of the OUTLIB= option. The DOWNLOAD procedure determines how to interpret the meaning of the OUT= option as follows:
>
> □ When you specify the DATA= option with the OUT= option, the OUT= option names the output SAS data set.
>   For example, if the USER= SAS system option is set to WORK, the following statement downloads the A data set from the WORK library on the remote host to the WORK library on the local host:
>
>   ```
>   proc download data=a out=a;
>   run;
>   ```
>
> □ If you specify only the OUT= option, the DOWNLOAD procedure downloads the last SAS data set created on the remote host. For example, the following statement downloads the last data set created on the remote host to the JUNK data set in the WORK library on the local host (assuming USER=WORK):
>
>   ```
>   proc download out=junk;
>   run;
>   ```
>
> See "Default Naming Conventions for Downloaded Data Sets" on page 212 for information on the effect of omitting the OUT= option.

OUTLIB=*local-SAS-library*
OUT=*local-SAS-library*
OUTDD=*local-SAS-library*
> names the destination SAS data library where the downloaded data sets and catalogs from the remote host are stored on your local host. All three forms of this option are equivalent. This option must be used with the INLIB= option (in any of its forms). Before using this option, you must define the libref used for *local-SAS-library*. Note that the OUT= form of this option is the same as the OUT= option used to specify a SAS data set. When you use this option, the DOWNLOAD procedure determines whether the input option was DATA= or INLIB= and processes the downloaded objects appropriately.
>
> The OUTLIB= option must be used with the INLIB= option, but you can use any form of the OUTLIB= option with any form of the INLIB= option. Refer to the description of the INLIB= option for examples that illustrate some valid pairs of these options.
>
> When you specify the INLIB= option (or some other form of this option) with the OUT= option, the OUT= option specifies the name of a SAS data library. For example,

the following statement downloads all of the data sets and catalogs in the A library on the remote host to the WORK library on the local host:

```
proc download inlib=a out=work;
run;
```

OUTCAT=*local-SAS-catalog*
: names the local host SAS catalog to which you want the downloaded catalog written. If you want to create a permanent SAS catalog, you must define the libref before the PROC DOWNLOAD statement and specify a two-level SAS catalog name. To download all of the catalogs in a SAS data library, specify

OUTCAT=*libref*._ALL_

If you specify this form for the OUTCAT= value, you must specify the same form for the INCAT= value.
 If you use the OUTCAT= option, you must also use the INCAT= option.

OUTFILE=*local-file-identifier*
: identifies an external file on the local host to which you want a downloaded external file written; *local-file-identifier* can be one of the following:

  fileref
  : is used if you have defined a fileref on the local host that is associated with a single file. You must define the fileref before the PROC DOWNLOAD statement.

  fileref(member)
  : is used if you have defined a fileref on the local host that is associated with an aggregate storage location such as a directory; *member* then specifies the particular file in that aggregate storage location. You must define the fileref before the PROC DOWNLOAD statement. Refer to the SAS documentation for your local host for more information on this use of filerefs.

  external-file-name
  : is used to define explicitly the file to be downloaded.

  If you use the OUTFILE= option, you must also use the INFILE= option.

STATUS=NO
: specifies that the status window should not be displayed while the data set, catalog, library, or external file is being downloaded. By default, the DOWNLOAD procedure displays the Transfer Status window.

Default Naming Conventions for Downloaded Data Sets

Follow these rules for cases in which you download a SAS data set and do not specify the name of the data set in the OUT= option:

- If the input data set (the data set specified in the DATA= option) has a two-level name and the same libref that is defined for the input data set is also defined in the local host environment, the data set is downloaded to the library on the local host that is associated with that libref. The data set has the same member name on the local host. For example, suppose you submit the following statement:

```
libname orders local-host-SAS-data-library ;
```

If you remote submit the following statements, the data set ORDERS.QTR1 is downloaded to ORDERS.QTR1 on the local host.

```
/* ORDERS libref defined on both hosts */
libname orders remote-host-SAS-data-library ;
proc download data=orders.qtr1;
run;
```

- If the input data set has a two-level name but the libref for the input data set is not also defined in the local host environment, the data set is downloaded to the library on the local host that is defined with the USER= SAS system option (usually the WORK library). The data set retains the same data set name that it had on the remote host. For example, if you remote submit the following statements, the data set is downloaded to WORK.QTR2 on the local host.

```
/* ORDERS libref defined only on the remote host */
libname orders remote-host-SAS-data-library;
proc download data=orders.qtr2;
run;
```

- If the input data set has a one-level name and the libref that is assigned to the USER= option on the remote host also exists on the local host, the data set is downloaded to that library. For example, suppose you submit the following statement:

```
libname orders local-host-SAS-data-library;
libname local local-host-SAS-data-library;

    /* this option has no effect in this case */
options user=local;
```

If you remote submit the following statements, the data set ORDERS.QTR1 is downloaded to ORDERS.QTR1 on the local host.

```
/* ORDERS libref defined on both hosts */
libname orders remote-host-SAS-data-library;
options user=orders;
proc download data=qtr1;
run;
```

- If the input data set has a one-level name and the libref assigned to the USER= option on the remote host does not exist on the local host, the data set is downloaded to the library assigned to the USER= option on the local host. That is, the USER= option on the local host is used only if the libref for the USER= option on the remote host does not exist on the local host. For example, suppose you submit these statements:

```
libname local local-host-SAS-data-library;
options user=local;
```

When you remote submit the following statements, the data set ORDERS.QTR1 is downloaded to LOCAL.QTR1 on the local host.

```
/* ORDERS libref defined only on the remote hosts */
libname orders remote-host-SAS-data-library;
options user=orders;
proc download data=qtr1;
run;
```

☐ If you omit the DATA= option, as in this example:

```
proc download;
run;
```

the last data set created on the remote host during the SAS session is downloaded to the local host. The naming conventions on the local host follow one of the rules described above, depending on how the last data set created was named.

Data Set Options and Attributes for the DOWNLOAD Statement

PROC DOWNLOAD permits you to specify SAS data set options in the DATA= and OUT= options. Note that SAS data set options are not supported with the INLIB= and OUTLIB= options, even when you download only data sets. The data set options must be associated with a specific SAS data set, so they must be used in the DATA= or OUT= options.

In addition, when you download SAS data sets using the DATA= option (omitting the OUT= option) or the INLIB= and OUTLIB= options, or if you omit all of these options, the following characteristics are inherited by the downloaded data set.

Note: The following list of characteristics indicates the SAS data set option used to create the characteristic for the original data set. You do not have to specify the option to have it inherited when the data set is downloaded.

☐ password for ALTER protection (ALTER= SAS data set option).

☐ compressed observations (COMPRESS= SAS data set option).

☐ indexes (INDEX= SAS system option or other methods of creating indexes). Note that the index for a downloaded SAS data set is re-created on the local host, not copied from the remote host. To prevent the re-creation of the index, you can specify the INDEX=NO option in the PROC DOWNLOAD statement, as described in "PROC DOWNLOAD Statement Options" on page 209.

☐ data set label (LABEL= SAS data set option).

☐ password for READ protection (READ= SAS data set option).

☐ reuse of free space in compressed data sets (REUSE= SAS data set option).

☐ list of variables the data set is sorted by (SORTEDBY= SAS data set option).

☐ data set type (TYPE= SAS data set option).

☐ password for WRITE protection (WRITE= SAS data set option).

If you specify the OUT= option when downloading a single data set, only the following characteristics are inherited by the downloaded data set:

- data set type
- data set label.

The following example illustrates using the DATA= option and the INDEX=NO option. The example also shows the use of the DROP= SAS data set option. Note that because no OUT= option is specified, the downloaded data set inherits the characteristics of the input data set except the index (since the INDEX=NO option is specified).

```
proc download data=idx(drop=sex) index=no;
run;
```

Syntax for the WHERE Statement

WHERE *where-expression-1* <*logical-operator where-expression-n*>

The DOWNLOAD procedure processes WHERE statements and the WHERE= data set option when you transfer a single SAS data set. WHERE statements allow multiple WHERE expressions joined by logical operators. *Logical-operator* can be AND, AND NOT, OR, or OR NOT.

You can use SAS functions in a WHERE expression. Also, note that a DATA or PROC step attempts to use an available index to optimize the selection of data when an indexed variable is used in combination with one of the following:

- CONTAINS operator
- LIKE operator
- colon modifier with a comparison operator
- TRIM function
- SUBSTR function (in some cases).

To understand when use of the SUBSTR function causes an index to be used, look at the format of the SUBSTR function in a WHERE statement:

```
where substr(variable, position, length)='character-string';
```

An index is used in processing when all of the following conditions are met:

- *position* is equal to 1
- *length* is less than or equal to the length of *variable*
- *length* is equal to the length of *character-string*.

The following example illustrates using a WHERE statement with the DOWNLOAD procedure. The downloaded data set contains only the observations that meet the WHERE condition.

```
proc download data=labeled out=new;
   where lname < 'K';
run;
```

For more information about the WHERE statement, refer to *SAS Language: Reference, Version 6, First Edition*.

Syntax for the EXCLUDE Statement

EXCLUDE *list*</ MEMTYPE=*mtype*| ENTRYTYPE=*etype*>;

The EXCLUDE statement enables you to exclude from downloading specific members in a SAS data library or specific entries in a SAS catalog. You cannot use both the EXCLUDE and SELECT statements in the same PROC DOWNLOAD step, but you can specify multiple EXCLUDE statements.

The EXCLUDE statement can have two forms. These forms are discussed in detail in the next two sections.

Members of a SAS Data Library

You can use the following form of the EXCLUDE statement with the INLIB= and OUTLIB= options in the PROC DOWNLOAD statement:

EXCLUDE *list*</ MEMTYPE=*mtype*>;

When you use the EXCLUDE statement to exclude members of a library from downloading, *list* specifies the members to exclude from downloading. You can explicitly name all members to exclude or use one of the following forms of name lists:

: (colon)   specifies all member names beginning with the string of characters immediately preceding the colon. For example, if you specify `TEST:`, none of the members beginning with the letters `TEST` are downloaded.

- (hyphen) specifies all member names falling lexigraphically between the names on either side of the hyphen. You can use this wild-card character only between two names that begin with the same string of characters and end in a number, for example, `TEST1-TEST5`.

For information on using the MEMTYPE= option, see "Using the MEMTYPE= Option" on page 219.

Entries in a SAS Catalog

You can use the following form of the EXCLUDE statement with the INCAT= and OUTCAT= options in the PROC DOWNLOAD statement:

EXCLUDE *list*</ ENTRYTYPE=*etype*>;

When you use the EXCLUDE statement to exclude catalog entries from downloading, each element of *list* has the form *entry.type*. In this form,

entry is the name of an entry in *member* to exclude from downloading.

.type is the type of the catalog entry. This part of the name is optional.

The ENTRYTYPE= option in the EXCLUDE statement works like the ENTRYTYPE= option in the PROC DOWNLOAD statement. For a complete list of entry types and for detailed information on how to use the ENTRYTYPE= option, see "Using the ENTRYTYPE= Option" on page 220.

Syntax for the SELECT Statement

SELECT *list</* MEMTYPE=*mtype*| ENTRYTYPE=*etype*>;

The SELECT statement enables you to select for downloading specific members in a SAS data library or specific entries in a SAS catalog. You cannot use both the EXCLUDE and SELECT statements in the same PROC DOWNLOAD step, but you can specify multiple SELECT statements.

The SELECT statement can have two forms. These forms are discussed in detail in the next two sections.

Members of a SAS Data Library

You can use the following form of the SELECT statement with the INLIB= and OUTLIB= options in the PROC DOWNLOAD statement:

SELECT *list</* MEMTYPE=*mtype*>;

When you use the SELECT statement to select members of a library for downloading, *list* specifies the members to select for downloading. You can explicitly name all members to select or use one of the following forms of name lists:

: (colon) specifies all member names beginning with the string of characters immediately preceding the colon. For example, if you specify TEST:, all of the selected members begin with the letters TEST.

- (hyphen) specifies all member names falling lexigraphically between the names on either side of the hyphen. You can use this wild-card character only between two names that begin with the same string of characters and end in a number, for example, TEST1-TEST5.

For information on using the MEMTYPE= option, see "Using the MEMTYPE= Option" on page 219.

Entries in a SAS Catalog

You can use the following form of the SELECT statement with the INCAT= and OUTCAT= options in the PROC DOWNLOAD statement:

SELECT *list</* ENTRYTYPE=*etype*>;

When you use the SELECT statement to select catalog entries for downloading, each element of *list* has the form *entry.type*. In this form,

entry is the name of an entry in *member* to select for downloading.

.type is the type of the catalog entry. This part of the name is optional.

The ENTRYTYPE= option in the SELECT statement works like the ENTRYTYPE= option in the PROC DOWNLOAD statement. For a complete list of entry types and for detailed information on how to use the ENTRYTYPE= option, see "Using the ENTRYTYPE= Option" on page 220.

Note: The SELECT statement also enables you to maintain an ordering and grouping of catalog entries containing graphics output because entries are downloaded into the local SAS catalog in the order that you specify in the SELECT statement. See "Ways to Use SAS/CONNECT Software" on page 17 for examples that illustrate how to use the SELECT statement to maintain the order and grouping of catalog entries containing graphics output.

Syntax for the TRANTAB Statement

TRANTAB NAME=*translation-table-name*
   <TYPE=(*etype-list*)>
   <OPT=DISP SRC (DISP SRC)>;

The TRANTAB statement enables you to specify translation tables to use for translating characters in catalog entries you want to download. The TRANTAB statement also enables you to specify the particular types of SAS/AF or SCL catalog entries to which you want to apply a translation. You can specify one translation table per statement, but there is no limit to the number of TRANTAB statements you can use in one invocation of the DOWNLOAD procedure. If you specify the TRANTAB statement, you must also specify the INCAT= and OUTCAT= options in the PROC DOWNLOAD statement.

Requirements for the TRANTAB Statement

A TRANTAB statement must include the following argument:

NAME=*translation-table-name*
   specifies the name of the translation table to apply to the SAS catalog you want to download. The *translation-table-name* you specify is the name of a catalog entry in either your SASUSER.PROFILE catalog or the SASHELP.HOST catalog. The DOWNLOAD procedure searches the SASUSER.PROFILE catalog first and the SASHELP.HOST catalog second.
   See "TRANTAB= System Option" on page 186 for more information about translation tables.
   By default, whenever you invoke PROC DOWNLOAD, the procedure uses the table that translates host-to-transport format. In most cases, the default translation table is the correct one to use, but you may need to apply additional translation tables if, for example, your application requires different national language characters.

You can specify a translation table other than the default in two ways:

☐ To specify a translation table for an invocation of PROC DOWNLOAD, use the TRANTAB statement in the DOWNLOAD procedure.

☐ To specify a translation table for your entire SAS session or job (including all file transfers you do), use the TRANTAB= system option. You use this system option to define which default translation tables to use in place of those supplied by SAS Institute. See "TRANTAB= System Option" on page 186 for a discussion of the TRANTAB= SAS system option.

See SAS Technical Report P-197, *The TRANTAB Procedure, Release 6.06* and Chapter 39, "The TRANTAB Procedure," of SAS Technical Report P-222 for information on creating translation tables with PROC TRANTAB.

Options for the TRANTAB Statement

You can use the following options in the TRANTAB statement:

TYPE=(*etype-list*)
    specifies that the DOWNLOAD procedure apply the translation table to only the entries with the type or types you specify. Note that *etype-list* can be one or more entry types. If *etype-list* is a simple entry type, omit the parentheses.
    See Table 15.1 for a list of entry types valid for the DOWNLOAD procedure. By default, the DOWNLOAD procedure applies the translation table to all of the entries in the catalog you specify.

OPT=DISP SRC (DISP SRC)
    specifies one of the following:

    ☐ when OPT=DISP, the DOWNLOAD procedure applies the translation table only to those entries of the catalog you specified that produce window displays.

    ☐ when OPT=SRC, the DOWNLOAD procedure applies the translation table only to those entries of the catalog you specified of the type SOURCE.

    ☐ when OPT=(DISP SRC), the DOWNLOAD procedure applies the translation table only to those entries of the catalog you specified that either produce window displays or have a type of SOURCE.

When you omit the OPT= option, the DOWNLOAD procedure applies the translation table to all of the entries in the catalog you specify.

Using the MEMTYPE= Option

If you specify the INLIB= and OUTLIB= options in the PROC DOWNLOAD statement, you can use the MEMTYPE= option to indicate what member types to download. You can specify the MEMTYPE= option in the following places:

☐ the PROC DOWNLOAD statement.

- the SELECT or EXCLUDE statement in parentheses immediately after a member name. If the type is enclosed in parentheses, it refers only to the member name immediately preceding the option.

- the SELECT or EXCLUDE statement after a slash (/) at the end of the statement. When used following a slash, the MEMTYPE= option refers to all members named in the statement unless the same option appears in parentheses after a name.

Valid values of the MEMTYPE= option are DATA, CATALOG (or CAT), and ALL.
If you use this option in the SELECT and EXCLUDE statements, you can specify only one value. If you use this option in the PROC DOWNLOAD statement, you can specify a list of values enclosed in parentheses, as shown here:

```
proc download inlib=this outlib=that memtype=(data catalog);
```

You can use the MEMTYPE= option in multiple places. When you do so, the DOWNLOAD procedure determines the type of each member as described below:

1. By the value of the option in parentheses immediately following the member name, if present
2. Otherwise, by the value of the option after the slash in the SELECT or EXCLUDE statement, if present
3. Otherwise, by the value of the option in the PROC DOWNLOAD statement, if present
4. If you do not specify a member type, the DOWNLOAD procedure uses the default type, ALL.

See "Purpose" on page 42 for examples that illustrate the use of the MEMTYPE= option.

Using the ENTRYTYPE= Option

This section describes the rules for specifying entry types and lists the valid entry types. See "Purpose" on page 43 for examples of using the ENTRYTYPE= option.

Rules for Specifying Entry Types

When you specify the INCAT= and OUTCAT= options in the PROC DOWNLOAD statement, you can use the ENTRYTYPE= option in the PROC DOWNLOAD statement, the SELECT statement, or the EXCLUDE statement to specify which entry types to download. The ENTRYTYPE= option is required only if you use a SELECT or EXCLUDE statement. If you omit the entry type and also omit the SELECT and EXCLUDE statements, all catalog entries are downloaded. You can specify a single entry type in any of the following places:

- in the PROC DOWNLOAD statement, specify the ENTRYTYPE= option.
- in the SELECT or EXCLUDE statement, specify the ENTRYTYPE= option in parentheses immediately after an entry name. If the type is enclosed in parentheses, it refers only to the entry name immediately preceding the option.

- in the SELECT or EXCLUDE statement, specify the ENTRYTYPE= option after a slash (/) at the end of the statement. When used following a slash, the ENTRYTYPE= option refers to all entries named in the statement unless the same option appears in parentheses after an entry name.
- in the SELECT or EXCLUDE statement, specify the entry type as part of the entry name. For example, you can specify TEST.MENU in the list of entries.

You can use the ENTRYTYPE= option in multiple places. When you do so, the DOWNLOAD procedure determines the type of each entry as described below:

1. by the entry type given as part of the entry name, such as XYZ.FORMAT
2. by the value of the option in parentheses immediately following the entry name, if present
3. otherwise, by the value of the option after the slash in the SELECT or EXCLUDE statement, if present
4. otherwise, by the value of the option in the PROC DOWNLOAD statement, if present.

Note: If you use the ENTRYTYPE= option in both the PROC DOWNLOAD statement and a SELECT or EXCLUDE statement, the values must be the same. In most cases, if you are using the ENTRYTYPE= option in a SELECT or EXCLUDE statement, you should omit it from the PROC DOWNLOAD statement.

Valid Entry Types

Table 15.1 indicates the entry types that can be downloaded between the different releases of the SAS System.

Note: For releases after Release 6.08, the following message is displayed if you try to download an entry that is not compatible with an earlier release:

```
ERROR: Catalog download to earlier version not allowed.
       Backward compatibility not supported.
```

Table 15.1 Catalog Entries That Can Be Downloaded

From This Remote Host	To This Local Host			
	Release 6.08	Release 6.07 (except UNIX)	Release 6.06, and UNIX Release 6.07	Release 6.04
Release 6.08	List A	List B	List E	none
Release 6.07 (except UNIX)	List C	List C	List E	none
Release 6.06 and UNIX Release 6.07	List D	List D	List D	none
Release 5.18	List F	List F	List F	List F

List A

AFCBT	EDPARMS	GRSEG	MENU	RESOURCE
AFGO	EIS	HELP	MODEL	SCL
AFMACRO	FILEFMT	INFMT	OUTPUT	SCREEN
CALC	FONT	INFMTC	PARMS	SLIST
CBT	FORM	KEYMAP	PGM	SOURCE
CLASS	FORMAT	KEYS	PMENU	TEMPLATE
CMAP	FORMATC	LETTER	PROGRAM	TRANTAB
DEV	FORMULA	LIST	RANGE	
DEVMAP	FRAME	LOG	REPORT	

List B

AFCBT	DEVMAP	HELP	LOG	PROGRAM
AFGO	EDPARMS	INFMT	MENU	SCL
AFMACRO	FONT	INFMTC	MODEL	SCREEN
CALC	FORM	KEYMAP	OUTPUT	SLIST
CBT	FORMAT	KEYS	PARMS	SOURCE
CMAP	FORMATC	LETTER	PGM	TEMPLATE
DEV	GRSEG	LIST	PMENU	TRANTAB

List C

AFCBT	EDPARMS	INFMT	MODEL	SCREEN
AFGO	FONT	INFMTC	OUTPUT	SLIST
AFMACRO	FORM	KEYMAP	PARMS	SOURCE
CALC	FORMAT	KEYS	PGM	TEMPLATE
CBT	FORMATC	LETTER	PMENU	TRANTAB
CMAP	FORMULA	LIST	PROGRAM	
DEV	GRSEG	LOG	REPORT	
DEVMAP	HELP	MENU	SCL	

List D

AFCBT	EDPARMS	GRSEG	LIST	SCREEN
AFGO	FONT	HELP	LOG	SOURCE
AFMACRO	FORM	INFMT	MENU	TEMPLATE
CBT	FORMAT	INFMTC	OUTPUT	TRANTAB
CMAP	FORMATC	KEYS	PMENU	
DEV	FORMULA	LETTER	PROGRAM	

List E

AFCBT	CMAP	KEYS	MENU
AFGO	EDPARMS	LETTER	SOURCE
AFMACRO	FORM	LIST	TEMPLATE
CBT	HELP	LOG	TRANTAB

List F

CBT	LETTER
CBTGO (becomes AFGO)	LIST
CBTSAVE (becomes AFCBT)	MENU
FORM	PROGRAM
HELP	TRANSAVE (becomes AFGO)
KEYS	

Compiling PROGRAM Entries

If you download a catalog that contains entries of type PROGRAM, you must compile the entries on the local host before execution. To compile all the PROGRAM entries in a catalog, submit the following statements to the SAS System:

```
proc build cat=libref.member-name batch;
    compile;
run;
```

where *libref* identifies the SAS data library containing the catalog and *member-name* identifies the catalog. Refer to *SAS/AF Software: Usage and Reference, Version 6, First Edition* for more information on compiling PROGRAM entries.

Transfer Status Windows

The transfer status window displays information describing the status of the downloading process. The window's display changes as the download proceeds. The information on the display includes

- the type of file being downloaded (SAS data set, SAS catalog, catalog entry containing graphics output, or external file).
- the name of the target SAS data set, SAS catalog, or external file. If the target is a SAS data set, the name has the form *libref.SAS-data-set*. If the target is a SAS catalog, the name has the form *libref.SAS-catalog*. If the target is an external file, the name is the external file name.
- the number of the byte being downloaded (updated as each new buffer is sent).
- the number of the observation being downloaded (for SAS data sets only).
- the time elapsed since the beginning of the transfer, in *hh:mm:ss* form.
- the percentage of the file already downloaded.
- an estimate of the amount of time required to complete the download, in *hh:mm:ss* form.
- a horizontal bar chart depicting the percentage of the file already downloaded.

   Note: For some types of files, the percentage completed, estimated time to completion, and the bar chart are not always available. Some operating systems cannot efficiently provide the size of the file, which is necessary to calculate these estimates. In other cases, the information provided by the operating system results in estimates that are greater than the actual time needed for the transfer. Thus, the percentage completed, estimated time to completion and bar chart may show exaggerated estimates, but they will show 100% when the transfer is completed.

Display 15.1 is a sample of the transfer status window during a SAS data set download. The target SAS data set is PS2DIR.MOVER.

Display 15.1
Transfer Status Window for Downloading a SAS Data Set

```
                           DOWNLOAD
The SAS data set PS2DIR.MOVER is being created

Currently transferring byte #        16776 observation #        699
Elapsed time   0:00:09
69.9 % of transfer completed
Estimated time to completion    0:00:04
0% ******************************************* 100%
```

Display 15.2 is a sample of the transfer status window when an external text file is downloading. The target file is C:PMCAPTEXTDOWN. In this example, the remote host is unable to provide the size of the input file, so the transfer status window omits the percentage of transfer completed, the estimated time to completion, and the bar chart.

Display 15.2
Transfer Status Window for Downloading an External File

```
                         TEXT DOWNLOAD
The file c:\pmcap\textdown  is being created

Currently transferring byte #        104108
Elapsed time   0:00:57
```

The BINARY Option

Normally, SAS/CONNECT assumes that external files being uploaded and downloaded are text files and alters them so that they can be used on the target machine. Two features are affected:

- Each operating system has its own type of record delimiters in external files. The record delimiters are incompatible between operating systems. Therefore, record delimiters appropriate to the target system are added to the copied file by the DOWNLOAD procedure.

- CMS, MVS, and VSE hosts use the EBCDIC character set; other operating systems use an ASCII character set. Consequently, if files are downloaded from CMS, MVS, or VSE to an ASCII-based system without any character translation, the downloaded files cannot be interpreted by the target system.

SAS/CONNECT solves the EBCDIC/ASCII problem by converting files automatically. The DOWNLOAD procedure converts text to the format of the local host.

There are times when these file conversions are not desirable. For example, you may need to upload executable files from the local host to the remote host and later download them to the same or a different local host. You may want to do this for backup purposes or to send files to other users. In cases where you do not want a file translated to another character set or record delimiters inserted, you can use the BINARY option to prevent automatic conversion. When you specify the BINARY option in a PROC DOWNLOAD statement, SAS/CONNECT transfers the file in *binary* image form (hence, the keyword BINARY).

Example of the BINARY Option

This example uses a PROC DOWNLOAD statement for downloading an external file from the remote host to the local host. Note that the BINARY option is included to suppress character-set translation and to prevent record-delimiter insertion:

```
proc download infile=hostmod
               outfile='external-file-name' binary;
run;
```

This PROC DOWNLOAD step is excerpted from "Example 17. Data Transfer Services: Distributing a .EXE File from the Remote Host to Multiple Local Hosts" on page 45.

PROC DOWNLOAD Output

The DOWNLOAD procedure writes a series of informative messages to the SAS log when it executes. Examples of these messages are shown in Output 15.1.

Output 15.1
SAS Log Messages
from the
DOWNLOAD
Procedure

```
NOTE: Remote submit to B commencing.
1    proc download outfile='local-external-file'
2        infile='remote-external-file';run;

NOTE: TEXT download in progress from
      infile=remote-external-file to
      outfile=local-external-file
NOTE: Downloaded 4 records and 136 bytes.
NOTE: 4 records were written to the file local-external-file.
      The maximum record length was 65.
      The minimum record length was 0.
NOTE: 136 bytes were transferred at 136 bytes/second.
NOTE: The PROCEDURE DOWNLOAD used 0.05 CPU seconds and 1455K.

NOTE: Remote submit to B complete.
$
```

Defining Librefs and Filerefs

As is true in all SAS programming, permanent SAS data sets, SAS catalogs, and external files must be defined correctly in order to be accessed. Defining a file means that you associate a shorthand, symbolic name with a file. The method you use to define a file depends on the operating system and whether it is a SAS file or an external file.

- Librefs for permanent SAS data libraries are defined with the LIBNAME statement.
- Filerefs for external files are defined with the FILENAME statement.

If you do not know how to use the LIBNAME and FILENAME statements, refer to Chapter 9, "SAS Language Statements," in *SAS Language: Reference, Version 6, First Edition*.

There are some special considerations to be aware of when you define files to use with the DOWNLOAD and UPLOAD procedures.

- Statements defining librefs and filerefs for files on the local host must be executed in the local SAS session with the SUBMIT command. They cannot be executed with the PROC DOWNLOAD or PROC UPLOAD steps with an RSUBMIT command or statement.
- Statements defining librefs or filerefs for files on the remote host must be executed on the remote host with the RSUBMIT command or statement. Therefore, these statements can be executed along with the PROC DOWNLOAD or PROC UPLOAD step, as long as they precede the PROC statement.

Non-English Keyboards

If you use a local host with a non-English keyboard, you probably have some external files with non-English characters in them. If your remote host is CMS or TSO, some specially accented characters may be translated incorrectly using the DOWNLOAD and UPLOAD procedures. This occurs because of the default translations from ASCII to EBCDIC and from EBCDIC to ASCII. To solve the problem, you can do one of the following:

- If SAS/CONNECT is used frequently, you should use an alternate EBCDIC/ASCII translation table on the remote host. The SAS Software Representative for the remote host should create the alternate table. See "Details for Micro-to-Host Link Releases" on page 289.
- If SAS/CONNECT is not used frequently, you can manage problematic characters by assigning the correct hex values through DATA step programming statements after the file is copied. For example, suppose you have a German keyboard and a CMS host. You want a file to contain umlaut-A characters after an upload. By default, the ASCII representation of umlaut-A, which is X'84', is translated to EBCDIC X'24'. However, the EBCDIC representation of umlaut-A is X'CO', so you need to translate EBCDIC

X'24' to EBCDIC X'CO'. The following DATA step performs this translation, where NAME is a variable containing umlaut-A characters:

```
data new;
   set old;
   retain to 'CO'x from '24'x;
   drop to from;
   name=translate(name,to,from);
run;
```

General Tips for DOWNLOAD

- When downloading variable block records from a remote MVS host to a local host, you must specify RECFM=U in the remote host FILENAME statement that points to the variable block record. For example, if the file you are downloading is called MYFILE, you would use:

    ```
    rsubmit;
      filename myfile 'vb.block.record' recfm=u;
      proc download infile=myfile outfile='c:vb.rec' binary;run;
    endrsubmit;
    ```

    After the local host's LOG window shows the number of bytes transferred, you would issue the following local FILENAME statement using a RECFM and a LRECL parameter, where LRECL is the number of bytes transferred:

    ```
    filename myfile 'c:vb.rec' recfm=s370vb and lrecl=xxxx;
    ```

- You cannot download a SAS data set to an external file or an external file to a SAS data set.

- Remember that the DOWNLOAD procedure executes on the remote SAS System. You must use the RSUBMIT command, not the SUBMIT command, to execute the PROC DOWNLOAD step.

- The rate at which files are transferred varies depending upon the size and number of files being transferred and the processing load on the remote host. The transfer status window keeps you informed of the progress of the transfer. See "Transfer Status Windows" on page 223 for more information.

- If the PROC DOWNLOAD step successfully completes the file transfer, the macro variable SYSINFO is set to 0. If the file transfer is not successfully completed, the SYSINFO macro variable is set to a value greater than 0. You can pass the value of the SYSINFO macro variable back to the local host by using the %SYSRPUT statement. See "%SYSRPUT Statement" on page 200 for detailed information on the %SYSRPUT statement.

- To download a text file with a record length greater than 132 bytes, the LRECL= option must be specified on both the local and remote FILENAME statements.

Chapter 16 The UPLOAD Procedure

Introduction 229

Syntax for the UPLOAD Procedure 230

Syntax for the PROC UPLOAD Statement 230
PROC UPLOAD Statement Options 231
Default Naming Conventions for Uploaded Data Sets 234
Data Set Options and Attributes for the UPLOAD Statement 236

Syntax for the WHERE Statement 237

Syntax for the EXCLUDE Statement 238
Members of a SAS Data Library 238
Entries in a SAS Catalog 238

Syntax for the SELECT Statement 239
Members of a SAS Data Library 239
Entries in a SAS Catalog 239

Syntax for the TRANTAB Statement 240
Requirements for the TRANTAB Statement 240
Options for the TRANTAB Statement 241

Using the MEMTYPE= Option 241

Using the ENTRYTYPE= Option 242
Rules for Specifying Entry Types 242
Valid Entry Types 243

Compiling PROGRAM Entries 245

Transfer Status Windows 245

The BINARY Option 246
Example of the BINARY Option 247

PROC UPLOAD Output 247

Defining Librefs and Filerefs 248

Non-English Keyboards 248

General Tips for UPLOAD 249

Introduction

Once you have started SAS/CONNECT, you can transfer files between your local session and the remote host. The UPLOAD procedure sends files from the local host to the remote host.

With SAS/CONNECT you can:

- transfer multiple SAS files in a single step by using the INLIB= and OUTLIB= options. This capability enables you to transfer an entire library or selected members of a library in a single PROC UPLOAD step.

- specify certain entries in a catalog or certain members in a library that should be uploaded by using the SELECT and EXCLUDE statements.
- specify a specific translation table that should be used when uploading a SAS catalog.
- use WHERE processing and SAS data set options when uploading individual SAS data sets.
- replicate certain data set attributes when you upload a data set.

This chapter describes the syntax and specifications for the UPLOAD procedure. For examples that use this syntax, see "Ways to Use SAS/CONNECT Software" on page 17.

Syntax for the UPLOAD Procedure

The UPLOAD procedure is controlled by the following statements:

PROC UPLOAD <*data-set-option(s)*>
         <*catalog-option(s)*>
         <*library-option(s)*>
         <*external-file-option(s)*>
         <STATUS=NO>;
WHERE *where-expression-1* <*logical-operator where-expression-n*>;
EXCLUDE *list* </MEMTYPE=*mtype* | ENTRYTYPE=*etype*>;
SELECT </MEMTYPE=*mtype* | ENTRYTYPE=*etype*>;
TRANTAB NAME=*translation-table-name*
         <TYPE=(*etype-list*)>
         <OPT=DISP SRC (DISP SRC)>;

The following sections give the syntax for these statements.

Syntax for the PROC UPLOAD Statement

PROC UPLOAD <*data-set-option(s)*>
         <*catalog-option(s)*>
         <*library-option(s)*>
         <*external-file-option(s)*>
         <STATUS=NO>;

- *data-set-options* can be one or more of the following:

  DATA=*local-SAS-data-set* OUT=*remote-SAS-data-set*
  INDEX=NO

- *catalog-options* can be one or more of the following:

  ENTRYTYPE=*etype*
  INCAT=*local-SAS-catalog* OUTCAT=*remote-SAS-catalog*

☐ *library-options* can be one or more of the following:

INDEX=NO
INLIB=*local-SAS-library* OUTLIB=*remote-SAS-library*
MEMTYPE=(*mtype-list*)

☐ *external-file-options* are the following:

BINARY
INFILE=*local-file-identifier* OUTFILE=*remote-file-identifier*

PROC UPLOAD Statement Options

The following options can be used with the PROC UPLOAD statement:

BINARY
: specifies that you want to upload a binary image (an exact copy) of an external file. Use this option only for uploading external files.
    The BINARY option prevents record delimiters from being inserted at each remote host record. In addition, if the remote host uses a different method of data representation, the BINARY option prevents any data translation such as conversion from ASCII to EBCDIC. See "The BINARY Option" on page 246 for more information.

DATA=*local-SAS-data-set*
: names a SAS data set you want to upload to the remote host from your local host. If the data set is a permanent SAS data set, you must define a libref before the PROC UPLOAD statement and specify the data set's two-level name.
    If you specify the name of a data view in the DATA= option, the materialized data are uploaded to the remote host, not the view definition.
    If you do not use the DATA=, INCAT=, or INFILE= option, the last SAS data set created on the local host during your SAS session is uploaded.
    If you use the DATA= option, you must either use the OUT= option or omit all other options.

ENTRYTYPE=*etype*
ETYPE=*etype*
ET=*etype*
: specifies a catalog entry type to be uploaded. You can use this option only when you specify the INCAT= and OUTCAT= options. See "Using the ENTRYTYPE= Option" on page 242 for more information.

INCAT=*local-SAS-catalog*
: names a SAS catalog you want to upload to the remote host from your local host. If the catalog is stored in a permanent SAS data library, you must define a libref before the PROC UPLOAD statement and specify the catalog's two-level name. To upload all of the catalogs in a SAS data library, specify

    INCAT=*libref*._ALL_

    If you specify this form for the INCAT= value, you must specify the same form for the OUTCAT= value.

You can transfer catalogs with entries containing graphics output as well as other catalog entries. Table 16.1 summarizes the catalog entries that can be transferred between different releases of the SAS System.

If you use the INCAT= option, you must also use the OUTCAT= option.

IN=*local-SAS-library*
INLIB=*local-SAS-library*
INDD=*local-SAS-library*

    names a SAS data library you want to upload from the local host to your remote host. All three forms of this option are equivalent. This option must be used with the OUTLIB= option (in any of its forms). Before using this option, you must define the libref used for *local-SAS-library*.

    The INLIB= option must be used with the OUTLIB= option, but you can use any form of the INLIB= option with any form of the OUTLIB= option. The following examples illustrate some valid pairs of these options:

INLIB= OUTLIB=
INLIB= OUT=
IN= OUT=
IN= OUTDD=
INDD= OUTDD=
INDD= OUTLIB=

INDEX=NO

    specifies that when you upload a SAS data set that has an index, the index is not re-created on the remote host. You can specify this option with the DATA= option (if you omit the OUT= option) or with the INLIB= and OUTLIB= options. Note that the index is re-created by default when you upload a single data set and omit the OUT= option or when you upload a SAS data library.

    If you specify the OUT= option with the DATA= option, the index is not re-created. To create an index for the output data set, use the INDEX= data set option in the data set name you specify in the OUT= option to define the index. The INDEX= data set option is described in Chapter 8, "SAS Data Set Options," in SAS Technical Report P-222, *Changes and Enhancements to Base SAS Software, Release 6.07*.

INFILE=*local-file-identifier*

    specifies the external file you want to upload to the remote host from the local host; *local-file-identifier* can be one of the following:

fileref	is used if you have defined a fileref on the local host that is associated with a single file. You must define the fileref before the PROC UPLOAD statement.
fileref(member)	is used if you have defined a fileref on the local host that is associated with an aggregate storage location, such as a directory; *member* then specifies the particular file in that aggregate storage location. You must define the fileref before the PROC UPLOAD statement. Refer to the SAS documentation for your local host for more information on this use of filerefs.
'external-file-name'	is used to explicitly define the file to be uploaded.

If you use the INFILE= option, you must also use the OUTFILE= option.

MEMTYPE=(*mtype-list*)
MTYPE=(*mtype-list*)
MT=(*mtype-list*)
> specifies one or more member types to be uploaded. You can specify this option only with the INLIB= and OUTLIB= options. See "Using the MEMTYPE= Option" on page 241 for more information.

OUT=*remote-SAS-data-set*
> names the SAS data set on the remote host to which you want the uploaded data set written. If you want to create a permanent SAS data set, you must define the libref before the PROC UPLOAD statement and specify a two-level SAS data set name.
>
> The OUT= option is a valid form of the OUTLIB= option. The UPLOAD procedure determines how to interpret the meaning of the OUT= option as follows:
>
> - When you specify the DATA= option with the OUT= option, the OUT= option names the output SAS data set. For example, if the USER= SAS system option is set to WORK, the following statement uploads the A data set from the WORK library on the local host to the WORK library on the remote host:
>
>   ```
>   proc upload data=a out=a;
>   run;
>   ```
>
> - If you specify only the OUT= option, the UPLOAD procedure uploads the last SAS data set created on the local host. For example, the following statement uploads the last data set created on the local host to the JUNK data set in the WORK library on the remote host (assuming USER=WORK):
>
>   ```
>   proc upload out=junk;
>   run;
>   ```
>
> See "Default Naming Conventions for Uploaded Data Sets" on page 234 for information on the effect of omitting the OUT= option.

OUTCAT=*remote-SAS-catalog*
> names the remote host SAS catalog to which you want the uploaded catalog written. If you want to create a permanent SAS catalog, you must define the libref before the PROC UPLOAD statement and specify a two-level SAS catalog name. To upload all of the catalogs in a SAS data library, specify
>
> OUTCAT=*libref*._ALL_
>
> If you specify this form for the OUTCAT= value, you must specify the same form for the INCAT= value.
>
> If you use the OUTCAT= option, you must also use the INCAT= option.

OUTLIB=*remote-SAS-library*
OUT=*remote-SAS-library*
OUTDD=*remote-SAS-library*
> names the destination SAS data library where the uploaded data sets and catalogs from the local host are stored on your remote host. All three forms of this option are equivalent. This option must be used with the INLIB= option (in any of its forms). Before using this option, you must define the libref used for *remote-SAS-library*. Note that the OUT= form of this option is the same as the OUT= option used to specify a SAS data set. When you use this option, the UPLOAD procedure determines whether

the input option was DATA= or INLIB= and processes the uploaded objects appropriately.

The OUTLIB= option must be used with the INLIB= option, but you can use any form of the OUTLIB= option with any form of the INLIB= option. Refer to the description of the INLIB= option for examples that illustrate some valid pairs of these options.

When you specify the INLIB= option (or some other form of this option) with the OUT= option, the OUT= option specifies the name of a SAS data library. For example, the following statement uploads all of the data sets and catalogs in the A library on the local host to the WORK library on the remote host:

```
proc upload inlib=a out=work;
run;
```

OUTFILE=*remote-file-identifier*
identifies an external file on the remote host to which you want an uploaded external file written; *remote-file-identifier* can be one of the following:

fileref
is used if you have defined a fileref on the remote host that is associated with a single file. You must define the fileref before the PROC UPLOAD statement.

fileref(member)
is used if you have defined a fileref on the remote host that is associated with an aggregate storage location, such as a directory or a partitioned data set; *member* then specifies the particular file in that aggregate storage location. You must define the fileref before the PROC UPLOAD statement. Refer to the SAS documentation for your remote host for more information on this use of filerefs.

external-file-name
is used to explicitly define the file to be uploaded.

If you use the OUTFILE= option, you must also use INFILE= option.

STATUS=NO
specifies that the status window should not be displayed while the data set, catalog, library, or external file is being uploaded. By default, the UPLOAD procedure displays the Transfer Status window.

Default Naming Conventions for Uploaded Data Sets

Follow these rules for cases in which you upload a SAS data set and do not specify the name of the data set in the OUT= option:

- If the input data set (the data set specified in the DATA= option) has a two-level name and the same libref that is defined for the input data set is also defined in the remote host environment, the data set is uploaded to the library on the remote host that is associated with that libref. The data set has the same member name on the remote host. For example, suppose you submit the following statement:

```
libname orders local-host-SAS-data-library;
```

If you remote submit the following statements, the data set ORDERS.QTR1 is uploaded to ORDERS.QTR1 on the remote host.

```
/* ORDERS libref defined on both hosts */
libname orders remote-host-SAS-data-library;
proc upload data=orders.qtr1;
run;
```

- If the input data set has a two-level name but the libref for the input data set is not also defined in the remote host environment, the data set is uploaded to the library on the remote host that is defined with the USER= SAS system option (usually the WORK library). The data set retains the same data set name that it had on the local host. For example, if you remote submit the following statement, the data set is uploaded to WORK.QTR2 on the remote host.

    ```
    /* ORDERS libref defined only on the local host */
    proc upload data=orders.qtr2;
    run;
    ```

- If the input data set has a one-level name and the libref that is assigned to the USER= option on the local host also exists on the remote host, the data set is uploaded to that library. For example, suppose you submit the following statements:

    ```
    libname orders local-host-SAS-data-library;

    options user=order;
    ```

If you remote submit the following statements, the data set ORDERS.QTR1 is uploaded to ORDERS.QTR1 on the remote host.

```
/* ORDERS libref defined on both hosts */
libname orders remote-host-SAS-data-library;
libname remote remote-host-SAS-data-library;

/* this option has no effect in this case */
options user=remote;
proc upload data=qtr1;
run;
```

- If the input data set has a one-level name and the libref assigned to the USER= option on the local host does not exist on the remote host, the data set is uploaded to the library assigned to the USER= option on the remote host. That is, the USER= option on the remote host is used only if the libref for the USER= option on the local host does not exist on the remote host. For example, suppose you submit these statements:

    ```
    libname orders local-host-SAS-data-library;
    options user=orders;
    ```

When you remote submit the following statements, the data set ORDERS.QTR1 is uploaded to REMOTE.QTR1 on the remote host.

```
   /* ORDERS libref defined only on the remote host */
libname remote remote-host-SAS-data-library;
options user=remote;
proc upload data=qtr1;
run;
```

- If you omit the DATA= option, as in this example:

```
proc upload;
run;
```

the last data set created on the local host during the SAS session is uploaded to the remote host.

The naming conventions on the remote host follow one of the rules described above, depending on how the last data set created was named.

Data Set Options and Attributes for the UPLOAD Statement

PROC UPLOAD permits you to specify SAS data set options in the DATA= and OUT= options. Note that SAS data set options are not supported with the INLIB= and OUTLIB= options, even when you upload only data sets. The data set options must be associated with a specific SAS data set, so they must be used in the DATA= or OUT= options.

In addition, when you upload SAS data sets using the DATA= option (omitting the OUT= option) or the INLIB= and OUTLIB= options, or if you omit all of these options, the following characteristics are inherited by the uploaded data set.

Note: The following list of characteristics indicates the SAS data set option used to create the characteristic for the original data set. You do not have to specify the option to have it inherited when the data set is uploaded.

- password for ALTER protection (ALTER= SAS data set option).
- compressed observations (COMPRESS= SAS data set option).
- indexes (INDEX= SAS system option or other methods of creating indexes). Note that the index for an uploaded SAS data set is re-created on the remote host, not copied from the local host. To prevent the re-creation of the index, you can specify the INDEX=NO option in the PROC UPLOAD statement, as described in "PROC UPLOAD Statement Options" on page 231.
- data set label (LABEL= SAS data set option).
- password for READ protection (READ= SAS data set option).
- reuse of free space in compressed data sets (REUSE= SAS data set option).
- list of variables the data set is sorted by (SORTEDBY= SAS data set option).
- data set type (TYPE= SAS data set option).
- password for WRITE protection (WRITE= SAS data set option).

If you specify the OUT= option when uploading a single data set, only the following characteristics are inherited by the uploaded data set:

- data set type
- data set label.

The following example illustrates using the DATA= option and the INDEX=NO option. The example also shows the use of the KEEP= SAS data set option. Note that because no OUT= option is specified, the uploaded data set will inherit the characteristics of the input data set except the index (since the INDEX=NO option is specified).

```
proc upload data=idx(keep=age) index=no;
run;
```

Syntax for the WHERE Statement

WHERE *where-expression-1 <logical-operator where-expression-n>*

The UPLOAD procedure processes WHERE statements and the WHERE= data set option when you transfer a single SAS data set. WHERE statements allow multiple WHERE expressions joined by logical operators. *Logical-operator* can be AND, AND NOT, OR, or OR NOT.

You can use SAS functions in a WHERE expression. Also, note that a DATA or PROC step attempts to use an available index to optimize the selection of data when an indexed variable is used in combination with one of the following:

- CONTAINS operator
- LIKE operator
- colon modifier with a comparison operator
- TRIM function
- SUBSTR function (in some cases)

To understand when use of the SUBSTR function causes an index to be used, look at the format of the SUBSTR function in a WHERE statement:

```
where substr(variable, position, length)='character-string';
```

An index is used in processing when all of the following conditions are met:

- *position* is equal to 1
- *length* is less than or equal to the length of *variable*
- *length* is equal to the length of *character-string*

The following example illustrates using a WHERE statement with the UPLOAD procedure. The uploaded data set contains only the observations that meet the WHERE condition.

```
proc upload data=labeled out=new;
   where origin='Atlanta' and revenue < 10,000;
run;
```

For more information about the WHERE statement, refer to *SAS Language: Reference, Version 6, First Edition*.

Syntax for the EXCLUDE Statement

EXCLUDE *list*</ MEMTYPE=*mtype*| ENTRYTYPE=*etype*>;

The EXCLUDE statement enables you to exclude from uploading specific members in a SAS data library or specific entries in a SAS catalog. You cannot use both the EXCLUDE and SELECT statements in the same PROC UPLOAD step, but you can specify multiple EXCLUDE statements.

The EXCLUDE statement can have two forms. These forms are discussed in detail in the next two sections.

Members of a SAS Data Library

You can use the following form of the EXCLUDE statement with the INLIB= and OUTLIB= options in the PROC UPLOAD statement:

EXCLUDE *list*</ MEMTYPE=*mtype*>;

When you use the EXCLUDE statement to exclude members of a library from uploading, *list* specifies the members to exclude from uploading. You can explicitly name all members to exclude or use one of the following forms of name lists:

: (colon)   specifies all member names beginning with the string of characters immediately preceding the colon. For example, if you specify **TEST:**, none of the members beginning with the letters **TEST** are uploaded.

- (hyphen) specifies all member names falling lexigraphically between the names on either side of the hyphen. You can use this wild-card character only between two names that begin with the same string of characters and end in a number, for example, **TEST1-TEST5**.

For information on using the MEMTYPE= option, see "Using the MEMTYPE= Option" on page 241.

Entries in a SAS Catalog

You can use the following form of the EXCLUDE statement with the INCAT= and OUTCAT= options in the PROC UPLOAD statement:

EXCLUDE *list*</ ENTRYTYPE=*etype*>;

When you use the EXCLUDE statement to exclude catalog entries from uploading, each element of *list* has the form *entry.type*. In this form,

entry   is the name of an entry in *member* to exclude from uploading.

.type   is the type of the catalog entry. This part of the name is optional.

The ENTRYTYPE= option in the EXCLUDE statement works like the ENTRYTYPE= option in the PROC UPLOAD statement. For a complete list of entry types and for detailed information on how to use the ENTRYTYPE= option, see "Using the ENTRYTYPE= Option" on page 242.

Syntax for the SELECT Statement

SELECT *list*</ MEMTYPE=*mtype*| ENTRYTYPE=*etype*>;

The SELECT statement enables you to select for uploading specific members in a SAS data library or specific entries in a SAS catalog. You cannot use both the EXCLUDE and SELECT statements in the same PROC UPLOAD step, but you can specify multiple SELECT statements.

The SELECT statement can have two forms. These forms are discussed in detail in the next two sections.

Members of a SAS Data Library

You can use the following form of the SELECT statement with the INLIB= and OUTLIB= options in the PROC UPLOAD statement:

SELECT *list*</ MEMTYPE=*mtype*>;

When you use the SELECT statement to select members of a library for uploading, *list* specifies the members to select for uploading. You can explicitly name all members to select or use one of the following forms of name lists:

: (colon)   specifies all member names beginning with the string of characters immediately preceding the colon. For example, if you specify **TEST:**, all of the selected members begin with the letters **TEST**.

- (hyphen)   specifies all member names falling lexigraphically between the names on either side of the hyphen. You can use this wild-card character only between two names that begin with the same string of characters and end in a number, for example, **TEST1-TEST5**.

For information on using the MEMTYPE= option, see "Using the MEMTYPE= Option" on page 241.

Entries in a SAS Catalog

You can use the following form of the SELECT statement with the INCAT= and OUTCAT= options in the PROC UPLOAD statement:

SELECT *list*</ ENTRYTYPE=*etype*>;

When you use the SELECT statement to select catalog entries for uploading, each element of *list* has the form *entry.type*. In this form,

entry is the name of an entry in *member* to select for uploading.

.type is the type of the catalog entry. This part of the name is optional.

The ENTRYTYPE= option in the SELECT statement works like the ENTRYTYPE= option in the PROC UPLOAD statement. For a complete list of entry types and for detailed information on how to use the ENTRYTYPE= option, see "Using the ENTRYTYPE= Option" on page 242.

Note: The SELECT statement also enables you to maintain an ordering and grouping of catalog entries containing graphics output because entries are uploaded into the remote SAS catalog in the order that you specify in the SELECT statement. See "Ways to Use SAS/CONNECT Software" on page 17 for an example that illustrates how to use the SELECT statement to maintain the order and grouping of catalog entries containing graphics output.

Syntax for the TRANTAB Statement

TRANTAB NAME=*translation-table-name*
        <TYPE=(*etype-list*)>
        <OPT=DISP SRC (DISP SRC)>;

The TRANTAB statement enables you to specify translation tables to use for translating characters in catalog entries you want to upload. The TRANTAB statement also enables you to specify the particular types of SAS/AF or SCL catalog entries to which you want to apply a translation. You can specify one translation table per statement, but there is no limit to the number of TRANTAB statements you can use in one invocation of the UPLOAD procedure. If you specify the TRANTAB statement, you must also specify the INCAT= and OUTCAT= options in the PROC UPLOAD statement.

Requirements for the TRANTAB Statement

A TRANTAB statement must include the following argument:

NAME=*translation-table-name*
    specifies the name of the translation table to apply to the SAS catalog you want to upload. The *translation-table-name* you specify is the name of a catalog entry in either your SASUSER.PROFILE catalog or the SASHELP.HOST catalog. The UPLOAD procedure searches the SASUSER.PROFILE catalog first, and the SASHELP.HOST catalog second.
        See "TRANTAB= System Option" on page 186 for more information about translation tables.
        By default, whenever you invoke PROC UPLOAD, the procedure uses the table that translates host-to-transport format. In most cases, the default translation table is the correct one to use, but you may need to apply additional translation tables if, for example, your application requires different national language characters.

You can specify a translation table other than the default in two ways:

- To specify a translation table for an invocation of PROC UPLOAD, use the TRANTAB statement in the UPLOAD procedure.

- To specify a translation table for your entire SAS session or job (including all file transfers you do), use the TRANTAB= system option. You use this system option to define which default translation tables to use in place of those supplied by SAS Institute. See "TRANTAB= System Option" on page 186 for a discussion of the TRANTAB= SAS system option.

See SAS Technical Report P-197, *The TRANTAB Procedure, Release 6.06* and Chapter 39, "The TRANTAB Procedure," of SAS Technical Report P-222 for information on creating translation tables with PROC TRANTAB.

Options for the TRANTAB Statement

You can use the following options in the TRANTAB statement:

TYPE=(*etype-list*)
> specifies that the UPLOAD procedure apply the translation table to only the entries with the type or types you specify. Note that *etype-list* can be one or more entry types. If *etype-list* is a simple entry type, omit the parentheses.
> See Table 16.1 on page 243 for a list of entry types valid for the UPLOAD procedure. By default, the UPLOAD procedure applies the translation table to all of the entries in the catalog you specify.

OPT=DISP SRC (DISP SRC)
> specifies one of the following:

- when OPT=DISP, the UPLOAD procedure applies the translation table only to those entries of the catalog you specified that produce window displays.

- when OPT=SRC, the UPLOAD procedure applies the translation table only to those entries of the catalog you specified of the type SOURCE.

- when OPT=(DISP SRC), the UPLOAD procedure applies the translation table only to those entries of the catalog you specified that either produce window displays or have a type of SOURCE.

When you do not specify the OPT= option, the UPLOAD procedure applies the translation table to all of the entries in the catalog you specify.

Using the MEMTYPE= Option

If you specify the INLIB= and OUTLIB= options in the PROC UPLOAD statement, you can use the MEMTYPE= option to indicate what member types to upload. You can specify the MEMTYPE= option in the following places:

- in the PROC UPLOAD statement.

□ in the SELECT or EXCLUDE statement in parentheses immediately after a member name. If the type is enclosed in parentheses, it refers only to the member name immediately preceding the option.

□ in the SELECT or EXCLUDE statement after a slash (/) at the end of the statement. When used following a slash, the MEMTYPE= option refers to all members named in the statement unless the same option appears in parentheses after a name.

Valid values of the MEMTYPE= option are DATA, CATALOG (or CAT), and ALL. If you use this option in the SELECT and EXCLUDE statements, you can specify only one value. If you use this option in the PROC UPLOAD statement, you can specify a list of values enclosed in parentheses, as shown here:

```
proc upload inlib=this outlib=that memtype=(data catalog);
```

You can use the MEMTYPE= option in multiple places. When you do so, the UPLOAD procedure determines the type of each member as described below:

1. By the value of the option in parentheses immediately following the member name, if present

2. Otherwise, by the value of the option after the slash in the SELECT or EXCLUDE statement, if present

3. Otherwise, by the value of the option in the PROC UPLOAD statement, if present

4. If you do not specify a member type, the UPLOAD procedure uses the default type, ALL.

See "Purpose" on page 42 for examples that illustrate the use of the MEMTYPE= option.

Using the ENTRYTYPE= Option

This section describes the rules for specifying entry types and lists the valid entry types. See "Purpose" on page 43 for examples of using the ENTRYTYPE= option.

Rules for Specifying Entry Types

When you specify the INCAT= and OUTCAT= options in the PROC UPLOAD statement, use the ENTRYTYPE= option in the PROC UPLOAD statement, the SELECT statement, or the EXCLUDE statement to specify which entry types to upload. The ENTRYTYPE= option is required only if you use a SELECT or EXCLUDE statement. If you omit the entry type and also omit the SELECT and EXCLUDE statements, all catalog entries are uploaded. You can specify a single entry type in any of the following places:

□ in the PROC UPLOAD statement, specify the ENTRYTYPE= option.

□ in the SELECT or EXCLUDE statement, specify the ENTRYTYPE= option in parentheses immediately after an entry name. If the type is enclosed in parentheses, it refers only to the entry name immediately preceding the option.

□ in the SELECT or EXCLUDE statement, specify the ENTRYTYPE= option after a slash (/) at the end of the statement. When used following a slash, the ENTRYTYPE=

option refers to all entries named in the statement unless the same option appears in parentheses after an entry name.

- in the SELECT or EXCLUDE statement, specify the entry type as part of the entry name. For example, you can specify TEST.MENU in the list of entries.

You can use the ENTRYTYPE= option in multiple places. When you do so, the UPLOAD procedure determines the type of each entry as described below:

1. by the entry type given as part of the entry name, such as XYZ.FORMAT
2. by the value of the option in parentheses immediately following the entry name, if present
3. otherwise, by the value of the option after the slash in the SELECT or EXCLUDE statement, if present
4. otherwise, by the value of the option in the PROC UPLOAD statement, if present.
   Note: If you use the ENTRYTYPE= option in both the PROC UPLOAD statement and a SELECT or EXCLUDE statement, the values must be the same. In most cases, if you are using the ENTRYTYPE= option in a SELECT or EXCLUDE statement, you should omit it from the PROC UPLOAD statement.

Valid Entry Types

Table 16.1 indicates the entry types that can be uploaded between the different releases of the SAS System.
Note: For releases after Release 6.08, the following message is displayed if you try to upload an entry that is not compatible with an earlier release:

```
ERROR: Catalog upload to earlier version not allowed.
       Backward compatibility not supported.
```

Table 16.1 Catalog Entries That Can Be Uploaded

To This Remote Host	From This Local Host			
	Release 6.08	Release 6.07 (except UNIX)	Release 6.06, and UNIX Release 6.07	Release 6.04
Release 6.08	List A	List C	List D	List F
Release 6.07 (except UNIX)	List B	List C	List D	List F
Release 6.06 and UNIX, Release 6.07	List E	List E	List D	List F
Release 5.18	none	none	none	none

List A

AFCBT	EDPARMS	GRSEG	MENU	RESOURCE
AFGO	EIS	HELP	MODEL	SCL
AFMACRO	FILEFMT	INFMT	OUTPUT	SCREEN
CALC	FONT	INFMTC	PARMS	SLIST
CBT	FORM	KEYMAP	PGM	SOURCE
CLASS	FORMAT	KEYS	PMENU	TEMPLATE
CMAP	FORMATC	LETTER	PROGRAM	TRANTAB
DEV	FORMULA	LIST	RANGE	
DEVMAP	FRAME	LOG	REPORT	

List B

AFCBT	DEVMAP	HELP	LOG	PROGRAM
AFGO	EDPARMS	INFMT	MENU	SCL
AFMACRO	FONT	INFMTC	MODEL	SCREEN
CALC	FORM	KEYMAP	OUTPUT	SLIST
CBT	FORMAT	KEYS	PARMS	SOURCE
CMAP	FORMATC	LETTER	PGM	TEMPLATE
DEV	GRSEG	LIST	PMENU	TRANTAB

List C

AFCBT	EDPARMS	INFMT	MODEL	SCREEN
AFGO	FONT	INFMTC	OUTPUT	SLIST
AFMACRO	FORM	KEYMAP	PARMS	SOURCE
CALC	FORMAT	KEYS	PGM	TEMPLATE
CBT	FORMATC	LETTER	PMENU	TRANTAB
CMAP	FORMULA	LIST	PROGRAM	
DEV	GRSEG	LOG	REPORT	
DEVMAP	HELP	MENU	SCL	

List D

AFCBT	EDPARMS	GRSEG	LIST	SCREEN
AFGO	FONT	HELP	LOG	SOURCE
AFMACRO	FORM	INFMT	MENU	TEMPLATE
CBT	FORMAT	INFMTC	OUTPUT	TRANTAB
CMAP	FORMATC	KEYS	PMENU	
DEV	FORMULA	LETTER	PROGRAM	

List E

AFCBT	CMAP	KEYS	MENU
AFGO	EDPARMS	LETTER	SOURCE
AFMACRO	FORM	LIST	TEMPLATE
CBT	HELP	LOG	TRANTAB

List F

AFCBT	CBT	FORM	LIST
AFGO	DEV	HELP	MENU
AFMACRO	EDPARMS	LETTER	PROGRAM

Compiling PROGRAM Entries

If you upload a catalog that contains entries of type PROGRAM, you must compile the entries on the remote host before execution. To compile all the PROGRAM entries in a catalog, remote submit the following statements to the SAS System:

```
proc build cat=libref.member-name  batch;
    compile;
run;
```

where *libref* identifies the SAS data library containing the catalog and *member-name* identifies the catalog. Refer to *SAS/AF Software: Usage and Reference, Version 6, First Edition* for more information on compiling PROGRAM entries.

Transfer Status Windows

The transfer status window displays information describing the status of the uploading process. The window's display changes as the upload proceeds. The information on the display includes

- the type of file being uploaded (SAS data set, SAS catalog, catalog entry containing graphics output, or external file).

- the name of the SAS data set, SAS catalog, or external file being uploaded. SAS data set names are displayed in the form *libref.SAS-data-set*. SAS catalogs are displayed in the form *libref.SAS-catalog*. External file names are displayed with the complete filename.

- the number of the byte being uploaded (updated as each new buffer is sent).

- the number of the observation being uploaded (for SAS data sets only).

- the time elapsed since the beginning of the transfer, in *hh:mm:ss* form.

- the percentage of the file already uploaded.

- an estimate of the amount of time required to complete the upload, in *hh:mm:ss* form.

- a horizontal bar chart depicting the percentage of the file already uploaded.

Note: For some types of files, the percentage completed, estimated time to completion, and the bar chart are not always available. Some operating systems cannot efficiently provide the size of the file, which is necessary to calculate these estimates. In other cases, the information provided by the operating system results in estimates that are greater than the actual time needed for the transfer. Thus, the percentage completed, estimated time to completion and bar chart may show exaggerated estimates, but they will show 100% when the transfer is completed.

Display 16.1 is a sample of the transfer status window during a SAS data set upload. The SAS data set name is PS2DIR.MOVER.

Display 16.1
Transfer Status Window for Uploading a SAS Data Set

```
                              UPLOAD
    The SAS data set PS2DIR.MOVER is being uploaded

    Currently transferring byte #      11280 observation #    471
    Elapsed time   0:00:06
    47.1 % of transfer completed
    Estimated time to completion       0:00:07
    0% ***********************                              100%
```

Display 16.2 is a sample of the transfer status window during an external text file upload. The OS/2 pathname is C:\ PMCAP\ TEST.

Display 16.2
Transfer Status Window for Uploading an External File

```
                            TEXT UPLOAD
    The file c:\pmcap\test is being uploaded

    Currently transferring byte #      68972
    Elapsed time   0:00:36
    37.9 % of transfer completed
    Estimated time to completion       0:00:59
    0% *****************                                    100%
```

The BINARY Option

Normally, SAS/CONNECT assumes that external files being uploaded are text files and alters them so that they can be used on the target machine. Two features are affected.

- Each operating system has its own type of record delimiters in external files. The record delimiters are incompatible between operating systems. Therefore, record delimiters appropriate to the target system are added to the copied file by the UPLOAD procedure.

- CMS, MVS, and VSE hosts use the EBCDIC character set; other operating systems use an ASCII character set. Consequently, if files are uploaded from an ASCII-based system to CMS, MVS, or VSE without character translations, the uploaded files cannot be interpreted by the target system.
  SAS/CONNECT solves the EBCDIC/ASCII problem by converting files automatically. The UPLOAD procedure converts text to the format of the remote host.

There are times when these file conversions are not desirable. For example, you may need to upload executable files from the local host to the remote host and later download them to the same or a different local host. You may want to do this for backup purposes or to send files to other users. In cases where you do not want a file translated to another character set or record delimiters inserted, you can use the BINARY option to prevent automatic conversion. When you specify the BINARY option in a PROC UPLOAD statement, SAS/CONNECT transfers the file in *binary* image form (hence, the keyword BINARY).

Example of the BINARY Option

Here is an example of a PROC UPLOAD statement for uploading an external file to the remote host. Note that the BINARY option is included to suppress character-set translation and to prevent record-delimiter insertion:

```
proc upload infile='external-file-name' outfile=hostmod binary;

run;
```

This PROC UPLOAD step is excerpted from "Example 17. Data Transfer Services: Distributing a .EXE File from the Remote Host to Multiple Local Hosts" on page 45.

The next example is a PROC UPLOAD statement for uploading a local SAS data set to the remote host:

```
proc upload data=pcnote.usage out=hostnote.usage;
run;
```

This PROC UPLOAD step is excerpted from "Example 19. Data Transfer Services: Downloading a Partitioned Data Set from an MVS Host" on page 47.

PROC UPLOAD Output

The UPLOAD procedure writes a series of informative messages to the SAS log when it executes. Examples of these messages are shown in Output 16.1.

Output 16.1
SAS Log Messages from the UPLOAD Procedure

```
NOTE: Remote submit to B commencing.

1    proc upload infile='local-external-file'
2        outfile='remote-external-file';run;

NOTE: TEXT upload in progress from infile=local-external-file to
      outfile=remote-external-file
NOTE: Uploaded 4 records and 136 bytes.
NOTE: 4 records were read from the file local-external-file
      The maximum record length was 65.
      The minimum record length was 0.
NOTE: 136 bytes were transferred at 68 bytes/second.
NOTE: The PROCEDURE UPLOAD used 0.04 CPU seconds and 1431K.

NOTE: Remote submit to B complete.
$
```

Defining Librefs and Filerefs

As is true in all SAS programming, permanent SAS data sets, SAS catalogs, and external files must be defined correctly in order to be accessed. Defining a file means that you associate a shorthand, symbolic name with a file. The method you use to define a file depends on the operating system and whether it is a SAS file or an external file.

- Librefs for permanent SAS data libraries are defined with the LIBNAME statement.
- Filerefs for external files are defined with the FILENAME statement.

If you do not know how to use the LIBNAME and FILENAME statements, refer to Chapter 9, "SAS Language Statements," in *SAS Language: Reference, Version 6, First Edition*.

There are some special considerations to be aware of when you define files to use with the DOWNLOAD and UPLOAD procedures.

- Statements defining librefs and filerefs for files on the local host must be executed in the local SAS session with the SUBMIT command. They cannot be executed with the PROC DOWNLOAD or PROC UPLOAD steps with an RSUBMIT command or statement.
- Statements defining librefs or filerefs for files on the remote host must be executed on the remote host with the RSUBMIT command or statement. Therefore, these statements can be executed along with the PROC DOWNLOAD or PROC UPLOAD step, as long as they precede the PROC statement.

Non-English Keyboards

If you use a local host with a non-English keyboard, you probably have some external files with non-English characters in them. If your remote host is CMS or TSO, some specially accented characters may be translated incorrectly using the DOWNLOAD and UPLOAD procedures. This occurs because of the default translations from ASCII to EBCDIC and from EBCDIC to ASCII. To solve the problem, you can do one of the following:

- If SAS/CONNECT is used frequently, you should use an alternate EBCDIC/ASCII translation table on the remote host. The SAS Software Representative for the remote host should create the alternate table. See "Details for Micro-to-Host Link Releases" on page 289.
- If SAS/CONNECT is not used frequently, you can manage problematic characters by assigning the correct hex values through DATA step programming statements after the file is copied. For example, suppose you have a German keyboard and a CMS host. You want a file to contain umlaut-A characters after an upload. By default, the ASCII representation of umlaut-A, which is X'84', is translated to EBCDIC X'24'. However, the EBCDIC representation of umlaut-A is X'C0', so you need to translate EBCDIC X'24' to EBCDIC X'C0'. The following DATA step performs this translation, where NAME is a variable containing umlaut-A characters:

```
data new;
   set old;
   retain to 'C0'x from '24'x;
```

```
        drop to from;
        name=translate(name,to,from);
run;
```

General Tips for UPLOAD

- You cannot upload a SAS data set to an external file or an external file to a SAS data set.

- If you upload to a remote host file that is defined with a fixed (F) record format, all records in the file are padded with blanks to the logical record length.

- Remember that the UPLOAD procedure executes on the remote host SAS System. You must use the RSUBMIT command, not the SUBMIT command, to execute the PROC UPLOAD step.

- The rate at which files are transferred varies depending upon the size and number of files being transferred and the processing load on the remote host. The transfer status window keeps you informed of the progress of the transfer. See "Transfer Status Windows" on page 245 for more information.

- If PROC UPLOAD successfully completes the file transfer, the macro variable SYSINFO is set to 0. If the file transfer is not successfully completed, the SYSINFO macro variable is set to a value greater than 0. You can pass the value of the SYSINFO macro variable back to the local host by using the %SYSRPUT statement. See "%SYSRPUT Statement" on page 200 for detailed information on the %SYSRPUT statement.

- To upload a text file with a record length greater than 132 bytes, the LRECL option must be specified in both the local and remote FILENAME statements.

Chapter 17 Script Statements

Introduction 251
Summary of Script Statements 251

Statement Descriptions 253
 ASCII Control Character Mnemonics 272
 ASYNC TYPE Statement Examples 274
 3270 Key Mnemonics 274
 3270 TYPE Statement Example 274

Introduction

This chapter begins with a table showing the name, purpose, and other summary information for each script statement. The table is a quick reference tool to help you identify the script statements you need to read about. The rest of the chapter consists of an alphabetical list of all script statements and their complete descriptions.

For examples of scripts that use these statements, see "Starting and Stopping SAS/CONNECT Software" on page 61.

Summary of Script Statements

Table 17.1 can help you decide which statements you need to use in your script. The table provides the following information:

- Statement is the statement name.
- Purpose is a brief description of the statement.
- Connection Type indicates the type of connection the statement applies to: TCP, TELNET, 3270, or ASYNC.
- Frequent or Infrequent indicates which statements are frequently used in scripts and which statements are infrequently used.

Table 17.1 Summary of Script Statements

Statement	Purpose	Connection Type	Frequent (F) or Infrequent (I)
ABORT	stops execution of a script; signals an error condition	all	F
BAUD	sets the baud rate	ASYNC	F
BREAK	sets the duration of the break signal for ASCII transmission	ASYNC	I
CALL	invokes a routine	all	F

(continued)

Table 17.1 (continued)

Statement	Purpose	Connection Type	Frequent (F) or Infrequent (I)
CHARWAIT	specifies the time to wait for a prompt or for packet characters from the remote host	ASYNC	I
DATABITS	sets the number of bits per character transmitted by the ASYNC port	ASYNC	F
DELAY	specifies the time to pause between characters being sent to the remote host	ASYNC, 3270	I
ECHO	controls display of characters sent from the remote host while a WAITFOR statement executes	ASYNC, TELNET, TCP	I
EOPCHAR	specifies an end-of-packet character	ASYNC, TELNET	I
GOTO	jumps execution to the specified script statement	all	F
HANDSHAKING	specifies the handshaking method between the remote host and the local host	ASYNC	F
IF	checks conditions before execution of labeled script statements	all	F
INPUT	displays a prompt to the user that requests a response for the remote system	all	F
LINEWAIT	specifies the time to wait after a prompt or after the last character in a packet from the remote host	ASYNC, TELNET, 3270	I
LOG	sends a message to the local host SAS LOG window	all	F
MAXI	specifies the maximum packet length going from the local host to the remote host (inbound packet)	ASYNC, TELNET	I
MAXO	specifies the maximum packet length going from the remote host to the local host (outbound packet)	ASYNC, TELNET	I
MODEL	specifies the IBM 3270 model being emulated	3270	I
MSG	controls remote host messages while the link is active	all	I
NOTIFY	sends a message in a window to the local SAS session	all	F
PARITY	sets the parity	ASYNC	F

(continued)

Table 17.1 (continued)

Statement	Purpose	Connection Type	Frequent (F) or Infrequent (I)
PROMPT	overrides the default prompt the local host receives before sending a packet	ASYNC	I
RETRY	specifies the number of attempts to resend a packet when an error occurs	all	I
RETURN	signals the end of a routine	all	F
SCANFOR	is an alias for WAITFOR	all	I
SNAPSHOT	copies the contents of the remote host session screen to the local SAS LOG window	3270	F
SOPCHAR	changes the start-of-packet character	ASYNC, TELNET, 3270	I
STOP	stops script execution normally	all	F
STOPBITS	specifies the number of stop bits	ASYNC	F
TIMEOUT	sets the time the local host waits for a packet from the remote host before resending the last local host packet	ASYNC, TELNET	F
TRACE	displays script statements as they execute	all	F
TYPE	sends characters to the remote host as if they were typed at a terminal	all	F
WAITFOR	specifies a pause until conditions are met	all	F
XCLOCK	specifies time to wait for the status line X-clock after typing an AID key	3270	I
XTIME	specifies time to wait after the status line X-clock disappears	3270	I

Statement Descriptions

The statements that can be used in writing scripts are described alphabetically in the following sections. The heading for each script statement contains the following information:

- the purpose of the script statement
- the type of connection you can use with the script statement.

ABORT

Stops execution of a script; signals an error condition

All connections

Syntax

ABORT;

Description

The ABORT statement immediately stops execution of a script and terminates the SIGNON or SIGNOFF function. ABORT prevents other script statements from executing when the communication link has not been established successfully. The ABORT statement is intended to signal an error condition; therefore, an error message is issued and displayed in the SAS LOG window when the ABORT statement executes. To terminate script execution under normal conditions, use the STOP statement.

BAUD

Sets the baud rate

ASYNC

Syntax

BAUD *baud-rate*;

Description

The BAUD statement sets the baud rate. Baud rate is a measure of data transmission speed. It is one of five communications parameters that must be set in order to use SAS/CONNECT over an asynchronous connection. The other parameters are data bits, handshaking, parity, and stop bits. For the DATABITS, PARITY, and STOPBITS script statements to take effect, you must first set the baud rate with the BAUD statement.

The value for *baud-rate* can be 110, 150, 300, 600, 1200, 2400, 4800, 9600, or 19200. There is no default value for *baud-rate*.

BREAK

Sets the duration of the break signal for ASCII transmission

ASYNC

Syntax

BREAK *n* SECONDS;

Description

The BREAK statement specifies the duration of an asynchronous break signal sent over the link by a TYPE script statement. (The TYPE statement can send a break signal by specifying the mnemonic BREAK.)

The number *n* is the duration of the signal in seconds. The default is 0.220 seconds. SECOND can be used instead of SECONDS.

CALL

Invokes a routine

All connections

Release 6.06 and later

Syntax

CALL *label*;

Description

The CALL statement causes the statements following *label* to be executed until a RETURN statement is encountered. When a RETURN statement is reached, script processing resumes at the statement following the CALL statement.

CHARWAIT

Specifies the time to wait for a prompt or for packet characters from the remote host

ASYNC

Syntax

CHARWAIT *n* SECONDS;

Description

The CHARWAIT statement specifies the number of seconds that the local host waits for either of the following:

- successive characters in a packet the remote host has begun to transmit. CHARWAIT does not specify a time to wait for a new packet from the remote host, but how long to wait for more characters in the current packet.

- a prompt from the remote host, where the prompt is either the default prompt or a character specified by the PROMPT script statement. This use is seldom needed. You do not need to specify the PROMPT statement unless the remote system's prompt has been modified from the standard prompt.

The number *n* specifies the seconds the local host is to wait. When the value of *n* is 0, the local host waits indefinitely for the prompt or packet characters. The default value is 0 for successive packet characters and 5 for the prompt. SECOND can be used instead of SECONDS.

When a prompt or packet characters are not received within the seconds specified, a timeout occurs.

- If the local host is waiting for packet characters, a timeout causes SAS/CONNECT to resend the last packet sent by the local host.

- If the local host is waiting for a prompt character, a timeout simply resumes execution.

Note: If you specify the wrong prompt character for the remote host with the PROMPT statement, the CHARWAIT time causes frequent delays because the local host waits for the wrong character.

DATABITS

Sets the number of bits per character transmitted by the ASYNC port

ASYNC

Syntax

DATABITS *data-bits*;

Description

The DATABITS statement sets the number of bits per character transmitted by the ASYNC port. Data bits is one of five communications parameters that must be set in order to use SAS/CONNECT over an asynchronous connection. The other parameters are baud, handshaking, parity, and stop bits. The DATABITS, PARITY, and STOPBITS script statements do not take effect unless you set the baud rate with the BAUD statement.

The value of *data-bits* can be 7 or 8. The value should be 7 if the PARITY statement is set to EVEN, ODD, SPACE, or MARK. If parity is set to NONE, the *data-bits* value should be 8.

DELAY

Specifies the time to pause between characters being sent to the remote host

ASYNC, 3270

Syntax

DELAY *n* SECONDS;

Description

The DELAY statement's purpose is somewhat different for ASYNC and 3270 connections. For ASYNC connections, the DELAY statement specifies the number of seconds to delay between characters being sent from the local host to the remote host. For 3270 connections, the DELAY statement specifies the delay between characters being sent from the local host to the remote host by the TYPE script statement. The DELAY statement is especially useful for correcting inhibited input problems with slow 3270 controllers.

The number *n* specifies the seconds to delay. For ASYNC connections, the default value is 0; that is, normally there is no delay. For 3270 connections, the default value is .1. SECOND can be used instead of SECONDS.

ASYNC connections do not normally need a delay; therefore, the default value of 0 is usually appropriate. However, if the connection to the remote host involves a modem or intermediate hardware such as data switches or protocol converters, a delay may be needed during the sign-on process. In this case, you should set a delay time in the script, but be sure to reset DELAY to 0 after the remote host connection is made. Otherwise, all transmissions to the remote host throughout your session are unnecessarily delayed.

ECHO

Controls display of characters sent from the remote host while a WAITFOR statement executes

ASYNC, TELNET, TCP

Syntax

ECHO ON | OFF;

Description

The ECHO statement determines whether or not characters sent by the remote host are displayed while a WAITFOR statement executes. The ECHO statement is useful when you are debugging a script.

When you specify ON, the characters are displayed. The default setting is OFF.

EOPCHAR

Specifies an end-of-packet character

ASYNC, TELNET

Syntax

EOPCHAR *character*;

Description

The EOPCHAR statement specifies the end-of-packet character for packets going from the local host to the remote host. This statement is used only for asynchronous connections that do not terminate input with a carriage return character (CR). This statement is seldom needed.

The value of *character* is the ASCII character used by the remote host to detect the end of a terminal input message. You can specify *character* in one of the following forms:

- a literal character enclosed in quotes, such as '?'
- a hex constant enclosed in quotes, such as '0D'X'
- an ASCII mnemonic, such as CR.*

---

* See the information on ASCII control character mnemonics in the description of the TYPE script statement later in this chapter.

The default is CR (carriage return).

The end-of-packet character cannot be an alphanumeric character, a period (.), a slash (/), or the same character used for the start-of-packet character.

GOTO

Jumps execution to the specified script statement

All connections

Syntax

GOTO *label*;

Description

The GOTO statement causes script execution to jump to the specified script statement. The GOTO statement can also be written as GO TO.

The value of *label* is the label of a statement elsewhere in the script.

HANDSHAKING

Specifies the handshaking method between the remote host and the local host

ASYNC

Syntax

HANDSHAKING *method*;

Description

The HANDSHAKING statement specifies the handshaking method (protocol) between your local host and the remote host. Handshaking is an exchange of predetermined signals transmitted between the remote host and the local host, and it is one of five communications parameters that are set before using SAS/CONNECT over an asynchronous connection. The other parameters are baud, data bits, parity, and stop bits. Unlike the other communications parameters, the handshaking method is not required.

The value of *method* can be one of the following:

NONE	specifies no handshaking method. This is the default value.
HARDWARE	specifies a flow control, or pacing, method called CTS/RTS (Clear to Send/Request to Send).
SOFTWARE	specifies a flow control method that uses the ASCII characters XON and XOFF for transmit on and transmit off, respectively.

IF

Checks conditions before execution of labeled script statements

All connections

Syntax

IF *condition* **GOTO** *label*;
IF NOT *condition* **GOTO** *label*;

Description

The IF statement conditionally jumps to another statement in the script. The IF statement can check two conditions: connection type and whether the script has been called by the SIGNON command or the SIGNOFF command.

If the statement is testing for sign on or sign off, *condition* should be one of the following:

SIGNON   specifies that the SIGNON command invoked this script.

SIGNOFF   specifies that the SIGNOFF command invoked this script.

If the statement is testing for connection type, *condition* should be either FULLSCREEN or one of the values for the COMAMID= system option.

The value FULLSCREEN can be used to detect any full-screen 3270 connection. The remaining values correspond to values for the COMAMID= system option. For more information on COMAMID= values for emulation software, see the description of the COMAMID= option in "System Options, Statements, Commands, and SCL Functions" on page 173.

The value of *label* must be a reference to a labeled statement in the script. For example, in the following IF statement, ENDIT is a label followed by one or more statements that terminate the link when the user has issued a SIGNOFF command:

```
if signoff then goto endit;
```

INPUT

Displays a prompt to the user that requests a response for the remote system

All connections

Syntax

INPUT *'prompt'*;

Description

The INPUT statement specifies a character string that is displayed to the user when the script executes. The specified string should be a prompt requesting a response from the user, and the user must respond by at least pressing ENTER or RETURN before script execution can continue. For example, in automatic logon scripts, the INPUT statement is used to issue prompts to the user for the userid and password needed to log on to the remote host.

The value of *prompt* is a character string and must be enclosed in quotes.

The INPUT statement does not automatically transmit a carriage return or ENTER key. Therefore, when writing a script, you must follow an INPUT statement with a TYPE statement if you want to transmit a carriage return or ENTER key to the remote session.

LINEWAIT

Specifies the time to wait after a prompt or after the last character in a packet from the remote host

ASYNC, TELNET, 3270

Syntax

LINEWAIT *n* SECONDS;

Description

The LINEWAIT statement specifies the number of seconds that the local host waits after receiving a prompt from the remote host or the last character in a packet from the remote host. If the LINEWAIT time is too short, information sent by the remote host can be lost.

The number *n* specifies the seconds to wait. The default value is .25. After the LINEWAIT time elapses, normal execution resumes. SECOND can be used instead of SECONDS.

Do not confuse the LINEWAIT statement with the CHARWAIT statement. CHARWAIT specifies how long the local host waits for a prompt from the remote host or for successive characters in a packet from the remote host. LINEWAIT specifies how long the local host waits after receiving a prompt or complete packet.

LOG

Sends a message to the local host SAS log

All connections

Syntax

LOG *'message'*;

Description

The LOG statement specifies a message to be written to the SAS log. You can use this statement to issue informative notes or error messages to the user as the script executes.

The value of *message* is a text string that must be enclosed in quotes. For example, the sample scripts from SAS Institute use the following LOG statement to inform users that the SIGNOFF completed successfully:

```
log 'NOTE: SAS/CONNECT conversation terminated.';
```

MAXI

Specifies the maximum packet length from the local host to the remote host

ASYNC, TELNET

Syntax

MAXI *bytes*;

Description

The MAXI statement specifies the maximum packet length for data sent from the local host to the remote host (an inbound packet). The value of *bytes* can be an integer from 72 through 4100. The default value is 512.

This statement is typically used in conjunction with the MAXO statement. The MAXI and MAXO statements can be used to restrict packet lengths when the length of the packet is limited by the hardware connections or maximum message sizes.

You can also indirectly control the transmission time between the local host and the remote host with the MAXI and MAXO statements. For example, suppose you specify 600 bytes for both the MAXI and MAXO statements and the baud rate is 1200. With 600-byte packets at 1200 baud, it takes about 6 seconds to transmit one packet between the local host and the remote host. If you specify a packet length less than 600 in the MAXI and MAXO statements, the packets are smaller and more of them are necessary to send the same data, but the transmission time for each packet is less. However, the total time may increase because of the overhead required to process the extra packets.

You may want to change the default value to smaller values when there is interference in the communication line. The advantage is that fewer errors can occur with smaller data packets, which means fewer repeat transmissions are needed.

MAXO

Specifies the maximum packet length from the remote host to the local host

ASYNC, TELNET

Syntax

MAXO *bytes*;

Description

The MAXO statement specifies the maximum packet length for data sent from the remote host to the local host (outbound packet). Typically, this statement is used in conjunction with the MAXI statement.

The value of *bytes* can be an integer from 72 through 4100. The default value is 512. You can restrict packet lengths or indirectly control the transmission time between the local host and the remote host with the MAXI and MAXO statements, as described in the previous section.

MODEL

Specifies the IBM 3270 model being emulated

3270

Syntax

MODEL *n*;

Description

The MODEL statement is usually unnecessary and is ignored when not needed. You may need to specify it with an older version of IRMA software if SAS/CONNECT cannot detect the appropriate number of the 3270 model that you are emulating.

The value of *n* is the number of the 3270 model to be emulated. The model number can be 2, 3, 4, or 5. The default model number is 2.

MSG

Controls the remote host messages while the link is active

All connections

Syntax

MSG ON | OFF;

Description

The MSG statement determines whether or not remote host messages from the operator or other users are ignored while SAS/CONNECT is in effect. The value ON specifies that messages will be detected, and OFF means messages are ignored. The default value is ON; this value is recommended.

The effect of the MSG statement is somewhat different for ASYNC and 3270 connections. When MSG is set to ON

- with ASYNC connections, any character string that is 80 bytes or that ends with a carriage return is displayed in the SAS LOG window. This includes any stray, noncontrol characters, as well as operator messages. (Display of remote host operator messages does not automatically cause the BREAK window to appear. The user must issue a break signal before responding to messages from the remote host.)

- with 3270 connections, any remote host messages cause the BREAK window to appear. You can switch to the remote host display to view the message.

When MSG is set to OFF

- with ASYNC connections, all characters and messages between packets are discarded

- with 3270 connections, any messages are discarded, the Break window is suppressed, and the link attempts to recover automatically.

NOTIFY

Sends a message in a window to the local SAS session

All connections

Release 6.06 and later

Syntax

NOTIFY 'message';

Description

The NOTIFY statement sends a message to the user on the local host by creating a window that displays the message. The user must select CONTINUE to clear the window. The NOTIFY statement is similar to the LOG statement but enables you to highlight messages that might not be noticed in the log.

PARITY

Sets the parity

ASYNC

Syntax

PARITY *parity*;

Description

The PARITY statement sets the parity. Parity is one of five communications parameters that must be set in order to use SAS/CONNECT over an asynchronous connection. The other parameters are baud, data bits, handshaking, and stop bits. The DATABITS, PARITY, and STOPBITS script statements do not take effect unless you set the baud rate with the BAUD statement.

Valid values for *parity* are EVEN, ODD, MARK, SPACE, and NONE. The default value is NONE. Refer to the documentation provided by the vendor of your remote host, or consult the SAS Software Representative at your site to determine the parity value to specify.

The settings for the parity and data bits parameters are related. In general, if the PARITY statement specifies NONE, the DATABITS statement should specify 8. For any other PARITY statement setting, DATABITS should specify 7.

SAS/CONNECT ignores parity errors and does not report them.[*]

---

[*] All error detection is performed with the CRC checksum embedded in all packets.

PROMPT

Overrides the default prompt the local host receives before sending data

ASYNC

Syntax

PROMPT *character*;

Description

The PROMPT statement overrides the default prompt that the local host receives from the remote host before sending the next data packet to the remote host.

The value of *character* is the last ASCII character used as the remote host prompt by your computing installation. Specify the character in one of the following forms:

- a literal character enclosed in quotes such as ?
- a hex character enclosed in quotes such as '3F'X
- an ASCII mnemonic such as DC1.*

The default prompts are as follows:

- For CMS hosts, it is '11'X or DC1.
- UNIX and TSO hosts normally do not require a prompt character; therefore, the default for UNIX and TSO hosts is '00'X or NUL.
- For VMS hosts, it is '24'X or $.
- For AOS/VS hosts, it is '29'X or) .
- For PRIMOS hosts, it is '2C'X or , .

Contact your SAS Software Representative if you encounter problems with the prompt character for your remote host.

When the PROMPT statement specifies NUL or '00'X, the local host does not expect a prompt character and, therefore, does not wait for it before sending an inbound packet to the remote host in response to the last outbound packet.

See also the section on the LINEWAIT statement earlier in this chapter.

---

* See the information on ASCII control character mnemonics in the description of the TYPE script statement.

RETRY

Specifies the number of attempts to resend a packet when an error occurs

All connections

Syntax

RETRY *n*;

Description

The RETRY statement specifies how many attempts the local host makes to resend a packet to the remote host when an error occurs. Typically, the remote host waits as long as the local host tries to resend, or there may be a host-dependent number of retries. Setting a limit on retries with the RETRY statement can prevent excessive line charges when communication problems occur.

The number *n* is an integer that specifies the number of retries. The default value is 5.

The RETRY statement is related to the TIMEOUT statement for ASYNC connections. See also the description of the TIMEOUT statement later in this chapter.

RETURN

Signals the end of a routine

All connections

Syntax

RETURN;

Description

The RETURN statement indicates the end of a group of statements that form a routine in a script. The routine begins with a statement label and is invoked by a CALL statement.

SCANFOR

Is an alias for WAITFOR

All connections

Syntax

SCANFOR *pause-specification-1*<. . . *pause-specification-n*>;

Description

The SCANFOR statement is a synonym for the WAITFOR statement. See the description of the WAITFOR statement.

SNAPSHOT

Copies the contents of the remote host screen to the local SAS LOG window

3270

Syntax

SNAPSHOT;

Description

The SNAPSHOT statement copies the contents of the remote host 3270 screen to the SAS log. Any remote host messages, including error or operator messages, are written to the SAS LOG window. Blank lines are not written to the log. The SNAPSHOT statement is used primarily for debugging a script or saving error messages from the remote host for problem reports.

SOPCHAR

Changes the start-of-packet character

ASYNC, TELNET, 3270

Syntax

SOPCHAR *character*;

Description

The SOPCHAR statement enables you to change the start-of-packet character from $ (the default) to some other ASCII character. Do not change the start-of-packet character unless directed to do so by your SAS Software Consultant in an attempt to resolve unusual ASYNC translation problems.

The value of *character* specifies the desired ASYNC start-of-packet character. For remote hosts running Release 5.18, a special zap must also be applied to change the remote host start-of-packet character to the same character specified in the SOPCHAR statement. The zap can be obtained from the Technical Support Department at SAS Institute.

STOP

Stops script execution normally

All connections

Syntax

STOP;

Description

The STOP statement halts execution of remaining script statements. The STOP statement is used to terminate script execution under normal conditions. Typically, you use the STOP statement at the end of a group of statements that perform sign-on tasks or sign-off tasks.

To halt execution under abnormal conditions, use the ABORT statement.

STOPBITS

Specifies the number of stop bits

ASYNC

Syntax

STOPBITS *stop-bits*;

Description

The STOPBITS statement specifies the number of stop bits. Stop bits is one of five communications parameters that must be set in order to use SAS/CONNECT over an asynchronous connection. The other parameters are baud, data bits, handshaking, and parity. The DATABITS, PARITY, and STOPBITS script statements do not take effect unless you set the baud rate with the BAUD statement.

Valid values for *stop-bits* are 1 and 2. The default is 1.

TIMEOUT

Sets the time the local host waits for a packet from the remote host before resending the last local host packet

ASYNC, TELNET

Syntax

TIMEOUT *n* SECONDS;

Description

The TIMEOUT statement specifies the length of time the local host waits for a packet of data from the remote host. This is also called the packet timeout period. A *timeout* is an error condition produced when a response is not received within a specified time period. When a timeout occurs, the link either

- tries to resend the last local host packet to the remote host
- terminates the link if the retry number is exceeded.

The number *n* specifies the packet timeout period. When the value of *n* is 0, the timeout period is 0; that is, the local host waits indefinitely for a data packet from the remote host. If you will be using the script to run the link interactively, the recommended TIMEOUT value is 0. If the remote host appears not to be responding, you can issue a break signal (usually CTRL-C) to interrupt the timeout. Abort the link and try to sign on again. Do not use this process unless you are sure the remote host is not responding.

The default value for TIMEOUT is 0. SECOND can be used instead of SECONDS.

If the timeout period specified is too short, a timeout may occur before the remote host can respond to the local host. In this case, a packet re-sent by the local host is discarded by the remote host. If the timeout period specified is too long, the system may wait longer than necessary before responding to errors resulting from an unstable communications line.

The best reason for resetting the TIMEOUT value to something other than 0 is when the local host needs to run unattended. In this case, set TIMEOUT to a value greater than the maximum time that the remote host needs to respond to a request from the local host. For example, if you remote-submit a PROC step that requires 2 minutes for the remote host to complete, the TIMEOUT value must be at least 120 seconds. See also the sections on the MAXI and MAXO statements earlier in this chapter.

TRACE

Displays script statements as they execute

All connections

Syntax

TRACE ON | OFF;

Description

The TRACE statement specifies whether or not script statements are displayed in the SAS LOG window as the script executes. This statement is most useful when debugging a script.

ON specifies that statements are displayed. The default value is OFF. You can set the TRACE statement on and off several times in a script in order to trace execution of selected statements.

TYPE

Sends characters to the remote host as if they were typed at a terminal

All connections

Syntax

TYPE *text*;

Description

The TYPE statement sends characters to the remote host as if they had been typed on a terminal attached to that system. For example, in a script that automatically logs on to the remote host, you use a TYPE statement to issue the remote host logon command.

TYPE *continued*

The value of *text* can be any combination of the following:

- literal string(s) enclosed in quotes, such as 'any string'.
- hex character string(s) enclosed in quotes, such as '01020304X'.
- ASCII control character mnemonics if you have an ASYNC connection (see the next section).
- the mnemonic BREAK to indicate a break tone for ASYNC connections. (This is a mnemonic and should not be enclosed in quotes.)
- 3270 key mnemonics if you have a 3270 connection (see the next section).

If you use TYPE statements in the script and some characters specified by the statement are not typed, try using the WAITFOR statement to establish a pause in script execution between TYPE statements.

To use a TYPE statement greater than 80 characters in a signon script, divide the TYPE statement into two or more TYPE statements. To divide the TYPE statement, insert a hyphen (-) at the division point. For example, to divide the following TYPE statement:

```
type "sas options ('dmr comamid=pclink')" enter;
```

change it to:

```
type "sas options ('dmr comamid=-" enter;
type "pclink')" enter;
```

Remember not to add any spaces around the hyphen.

ASCII Control Character Mnemonics

To specify an ASCII control character in the TYPE statement, use a mnemonic representation of the character. Table 17.2 lists the ASCII control characters and corresponding mnemonics, decimal codes, and hex values. As you use these control characters, keep in mind:

- Do not enclose an ASCII mnemonic in quotes.
- In the TYPE statement, use only the values from decimal 0 to 127 (hex 0 to 7F). Do not use any of the extended ASCII characters above decimal 127.

Table 17.2
ASCII Character Mnemonics for ASYNC Connections

ASCII Control Character	Mnemonic Representation	Decimal Value	Hexadecimal Value
Null character	NUL	0	00
Start of header	SOH or CTL_A	1	01
Start of text	STX or CTL_B	2	02
End of text	ETX or CTL_C	3	03

(continued)

Table 17.2 *(continued)*

ASCII Control Character	Mnemonic Representation	Decimal Value	Hexadecimal Value
End of transmission	EOT or CTL_D	4	04
Enquiry	ENQ or CTL_E	5	05
Acknowledge positive	ACK or CTL_F	6	06
Bell	BEL or CTL_G	7	07
Backspace	BS or CTL_H	8	08
Horizontal tabulation	HT or CTL_I	9	09
Line feed	LF or CTL_J	10	0A
Vertical tabulation	VT or CTL_K	11	0B
Form feed	FF or CTL_L	12	0C
Carriage return	CR or CTL_M	13	0D
Shift out	SO or CTL_N	14	0E
Shift in	SI or CTL_O	15	0F
Data link escape	DLE or CTL_P	16	10
Device control 1 (XON)	DC1 or CTL_Q	17	11
Device control 2	DC2 or CTL_R	18	12
Device control 3 (XOFF)	DC3 or CTL_S	19	13
Device control 4	DC4 or CTL_T	20	14
Negative acknowledge	NAK or CTL_U	21	15
Synchronization	SYN or CTL_V	22	16
End of text block	ETB or CTL_W	23	17
Cancel	CAN or CTL_X	24	18
End of medium	EM or CTL_Y	25	19
Substitute	SUB or CTL_Z	26	1A
Escape	ESC	27	1B
File separator	FS	28	1C
Group separator	GS	29	1D
Record separator	RS	30	1E
Unit separator	US	31	1F
Blank space	SP	32	20
Delete or rubout	DEL	127	7F

TYPE continued

ASYNC TYPE Statement Examples

Here are some examples of the TYPE statement for ASYNC connections. The first example combines a literal and a mnemonic in one statement and sends the string **'logoff'** (a literal) followed by a carriage return (represented as an ASCII control character mnemonic):

```
type 'logoff' CR;
```

The next example sends the string 'ABCABCABC' by combining two literal ABC strings with a hex representation of the characters A, B, and C:

```
type 'ABC' '414243'x 'ABC';
```

3270 Key Mnemonics

Users with 3270 connections can specify certain 3270 keyboard keys in the TYPE statement by specifying a mnemonic representation of the key. One type of key that can be specified is an attention ID key (abbreviated AID key). An *AID key* requests the attention of the remote host so that the remote host receives input from the emulated 3270 terminal. The other type of key that can be specified is one that performs a local 3270 function, for example, cursor keys. Keys performing local functions do not solicit a response from the remote host.

The following list shows the mnemonics for AID keys. Note that the mnemonics correspond to the names of the keys on the 3270 keyboard.

PA1	PF1	PF9	PF17
PA2	PF2	PF10	PF18
PA3	PF3	PF11	PF19
CLEAR	PF4	PF12	PF20
ATTN	PF5	PF13	PF21
ENTER	PF6	PF14	PF22
CURSEL	PF7	PF15	PF23
SYSREQ	PF8	PF16	PF24

AID keys cannot always be used in rapid succession, just as you cannot necessarily press them in succession on your keyboard. You may need to use a WAITFOR statement between TYPE statements that specify successive AID keys in order to wait for the appropriate response from the remote host. This is particularly true for CMS hosts.

Figure 17.1 shows the 3270 local function key mnemonics and the corresponding 3270 keys.

3270 TYPE Statement Example

Here is an example of the TYPE statement for 3270 connections that combines a literal string with an AID key mnemonic:

```
type 'sas options(dmr comamid=pclink)' ENTER;
```

Figure 17.1
3270 Function Keys and Mnemonics

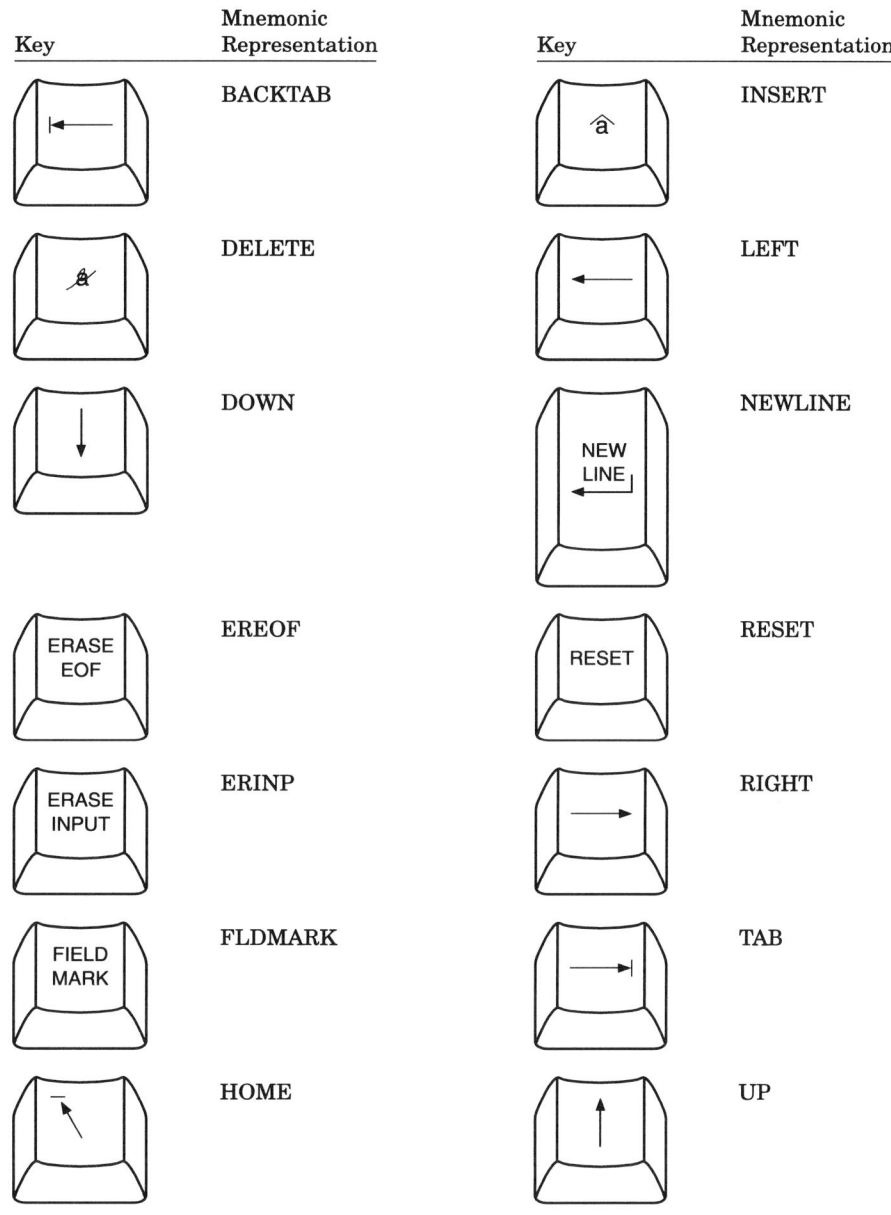

WAITFOR

Specifies a pause until conditions are met

All connections

Syntax

WAITFOR *pause-specification-1*<*... pause-specification-n*>;

Description

The WAITFOR statement directs the SAS System on the local host to do one of the following:

- pause for a specified time
- pause for a specified time or until specified characters from the remote host are received
- pause until specified characters from the remote host are received.

Typically, a WAITFOR statement is used after a TYPE statement sends input to the remote host causing the local host to wait for the remote host's response to the input. For example, a WAITFOR statement follows the TYPE statement that invokes the SAS System on the remote host in the sample scripts in "Starting and Stopping SAS/CONNECT Software" on page 61. The WAITFOR statement is also used after any TYPE statement that sends an ASYNC carriage return or a 3270 AID key to the remote host.

You can include one or more pause specifications in a WAITFOR statement. When you include more than one pause specification, use commas to separate the clauses. The value of *pause-specification* can be either of the following:

- *time-clause*<*:timeout-label*>

    where

    time-clause specifies a time period in the form

    n SECONDS

    The number *n* is the number of seconds that the local host is to wait. If you specify 0 SECONDS, a timeout occurs almost immediately. In most cases, you should specify a value greater than 0. You can specify only one time clause in a WAITFOR statement.

    :timeout-label specifies the label of a statement later in the script. The label must be preceded by a colon (:). When you specify a label, script execution passes to the labeled statement after a timeout occurs. If no label is specified, execution proceeds with the statement following the WAITFOR statement.

□ <*screen-location*> *text-clause*<:*text-label*>

where

screen-location indicates the screen location at which the specified text clause should be found. This specification applies only to 3270 connections. If *screen-location* is specified, it must precede the *text-clause* to which it applies. The screen location is specified by the following, where *n* is any valid column or row number:

<COL *n*> <ROW *n*>

Maximum values depend on the 3270 model being emulated (see Table 17.3). If you specify a row without a column, the WAITFOR statement scans all columns of the given row. If you specify a column without a row, all rows of the column are scanned. The entire screen is scanned if you do not include a screen specification.

Text-clause specifies a string the local host waits to receive from the remote host. The string can be

- □ a character literal enclosed in quotes
- □ a hex string enclosed in quotes
- □ an ASCII control character mnemonic if you have an ASYNC connection.*

When *text-clause* is specified, the SAS System on the local host reads input from the remote host, searching for the specified string. With ASYNC connections, the SAS System on the local host reads all characters from the remote host sequentially. With 3270 connections, the SAS System on the local host scans the remote host screen (instead of reading characters sequentially).

:*text-label* specifies the label of a statement later in the script. The label must be preceded by a colon (:). When you specify a label, script execution passes to the labeled statement after a timeout (if the label follows a time clause) or after the specified string has been read (if the label follows a text clause). If no label is specified, execution proceeds with the statement following the WAITFOR statement.

Table 17.3
Maximum Values for Screen Rows and Columns by 3270 Model Number

3270 Model	Maximum Row	Maximum Column
model 2	24	80
model 3	32	80
model 4	43	80
model 5	27	132

---

* See the discussion of ASCII mnemonics in the description of the TYPE statement.

WAITFOR   *continued*

Usage Notes

- You must specify either a time clause or a text clause in the WAITFOR statement. Optionally, you can specify multiple text clauses, or you can combine a time clause and one or more text clauses. Labels and screen location specifications are optional.

- If the only specification in the WAITFOR statement is a time clause, there is a pause during the script's execution. When the specified time has elapsed, control passes to the next statement in the script. For example, the following WAITFOR statement causes a 2-second pause in script execution:

    ```
    waitfor 2 seconds;
    ```

- If the WAITFOR statement contains a time clause followed by a label, a pause occurs, and control passes to the labeled statement. The following WAITFOR statement causes a 2-second pause and then passes control to the script statement labeled STARTUP:

    ```
    waitfor 2 seconds :startup;
    ```

- If the WAITFOR statement contains a time clause and a text clause, the local host waits the specified time for the specified characters from the remote host. If the local host does not receive the expected characters before the time expires, a timeout occurs and control passes to the next statement or to the labeled statement (if a label is specified with the time clause). For example, when the following WAITFOR statement executes, the local host pauses for 5 seconds, reading any input sent by the remote host:

    ```
    waitfor 'Enter your password', 5 seconds :nohost;
    ```

    If the following string is sent by the remote host within 5 seconds, no timeout occurs and control passes to the next statement in the script:

    ```
    Enter your password
    ```

    If the string is not received within 5 seconds, a timeout occurs and control passes to the statement labeled NOHOST.

- You can specify labels for both text clauses and time clauses, as in this example:

    ```
    waitfor 'Enter your password' :startlnk, 5 seconds :nohost;
    ```

    This WAITFOR statement is like the preceding example except that a label is specified after the text clause. Therefore, if the following string is sent by the remote host within 5 seconds, no timeout occurs and control passes to the statement labeled STARTLNK:

    ```
    Enter your password
    ```

    If the string is not received within 5 seconds, a timeout occurs a nd control passes to the statement labeled NOHOST, as in the previous example.

- If you do not specify a time clause (that is, if you specify only a text clause), a timeout cannot occur and the local host waits indefinitely for the specified text response from the remote host. Therefore, you should generally specify a time clause to avoid being trapped in an infinite wait.

- If you specify multiple text clauses in a WAITFOR statement, the commas that separate the clauses imply a logical OR operator. In other words, only one of the text clauses needs to be satisfied (true).

- The following is an example of a WAITFOR statement that uses a screen location specification (applicable to 3270 connections only):

```
waitfor  row 20 'ready' 8 seconds: noready;
```

This statement directs the local host to wait for the string READY to appear somewhere on row 20. If the string is found, execution continues with the next script statement. If the string is not found, a timeout occurs after 8 seconds and control passes to the statement labeled NOREADY.

XCLOCK

Specifies time to wait for the status line X-clock after typing an AID key

3270 (does not apply to CXI or PC 3270 interfaces)

Syntax

XCLOCK *n* SECONDS;

Description

The XCLOCK statement specifies the number of seconds to wait for the 3270 status line X-clock to appear after a TYPE statement sends a 3270 AID key, such as ENTER. The X-clock appears when an AID key is sent to the remote host and disappears when the remote host responds.

The number *n* is the number of seconds to wait. The default value is .25 seconds. If the X-clock does not appear within the specified time, a timeout occurs and script processing resumes.

The X-clock normally appears within a fraction of a second. In fact, it is possible for the X-clock to appear and disappear so rapidly that the link cannot detect its presence. In this case, the link waits for a timeout and processing resumes.

XTIME

Specifies time to wait after the status line X-clock disappears

3270 (does not apply to CXI or PC 3270 interfaces)

Syntax

XTIME *n* SECONDS;

Description

The XTIME statement specifies how long the local host waits after the 3270 X-clock symbol disappears. The local host waits the specified time before sending input to the remote host or reading output from the remote host. Normally, the 3270 X-clock appears when you send a 3270 AID key to the remote host (for example, the ENTER key) and disappears after the remote host responds. Sometimes the X-clock reappears when the remote host updates a 3270 screen in a line-mode session; this is most likely to happen while you are signing on. This statement enables you to specify the minimum time the local host waits after the X-clock disappears in order to reduce keyboard-inhibited problems caused by an unexpected display of the X-clock.

The number *n* specifies the amount of time the local host should wait after the X-clock disappears. The default is 0.

The XTIME statement is not commonly used in scripts. It is not necessary to include XTIME in a script unless you are having problems with the X-clock display.

Part 4
Appendices

Appendix 1	Using the Services of SAS/CONNECT® and SAS/SHARE® Software
Appendix 2	ASCII and EBCDIC Character Set Translation
Appendix 3	Details for Micro-to-Host Link Releases

Appendix 1 Using the Services of SAS/CONNECT® and SAS/SHARE® Software

Introduction 283

Differences in Implementation Between a Single-user Server and a Multi-user Server 283
Access to the Server 283
Server Initialization 284
Client/Server Configurations 284
Usage with Access Methods 284

Introduction

Both SAS/CONNECT and SAS/SHARE provide services in a client/server environment. However, there are well-defined differences between the functionality of SAS/CONNECT and that of SAS/SHARE. Mapping these characteristics with the requirements of an application should enable you to determine which product you need to get the job done. In many cases, you might find that you want to combine functionality from both products.

The most obvious distinguishing characteristic of SAS/SHARE software is that it is the only piece of the SAS System that provides multi-user update access to SAS data libraries or SAS files. On the other hand, SAS/CONNECT software is the only piece of the SAS System that gives you compute services, data transfer services, and single-user RLS.

Differences in Implementation Between a Single-user Server and a Multi-user Server

The capabilities and setup of these two types of servers are different. This section highlights these server differences.

Access to the Server

Single-user Server

- Single-user access to a dedicated server
- With SAS/ACCESS, access to data is read or write (the user can update data)
- Connecting to the server requires SIGNON followed by a LIBNAME statement naming the REMOTE engine:

    ```
    SIGNON <rsessid>;
    LIBNAME <libref> REMOTE
    <'datalib'> SERVER=<rsessid>;
    ```

Multi-user Server

- Multi-user, concurrent access to a server
- With SAS/ACCESS, access to data is read only (users cannot update data)
- Connecting to the server requires a LIBNAME statement naming the REMOTE engine:

```
LIBNAME <libref> REMOTE <'datalib'> SERVER=serverid;
```

Server Initialization

Single-user Server
Execution of LIBNAME statement initializes the server.

Multi-user Server
Server is initialized and controlled by the system administrator. The LIBNAME statement connects to a pre-existing server.

Client/Server Configurations

SAS/CONNECT provides the single-user server and SAS/SHARE provides the multi-user server. However, the REMOTE engine is present with both products. This means that if you have SAS/CONNECT locally and SAS/SHARE on the remote host, you can access a multi-user server from your local session.

Usage with Access Methods

For SAS/SHARE, the following error message occurs if the local TCP services file is not set up correctly when using RLS:

```
You cannot connect to server xxxxx.xxxx because

ERROR: No TCP server 'xxxx' on this host
ERROR: Error in the LIBNAME or FILENAME statement
```

To use RLS through the TCP/IP access method to access data through a multi-user SAS server, you must identify the port number(s) of the multi-user SAS server(s) to the TCP/IP software used by your local SAS/CONNECT session.

Refer to the documentation for your TCP/IP software for the location of the *services* file. Add the port assignment(s) of your multi-user SAS server(s) to it.

An example of an entry in a services file for a server named MKTSERV is:

```
mktserv         5000/tcp        # SAS server for Marketing and Sales
```

The server name must be one to eight characters in length. The first character must be a letter or underscore. The remaining seven characters can include letters, digits, underscores, the dollar ($) sign, or the at (@) sign.

Appendix 2 ASCII and EBCDIC Character Set Translation

Introduction 285

Translation Tables 285

Introduction

The SAS System and SAS/CONNECT on AOS/VS, DOS, OS/2, Windows, PRIMOS, UNIX, and VMS hosts use the extended ASCII character set. CMS, MVS, and VSE hosts use EBCDIC. Because ASCII and EBCDIC character sets differ, when files are transferred between two hosts using different characters sets, characters must be translated. This appendix shows the default character-set translation tables for EBCDIC and ASCII translations.

Users working in languages other than English may need to refer to the tables in this appendix.

Translation Tables

If character translation problems occur, they can be corrected by modifying the ASCII and EBCDIC translation tables that are part of base SAS software. One table is for ASCII-to-EBCDIC translation, and the other is for EBCDIC-to-ASCII translation. Consult your SAS Software Representative for the location of these tables and for help in making changes to these translation tables.

Note that most SAS/CONNECT users will not experience any translation problems. Character translations are not necessary when both the local host and the remote host use the ASCII character set because the SAS System uses the ASCII character set as the transport format when transferring files. If you are moving files to or from an EBCDIC host, character values are translated using standard character equivalents. If you are working in a language other than English, you may sometimes use characters with special accent marks. This situation is more likely to encounter ASCII and EBCDIC translation problems. *

If there are problems, they will probably occur when you upload or download SAS data sets with character variables, upload or download external files without the BINARY option, or remote-submit SAS programs to the remote host.

Table A2.1 shows the standard ASCII-to-EBCDIC translation table. Note that some translations are different if you use Version 5 of the SAS System on the remote host. These differences are marked with an asterisk in the table and explained in detail after the table.

---

* Do not confuse ASCII and EBCDIC translation tables with 3270 keyboard scan-code translation tables. A keyboard translation table only defines the 3270 keystrokes sent to a 3274 controller; it does not affect the transmission of data over the link. Therefore, a scan-code translation table cannot correct ASCII-to-EBCDIC or EBCDIC-to-ASCII errors. For a discussion of 3270 keyboard translation tables, see "Details for Micro-to-Host Link Releases" on page 289.

Table A2.1
ASCII-to-EBCDIC Translation Table

	ASCII 2nd Digit															
	0	1	2	3	4	5	6	7	8	9	A	B	C	D	E	F
0	00	01	02	03	37	2D	2E	2F	16	05	25	0B	0C	0D	0E	0F
1	10	11	12	13	3C	3D	32	26	18	19	3F	27	1C	1D	1E	1F
2	40	5A	7F	7B	5B	6C	50	7D	4D	5D	5C	4E	6B	60	4B	61
3	F0	F1	F2	F3	F4	F5	F6	F7	F8	F9	7A	5E	4C	7E	6E	6F
4	7C	C1	C2	C3	C4	C5	C6	C7	C8	C9	D1	D2	D3	D4	D5	D6
5	D7	D8	D9	E2	E3	E4	E5	E6	E7	E8	E9	*	E0	*	5F	6D
6	79	81	82	83	84	85	86	87	88	89	91	92	93	94	95	96
7	97	98	99	A2	A3	A4	A5	A6	A7	A8	A9	C0	4F	D0	A1	07
8	20	21	22	23	24	15	06	17	28	29	2A	2B	2C	09	0A	1B
9	30	31	1A	33	34	35	36	08	38	39	3A	3B	04	14	3E	E1
A	41	42	43	44	45	46	47	48	49	51	52	53	54	55	56	57
B	58	59	62	63	64	65	66	67	68	69	70	71	72	73	74	75
C	76	77	78	80	8A	8B	8C	8D	8E	8F	90	9A	9B	9C	9D	9E
D	9F	A0	AA	AB	AC	*	AE	AF	B0	B1	B2	B3	B4	B5	B6	B7
E	B8	B9	BA	BB	BC	*	BE	BF	CA	CB	CC	CD	CE	CF	DA	DB
F	DC	DD	DE	DF	EA	EB	EC	ED	EE	EF	FA	FB	FC	FD	FE	FF

(ASCII 1st Digit: rows 0–F)

EBCDIC Values

For all releases of the SAS System except Version 5 on the remote host, the following translations occur:

ASCII value	translates to	EBCDIC value
5B ([ )		AD (nonprintable)
5D ( ])		BD (nonprintable)
D5 (nonprintable)		4A ( )
E5 (nonprintable)		6A ( )

If you are running Version 5 of the SAS System on the remote host, the following translations occur:

ASCII value	translates to	EBCDIC value
5B ([ )		4A ( )
5D ( ])		6A ( )
D5 (nonprintable)		AD (nonprintable)
E5 (nonprintable)		BD (nonprintable)

Table A2.2 shows the standard EBCDIC-to-ASCII translation table. Note that some translations are different if you use Version 5 of the SAS System on the remote host. These differences are marked with an asterisk in the table and explained in detail after the table.

Table A2.2 EBCDIC-to-ASCII Translation Table

EBCDIC 2nd Digit

EBCDIC 1st Digit	0	1	2	3	4	5	6	7	8	9	A	B	C	D	E	F
0	00	01	02	03	9C	09	86	7F	97	8D	8E	0B	0C	0D	0E	0F
1	10	11	12	13	9D	85	08	87	18	19	92	8F	1C	1D	1E	1F
2	80	81	82	83	84	0A	17	1B	88	89	8A	8B	8C	05	06	07
3	90	91	16	93	94	95	96	04	98	99	9A	9B	14	15	9E	1A
4	20	A0	A1	A2	A3	A4	A5	A6	A7	A8	*	2E	3C	28	2B	7C
5	26	A9	AA	AB	AC	AD	AE	AF	B0	B1	21	24	2A	29	3B	5E
6	2D	2F	B2	B3	B4	B5	B6	B7	B8	B9	*	2C	25	5F	3E	3F
7	BA	BB	BC	BD	BE	BF	C0	C1	C2	60	3A	23	40	27	3D	22
8	C3	61	62	63	64	65	66	67	68	69	C4	C5	C6	C7	C8	C9
9	CA	6A	6B	6C	6D	6E	6F	70	71	72	CB	CC	CD	CE	CF	D0
A	D1	7E	73	74	75	76	77	78	79	7A	D2	D3	D4	*	D6	D7
B	D8	D9	DA	DB	DC	DD	DE	DF	E0	E1	E2	E3	E4	*	E6	E7
C	7B	41	42	43	44	45	46	47	48	49	E8	E9	EA	EB	EC	ED
D	7D	4A	4B	4C	4D	4E	4F	50	51	52	EE	EF	F0	F1	F2	F3
E	5C	9F	53	54	55	56	57	58	59	5A	F4	F5	F6	F7	F8	F9
F	30	31	32	33	34	35	36	37	38	39	FA	FB	FC	FD	FE	FF

ASCII Values

For all releases of the SAS System except Version 5 on the remote host, the following translations occur:

EBCDIC value	translates to	ASCII value
4A ( )		D5 (nonprintable)
6A ( )		E5 (nonprintable)
AD (nonprintable)		5B ([ )
BD (nonprintable)		5D ( ])

If you are running Version 5 of the SAS System on the remote host, the following translations occur:

EBCDIC value	translates to	ASCII value
4A ( )		5B ([ )
6A ( )		5D ( ])
AD (nonprintable)		D5 (nonprintable)
BD (nonprintable)		E5 (nonprintable)

Appendix 3 Details for Micro-to-Host Link Releases

Introduction 289

Hardware Requirements for the Micro-to-Host Link Connection 290

Software Requirements 290

Required SAS Software 293

Scripts and Script Statements for Micro-to-Host Link Access Methods 295

Checklist for Release 6.04 on PC DOS 297
    General Information 297
    Communications Hardware and Software 297
    SAS Software 298
    Script Information 298

ASYNC Terminal Emulator Program 298

3270 Keyboard Translation Tables 300

Creating a Keyboard Translation Table 303

Using a Keyboard Translation Table 306

Sample Keyboard Translation Table 306

Micro-to-Host Link Information for the Examples in This Book 312

Break Window for Release 6.04 316

Using Protocol Converters with Micro-to-Host Link Releases 321

System Commands, Options, and Reference Tables for Micro-to-Host Link Releases 322

Troubleshooting Problems in Micro-to-Host Link Releases 331

Introduction

In Release 6.04 and earlier releases of the SAS System for personal computers, the micro-to-host link provides some of the capabilities that SAS/CONNECT provides for Release 6.06 and later releases of the SAS System. To use the micro-to-host link, you must have the correct hardware and software components on your PC and the remote host. If you can complete the checklist provided in "Checklist for Release 6.04 on PC DOS" on page 297, you have all of the necessary hardware, software, and information for starting, using, and stopping the link. There may be items in the checklist that need more explanation; you can find the explanations in this appendix.

This appendix also discusses the TTY program and keyboard translation tables for Release 6.04. Finally, this appendix contains specific information about SAS/CONNECT examples and procedures that relate to micro-to-host link environments.

If you have not worked with communications hardware and software before, you may encounter new concepts and terminology in this appendix. Refer to the Glossary for help with new terminology.

Hardware Requirements for the Micro-to-Host Link Connection

There are three basic hardware requirements for using the micro-to-host link:

- a PC with at least 450K of free DOS memory after any resident software has been loaded, including DOS and any terminal emulator or control program. *Resident software* is software that is loaded into memory and remains there as long as you do not turn off the PC or restart (reboot) PC DOS. You can determine how much memory is available with the DOS command CHKDSK.
- a remote host running AOS/VS, CMS, MVS, PRIMOS, VMS, or VSE.
- Asynchronous or 3270 communications hardware to connect the PC and the remote host.

Adapters

You are probably familiar with the PC and the remote host, but you may not be familiar with communications hardware. There are three, interchangeable, commonly used terms for communications hardware for microcomputers. They are *adapter*, *board*, and *card*. This book uses the term adapter. The adapter is in your PC.

The micro-to-host link supports two categories of adapters: asynchronous adapters and 3270 adapters. PCs with asynchronous (ASYNC) adapters normally operate in line mode; that is, they send lines of data rather than screens of data. In contrast, PCs with 3270 adapters operate in full-screen mode; that is, they are capable of sending and receiving a whole screen of data. The capabilities of the micro-to-host link are the same, regardless of the type of adapter.

Keyboards

For 3270 connections, the micro-to-host link is designed to be used with standard U.S. typewriter keyboards. If you use another type of keyboard, you may need to use a keyboard translation table to redefine the keyboard scan codes. See "3270 Keyboard Translation Tables" on page 300.

Software Requirements

3270 communications adapters are used in conjunction with specialized 3270 emulation software, which may be called *control programs* or *terminal emulators*. Emulation software makes the PC behave as if it were a 3270 terminal connected to the remote host.

The following list describes the emulation software supported by each value of the REMOTE= system option on the SAS System for personal computers:

ASYNC   uses asynchronous lines to connect to a remote host.

CXL*x*   uses the CXI applications program interface (API). Specify this value if you have a CXI Control Program with a CXI adapter. Because of memory constraints, you will probably need to run in CUT mode, not in DFT mode. With EMS and sufficient memory, it may be possible to configure this control program in DFT mode.

EPAPI*x*   uses the IBM low-level applications program interface (LLAPI). Specify this value if you have the IBM Emulation Program Version 3 (in either DFT or CUT mode) or the IBM Personal Communication/3270.

FORTE   uses the FORTE board-level interface for 3270 CUT mode. Specify this value if you have the Forte PC7879 terminal emulator with the 3270 Forte PJ adapter or the GRAPH terminal emulator with the ForteGraph adapter.

HLLAPI*x*   uses the IBM high-level language applications program interface (HLLAPI). Specify this value if you are using 3270 emulation software that supports IBM's HLLAPI standard.

IRMA   uses the IRMA board-level interface for CUT mode 3270 emulation. Specify this value if you have an IRMA adapter in CUT mode. It is recommended that you use Release 1.32 or later of the E78 terminal emulator.

IRMADFT*x*   uses the IRMA CSUBS interface for DFT mode 3270 emulation. Specify this value if you have an IRMA emulator operating in DFT mode.

PC3270*x*   uses IBM LLAPI structured fields. Specify this value if you have the 3270 PC Control Program 3.0 or 1.22, the IBM Workstation Program, or Attachmate Extra running in DFT mode. Earlier versions of the 3270 PC Control Program do not work, and Version 2 does not leave enough memory for the SAS System.

    You can run the SAS System under Version 3.00 or later of the 3270 PC Control Program but only if you have an IBM XMA adapter installed in your PC.

PC7879   uses the IBM board-level interface for CUT mode 3270 emulation. Specify this value if you have either the IBM 3278/79 adapter (for a PC AT) or the 3270 connection adapter (for a PS/2) and the IBM PC 3270 Emulation Program Entry Level.

RABBIT   uses the Rabbit board-level interface for CUT mode 3270 emulation. Specify this value for a Rabbit board in CUT mode. In previous releases of SAS software, the REMOTE= value for this board was MPLUS.

WSAPI*x*   uses the IBM LLAPI for the IBM Workstation Program (without structured fields). Specify this value if you have the IBM Workstation Program running in CUT mode (that is, with no structured field support).

▶ *Caution* . . . . *Some large 3270 emulation software* configured with large screen sizes, graphics, or multiple host sessions may take too much memory to be run with the SAS System. ▲

In general, 3270 emulation software running concurrent with the SAS System requires the use of EMS memory. Specify the following in your CONFIG.SAS file:

```
-ems all
```

Notes on Using Communications Software

As you use your emulation software with SAS/CONNECT software, you should be aware of the following:

- If you use an adapter that comes with a control program, you must invoke that control program first in order to use SAS/CONNECT software.

- Control programs are always resident, which means that once loaded, the program remains in memory as long as your DOS session lasts. Because control programs are resident, you must be sure to invoke the control program before you invoke the SAS System on your PC. You cannot load resident software after you begin a SAS session on the PC.

- If you use an adapter that has a terminal emulator, use the emulator with the micro-to-host link.

- Some 3270 terminal emulators become resident by default, but other 3270 emulators let you choose whether or not to make the emulator resident. In most cases, you must use terminal emulators in resident mode. For IRMA CUT mode and the IBM PC 3270 Emulation Program, Entry Level Version 1, you are not required to make the emulator resident, but it is recommended that you do so because the remote host session is available to you at any time in your session through the use of hot keys. See "Special Topic: Hot Keys" for more information.

    If you use a resident emulator, you must load it before you invoke the SAS System on the PC. Do not load a resident terminal emulator after you begin a SAS session on the PC.

- Any terminal emulator used with an ASYNC connection must be able to maintain the remote host session when you exit from the emulator. That is, the emulator must be able to hold the DTR signal high. Otherwise, you will be disconnected from the remote host.

> **Special Topic: Hot Keys**
>
> If you have a 3270 adapter and are using a control program or resident terminal emulator, you can access the remote host session at any time by using hot keys. *Hot keys* are special keys or combination keys that take you back and forth between a DOS or SAS session on the PC and the remote host session. The key or keys you use to switch between sessions depends on your adapter. Refer to the documentation provided by the vendor for your adapter for the key or keys you can use as a hot key.

Required SAS Software

In Release 6.04, the micro-to-host link is a facility in the SAS System's base SAS software. (In later releases of the SAS System, this facility has been expanded into the SAS/CONNECT product.) The SAS software that controls the link is actually in two parts: one part is found in the SAS System for PCs and the other part is in the remote host's SAS System. Thus, in order to be able to use the micro-to-host link, you must have SAS software on both machines. The software releases you need are

- Release 6.04 (or later) of the SAS System for PCs on your microcomputer. Be sure that you have the latest release of the SAS System for PCs and the micro-to-host link installed on your PC.

- Release 5.16 of the SAS System under VSE, or Release 5.18 or later under AOS/VS, CMS, PRIMOS, MVS, or VMS. If you are running Release 6.06 or later on your remote host, you must also have SAS/CONNECT software installed on the remote host.

In addition to the appropriate releases of the SAS System on the remote host and the PC, you also need a script with which to initiate and terminate the link.

What Is a Script?

A *script* is a program composed of special SAS statements called script statements. These statements direct the link software to perform special processing while initiating or terminating the connection between the SAS session on the PC and the remote host. Scripts are stored in PC DOS files like other SAS programs. Scripts that initiate the link are executed by issuing the SIGNON command, and scripts that terminate the link are executed by issuing the SIGNOFF command.

A script can be simple or complex, depending on how much you want the script to do. For example, a script can be written that combines the sign-on and sign-off functions so you can initiate and terminate the link with the same script. Scripts can also be designed for use with both ASYNC adapters and 3270 adapters.

Kinds of Scripts

There are two basic categories of scripts:

- Some scripts assume that you are already logged on to the remote host and at the remote host's prompt before you execute the SIGNON command to start the link. Such scripts are referred to as manual logon scripts because you type the logon command yourself. Manual logon implies that you first invoke a terminal emulator or control program (depending on your adapter); otherwise, you cannot log on to the remote host manually.

- Other scripts assume that you are not logged on to the remote host when you execute the SIGNON command; these scripts issue the remote host's logon command for you and prompt you to supply your userid and password. Such scripts are referred to as automatic logon scripts. Automatic logon scripts are relatively complex and contain information that is specific to your computing installation.

  If you do not log on to the remote host before executing the SIGNON command, you must use an automatic logon script.

What Script Will You Use?

You probably do not need to worry about writing your own script for the micro-to-host link. At many computing installations, scripts are provided by systems personnel, by the SAS Software Representative, or by the SAS Software Consultant. Ask your SAS Software Representative or Consultant what scripts are available to you. If you will use a script written or modified by your computing installation, you may need to copy the script to your PC.

If someone at your installation has not written a script for you, you can use one of the sample scripts provided with the micro-to-host link. (See "Sample Scripts" for more information.) If your computing installation does not provide a script suitable for your use and you do not want to use one of the sample scripts, you can write your own script. See "Starting and Stopping SAS/CONNECT Software" on page 61 for instructions.

Sample Scripts

The sample scripts are installed in the *sasroot*\SASLINK directory when the link is installed on your PC; they have the extension .SCR. "EHLLAPI and 3270 Access Methods" on page 141 presents instructions on using the sample scripts. "Starting and Stopping SAS/CONNECT Software" on page 61 contains listings of sample scripts. "Script Statements" on page 251 provides reference information on all script statements.

Note: Scripts for some of the remote hosts may not be included with the SAS System on your PC. Ask your SAS Software Representative for the location of any scripts you do not have.

These sample scripts are manual logon scripts:

- AOS.SCR (for users with an AOS/VS remote host)
- CMS.SCR (for users with a CMS remote host)
- PRIM.SCR (for users with a PRIMOS remote host)
- TSO.SCR (for users with a TSO remote host)
- VMS.SCR (for users with a VMS remote host)
- VSE.SCR (for users with a VSE remote host).

These sample scripts are automatic logon scripts:

- LOGAOS.SCR (for users with an AOS/VS remote host)
- LOGCMS.SCR (for users with a CMS remote host)
- LOGPRIM.SCR (for users with a PRIMOS remote host)
- LOGTSO.SCR (for users with a TSO remote host)
- LOGVMS.SCR (for users with a VMS remote host)
- LOGVSE.SCR (for users with a VSE remote host).

The manual logon sample scripts are especially easy to use. The automatic logon sample scripts must be modified to add information that is specific to your site. Do not attempt to start the link with an automatic logon script until the necessary modifications have been made. (Your SAS Software Representative or Consultant may have altered these scripts as needed.) If someone has altered an automatic logon sample script for users at your installation, you need to load a copy of the modified file on your PC. Copy the file to the *sasroot*\SASLINK directory, and make sure it replaces the unmodified version.

Note: If you are using Release 6.04 or a later release to access Release 6.06 on the remote host, you must alter the scripts provided with the SAS System for PCs. The TYPE statement that issues the command to invoke the Release 6.06 SAS System must contain the DMR and COMAMID= system options. These two options replace the REMOTE= system option that is currently in the scripts for Release 6.04. For example, in LOGTSO.SCR or TSO.SCR, change the TYPE statement to the following:

```
type "sas options('dmr,comamid=pclink')" enter;
```

In LOGVMS.SCR or VMS.SCR, change the TYPE statement to the following:

```
type "sas/dmr/comamid=rasync" cr;
```

What You Need to Know about Your Script

To use the micro-to-host link, you do not need to understand all the details of your script. However, you do need answers to these questions:

- What is the complete pathname of the script file?
- Does the script issue the remote host's logon command automatically?
- Does the SAS command on the remote host include the correct setting for the REMOTE= or COMAMID= system option? For more information, see "System Options, Statements, Commands, and SCL Functions" on page 173.
- If you use an ASYNC connection, are the asynchronous communications parameters (baud rate, data bits, handshaking, parity, and stop bits) set up correctly for your computing installation?
  The parameters must be specified in your script by the BAUD, DATABITS, HANDSHAKING, PARITY, and STOPBITS script statements. If you do not know what the settings should be, ask the SAS Software Representative or Consultant.

Scripts and Script Statements for Micro-to-Host Link Access Methods

This section contains examples of scripts and describes differences in the use of scripts for micro-to-host link releases. This section also provides details about the use of specific script statements with these releases.

TELNET Scripts

If you are using Release 6.07 to access Release 5.18 on the remote host, you must alter the scripts provided with Release 6.07 of the SAS System. For Release 5.18, the TYPE statement that issues the command to invoke the Release 6.07 SAS System must contain the REMOTE= system option instead of the DMR and COMAMID= system options. In Release 5.18, the REMOTE= system option was used on the remote host in much the same way that the COMAMID= system option is used on the remote host in Release 6.07. For example, in the script teltso.scr, change the TYPE statement to the following:

```
type "sas options('remote=async')" enter;
```

In the script telvms.scr, change the TYPE statement to the following:

```
type "sas/remote=async" cr;
```

Automatic Logon Scripts

For the example described in "Starting SAS/CONNECT with an Automatic Logon Script" on page 66, the Release 6.04 OPTIONS statement includes only the REMOTE= system option, as follows:

```
options remote=device ;
```

where *device* is one of these keywords: ASYNC*n*, CXI, EPAPI*x*, FORTE, HLLAPI*x*, IRMA, IRMADFT*x*, PC3270*x*, PC7879, RABBIT, or WSAPI*x*.

Scripts for EHLLAPI or ASYNC Access

If you are using Release 6.06 to access Release 5.18 on the remote host, you must alter the scripts provided with Release 6.06 of the SAS System. For Release 5.18, the TYPE statement that issues the command to invoke the Release 6.06 SAS System must contain the REMOTE= system option instead of the DMR and COMAMID= system options. In Release 5.18, the REMOTE= system option is used on the remote host in much the same way that the COMAMID= option is used on the remote host in Release 6.06. For example, in LOGTSO.SCR or TSO.SCR, change the TYPE statement to the following:

```
type "sas options('remote=pclink')" enter;
```

In LOGVMS.SCR or VMS.SCR, change the TYPE statement to the following:

```
type "sas/remote=async" cr;
```

Script Statements

BAUD Statement for Release 6.04
    SAS/CONNECT software attempts to support 19200 baud communication. However, 19200 baud use cannot be guaranteed because PC DOS does not officially support 19200 baud; 19200 baud will probably not work unless you have at least a PC AT class machine.

SOPCHAR Statement
    The value of *character* specifies the desired ASYNC start-of-packet character. For remote hosts running Release 5.18, a special zap must also be applied to change the remote host start-of-packet character to the same character specified in the SOPCHAR statement. The zap can be obtained from the Technical Support Division at SAS Institute.

Checklist for Release 6.04 on PC DOS

This checklist summarizes the information you must be able to provide to use the link with Release 6.04 on PC DOS. For further assistance with the items on this checklist, you can ask the people at your computing installation who are designated as the SAS Software Representative and the SAS Software Consultant. These individuals can provide answers to many questions related to SAS software, especially SAS/CONNECT. In particular, they can help you with questions about issues specific to your computing environment, such as the names of script files required to run SAS/CONNECT.

General Information

Who is your SAS Software Representative? _____

Who is your SAS Software Consultant? _____

What operating system runs on your remote system?

    ☐ AOS/VS   ☐ MVS   ☐ VMS
    ☐ CMS   ☐ PRIMOS   ☐ VSE

Communications Hardware and Software

What kind of connection do you have?

    ☐ ASYNC   ☐ 3270

What terminal emulation software do you have? _____

What command do you use to invoke your emulation software? _____

What type of terminal does your emulation software emulate? _____

ASYNC Connection

Which port do you use?

    ☐ COM1   ☐ COM2

What are the settings for these communications parameters?

    Baud rate _____

    Data bits _____

    Handshaking method _____

    Parity _____

    Stop bits _____

Do you know how to exit your terminal emulator and leave the DTR signal high?
☐ Yes ☐ No

Are you using a protocol converter? ☐ Yes ☐ No

3270 Connection

What kind of communications software do you have? (Refer to "Software Requirements" on page 286 to see if your communications software is supported.)

What terminal model is emulated? (IBM 3278/79 model #) _____

If you have an IBM 3270 PC, what session do you use? (A-Z) _____

Is the terminal emulator or control program resident by default?
☐ Yes ☐ No

Do you know how to make the terminal emulator or control program resident?
☐ Yes ☐ No

SAS Software

Is SAS Release 6.04 installed on your local system? ☐ Yes ☐ No

Is SAS Release 5.18 or later (or Release 5.16 for VSE) installed on the remote system?
☐ Yes ☐ No

Script Information

Do you use

- ☐ a script provided by your computing installation?
- ☐ a sample script from SAS Institute?
- ☐ a script you wrote?

Does the script sign on and sign off the link? ☐ Yes ☐ No

Sign-on script name: _____

Sign-off script name (if different): _____

Does the script

- ☐ automatically log on to the remote system?
- ☐ require you to log on the remote system manually?

If you plan to use an automatic logon script, has it been modified as needed for your site's log-on process? ☐ Yes ☐ No

If you have an ASYNC connection,

- ☐ does the script contain the correct settings for the ASYNC communications parameters in the BAUD, DATABITS, HANDSHAKING, PARITY, and STOPBIT statements?
- ☐ do you have a .COM file that sets these parameters by using the MODE command?

ASYNC Terminal Emulator Program

Micro-to-host link users with ASYNC connections are not required to use a terminal emulation program with the link; however, terminal emulation programs are recommended. Without terminal emulation software, you are restricted to using scripts that perform automatic logon and logoff for the remote host. With a terminal emulator, you can use a script for automatic logon and logoff or for manual logon and logoff. In addition, you can easily view and respond to remote host messages.

The TTY.EXE Program

SAS software includes an asynchronous terminal emulation program named TTY.EXE, commonly referred to as the TTY program. The TTY.EXE program file is copied to the *sasroot* directory when the SAS System is installed on your PC. To invoke the TTY program, enter the following command from PC DOS: *

```
tty
```

The TTY program has the following defaults:

- communications port, COM1
- half duplex
- handshaking, NONE.

The TTY program assumes that the baud rate, parity, data bits, and stop bits have been set with the DOS MODE command if you do not specify these parameters with the TTY program.

TTY Functions

You can perform certain functions while the TTY program is running. These functions are initiated with the following key combinations:

ALT-B	signals a 220-millisecond break to the remote host.
ALT-D	toggles between full and half duplex.
ALT-F	opens and closes a PC DOS file that records all TTY activity.
ALT-H	displays help for the TTY program.
ALT-Q	quits (exits) the TTY program with DTR enabled (held high) so that you do not drop the remote host connection.
ALT-R	issues prompts enabling you to change communications parameters. Note that when you exit the TTY program (with ALT-Q), the communications port, baud, parity, data bits, and stop bits are reset to the status they had before you invoked the TTY program. Therefore, you cannot preset these communications parameters for SAS/CONNECT software with the TTY program.

---

* This command works if your AUTOEXEC.BAT file includes a PATH command that references the *sasroot* directory.

Using the TTY Program

You must exit the TTY program (using ALT-Q) to invoke the SAS System for personal computers and the micro-to-host link. However, once the link is started you can reinvoke the TTY program if necessary. For example, you may want to respond to messages from the remote host. To reinvoke the TTY program, press the CTRL-C keys or the CTRL-BREAK keys to enter the BREAK window. From the command line of the BREAK window, enter

```
x tty
```

With the TTY program running, you can respond to remote host messages or use the TTY program keys described in the previous section. To return to the SAS session on the PC, exit the TTY program (using ALT-Q) after the remote host responds with a $008NNN-type packet message (a negative acknowledge, or NAK). After exiting the TTY program, you return to the BREAK window. Enter the R BREAK action to resend the packet and then enter the C BREAK action to continue the SAS session on the PC.

3270 Keyboard Translation Tables

A keyboard translation table is a DOS file that maps the PC's character set to the corresponding 3270 keyboard scan codes. A *scan code* is a hex value specifying the position of a key on the keyboard.

For 3270 emulation software that does not offer alternate keyboard support through the applications program interface, a keyboard translation table is used to match the characters that are typed by a script TYPE statement with the correct scan codes. Then, the scan codes are sent to the 3274 controller where they are interpreted and transmitted to the remote system as EBCDIC characters.

When You Need a Keyboard Translation Table

By default, the micro-to-host link assumes that the keyboard for a 3270 connection is the standard U.S. typewriter keyboard. Figure A3.1 illustrates the standard U.S. typewriter keyboard, and Figure A3.2 shows the scan codes for the standard U.S. typewriter. The micro-to-host link also assumes that the PC is attached to a standard U.S. 3274 controller. You only need a keyboard translation table if one or more of the following are true:

- Your 3270 emulation software does not provide keyboard translation to the link. If your emulator has an applications program interface (API), you do not need to create a translation table because the keyboard translation is handled by the API. Emulators that may require a keyboard translation table are Rabbit, Forte, IRMA CUT mode, and the IBM Entry Level Emulation Program Version 1.

- Your PC has a non-U.S. typewriter keyboard. Examples of non-U.S. typewriter keyboards are the 3270 APL keyboard, which moves the function keys and others to different positions, and French keyboards, which use the AZERTY keyboard rather than QWERTY. Because the keys are not in the same relative positions on the non-U.S. typewriter keyboards, the scan codes assigned to the keys differ.

- Your PC communicates with the remote host through a non-U.S. controller. A non-U.S. controller assumes a non-U.S. keyboard and, therefore, interprets the scan codes it receives differently from the standard U.S. 3274 controller.

Figure A3.1 U.S. Typewriter Keyboard Layout: Characters

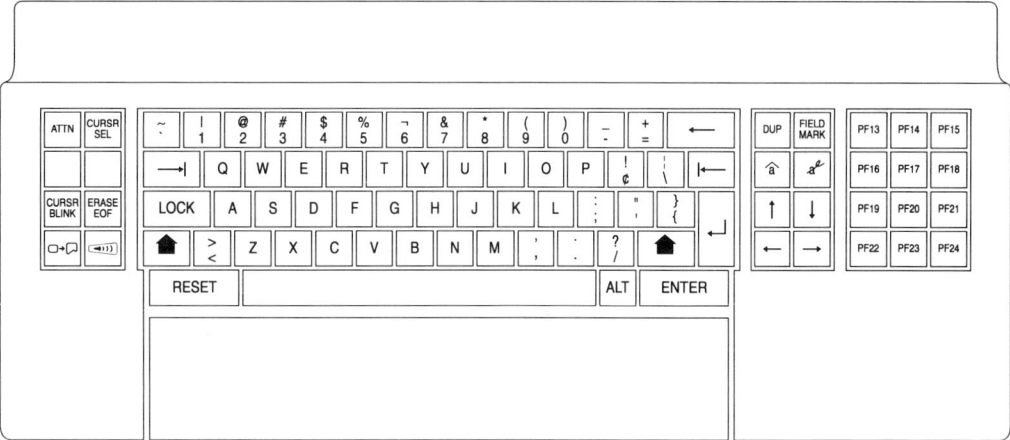

Figure A3.2 U.S. Typewriter Keyboard Layout: Scan Codes

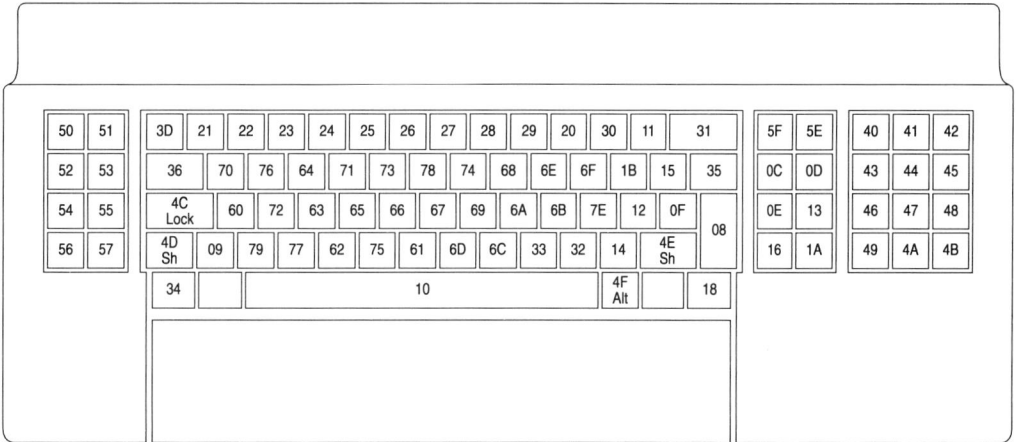

Sample Keyboard Translation Tables

The micro-to-host link includes a collection of sample keyboard translation tables. They are copied to the *sasroot*\SASLINK directory when the micro-to-host link is installed on your PC. Each translation table is a DOS file with the extension .XLT.

The sample table CUTMODE.XLT defines the U.S. typewriter keyboard (the default keyboard) used for board-level, CUT-mode 3270 interfaces. The CUTMODE.XLT table is provided to help you prepare your own translation table if necessary. See "Creating a Keyboard Translation Table" later in this appendix. You can copy the CUTMODE.XLT table and edit it to create your own keyboard translation table.

The list that follows shows the available sample translation tables.* If you need a keyboard translation table, you may be able to use one of the sample tables, or you may want to modify a sample table. Check with your SAS Software Representative or Consultant to find out if any of the samples are appropriate for your machine.

CUTMODE.XLT	defines standard U.S. typewriter keyboard.
I3270.XLT	defines Italian 3270 PC keyboard.
DK3270.XLT	defines Danish 3270 PC keyboard.
DKIRMA.XLT	defines Danish CUT-mode keyboard.
FIRMA.XLT	defines French CUT-mode keyboard.
S3270.XLT	defines Swedish 3270 PC keyboard.
DIRMA.XLT	defines German CUT-mode keyboard.
SIRMA.XLT	defines Swedish CUT-mode keyboard.
D3270.XLT	defines German 3270 PC keyboard.
F3270.XLT	defines French 3270 PC keyboard.
UKIRMA.XLT	defines UK CUT-mode keyboard.
UK3270.XLT	defines UK 3270 PC keyboard.

Table Content and Format

Keyboard translation tables have a specific format. The first row of the table is the following header:

```
0123456789RLINKXTABLE
```

After the header, there can be up to 256 translation entries, one for each character in the SAS character set for PCs (an ASCII character set). Each translation entry has five fields, as shown in Figure A3.3 and described after the figure.

---

* This list may not be exhaustive.

Figure A3.3 Translation Entry Fields

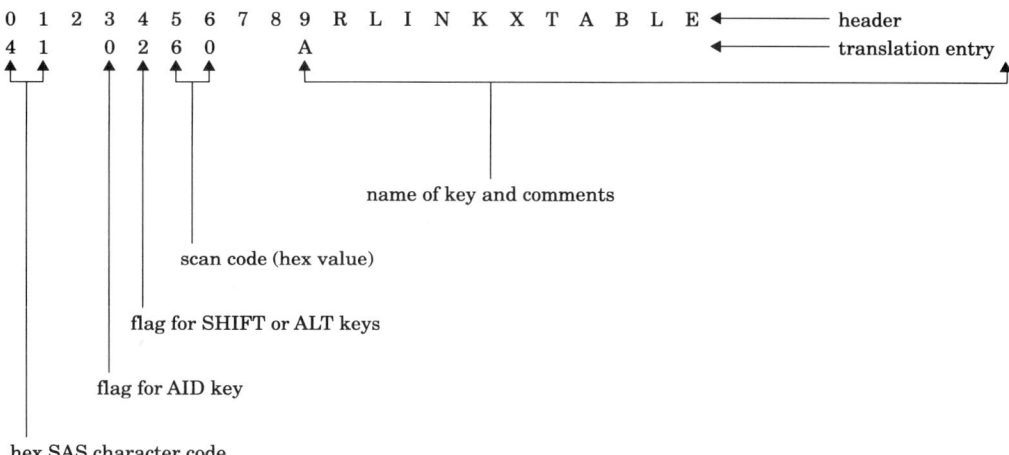

The information in a keyboard translation table is formatted as follows:

Columns 0 and 1	specify the hexadecimal ASCII character code. For the first 128 entries in the default table, these codes are for standard ASCII characters. The remaining 128 are special 3270 key values with meanings specific to SAS software.
Column 3	specifies the AID (attention) key flag. 0 means the key is buffered (that is, not immediately sent to the remote session), and a 1 means it is an AID key. The attention flag must be set for 3270 AID keys (function keys and the PA keys) but not for other keys.
Column 4	specifies the SHIFT/ALT key flag. 0 means neither key is pressed. 1 means the ALT key is pressed, and 2 means the SHIFT key is pressed.
Columns 5 and 6	specify the hex representation of the scan code. The scan code specifies the key's relative position on the keyboard.
Columns 9 through 79	specify optional information, such as the key's name (display character, AID function, or cursor motion), the ASCII meaning, or special comments. By convention, the key's name is shown first in this field.

If an entry is described with an unused comment and the 3270 scan code assigned is 0000 (the null character), then scan codes are not sent to the 3274 controller for the key.

Creating a Keyboard Translation Table

If you need a keyboard translation table and none of the sample tables is appropriate, you can create your own. For the best performance, your translation table need only include entries for keys that are different from the default U.S. typewriter keyboard. Figure A3.4 illustrates a nonstandard keyboard, the AZERTY keyboard.

304 *Creating a Keyboard Translation Table* □ *Appendix 3*

Figure A3.4 A Sample Nonstandard Keyboard: The AZERTY Keyboard

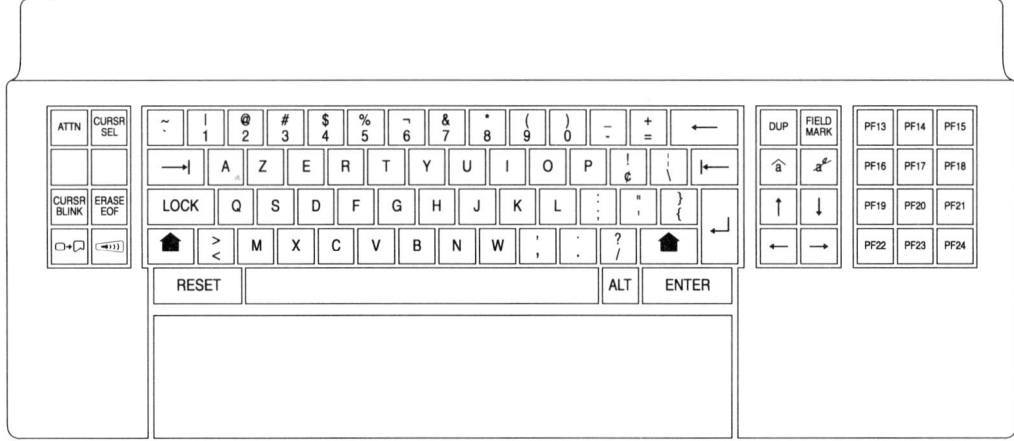

Create your own table by following these steps:

1. Create a DOS file for your table. As the first line in the file, type the keyboard translation table header entry, beginning at the leftmost position:

   ```
   0123456789RLINKXTABLE
   ```

2. Compare your keyboard (the non-U.S. typewriter keyboard) to the U.S. typewriter keyboard (shown in Figure A3.1). Make a list of any keys on your keyboard that are not in the same relative position on the U.S. typewriter keyboard. List these keys in column 9 under the header line.

   For example, suppose your keyboard is like the one in Figure A3.4, an AZERTY keyboard. Comparing the AZERTY and U.S. typewriter keyboards, you find the following keys are in different positions on the AZERTY keyboard:

   ```
   0123456789RLINKXTABLE
            A
            Z
            Q
            W
            M
            a
            z
            q
            w
            m
   ```

3. For each key in the list, write down the hex character code used by the SAS System for PCs. (You can get these codes from columns 0 and 1 of the sample CUTMODE.XLT table, shown in Figure A3.5.) Write the codes in columns 0 and 1.

   For example, the hex values for the characters A, Z, Q, W, M, a, z, q, w, and m are typed as follows:

   ```
   0123456789RLINKXTABLE
   41       A
   5A       Z
   ```

```
51  Q
57  W
4D  M
61  a
7A  z
71  q
77  w
6D  m
```

4. Make note of the keys on the U.S. typewriter keyboard (Figure A3.1) that are in the same relative position as the keys you listed from your keyboard.

   Again, using the AZERTY keyboard as an example, the corresponding keys are

AZERTY	U.S. Typewriter
Z	W
A	Q
Q	A
W	M
M	Z
z	w
a	q
q	a
w	m
m	z

5. Using the sample CUTMODE.XLT table (Figure A3.5), look up the AID flags, SHIFT/ALT flags, and scan codes for the U.S. typewriter keys that you listed in step 4. (These values are in columns 3 through 6 of the sample table.) Enter these values in columns 3, 4, 5, and 6 of your table in the translation entry for the AZERTY key in the same relative position.

   For example, the U.S. Q is in the same relative position as the AZERTY Z. Look up the Q in Figure A3.5. The values for the AID flag, SHIFT/ALT flag, and scan code for Q are 0270. Type these values in the translation entry for the AZERTY character Z.

   The completed table for the AZERTY keyboard is as follows:

   ```
   0123456789RLINKXTABLE
   41 0270  A
   5A 0276  Z
   51 0260  Q
   57 026c  W
   4D 0279  M
   61 0070  a
   7A 0076  z
   71 0060  q
   ```

```
                    77 006c  w
                    6D 0079  m
```

6. Optionally, you can add comments in columns 10 through 79 of the table.

Using a Keyboard Translation Table

When you invoke the micro-to-host link (SIGNON command), the SAS System for personal computers automatically checks for a keyboard translation table. In order for the SAS System to identify a keyboard translation table, the file must be assigned the fileref SASRXLAT.

Use a FILENAME statement to associate the keyboard translation table's filename with the SASRXLAT fileref. For example, if you use a translation table called \MYSASDIR\KEYDEF.XLT, use the following FILENAME statement:

```
filename sasrxlat '\mysasdir\keydef.xlt';
```

The FILENAME statement must execute before the SIGNON command executes. Execute the FILENAME statement with the SUBMIT command or key because it defines a fileref for a local file not a remote file.

If the SAS System cannot find the SASRXLAT fileref, no translation table is used, and the scan codes sent are for the default U.S. keyboard. If you have defined a translation table with the SASRXLAT fileref but the file cannot be found or is not properly formatted, the link terminates with appropriate error messages.

For convenience, you may want to add a FILENAME statement for your translation table to your AUTOEXEC.SAS file. Then you know the table is defined each time you invoke the SAS System for PCs.

With the exception of creating the translation table and defining SASRXLAT as its fileref, using the link with a keyboard translation table is the same as using the link without a keyboard translation table. To summarize, using a translation table involves

- determining if you need a keyboard translation table
- creating the table
- invoking the SAS System for PCs
- defining the SASRXLAT fileref with a FILENAME statement
- starting the micro-to-host link.

Sample Keyboard Translation Table

Figure A3.5 illustrates the CUTMODE.XLT table, which can be used as a model for creating your own translation table.

Figure A3.5
A Sample Keyboard Translation Table,
CUTMODE.XLT

```
0123456789RLINKXTABLE        Copyright 1986, SAS Institute, Cary, N.C. USA
00 0000    NUL
01 0000    SOH               RLINK optional "CUT" mode translate table for
02 0000    STX               the standard US 3278/79 typewriter keyboard.
03 0000    ETX
04 0000    EOT
05 0000    ENQ               - can be used by Irma, Forte and IBM 78/79RLINK.
06 0000    ACK
07 0000    BEL               First line must be left in original form.
08 0031    BS = left arrow   This translate table can be up to 257 lines long
09 0036    HT = tab          and need not have all 256 hex entries present.
0A 0008    LF
0B 0000    VT                Table format is as follows:
0C 0000    FF
0D 1018    CR = Enter        columns  0-1  hex index of char to be translated
0E 0000    SO                column   3    0 = buffered key 1 = attention key
0F 0000    SI                columns  4    0 = unshifted 1 = ALT 2 = SHIFTED
10 0000    DLE               columns  5-6  hex value of 3270 scan code
11 0000    DC1               columns  8... show the typical PC DOS display code
12 0000    DC2                             followed by comments
13 0000    DC3
14 0000    DC4               If a hex code shows -unused- it is assigned
15 0000    NAK               a 3270 scan code of 0000 or the NULL character.
16 0000    SYN
17 0000    ETB
18 0000    CAN
19 0000    EM                NOTE
1A 0000    SUB               ----
1B 0000    ESC
1C 0000    FS                As with any 3278/79 Emulation Program, there are
1D 0000    GS                certain translation problems between ASCIIand
1E 0000    RS                EBCDIC.
1F 0000    US
20 0010    space             There are 3 characters in ASCII that are not part
21 021b !  exclamation       of the official EBCDIC character set and translate
22 0212 "  double quote      as follows:
23 0223 #  number sign
24 0224 $  dollar sign           ASCII }^} (hat)          ==> EBCDIC ¬ (not sign)
25 0225 %  percent              ASCII [ (left  bracket) ==> EBCDIC   (cent sign)
26 0227 &  ampersand            ASCII ] (right bracket) ==> EBCDIC   (solid bar)
27 0012 '  single quote
28 0229 (  left  paren       You may also enter PC ascii codes for the cent
29 0220 )  right paren       sign (alt-155) and the not sign (alt-170) to get
2A 0228 *  asterisk          the EBCDIC equivalent.
2B 0211 +  plus sign
2C 0033 ,  comma             The 3270 Standard TW Keyboard does not contain the
2D 0030 -  dash              right or left square brackets and so they
2E 0032 .  period            cannot be entered from RLINK.
2F 0014 /  slash
30 0020 0 .
31 0021 1 .
32 0022 2 .
33 0023 3 .
```

```
34 0024 4 .
35 0025 5 . numerics
36 0026 6 .
37 0027 7 .
38 0028 8 .
39 0029 9 .
3A 027e : colon
3B 007e ; semi-colon
3C 0009 < less than
3D 0011 = equals
3E 0209 > greater than
3F 0214 ? question mark
40 0222 @ at sign
41 0260 A .
42 0261 B .
43 0262 C .
44 0263 D .
45 0264 E .
46 0265 F .
47 0266 G .
48 0267 H .
49 0268 I .
4A 0269 J .
4B 026a K .
4C 026b L . upper case letters
4D 026c M .
4E 026d N .
4F 026e O .
50 026f P .
51 0270 Q .
52 0271 R .
53 0272 S .
54 0273 T .
55 0274 U .
56 0275 V .
57 0276 W .
58 0277 X .
59 0278 Y .
5A 0279 Z .
5B 001b [ left square bracket    * inputs EBCDIC cent sign
5C 0015 \ reverse slash
5D 0221 ]    right square bracket  * inputs EBCDIC solid bar |
5E 0226 }^ hat                    * inputs EBCDIC logical not sign  ^
5F 0230 _ underscore
60 003d }   reverse single quote
61 0060 a .
62 0061 b .
63 0062 c .
64 0063 d .
65 0064 e .
66 0065 f .
67 0066 g .
68 0067 h .
```

```
69 0068 i .
6A 0069 j .
6B 006a k .
6C 006b l . lower case letters
6D 006c m .
6E 006d n .
6F 006e o .
70 006f p .
71 0070 q .
72 0071 r .
73 0072 s .
74 0073 t .
75 0074 u .
76 0075 v .
77 0076 w .
78 0077 x .
79 0078 y .
7A 0079 z .
7B 000f { left brace
7C 0215 | broken bar * There should be a broken vertical bar here */
7D 020f } right brace
7E 023d ~ tilda
7F 0031   rubout, delete = left arrow
80 0000 p0033; . /* fonts for following characters not available to PUBLISH yet */
81 0000 p331; .
82 0000 p333; .
83 0000 p331; .
84 0000 p331; .
85 0000 p333; .
86 0000 p331; .
87 0000 p331; .
88 0000 p333; .
89 0000 p331; .
8A 0000 p333; .
8B 0000 p331; .
8C 0000 p331; .
8D 0000   i    . foreign PC DOS symbols are unused in US translate table
8E 0000 p331; .
8F 0000   A    .
90 0000 p333; .
91 0000 p331; .
92 0000 p331; .
93 0000 p331; .
94 0000 p331; .
95 0000   o   .
96 0000 p331; .
97 0000 p333; .
98 0000   y   .
99 0000 p331; .
9A 0000 p331; .
9B 0000   cent sign   * not a normal ascii character
9C 0000 p331; .
9D 0000        .
```

```
9E 0000  Pt .
9F 0000  p331;  .
A0 0000  p331;  .
A1 0000  i .
A2 0000  o . foreign PC DOS symbols are unused in US translate table
A3 0000  u .
A4 0000  n .
A5 0000  N .
A6 0000  a .
A7 0000  o .
A8 0000  p331;  .
A9 0000    BREAK (used to signal an asynchronous "break")
AA 0226  ¬  logical not sign * not a normal ascii character
AB 0000    -unused-
AC 0000    -unused-
AD 0000    -unused-
AE 0000    -unused-
AF 0000    -unused-
B0 1121    PF1
B1 1122    PF2
B2 1123    PF3
B3 1124    PF4
B4 1125    PF5
B5 1126    PF6
B6 1127    PF7
B7 1128    PF8
B8 1129    PF9
B9 1120    PF10
BA 1130    PF11
BB 1111    PF12
BC 1040    PF13
BD 1041    PF14
BE 1042    PF15
BF 1043    PF16
C0 1044    PF17
C1 1045    PF18
C2 1046    PF19
C3 1047    PF20
C4 1048    PF21
C5 1049    PF22
C6 104a    PF23
C7 104b    PF24
C8 115f    PA1
C9 115e    PA2
CA 110c    PA3
CB 1151    clear
CC 1018    enter
CD 1050    attn
CE 1150    sys req
CF 1051    cursor select
D0 0034    reset
D1 000e    up arrow
D2 0013    dn arrow
```

```
D3 001a  rt arrow
D4 0016  lf arrow
D5 0036  tab
D6 0035  back tab
D7 0008  new line
D8 0135  home
D9 000c  insert
DA 000d  delete
DB 0053  erase input
DC 0055  erase eof
DD 005e  field mark
DE 0056  print
DF 005f  dup
E0 0000 α  .
E1 0000 β  .
E2 0000 Γ  .
E3 0000 π  .
E4 0000 Σ  .
E5 0000 σ  .
E6 0000 μ  .
E7 0000 τ  .          reserved for Greek alphabet or other special symbols
E8 0000 Φ  .
E9 0000 eta .
EA 0000 Ω  .
EB 0000 δ  .
EC 0000 ω  .
ED 0000 φ  .
EE 0000 ϵ  .
EF 0000 η  .
F0 0052  change format      .
F1 010e  cursor position    .
F2 0152  doc on/off         .
F3 010d  word delete        .
F4 0156  ident/wrap         . special purpose 3270 keys
F5 0116  fast cursor left   .
F6 011a  fast cursor right  .
F7 0134  device cancel      .
F8 0154  alt cursor         .
F9 016f  test               .
FA 0000  -unused-
FB 0000  -unused-
FC 0000  -unused-
FD 0000  -unused-   table need not have all 256 entries present
FE 0000  -unused-
FF 0000  -unused-   *** end of translate table ***
```

Micro-to-Host Link Information for the Examples in This Book

This section contains micro-to-host link details for examples in "Ways to Use SAS/CONNECT Software" on page 17.

Remote Graphics Processing with Release 6.04

This example is explained in "Example 4. Compute Services: Remote Graphics Processing" on page 22. Because this example is one of the most memory-intensive applications of the SAS System for personal computers, you may need EMS (Expanded Memory Specification) on the PC.

Distributing a .EXE File from the Remote Host to Multiple Local Hosts

This example is explained in "Example 17. Data Transfer Services: Distributing a .EXE File from the Remote Host to Multiple Local Hosts" on page 45. For Release 5.18 under VMS, AOS/VS, or PRIMOS, use a SAS FILENAME statement to identify the target file on the remote host.

Automated Remote Processing

This example is used only for micro-to-host link releases on the local host. These releases do not have the full capability of SAS/CONNECT procedures.

Purpose

The SAS/CONNECT commands SIGNON, SIGNOFF, and RSUBMIT can be used as part of a DM statement on your local host. With these statements, you can now do both local and remote processing with one local SUBMIT statement. You can also include these statements in a SAS program running under display manager on your local host, and the program will execute these statements on the remote host.

You can execute the SIGNON and SIGNOFF commands through a DM statement, such as the following:

```
dm 'signon';
dm 'signoff';
```

To begin submitting SAS statements to your remote host, enter RSUBMIT within a DM statement, as follows:

```
dm 'rsubmit';
```

After this statement, enter any SAS statements that you want to submit to the remote host. Your local SAS session will continue to submit statements to the remote host until it encounters the ENDRSUBMIT statement:

```
endrsubmit;
```

(Note that the ENDRSUBMIT statement is not included in a DM statement, but is itself a SAS statement.)

The Program

Suppose you want to automate the backup process described in the last example so that backups are performed each morning when you begin a SAS session.

Note: You should understand all of the steps in the previous example before attempting this example. The previous example explains how a SAS program can write other SAS programs. That concept is also used in this example.

You can add the following statements to your AUTOEXEC.SAS file, which executes when you start your SAS session. These statements include and submit the backup program (BACKUP.SAS), which creates the statements to upload the SAS data set you want. As before, the script file used in this example assumes that you have already logged on to the remote host.

```
options remote=device ;
filename rlink 'script-filename ';
dm 'inc "backup.sas"';
dm 'submit';
```

The program BACKUP.SAS (included by the previous AUTOEXEC.SAS statements) is shown here. The statements needed to establish the link, submit the job, and end the link are created and stored in a program named UPLOAD.SAS (as in the previous example) and then the UPLOAD.SAS program is executed by the DM 'SUBMIT' statement at the end of the BACKUP.SAS program. To see how the program works, read the explanations in the numbered list following the program listing. Match the boldface numbers in the program to the corresponding item in the list.

```
        /* BACKUP.SAS */
❶    x 'dir \ sales\ *.ssd > dir.dat';

     data _null_;
       infile 'dir.dat' length=len end=finish;
         length card $ 80.;
         input card $varying80. len;
         file '\ sales\ upload.sas';
         if _n_=1 then
           do;
❷           put "libname lhost '\ sales';";
❸           put "dm 'signon';";
              put "dm 'rsubmit';";
              put "libname rhost 'remote-SAS-data-library ';";
         end;
```

```
                    if substr(card,10,3)="SSD" then
                       do;
                          record=substr(card,1,8);
                          put "proc upload data=lhost." record " out=rhost." record ";";
                          put "run;";
                       end;
                    if finish then
                       do;
❹                        put "endrsubmit;";
                          put "dm 'signoff';";
                          put "run;";
                       end;
                run;


❺   dm "inc '\ sales\ upload.sas'";
    dm "submit";
    run;
```

❶ The BACKUP.SAS program is very similar to the BACKUP.SAS program discussed in the previous example. There are a few changes in this version of the program to more fully automate the backup process. The INFILE statement now has an additional option, END=, which detects the end of the DIR.DAT file. When all the filenames in DIR.DAT have been processed, some statements can be added to the end of the UPLOAD.SAS program to automatically submit the program after it has been built. See number 4 later in this example.

❷ The LIBNAME statement for the local host can be included in the UPLOAD.SAS program in this example. This LIBNAME statement is submitted to the local host. The LIBNAME statement that must be submitted to the remote host can be in the same program, following a DM 'SUBMIT' statement.

❸ The two DM statements that are added to the UPLOAD.SAS program tell the local system that the link should be established and the statements between the DM 'SUBMIT' and END 'SUBMIT' statements should all be processed by the remote host.

❹ When all of the filenames stored in DIR.DAT have been processed and the UPLOAD.SAS file contains all of the PROC UPLOAD statements needed to perform the backup, the END 'SUBMIT' and DM 'SIGNOFF' statements are added to the UPLOAD.SAS program to indicate the end of the remote processing and to sign off of the link.

❺ These two DM statements automatically include the program just built in BACKUP.SAS and submit it for processing. This step completes the automation of the backup process.

The UPLOAD.SAS program created by BACKUP.SAS now appears as follows:

```
libname lhost '\sales';
dm 'signon';
dm 'rsubmit';
libname rhost 'remote-SAS-data-library';

proc upload data=lhost.jan  out=rhost.jan ;
run;
```

```
proc upload data=lhost.mar    out=rhost.mar ;
run;
proc upload data=lhost.feb    out=rhost.feb ;
run;
proc upload data=lhost.apr    out=rhost.apr ;
run;
proc upload data=lhost.callback  out=rhost.callback ;
run;
proc upload data=lhost.orders   out=rhost.orders ;
run;
proc upload data=lhost.may    out=rhost.may ;
run;
proc upload data=lhost.clients  out=rhost.clients ;
run;
endrsubmit;
dm 'signoff';
run;
```

The statements in the AUTOEXEC.SAS file automatically include and submit BACKUP.SAS each time you start a SAS session on the local host.

Downloading Catalog Entries Containing Graphics Output

This example is used only for micro-to-host link releases on the local host. These releases do not have the full capability of SAS/CONNECT UPLOAD and DOWNLOAD procedures.

You can use the GRLINK driver to transfer catalog entries containing graphics output from the remote host to the local host by running the GREPLAY procedure on the remote host and sending the output to the local host via the GRLINK driver. This process places the picture in the catalog WORK.GSEG on your local host. Pictures replayed from the host catalog into WORK.GSEG on the local host can be replayed on the local host or copied to another catalog.

The Program

To download catalog entries containing graphics output through the link, follow these steps:

1. Establish the link between your local and remote hosts.

2. Submit the following statement to your local SAS session:

   ```
   goptions device=driver nodisplay;
   ```

   In this example, *driver* is the name of the device driver that you will use later to generate graphs.
   Note that the device driver you specify for the download affects how those catalog entries are displayed later. This is important because you can display downloaded catalog entries containing graphics output with any of the supported graphics device drivers. For example, if you download using a black-and-white device driver, then when you display the graphics output later, your graphs will have two colors at most.

3. Remote-submit the following statements to your remote host SAS session:

```
libname rhost 'remote-SAS-data-library' ;

goptions device=grlink;

proc greplay igout=rhost.catalog  nofs;
   replay _all_;
quit;
```

Use the LIBNAME statement to identify the catalog containing the graphics output. If you only want to download individual pictures from a catalog, replace the REPLAY _ALL_ statement with

```
replay entry-id ;
```

where *entry-id* is the number or name of the catalog entry containing the pictures that you want to download.

When these statements are executed, the graphs in your catalog on the remote host are copied to the catalog WORK.GSEG on your local host. Because you used the NODISPLAY option on the local host, the graphs are not displayed while they are copied. After the transfer takes place, you can use PROC GREPLAY on your local host to move the catalog containing graphics entries from WORK.GSEG to a permanent catalog.

Break Window for Release 6.04

A special SAS display manager window, the BREAK window, enables you to handle system interruptions and error conditions while using SAS/CONNECT. This window also enables you to interrupt processing if you need to. The BREAK window is shown in Display A3.1.

Display A3.1
The BREAK Window
for Release 6.04

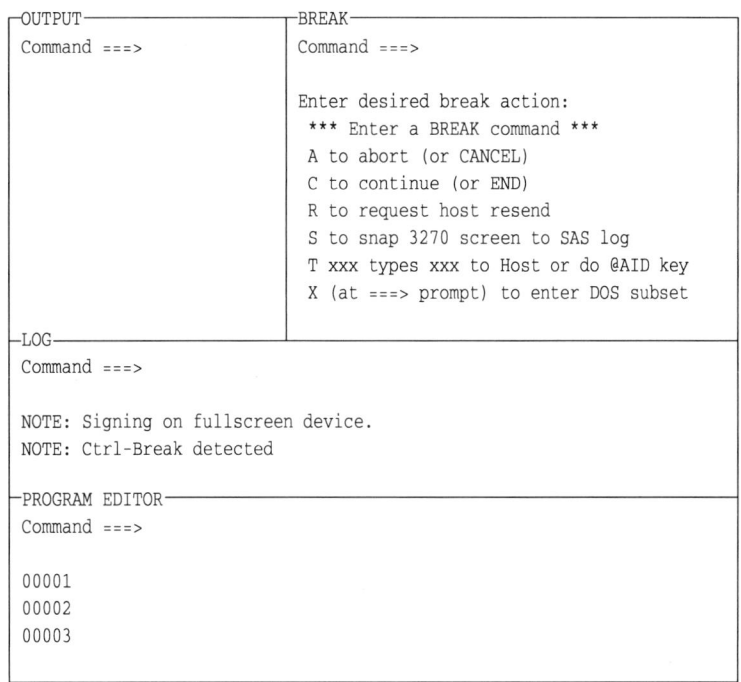

The SAS System displays the BREAK window

- when you send a *break signal* from your PC. You send a break signal by simultaneously pressing the CTRL-C keys or the CTRL-BREAK keys during execution of an RSUBMIT, SIGNON, or SIGNOFF command. Issue a break signal to interrupt processing of one of these commands.

- with 3270 connections when the host operating system issues a message, such as an error message, a message from the operator, or an incoming mail message. Note that messages from the host SAS System do not cause the BREAK window to appear; only host operating system messages cause this.

    Note: If you are using an ASYNC connection, host messages do not cause the BREAK window to appear, regardless of whether they are error messages, operator messages, or messages from other users. Instead, host messages are written to the SAS LOG window.

BREAK Window Commands

When the BREAK window is displayed, you can execute some special commands from the field labeled

        Enter desired break action:

These commands enable you to choose what happens next. The BREAK window commands are as follows:

A   aborts processing of the RSUBMIT, SIGNON, or SIGNOFF command and terminates the link.

C
: continues processing of the command or program running when the break signal occurred or the host message interrupted.

R
: causes a resend of the last information transmitted over the link. Information travels over the link in units called *packets*. Occasionally, a packet is lost or garbled, and link processing stalls. When this happens, use the R command to resend the previous packet so processing can resume.

S
: takes a snapshot of the host screen and displays it in the local SAS LOG window. Blank lines in the host screen are not copied. This command is applicable only for 3270 connections. In situations where a host message causes an interruption, use the S command to read the host message.

T *string*
: sends the specified string to the host for execution as though the string had been input (typed) from a terminal. After the string executes, the link prompts you for another BREAK window command. T is applicable when a host message interrupts processing. You can use T to respond to the host message so processing can resume.

    If you have a 3270 connection, you can type certain AID keys as well as other kinds of responses. Do this by specifying a mnemonic representation of the key as the string. These mnemonics can be specified:

    @PA1 (for PA1)

    @PA2 (for PA2)

    @CLEAR (for CLEAR)

    @ENTER (for ENTER)

    @PF3 (to terminate the host SAS session).

Display Manager Window Commands

In addition to special BREAK window commands, some standard display manager commands for the SAS System for personal computers can be executed from the command line of the BREAK window. Valid commands are PREVCMD, ZOOM, COLOR, and X.

The X command invokes DOS subset mode and is especially useful for handling a host message. Once you are in DOS subset mode, you can execute DOS commands. For example, you may invoke your terminal emulator to view and respond to host messages. (However, remember that you must not load a resident program once the SAS System has started on the PC.)

For more information on using display manager commands while a BREAK window is active, see "Special Topic: When the BREAK Window is Active."

> **Special Topic: When the BREAK Window Is Active**
>
> When the BREAK window is displayed, you must be careful about executing commands in other display manager windows. In particular, do not attempt to execute SUBMIT or RSUBMIT commands in the PROGRAM EDITOR window.
>
> You can execute display manager global commands, such as window management commands. However, if you bring up an accessory window, such as the HELP or KEYS window, you should end it before returning to the BREAK window.

When a Host Message Interrupts SAS/CONNECT

Messages from the host interrupt link processing. The interruption continues until the host message is resolved. Therefore, you must respond to host messages so that processing can resume.

There are several ways to handle host interruptions, but all of them involve

1. reading the host message
2. responding to the message
3. continuing SAS/CONNECT processing.

The next three sections explain how to carry out these steps.

Reading the Host Message

If you have an ASYNC connection, messages from the host are written to the SAS LOG window. To read them, go to the LOG window.

If you have a 3270 connection, a message sent by the host is not automatically displayed on the SAS session window of your PC. You must display the message first. The method you use to display the message depends on whether you are using a resident emulation software or a nonresident terminal emulator.

- If you are running resident emulation software, you can hot-key to the host session to view the message.

- If you are not running resident emulation software, you can do one of two things:

    - Execute the BREAK window's S command to snap the contents of the host message to the SAS LOG window on your PC.

    - Execute an X command from the BREAK window to enter DOS subset mode. In DOS subset mode, you can invoke the terminal emulator and then view the host display.

Responding to the Message

Once you have seen what the host message is, you must respond to the message before link processing can resume. If you are running a control program or terminal emulator, respond from the host session display. If you are not running an emulator, use the BREAK window T command to respond to the host.

If you have a 3270 connection, you may need to press the PA2 or ENTER key after you respond in order to completely resolve the host message.

Continuing SAS/CONNECT Processing

After you respond successfully to the host message, you can continue processing in one of the following ways:

- If you are using resident emulation software, hot-key back to the SAS session on your PC and execute the BREAK window C command to continue.

- If you are using a nonresident emulator, quit the emulation program and return to the SAS session on your PC. Then, execute the BREAK window C command to continue.

- If you are not using a control program or terminal emulator, simply execute the BREAK window C command to continue.

Example

Suppose you write a program to execute on the host, but you misspell the name of a host file referenced in the program. Without realizing your error, you invoke the RSUBMIT command to execute your program. The host cannot find the file referenced in the program and issues an error message. If you have an ASYNC connection, processing pauses. Issue a break signal to bring up the BREAK window. If you have a 3270 connection, the host message brings up the BREAK window automatically.

- If you have an ASYNC connection, read the host message in the LOG window. The message explains that the file cannot be found and prompts you for the correct filename. Go to the BREAK window and use the T command to respond to the host's prompt. Then select C to resume execution.

    Alternatively, you can execute an X command from the BREAK window, enter DOS subset mode, invoke your terminal emulator, respond to the host, quit the emulator, and return to the BREAK window.

- If you are using resident emulation software with a 3270 connection, you hot-key to the host session to view the message. The message explains that the file cannot be found and prompts you for the correct filename. You type in the correct name and press ENTER. The host indicates that the problem is resolved. You hot-key back to the SAS session on your PC and execute the BREAK window C command to continue processing. The program resumes execution.

- If you are not using resident emulation software with a 3270 connection, you can execute the X command from the BREAK window command line to enter DOS subset mode. From DOS subset mode, you invoke a terminal emulator (nonresident) and read the host messages. The messages tell you the file cannot be found and prompt you for the correct filename. You type in the correct name, and press the ENTER key. The host indicates that the problem is resolved, so you quit the emulator and return to the SAS session on your PC. Then you execute the BREAK window C command to continue processing. The program resumes execution.

Another way of handling the situation when you are not using a resident emulator with a 3270 connection is to execute a BREAK window S command so that the host messages appear in the SAS LOG window. Then execute a BREAK window T command to send your response to the host messages. Finally, execute the C command to continue processing.

Using Protocol Converters with Micro-to-Host Link Releases

MS-DOS or PC DOS running Release 6.04 of SAS software enables you to connect to:

☐ MVS or CMS Version 5.18 or later

☐ Release 6.08 under VSE

through a 3270 connection or asynchronously through the IBM 7171 or the Commtex Cx-80 protocol converters.

This section describes how to use a protocol converter with Release 6.04 of the SAS System under MS-DOS or PC DOS to connect to Release 6.08 of the SAS System under VSE. SAS software includes a simple terminal emulation program, called TTY, that provides the appropriate terminal emulation for SAS/CONNECT software. You must use this program to access the remote host when using a protocol converter.

Preparing to Use a Protocol Converter

Before using SAS/CONNECT software with a protocol converter, complete the following steps:

1. Make sure that you are using Release 6.04 of the SAS System on the local host.

2. Locate a script that signs you on to a remote VSE host through your protocol converter.

    A script to do this is included on the installation tape for MVS and CMS, Release 5.18 or later and Release 6.08 under VSE. To use this script, you must move the script from MVS, CMS, or VSE to your MS-DOS or PC DOS system. In addition, a sample script to connect from Release 6.04 under MS-DOS or PC DOS to Release 6.08 under VSE is described in "Using Protocol Converters and TTY with the ASYNC Access Method" on page 147.

    Be sure that the script you use contains a TYPE statement that includes DMR and COMAMID=RSAS7171 in the command that invokes the SAS System on the remote host, as shown in this example:

    ```
    type "sas 'dmr comamid=rsas7171 noterminal no$syntaxcheck', db32782" ENTER;
    ```

3. Determine the full pathname of the TTY program (usually SAS\SASEXE\TTY.EXE).

4. To use the TTY program, make sure a statement that defines the correct device driver is included in the CONFIG.SYS file when you boot MS-DOS or PC DOS. Specify the following DEVICE statement.

    ```
    device=ansi.sys
    ```

    This device driver must be installed before you can use the MODE command to set communications parameters for a serial port.

322 *System Commands, Options, and Reference Tables* ▫ *Appendix 3*

Steps for Using a Protocol Converter

Use SAS/CONNECT software with the IBM 7171 or the Commtex Cx-80 protocol converter by following these steps.

1. From an MS-DOS or PC DOS command prompt, invoke the TTY command.
2. Log on to the remote host.
3. Press ALT-Q, which quits the TTY program and holds the DTR signal high. This ensures that the host connection is not dropped. Doing this returns you to your MS-DOS or PC DOS session.
4. Invoke the SAS System under MS-DOS or PC DOS and locally submit the following SAS statement:

   ```
   options remote=async;
   ```

   A link established through a protocol converter is an asynchronous connection, so you must use REMOTE=ASYNC on the local side.

5. Submit the following SIGNON statement to sign on to the SAS System on the remote host, where *protocol-converter-script*.SCR is the pathname of the script file for your protocol converter:

   ```
   signon 'protocol-converter-script.scr';
   ```

6. When the link is established, this message appears in the LOG window:

   ```
   Remote signon complete
   ```

System Commands, Options, and Reference Tables for Micro-to-Host Link Releases

This section describes differences in the way you use some of the SAS/CONNECT system commands and options for micro-to-host link releases. This section also contains quick reference tables for commands, options, and scripts.

COMAMID= and the REMOTE= System Options

If the local host is running Release 6.04, you need to specify the COMAMID= system option only on the remote host.

If your local host is running Release 6.04 of the SAS System or your remote host is running Release 5.18 of the SAS System, refer to the list of values in the following sections.

REMOTE= System Option for Version 5 and Release 6.04

This option identifies the communications device on the local and remote hosts.

Syntax

REMOTE=*device*

Description

You must tell both the local SAS System and the remote SAS System what kind of communications device you are using for the link. For Version 5 and Release 6.04, you do this with the REMOTE= system option, a SAS system option used only with the link.*

The *device* specifies the hardware connection you have with the remote host. For Release 6.04 on the PC, *device* must be one of the values in the following list. See Table A3.2 for detailed information on when to use each of these values.

ASYNC*n*	where *n* is 1 or 2 depending on whether you use COM1 or COM2 **
CXI*x*	where *x* is the session letter
EPAPI*x*	where *x* is the session letter
FORTE	
HLLAPI*x*	where *x* is the session letter
IRMA	
IRMADFT*x*	where *x* is the session letter
PC3270*x*	where *x* is the session letter
PC7879	
RABBIT	
WSAPI*x*	where *x* is the session letter.

For Version 5 on the remote host, *device* must be one of the following:

ASYNC	is used when you are connecting to a remote host over an asynchronous line.
PC3270	is used for 3270 emulation software that uses IBM's low-level applications program interface (LLAPI). You specify this value only on a remote host running Release 5.18 and only when the local host is running Release 6.04 with a REMOTE= value of PC3270.
PCLINK	is used for all other 3270 emulation software. This is the only valid value for a remote host running VSE.

---

* If your PC is equipped with more than one communications card, you can also use the REMOTE= system option to select which communications card to use.

** The value ASYNC*n* is not valid if the remote host is running VSE.

Note: For Release 6.06 and later releases, the REMOTE= system option has a different purpose. The function that the REMOTE= system option has in Version 5 and Release 6.04 is provided by the COMAMID= and DMR system options in Release 6.06 and later releases.

Specifying the REMOTE= System Option on the Local Host, Release 6.04

Typically, you set up the AUTOEXEC.SAS file on the local host so that the REMOTE= system option executes automatically. You do this by including an OPTIONS statement in the AUTOEXEC.SAS file that sets the value of the REMOTE= system option for the local host each time the local SAS System is invoked.

If you do not include an OPTIONS statement specifying the REMOTE= system option in your AUTOEXEC.SAS file, you can use one of these methods to specify the system option on the local host:

- Type and submit the OPTIONS statement before executing a SIGNON command.
- Include the REMOTE= system option in the SAS command that starts the SAS session on the local host.
- Include the REMOTE= system option in the CONFIG.SAS file that is processed when you start the SAS session on the local host.

Specifying the REMOTE= System Option on the Remote Host, Version 5

For the remote host, you must specify the REMOTE= system option in the TYPE statement that contains the SAS command in the script you use to sign on. If you fail to specify the REMOTE= option, an error message is issued, and the link terminates.

Examples for Signing On

This section provides three examples of setting communications options for signing on. These examples show the OPTIONS statement you use on the local host and the TYPE script statement that invokes the SAS System on the remote host.

- Suppose you use an IRMA adapter and your remote system is CMS running Release 6.06 of the SAS System. You can specify the REMOTE= system option in a Release 6.04 SAS OPTIONS statement as follows:

    ```
    options remote=irma;
    ```

    In the TYPE statement that submits the remote SAS command, you can use the COMAMID= and DMR system options as follows:

    ```
    type "sas (dmr comamid=pclink)" enter;
    ```

- If your remote system is TSO running Release 5.18 of the SAS System and you use a 3270 PC with G as the active session, your Release 6.04 SAS OPTIONS statement is

    ```
    options remote=pc3270g;
    ```

The TYPE statement with the remote SAS command is

```
type "sas options('remote=pc3270')" enter;
```

☐ If your remote system is VMS running Release 5.18 of the SAS System and you use an ASYNC connection (COM2 port) from an OS/2 session running Release 6.06 of the SAS System, your local OPTIONS statement is

```
options comamid=rasync remote=com2;
```

The TYPE statement with the remote SAS command is

```
type "sas /remote=async" enter;
```

FILENAME Statement and the SAS Autoexec File

The AUTOEXEC.SAS file is copied to the SAS directory automatically when you install base SAS software for PCs. (You may have copied the AUTOEXEC.SAS file to your personal directory from the \ SAS directory, as suggested in step 6 of the installation instructions for the SAS System on PCs.) By default, the AUTOEXEC.SAS file already includes the following FILENAME statement:

```
filename rlink '!sasroot\saslink\tso.scr';
```

If you do not use the TSO.SCR sample script to start and terminate the link, edit this FILENAME statement to include the correct file specification for your script.

For Release 6.04, the AUTOEXEC.SAS file is discussed in more detail on pages 313 and 465 of the *SAS Language Guide, Release 6.03 Edition*.

DOWNLOAD Procedure

Release 5.18
  The form *fileref(member)* is not available in Release 5.18 of the SAS System.

Release 6.04
  The form *fileref(member)* is not available in Release 6.04 of the SAS System.

filerefs
  Filerefs for external files accessed by Version 5 under CMS, MVS, and VSE are defined using operating system control language for that host. If you do not know how to use the LIBNAME and FILENAME statements, refer to Chapter 9, "SAS Language Statements," in *SAS Language: Reference, Version 6, First Edition* or Chapter 18, "SAS Statements Used Anywhere," in *SAS Language Guide for Personal Computers, Release 6.03 Edition*, for Release 6.04 of the SAS System. For Version 5, refer to Appendix 2, "Operating System Notes," in the *SAS User's Guide: Basics, Version 5 Edition*.

UPLOAD Procedure

INFILE Option for Release 6.04
    The form *fileref(member)* is not available in Release 6.04 of the SAS System.

OUTFILE Option for Release 6.06 under CMS, or Release 5.18
    The form *fileref(member)* is not available in either Release 5.18 of the SAS System or in Release 6.06 under CMS.

OUTCAT Option for Version 5
    Do not specify a Version 5 catalog. You cannot upload a catalog entry from Version 6 to Version 5 of the SAS System.

Reference Tables for Commands, Options, and Scripts

Table A3.1 Summary of Scripts and Options

If your local host is ...	and your remote host is ...	then use this COMAMID= value on the local host ...[1]	use this REMOTE= value on the local host ...[1]	and use this supplied script.[2]
OpenVMS, Release, 6.08, and 6.07	MVS, Release 5.18	TELNET	*internet address*	teltso.scr[3]
	CMS, Release 5.18	TELNET	*internet address*	telcms.scr[3]
	PRIMOS, Release 5.18	TELNET	*internet-address*	telprim.scr[3]
	OpenVMS, Release 5.18	TELNET	*internet address*	telvms.scr[3]
	AOS/VS, Release and 5.18	TELNET	*internet-address*	telaos.scr[3]
UNIX, Release 6.09 and 6.07	MVS, Release 5.18	TELNET	*internet address*	teltso.scr[3]
	CMS, Release 5.18	TELNET	*internet address*	telcms.scr[3]
	OpenVMS, Release 5.18	TELNET	*internet address*	telvms.scr[3]

(continued)

Table A3.1 (continued)

If your local host is ...	and your remote host is ...	then use this COMAMID= value on the local host ...[1]	use this REMOTE= value on the local host ...[1]	and use this supplied script.[2]
	PRIMOS, Release 5.18	TELNET	*internet-address*	telprim.scr[3]
	AOS/VS, Release 5.18	TELNET	*internet-address*	telaos.scr[3]
OS/2, Release 6.08	MVS, Release 5.18	EHLLAPI	*name-of-remote-session*	tso.scr or logtso.scr[4]
		TELNET	*internet-address*	teltso.scr[4]
		RASYNC	COM*n*	tso.scr, logtso.scr, tso7171.scr, or tsoctex.scr[3]
	CMS, Release 5.18	EHLLAPI	*name-of-remote-session*	cms.scr or logcms.scr[4]
		TELNET	*internet-address*	telcms.scr[4]
		RASYNC	COM*n*	cms.scr, logcms.scr, cms7171.scr, or cmsctex.scr[3]
	OpenVMS, Release 5.18	RASYNC	COM*n*	vms.scr or logvms.scr[3]
		TELNET	*internet-address*	telvms.scr[3]
	VSE, Release 5.16	EHLLAPI	*name-of-remote-session*	vse.scr[5]
	PRIMOS, Release 5.18	TELNET	*internet-address*	telprim.scr[3]

(continued)

Table A3.1 (continued)

If your local host is ...	and your remote host is ...	then use this COMAMID= value on the local host ...[1]	use this REMOTE= value on the local host ...[1]	and use this supplied script.[2]
		RASYNC	COM*n*	prim.scr or logprim.scr[3]
	AOS/VS, Release 5.18	TELNET	*internet-address*	telaos.scr[3]
		RASYNC	COM*n*	aos.scr or logaos.scr[3]
OS/2, Release 6.06	MVS, Release 5.18	EHLLAPI	*name-of-remote-session*	tso.scr or
		RASYNC	COM*n*	tso.scr, logtso.scr, tso7171.scr, or tsoctex.scr[3]
	CMS, Release 5.18	EHLLAPI	*name-of-remote-session*	cms.scr or
		RASYNC	COM*n*	cms.scr, logcms.scr, cms7171.scr, or cmsctex.scr[3]
	OpenVMS, Release 5.18	RASYNC	COM*n*	vms.scr or logvms.scr[3]
	VSE, Release 5.16	EHLLAPI	*name-of-remote-session*	vse.scr[5]
	PRIMOS, Release 5.18	RASYNC	COM*n*	prim.scr or logprim.scr[3]
	AOS/VS, Release 5.18	RASYNC	COM*n*	aos.scr or logaos.scr[3]

(continued)

Table A3.1 (continued)

If your local host is ...	and your remote host is ...	then use this COMAMID= value on the local host ...[1]	use this REMOTE= value on the local host ...[1]	and use this supplied script.[2]
Windows 3.1, Release 6.08	MVS, Release 5.18	EHLLAPI	*name-of-remote-session*	tso.scr or logtso.scr[4]
		TELNET	*internet-address*	teltso.scr
	CMS, Release 5.18	EHLLAPI	*name-of-remote-session*	cms.scr or logcms.scr[4]
		TELNET	*internet-address*	telcms.scr
	VSE, Release 5.16	EHLLAPI	*name-of-remote-session*	vse.scr[5]
	PRIMOS, Release 5.18	TELNET	*internet-address*	telprim.scr[3]
	AOS/VS, Release 5.18	TELNET	*internet-address*	telaos.scr[3]
Windows NT, Release 6.09	MVS, Release 5.18	TELNET	*internet-address*	teltso.scr
	CMS, Release 5.18	TELNET	*internet-address*	telcms.scr
	OpenVMS, Release 5.18	TELNET	*internet-address*	telvms.scr
	PRIMOS, Release 5.18	TELNET	*internet-address*	telprim.scr
	AOS/VS, Release 5.18	TELNET	*internet-address*	telaos.scr

Table Notes

1. Submit these options in the OPTIONS statement on the local host.
2. Use a FILENAME statement to associate this script with the RLINK fileref or another fileref that you will use in the SIGNON and SIGNOFF commands.
3. If you are running Release 5.18 on the remote host, the script you use must be modified to invoke Version 5 of the SAS System and to specify REMOTE=ASYNC (or

REMOTE=RSAS7171 for protocol converters) instead of a COMAMID= value and the DMR option.

4. If you are running Release 5.18 on the remote host, the script you use must be modified to invoke Version 5 of the SAS System and to specify REMOTE=PCLINK or PC3270 instead of a COMAMID= value and the DMR option.

5. If you are running Release 5.16 under VSE, the script you use must be modified to invoke Version 5 of the SAS System and to specify REMOTE=PCLINK instead of a COMAMID= value and the DMR option.

Table A3.2 Summary of Scripts and Options for Release 6.04 under DOS on the Local Host

If your remote host is ...	then use this REMOTE= value on the local host ...[1]	and use this supplied script.[2]
MVS, Release 6.08, 6.07, 6.06, and 5.18	CXI, EPAPI, FORTE, EHLLAPI, IRMA, IRMADFT, PC3270, PC7879, RABBIT, or WSAPI[3]	tso.scr or logtso.scr[4]
	ASYNC	tso.scr, logtso.scr, tso7171.scr, or tsoctex.scr[5]
CMS, Release 6.08, 6.07, 6.06, and 5.18	CXI, EPAPI, FORTE, EHLLAPI, IRMA, IRMADFT, PC3270, PC7879, RABBIT, or WSAPI[3]	cms.scr or logcms.scr[4]
	ASYNC	cms.scr, logcms.scr, cms7171.scr, or cmsctex.scr[5]
OpenVMS, Release 6.08, 6.07, 6.06, and 5.18	ASYNC	vms.scr or logvms.scr[5]
UNIX, Release 6.09 and 6.07	ASYNC	unix.scr or logunix.scr
VSE, Release 6.07	CXI, EPAPI, FORTE, EHLLAPI, IRMA, IRMADFT, PC3270, PC7879, RABBIT, or WSAPI[3]	vse.scr[4]
	ASYNC	vse.scr

(continued)

Table A3.2 (continued)

If your remote host is ...	then use this REMOTE= value on the local host ...[1]	and use this supplied script.[2]
VSE, Release 5.16	CXI, EPAPI, FORTE, EHLLAPI, IRMA, IRMADFT, PC3270, PC7879, RABBIT, or WSAPI [3]	vse.scr
PRIMOS, Release 6.06 and 5.18	ASYNC	prim.scr or logprim.scr[5]
AOS/VS, Release 6.06 and 5.18	ASYNC	aos.scr or logaos.scr[5]

Table Notes

1. Submit these options in the OPTIONS statement on the local host.
2. Use a FILENAME statement to associate this script with the RLINK fileref or another fileref that you will use in the SIGNON and SIGNOFF commands.
3. See "Software Requirements" on page 290 for a list and description of the values that can be used here.
4. If you are running Version 6 on the remote host, the script you use must be modified to invoke Version 6 of the SAS System and to specify either PCLINK or PC3270 as the COMAMID= option and DMR instead of the REMOTE= option.
5. If you are running Version 6 on the remote host, the script you use must be modified to invoke Version 6 of the SAS System and to specify COMAMID=RASYNC (or COMAMID=RSAS7171 for protocol converters) and DMR instead of the REMOTE= option.

Troubleshooting Problems in Micro-to-Host Link Releases

This section describes problems you may encounter with micro-to-host link releases and provides answers to these problems.

Users of the link on PC DOS often have questions about messages that appear while signing on, failure during remote-submit, CXI/Graph adapters, and duplex warning messages. Some of the most frequently asked questions are addressed in the following sections.

Screen-Size Error

3270

Local: Release 6.04

Remote: all releases

Problem
You are signing on to a remote session from a PC DOS session running Release 6.04, and you receive the following message:

```
ERROR: Unexplained error reading screen size
```

Explanation
This message occurs if you are using the incorrect local device driver for the REMOTE= system option. See "Software Requirements" on page 290 for a list of valid values for the REMOTE= system option.

Screen-Erasure Messages for 3270 PC

3270

Local: Release 6.04

Remote: all releases

Problem
When you try to sign on from an IBM 3270 PC to a TSO host, you receive the following messages and the link does not start:

```
COMMUNICATIONS IN PROGRESS
IKT04051 SCREEN ERASURE CAUSED BY ERROR RECOVERY PROCEDURE
```

Explanation
You may be trying to connect in 3270 CUT mode, which is not supported by the link for 3270 PCs. Version 1.22 of the IBM 3270 PC Control Program must be used to configure the device as a DFT terminal. The 3274 control unit may need to be restarted for the port to support DFT mode if you have been running in CUT mode. In addition, VTAM must have the PSERVICE QUERY bit on.

QUERYID Message on IBM 3270 PC

3270

Local: Release 6.04

Remote: all releases

Problem
When you try to sign on, you receive the following message:

```
LLPCIN: QUERYID RC 2x
```

Explanation
The IBM 3270 PC must be connected to VTAM in DFT mode with the PSERVICE QUERY bit in the VTAM logmode table turned on. This enables VTAM and the 3270 PC to perform structured field communications. Contact your communications or systems personnel to perform this task.

RSUBMIT Failure

3270

Local: Release 6.04

Remote: all releases

Problem
You are linked to a TSO host as a 3270 CUT-mode session, and a system problem causes you to be disconnected. You log on to TSO again and receive a RECONNECTED message. However, the next RSUBMIT command fails, or you get messages about mismatched sequence numbers.

Explanation
After you log on to TSO and receive a RECONNECTED message, press ENTER. You should see the last screen displayed by SAS/CONNECT software before you were disconnected. Press ENTER again. You should now be able to resume normal use of the link.

Duplex Warning Message

ASYNC

Local: Release 6.04

Remote: all releases

Problem
You use an ASYNC connection. While the SIGNON command is executing, you receive the following message:

```
WARNING: RLINK host using full duplex echo
```

Explanation
This is an informational warning to let you know your remote host is using full duplex communications. To save CPU time and line charges during the sign-on process, use half duplex rather than full duplex. (The status of duplex is normally set at the remote host.)

Insufficient Memory Message

3270 and ASYNC

Local: Release 6.04

Remote: all releases

Question
When you attempt to display a graph in Release 6.04 of the SAS System for personal computers using the GRLINK device driver on the remote host, you receive one of the following messages:

```
ERROR: Cannot load SASXGSUB due to insufficient memory.
       Press any key to continue.

ERROR: Load device driver failed (rc=2) on the pc
       Device GRLINK cannot be used--please enter device name on host
```

Answer
Displaying remote graphics on the local host is a memory-intensive application. You may need to add an expanded memory specification (EMS) board to your PC to be able to display graphs successfully.

  Note: You may receive a message recommending you delete DOS files; deleting DOS files does not enable the graphs to be displayed.

SAS System Clock

3270

Local: Release 6.04

Remote: all releases

Problem
A clock appears on the PC DOS display when in DOS subset mode and on 3270 displays when in 3270-emulation mode.

Explanation
The clock is the SAS System's clock showing the time of day; it also appears in windows of the SAS Display Manager System. If you do not want the clock on the PC DOS or the 3270 displays, use the CLOCK display manager command to turn it off. Some users find that the clock reminds them that the SAS System is active, so they do not try to reinvoke the SAS System from DOS subset mode.

Degraded Response Time

3270

Local: Release 6.04

Remote: all releases

Problem
When you run SAS/CONNECT software with a remote 3274 controller, response time may slow down for other users.

Explanation
This problem can be minimized with system performance tuning that gives lower priority to SAS/CONNECT software users. Also, for TSO hosts, the MVS system resource manager (SRM) can be used to set up special userids to be used exclusively for downloading or uploading data. This can reduce the impact on other users.

CUT-mode 3270 users (not 3270 PC) can also help this problem somewhat by using model 2 screens rather than models 3, 4, or 5. Using a model 2 causes less data to be transferred at a time. When your remote processing is broken into smaller packets of data, other users' tasks can be interleaved between the packets sent for your remote processing.

Glossary

This section defines terms used in this book to document SAS/CONNECT. Some terms listed here may have other meanings in other contexts.

access method
See *communication access method.*

access pattern
the way that a particular file is being accessed: sequential, random, BY-group rewind, or two-pass sequential.

adapter
for PCs, one of several interchangeable terms for a piece of communications hardware. In this context, adapter is synonymous with board or card. The adapter is a printed circuit card that plugs into the PC expansion slot to attach the PC to some external connection.

aggregate storage location
a location on an operating system that can contain a group of distinct files. Different host operating systems call an aggregate grouping of files different names, such as a directory, a maclib, or a partitioned data set. The standard form for referencing an aggregate storage location from within the SAS System is *fileref(name)*, where the *fileref* is the entire aggregate and the *(name)* is a specific file or member of that aggregate. See also fileref.

AID key
an acronym for attention ID key. AID keys (for example, ENTER, PA1, PA2, and the function keys) are features of 3270 series terminals. The AID key requests the attention of the 3270 system. When you press an AID key, it becomes the first component in the 3270 data stream; it describes the action that caused the data stream to be sent.

API
an abbreviation for application programming interface. API is a formally defined programming language interface. Some 3270 emulation programs offer an API to enable an application to read and write 3270 screens and to type on the keyboard. An example is IBM's HLLAPI offered by most 3270 vendors as a standard program interface.

APPC*
an acronym for Advanced Program-to-Program Communication. This type of connection uses the LU6.2 protocol for distributed processing within an IBM Systems Network Architecture (SNA) network. The terms APPC and LU6.2 are often used interchangeably.

ASCII
an acronym for the American Standard Code for Information Interchange. ASCII is a 7-bit character coding scheme (8 bits when a parity check bit is included) including graphic (printable) and control (nonprintable) codes.

ASCII collating sequence
an ordering of characters that follows the order of the characters in the American Standard Code for Information Interchange (ASCII) character coding scheme. The SAS System uses the same collating sequence as its host operating system. See also EBCDIC collating sequence.

ASCII mnemonics
the names of ASCII control characters that you can specify in a program to invoke the associated function. For example, NUL represents the null character, CR represents carriage return, and so on.

async
See asynchronous communication.

asynchronous communication
a method of transferring data that does not require the information to be sent at a constant pace. Asynchronous (async) transmission enables data to be sent at irregular intervals by preceding each character code with a start bit and following it with a stop bit. Async communication is also called serial communication.

attention ID key
See AID key.

autoexec file
a file containing SAS statements that are executed automatically when the SAS System is invoked. The autoexec file can be used to specify some SAS system options, as well as librefs and filerefs that are commonly used.

base SAS software
software that includes a programming language that manages your data, procedures for data analysis and reporting, procedures for managing SAS files, a macro facility, help menus, and a windowing environment for text editing and file management.

batch mode
on mainframes and minicomputers, a method of running SAS programs in which you prepare a file containing SAS statements and any necessary operating system control statements and submit the file to the operating system. Execution is completely separate from other operations at your terminal and is sometimes referred to as running in background.

baud rate
the rate at which data are transmitted between two devices. Baud rate is a measure of data transmission speed equal to the number of signal changes per second. Baud rate expresses a quantity of signals traveling over a data link per second. You can roughly estimate the characters per second by dividing the baud rate by 10. Common baud rates are 1200, 2400, and 9600.

binary
the name of the base 2 number system. A binary digit can have one of two values: 0 or 1. A binary digit is called a bit and is considered to be off when its value is 0 and on when its value is 1.

board
See adapter.

break signal
in SAS/CONNECT and the micro-to-host link, a signal you send to your local host to interrupt an executing program. For PCs, you send a break signal by pressing the CONTROL and BREAK keys, or the CONTROL and C keys, simultaneously. While an RSUBMIT, SIGNON, or SIGNOFF command executes, a break signal from the local host

keyboard interrupts execution. The link software displays a break window to enable you to decide how to proceed by using special break window commands.

break window
a special class of display manager windows for SAS/CONNECT and the micro-to-host link. Break windows enable you to handle error conditions and interruptions you cause by issuing a control-break signal.

buffer
a portion of the computer's memory used for special holding purposes or processes. For example, a buffer might simply store information before sending it to main memory for processing. Or a buffer might hold data after they are read or before they are written.

card
a printed circuit board. See also adapter.

catalog
See SAS catalog.

catalog entry
See entry type and SAS catalog entry.

character set
a standardized way of representing alphabetic, numeric, and control characters. The most widely used character sets are ASCII and EBCDIC.

character set translation table
a file that contains ASCII-to-EBCDIC or EBCDIC-to-ASCII translation information. See also keyboard translation table.

client
in a network, a workstation requesting services from the server. See also server.

client/server*
an arrangement used on networks that treats both the server workstation and the individual client workstations as programmable devices. The processing of an application is distributed between the software running on the client and server workstations. The server software accepts data or requests for processing from client software and returns the data or results to the client. The client portion of the application is typically optimized for user interaction, whereas the server portion provides centralized, multi-user functionality.

coaxial cable
a type of communications cable used for networks and for connecting 3270 terminals to remote host 3270 controllers. Coaxial cable can carry data at high rates and is resistant to electrical interference.

collating sequence
See ASCII collating sequence and EBCDIC collating sequence.

COM port
a serial communication port supported by the DOS and OS/2 operating systems. The COM ports are named COM1, COM2, and COM3. A COM port is also called an async or serial port.

command file
in SAS software, a file that contains operating system commands to be executed in sequence.

Communication Services Break Handler window
one of two possible windows displayed when a remote session is interrupted by a control break or when there is an error in a statement submitted to the remote host. This window offers the following selections: **continue, disconnect link, debug, resend, snapshot screen, type, subset command**, and **invoke the Application Break Handler**. See also SAS/CONNECT Attention Handler window.

communications access method
the method your local session uses to communicate with a remote host. Values for the communications access method are specified with the COMAMID= system option.

communications adapter
See adapter and communications hardware.

communications board
See adapter and communications hardware.

communications card
See adapter and communications hardware.

communications controller
a machine that manages the control of communications lines so that CPU resources can be used for performing applications processing. A communications controller is also known as a communications processor, front end processor, or transaction processor.

communications hardware
computer hardware used in connections between a terminal and host computer or between two computers. Communications hardware usually refers to a communications adapter, also called a communications board or communications card. The kind of hardware you use determines the kind of connection you have, either async or 3270.

Communications Manager
the communications component for OS/2 Extended Edition software that provides multiple connections to hosts. This enables you to have several communications sessions active at the same time.

communications options
options that specify what communications method to use (EHLLAPI, RASYNC, TELNET, TCP) and which port or remote host to use in establishing the link (remote host session id, such as A or B; or COM1, COM2, COM3, or host name). Which options to use depends on the operating systems and communications methods involved.

compute services
services of the SAS System for distributed applications. These services use remote computing resources (hardware, software, and data) to execute an application more efficiently than execution on a single, local system would be. See also distributed application.

configuration file
an external file containing SAS system options that are put into effect when the SAS System is invoked.

configuration option
a SAS option that can be specified in the SAS command or in a configuration file. Configuration options affect how the SAS System interfaces with the computer hardware and operating system.

control character
a character, usually nonprintable, used for control purposes rather than for information exchange.

control program
a low-level software interface, such as SAS/CONNECT, between communications hardware and applications programs. A control program works in conjunction with an adapter.

crc checksum
one or more characters appended to the end of a data block for error checking purposes.

CUT
an acronym for Control Unit Terminal, an IBM 3270 network term. All control of data flow with CUT-mode 3270 terminals is done by the 3274 type controller, in contrast to DFTs, which perform some controller functions. See also DFT.

data representation
the format in which data of a particular type are represented on a computer architecture or operating system. For example, on the IBM mainframe under the MVS operating system, character data are represented by means of their EBCDIC encoding, while on the IBM PC, such data are represented by their ASCII encoding.

data transfer services
services of the SAS System for copying data to and from a remote system. By creating copies of the data on the local or remote machine, further transfer of the data across the network may not be required for subsequent analyses on either machine.

data translation
the conversion of data from one data representation to another data representation. See also data representation.

DECnet**
Digital Equipment Corporation's networking software that runs on nodes in both local and wide-area networks.

DFT
an abbreviation for Distributed Function Terminal, an IBM 3270 network term. In contrast with CUTs, DFTs participate with the 3274 controller in controlling the flow of data. DFT mode also enables you to run more than one remote host session. DFT-mode 3270 terminal emulation is more complicated than CUT-mode 3270 emulation and uses much more memory than CUT-mode emulation programs.

display manager
See SAS Display Manager System.

distributed application
an application, typically implemented in a client/server environment, whose components are distributed for execution over various nodes of the network. Depending on the specific update and retrieval traffic, distributing the application can significantly enhance overall performance. See also client/server.

download
to copy a file from the remote host to the local host.

DTR
an abbreviation for Data Terminal Ready, a signal indicating that the local host is functioning as a terminal in an async connection. The DTR signal must be held high (remain on) so the connection between the local host and remote host remains intact. This is especially important when you quit an async terminal emulator and then run a SAS/CONNECT async connection.

duplex
a feature of async communication in which a channel provides simultaneous transmission of data between remote host and local host (full duplex) or one-way transmission (half duplex).

EBCDIC
an acronym for Extended Binary Coded Decimal Interchange Code. EBCDIC is an 8-bit character coding scheme including graphic (printable) and control (nonprintable) codes.

EBCDIC collating sequence
an ordering of characters that follows the order in the Extended Binary Coded Decimal Interchange Code (EBCDIC) character coding scheme. The SAS System uses the same collating sequence as its host operating system. See also ASCII collating sequence.

echoplex
the remote echoing of characters typed at the local terminal as a form of confirmation of the character typed. Half duplex or echoplex off means that characters are not echoed but are displayed at the local terminal by the terminal hardware. Full and half duplex can also refer to the asychronous send and receive capabilities of the communications line.

EHLLAPI
an acronym for Emulator High-Level Language Applications Programming Interface, a Communications Manager application program interface that enables users and programmers to access the 3270 host presentation space. EHLLAPI is the same as HLLAPI, but IBM uses EHLLAPI in references to Extended Edition OS/2.

engine
a part of the SAS System that reads from or writes to a file. Each engine allows the SAS System to access files with a particular format. There are several types of engines. See also interface engine, library engine, native engine, and view engine.

entry
in SAS software, a unit of information stored in a SAS catalog. Catalog entries differ widely in content and purpose. See also entry type.

entry type
a characteristic of a SAS catalog entry that identifies its structure and attributes to the SAS System. When you create an entry, the SAS System automatically assigns the entry type as part of the name.

environment variable
(1) on some hosts, a named operating system variable that represents or contains a value. The value can be specified using an operating system option, an operating system command, or both. The environment variables that are defined in one operating system process are not available to other operating system processes. (2) in OS/2, a variable that equates one string with another under OS/2, using the SET system option or the OS/2 SET command. The environment variables that are defined in one OS/2 process are not available to other OS/2 processes.

external database
a database that stores data that are not part of the SAS System, for example DB2, ORACLE, and SYBASE.

external file
(1) a file maintained by the host operating system that the SAS System can read data from and route output to. External files can contain raw data, SAS programming statements, procedure output, or output created by the PUT statement. See also fileref. (2) in a DATA step, a file the SAS System can read using INFILE and INPUT statements or a file the SAS System can write to using FILE and PUT statements.

file specification
the name of an external file. This name is the name by which the host operating system recognizes the file. On directory-based systems, the file specification can be either the complete pathname or the relative pathname from the current working directory.

fileref
a name temporarily assigned to an external file or to an aggregate storage location that identifies it to the SAS System. You assign a fileref with a FILENAME statement or with an operating system command.

Do not confuse filerefs with librefs. Filerefs are used for external files; librefs are used for SAS data libraries. See also libref.

gateway*
a device that connects networks that use the same or different communications protocols, enabling information to be passed from one network to the other. If the protocols are different, a gateway both transfers information and converts it to a form compatible with the protocols that are used by the second network for transport and delivery.

graphical user interface (GUI)*
a type of computer display format that enables a user to choose commands, start programs, and see lists of files and other options by pointing to pictorial representations (icons) and to lists of menu items on the screen. Choices can typically be activated either with the keyboard or with a mouse.

GRLINK
a special device driver that you must always use on the remote host when using SAS/CONNECT to execute graphics statements on the remote host and display graphs on the local host.

handshaking
the exchange of signals between two devices over an interface for control or synchronization purposes. Data flow control is needed to ensure that data are not sent faster than the receiving device can process them. Handshaking usually involves sending signals between the device and the host computer in order to start and stop transmission of data.

HLLAPI
an acronym for High-Level Language Applications Programming Interface, a Communications Manager application program interface that enables users and programmers to access the 3270 host presentation space. EHLLAPI is the same as HLLAPI, but IBM uses EHLLAPI in references to Extended Edition OS/2.

host
the operating system that provides facilities, computer services, and the environment for software applications.

hot key
one or a combination of keys that enables you to switch from a local session to a remote host or from a remote host to a local session when you have a 3270 connection. The keys you use depend on your local host and terminal emulator, if any. You must be running a control program or a resident terminal emulator to use hot keys.

inbound packet
a unit of bytes transmitted from a local host to a remote host.

interactive line mode
a method of running SAS programs without using the SAS Display Manager System. You enter one line of a SAS program at a time. The SAS System processes each line immediately after you enter it.

keyboard translation table
a file that contains 3270 scan code translation information for use with non-U.S. 3274 controllers and non-U.S. typewriter keyboards. See also character set translation table.

libref
the name temporarily associated with a SAS data library. You assign a libref with a LIBNAME statement or with operating system control language.

line mode
See interactive line mode.

link
in SAS/CONNECT, intercomputer communication in which one computer is a local host and the other is a remote host. The link can be used to transfer files or to distribute processing to computers other than the local host.

local area network (LAN)*
a group of computers and other devices dispersed over a geographically limited area and connected by a communications link that enables any device to interact with any other on the network. Separate LANs can be connected to form larger networks. LANs that use the same physical and communications protocols are linked by bridges or gateways, whereas dissimilar LANs are linked by gateways. See also gateway.

local host
the computer on which you use a SAS session to initiate a link with a remote host. See also local session.

local session
a SAS session running on the local host. The local session accepts SAS statements and passes those that are remote-submitted to the remote host for processing. The local session manages the output and messages from both the local session and the remote session.

macro facility
a portion of the SAS System used for extending and customizing the SAS System and for reducing the amount of text that must be entered to do common tasks. It consists of the macro processor and the macro language.

macro variable
a variable belonging to the macro language whose value is a string that remains constant until you change it. A macro variable is also called a symbolic variable.

member
(1) a file in a SAS data library. (2) under CMS, a single file in a CMS LOADLIB, MACLIB, or TXTLIB. (3) under MVS, a single component of a partitioned data set. (4) under OpenVMS, a component of an OpenVMS text library.

member name
(1) a name given to a SAS file in a SAS data library. A member name can reference a SAS data set, catalog, access descriptor, or stored program. (2) under CMS, the name of a single file in a CMS LOADLIB, MACLIB, or TXTLIB. (3) under MVS, the name of a single component of a partitioned data set. (4) under OS/2, member name is equivalent to filename for files stored in a SAS data library. (5) under OpenVMS, member name is synonymous with filename for files stored in a SAS data library.

member type
a name assigned by the SAS System that identifies the type of information stored in a SAS file. Member types include ACCESS, DATA, CATALOG, PROGRAM, and VIEW.

methods of running the SAS System
(1) standard methods of operation used to run SAS System programs. These methods are SAS/ASSIST, display manager, interactive line mode, noninteractive mode, and batch mode. (2) in SAS/CONNECT, in addition to standard methods used to run SAS System programs, a special mode of operation is invoked when you initiate a link. This mode, called display manager remote, is initiated by using the DMR system option in the script that invokes the SAS System on the remote host. No output or log messages appear in the display manager remote session; they are passed back to the local SAS System session. (3) under Windows, only SAS/ASSIST, display manager, and batch mode are supported.

micro-to-host link
a facility of SAS software prior to Release 6.06 that allows communication between a SAS session under DOS and a SAS session on a remote host computer. In Release 6.06 and later releases of SAS software, the capabilities of the micro-to-host link are included in SAS/CONNECT.

multi-observation buffering
a method of transmitting more than one observation in each exchange with a SAS server. The TOBSNO= data set option is used to specify a different number of observations per exchange than the number calculated by SAS software.

NetBIOS*
an acronym for Network Basic Input/Output System. NetBIOS is an application programming interface (API) for application programs running on nodes in a local area network (LAN).

non-U.S. keyboard
a keyboard that is not a standard U.S. typewriter keyboard. Non-English language keyboards often have characters not found on U.S. keyboards and, likewise, may not have some characters found on U.S. keyboards.

noninteractive mode
a method of running SAS programs in which you prepare a file of SAS statements and submit the program to the computer system. The program runs immediately and occupies your current terminal session.

open mode
a way that a SAS task accesses and operates on a member in a SAS data library. There are three open modes for SAS files: input, update, and output.

outbound packet
a unit of bytes transmitted from a remote host to a local host.

packet
a grouping of printable characters, a sequence number, and a checksum, which are transmitted over the link as a unit. The SAS/CONNECT local and remote hosts use these specially formatted packets to communicate with each other.

parity
(1) a form of error-checking in which an extra bit is added to each byte so that the total number of bits in each byte forms a particular pattern or sum. For odd parity, the number of bits set to 1 in each byte is odd; for even parity, the number of bits set to 1 is even. (2) a simplistic technique for detecting async transmission errors.

peer-to-peer configuration***
data communications support that routes data in a network between two or more APPC systems that do not need to be adjacent. See also APPC and program-to-program communications.

permanent SAS data library
a library that is not deleted when the SAS session terminates; it is available for subsequent SAS sessions. Unless the USER libref is defined, you use a two-level name to access a file in a permanent library. The first-level name is the libref, and the second-level name is the member name.

permanent SAS file
a SAS file in a library that is not deleted when the SAS session or job terminates.

physical filename
the name the operating system uses to identify a file.

procedure output file
an external file that contains the result of the analysis or the report produced. Most procedures write output to the procedure output file by default. Reports that DATA steps

produce using PUT statements and a FILE statement with the PRINT destination also go to this file.

program generator
a SAS program that writes another SAS program. Most program generators are DATA step programs, but some procedures can also generate programs.

program-to-program communications
a communications protocol that allows interconnected systems, such as those in a peer-to-peer configuration, to communicate and to share the processing of programs. See also peer-to-peer configuration.

protocol converter
a device that enables ASCII terminals to communicate with host systems by converting the ASCII data stream to an IBM 3270 data stream and vice versa.

reboot
to reinitialize your PC or PS/2 (when it is already started) by pressing the CTRL, ALT, and DEL keys simultaneously. Rebooting aborts any application you are running at the time.

remote data services
Remote library services and data transfer services of the SAS System for distributed applications. These services enable access to data that are stored in a remote environment. These data can include SAS data sets, external database files, SAS catalogs, and external files. See also data transfer services, REMOTE engine, and remote library services.

REMOTE engine
a SAS library engine that enables a user's SAS session to access data by communicating with another SAS session. See also remote library services and remote session.

remote host
in SAS/CONNECT, the computer on which processing occurs when you execute a PROC DOWNLOAD, PROC UPLOAD, or other SAS statement that is executed with the RSUBMIT command or statement. The term remote is used to describe how you interact with the SAS session running on the computer; it is not related to the physical location of the computer. See also local host and remote session.

remote library services (RLS)
services of the SAS System for distributed applications. These services provide transparent access to remote data libraries and move data through the network as the local SAS session requests it. The data must pass through the network if they are needed subsequently by local processing. See also distributed application.

remote processing
the process of using communications software to process local jobs with the CPU resources of a remote host. With SAS/CONNECT, the output and messages from a program running on the remote host are displayed on the local host.

remote session
a SAS session running in a special mode on the remote host. No output or log messages are displayed on the remote host; instead, the results of a remote SAS session are transmitted back to the log and output files on the local host.

remote submit
to use the RSUBMIT command or statement to submit statements entered in a local SAS session to be executed by a remote SAS session.

resident software
software that is loaded into the PC's memory and remains there until the machine is turned off or rebooted. Resident software uses some of the memory available to your PC session. If too much memory is taken up by resident software, you may not be able to run certain applications, including SAS software.

return code
a code passed to the operating system that reports whether a command or job step has executed successfully.

RS-232
a particular kind of communications connector and hardware protocol that is usually used for async and SDLC connections.

SAS catalog
a SAS file that stores many different kinds of information in smaller units called catalog entries. A single SAS catalog can contain several different types of catalog entries. Some catalog entries contain system information such as key definitions. Other catalog entries contain application information such as window definitions, help windows, formats, informats, macros, or graphics output.

SAS catalog entry
a separate storage unit within a SAS catalog. Each entry has an entry type that identifies its structure to the SAS System. See also entry type.

SAS command
a command that invokes the SAS System. This command may vary depending on operating system and site. See also SAS invocation.

SAS/CONNECT Attention Handler window
one of two possible windows displayed when a remote session is interrupted by a break signal. This window offers the following selections: abort current remote processing or continue processing the current remote submit. See Communication Services Break Handler window.

SAS data file
(1) a SAS data set that contains both the data values and the descriptor information. (2) in the SAS data model, a SAS data set that is implemented in a form that contains both the data values and the descriptor information. SAS data files have the type DATA. (3) one of the formats of a SAS data set implemented in Version 6 of the SAS System. A SAS data file contains both the data values and the descriptor information associated with the data, such as the variable attributes. In previous releases of the SAS System, all SAS data sets were SAS data files. SAS data files are of member type DATA. In the SAS System, a PROC SQL table is a SAS data file.

SAS data library
a collection of one or more SAS files that are recognized by the SAS System and that are referenced and stored as a unit. Each file is a member of the library.

SAS data set
descriptor information and its related data values organized as a table of observations and variables that can be processed by the SAS System. A SAS data set can be either a SAS data file or a SAS data view.

SAS data view
a SAS data set in which the descriptor information and the observations are obtained from other files. SAS data views store only the information required to retrieve data values or descriptor information.

SAS Display Manager System
an interactive, windowing interface to SAS System software. Display manager commands can be issued by typing them on the command line, pressing function keys, or selecting items from the PMENU facility. Within one session, many different tasks can be accomplished, including preparing and submitting programs, viewing and printing results, and debugging and resubmitting programs.

SAS file
a specially structured file that is created, organized, and, optionally, maintained by the SAS System. A SAS file can be a SAS data set, a catalog, a stored program, or an access descriptor.

SAS invocation
the process of calling or starting up the SAS System by an individual user through execution of the SAS command. Invoking the SAS System initiates SAS initialization.

SAS log
a file that contains the SAS statements you have submitted, messages about the execution of your program, and in some cases, output from the DATA step and from certain procedures.

SAS server
a SAS session that provides data and processing services as part of a distributed application. See also distributed application.

SAS Software Consultant
an individual at your computing installation who is designated as a support person for SAS software users at the installation. The consultant can help you with questions about using SAS software.

SAS Software Representative
an individual at your computing installation who is designated as SAS Institute's contact for information on new and existing software. The representative receives any distribution package of software from the Institute. For SAS sites running DOS or OS/2, the representative coordinates distribution of software diskettes within the site. The representative can help you with questions about installing and configuring SAS software.

SAS system option
an option that affects processing the entire SAS program or interactive SAS session from the time the option is specified until it is changed. Examples of items controlled by SAS system options include appearance of SAS output, handling of some files used by the SAS System, use of system variables, processing observations in SAS data sets, features of SAS System initialization, and the SAS System's interface with your computer hardware and with the host operating system.

sasroot
a term that represents the name of the directory where the SAS System is installed at your site or on your workstation.

scan code
a number that a CUT-mode 3270 emulator sends to the 3270 controller to indicate a keystroke. The scan code is related to the key's position and not its label. Each relative key position on any 3270 keyboard always sends the same scan code, but the controller can interpret it differently. How the controller interprets the code depends on the keyboard type or foreign character set.

SCL function
in the SAS screen control language (SCL), a mathematical relationship between variables that assigns exactly one value of the dependent variable to each combination of values of the independent variables. See also Screen Control Language (SCL).

Screen Control Language (SCL)
a programming language provided in SAS/AF and SAS/FSP software to develop interactive applications that manipulate SAS data sets and external files; display tables, menus, and selection lists; generate SAS source code and submit it to the SAS System for execution; and generate code for execution by the host command processor.

script
an external file stored on the local host containing SAS script statements that provide the instructions needed to establish and terminate the SAS/CONNECT link. Scripts are executed by the SIGNON and SIGNOFF commands.

script statement
a special kind of SAS statement developed for use in scripts for SAS/CONNECT. Script statements are not used in any kind of SAS program except a script.

server
in a network, a special workstation, machine, or computer reserved for servicing other computers in the network. Servers can provide file services, communication services, and so on. Servers enable users to access common resources such as disks, data, and modems. See also client.

snapshot
a selection in the Communication Services Break Handler window that is displayed when a SAS/CONNECT session is interrupted and is applicable only to 3270 access methods. Snapshot copies the remote session's 3270 screen to the local SAS LOG window.

spawner
a program that listens for incoming requests to connect the requesting program to a program on the machine that is running the spawner.

SQL
See Structured Query Language (SQL).

start bit
a bit in asynchronous data transmission that indicates the start of a new character code.

statement label
a SAS name followed by a colon that prefixes a statement in a DATA step so that other statements can direct execution to that statement as necessary, bypassing other statements in the step.

stop bit
one or more bits in asynchronous data transmission that indicate the end of a character code. The most common number of stop bits is 1, with 2 sometimes used for transmission speeds below 300 baud.

Structured Query Language (SQL)
the standardized, high-level query language used in relational database management systems to create and manipulate database management system objects. The SAS System implements SQL through the SQL procedure.

subset mode
the local host environment available when you execute an X command with no operands in a local SAS session.

system option
See SAS system option.

TCP/IP
an abbreviation for a pair of networking protocols. Transmission Control Protocol (TCP) is a standard protocol for transferring information on local area networks such as Ethernets. TCP ensures that process-to-process information is delivered in the proper order. Internet Protocol (IP) is a protocol for managing connections between hosts. IP routes information through the network to a particular host and fragments and reassembles information in host-to-host transfers.

TELNET
an acronym for Teletypewriter Network Protocol. TELNET is a program that provides virtual terminal services that enable you to log on to a remote host from a terminal connected to a local host. The local terminal performs as if it were physically connected to the remote host. TELNET, as used with SAS/CONNECT, is always executed via an automatic log-on script, not directly by a user.

terminal-based communications
a communications protocol that is designed for displaying data on a terminal. Applications that use this protocol must put all data into a screen image, including data that are not intended to be read by a user. This requirement limits the efficiency of communications if the protocol is used for communication between two processes.

terminal emulation
the PC imitation of an ASCII terminal or 3270 terminal for the purpose of communicating with a remote host or communications network.

terminal emulator
software, hardware, or a combination of the two that simulates the operation of a particular model of terminal. For example, terminal emulators simulate VT100 and IBM 3270 terminals.

timeout
an error condition produced when a required response from a device is not received. Some SAS script statements control what happens when a timeout occurs.

toggle
an option, parameter, or other mechanism that enables you to turn on or turn off a processing feature.

token ring network*
a local area network (LAN) formed in a ring topology that passes tokens as a means of regulating traffic on the line. On a token ring network, a token that governs the right to transmit is passed from one station to the next in a physical circle.

translation table
See character set translation table and keyboard translation table.

transparent mode
the mode the converter operates in when using a protocol converter with SAS/CONNECT. Transparent mode enables the remote host to send ASCII data directly to the local host without performing the normal data conversion for 3270-type appearance.

TTY
an abbreviation for teletypewriter equipment. This term actually is used for any asynchronous terminal, not teletype equipment.

TTY program
a low-level asynchronous terminal emulator used with PC DOS or OS/2. This program does not provide full-function terminal emulation.

upload
to copy a file from the local host to the remote host.

view
See SAS data view.

WHERE expression
a type of SAS expression used to specify a condition for selecting observations for processing by a DATA or PROC step. WHERE expressions can contain special operators not available in other SAS expressions. WHERE expressions can appear in a WHERE statement, a WHERE= data set option, a WHERE clause, or a WHERE command.

WHERE statement
See WHERE expression.

3270
IBM's designation for a series of terminals, printers, and control units used primarily on its mainframes. With a 3270 adapter and emulation software, a PC can emulate a 3270 series terminal.

3270 connection
the link between local host and remote host if the adapter is a 3270 adapter.

---

* identifies terms whose definitions are taken directly or paraphrased from *Microsoft Press Computer Dictionary*, 4th Edition, 1991.

** identifies terms whose definitions are taken directly or paraphrased from *The Digital Dictionary*, published by Digital Equipment Corporation, 1984, 1986.

*** identifies terms whose definitions are from *IBM Dictionary of Computing*, Ninth Edition, 1991.

Index

A

ABORT script statement 254
Access Control Information (ACI)
   starting SAS/CONNECT with DECnet access method 116
access methods
   listing for current operating system 202
   specifying 174
   specifying with a spawner program 137
   summary of available connections 14
access pattern, definition 33
accessing remote data with WHERE statement
   example 36
ACF/VTAM, APPC on CMS 94
ACI (Access Control Information)
   See Access Control Information (ACI)
-ADAPTER option, spawner program 138
adapters 290
administration tasks for remote data sets
   example 20–21
alarm, OS/2
   turning off 162
API (applications programming interface)
   See applications programming interface (API)
APPC access method 11
   available connections 94
   CMS requirements 94–97
   CMS to MVS 105–106
   configuring CMS userids 95–97
   MVS requirements 97–99
   MVS to CMS 107
   MVS to OS/2 107
   OS/2 requirements 99–100
   OS/2 to MVS 108
   OS/2 to OS/2 108
   OS/2 to TSO 109
   OS/2 to VSE 109
   passing password or userid to remote host on MVS 98
   requirements for CMS 94–97
   specifying VTAM LOGMODE entry for VSE 104
   troubleshooting 110–113
   VSE definition, example 103
   VSE requirements 102–104
   Windows 32s requirements 101–102
   Windows 32s to MVS 106–107
APPC/VM VTAM Support (AVS) 94
APPC_LU62MODE environment variable, OS/2 100
APPC_PARTNER_COUNT 102
APPC_SECURE environment variable
   OS/2 100
   Windows 32s 102
APPC_SURROGATE_LUNAME environment variable
   OS/2 100
   Windows 32s 102
APPCAPPL= system option, VSE 104
APPCLOGM= system option, VSE 104
APPCPASS statement, CMS 96
APPCSEC= system option
   MVS 98
   VSE 104
applications programming interface (API) 12
ASCII
   control character mnemonics 272–273
   translation to EBCDIC 285–288
ASYNC access method
   handling host messages 89–91
   line noise 157
   losing data 156
   manual logon 65
   protocol converters 147
   troubleshooting 155–158
   TTY 147
asynchronous terminal
   simulating a 3270-type terminal 147
at sign (@)
   in userids and passwords 98
autoexec file 68–70
automated remote processing
   micro-to-host link connection 312–315
automatic logon, sample script 79–82
AVS (APPC/VM VTAM Support)
   See APPC/VM VTAM Support (AVS)

B

-B option, TTY 150
background color, changing 164
backing up data, local files to remote host 7
.BAT file name, specifying with a spawner program 138
batch file name, specifying with a spawner program 138
baud rate, setting for TTY under ASYNC 150
BAUD script statement 254
binary data
   downloading 209
   uploading 231
BINARY option
   DOWNLOAD procedure 45, 209, 224–225
   UPLOAD procedure 231, 246–247
boards
   See adapters
break, signal to host
   TTY under ASYNC 151
BREAK script statement 255

BREAK window, micro-to-host link connection 316–318
break windows 87

C

-C option, TTY 150
CALL script statement 255
CANCEL option, ENDRSUBMIT statement 188
cards
    See adapters
case sensitivity
    script statements 71
    userids and passwords 98
    WAITFOR statement 160–161
catalog entries
    downloading 44, 209
    excluding members from downloading 216–217
    excluding members from uploading 238–239
    recompiling PROGRAM type 223, 245
    selecting members for downloading 217–218
    selecting members for uploading 239–240
    selecting types for downloading 220–223
    selecting types for uploading 242–245
    transferring 7, 25
    transferring in original order 44
    uploading 231
    uploading or downloading 7
    valid types for downloading 221–223
    valid types for uploading 243–245
catalogs
    downloading 209
    naming destination when downloading 212
    naming destination when uploading 234
    uploading 231
    uploading graphics output 47
CBACK= option, remote graphics processing 25
Change Number of Sessions (CNOS)
    APPC protocol command 94
CHARWAIT script statement 256
CHKCODE macro 56–57
client/server environment
    copying data 6
    data transfer services diagram 7
    remote library services (RLS) 8
    SAS/CONNECT vs. SAS/SHARE 283–284
.CMD file name, specifying with a spawner program 138
CMS
    APPC access method 94–97
    APPC aliasing restrictions 95
    communications directory files 95
    configuring userids for APPC 95–97
    EHLLAPI access method 141
    interrupting processing 88
    script directory 65
    SET commands for APPC 97
    signing on to MVS with APPC, example 105
    specifying UNIX domain with GLOBALV statement 125
    TCP/IP 122–123
CMS communications directory entry 95

CNOS (Change Number of Sessions)
    See Change Number of Sessions (CNOS)
colon (:)
    in macro variable 117
    on EXCLUDE statement 216, 238
    script label delimiter 71
color, background
    changing 164
COM port sharing
    not allowed with TTY under ASYNC 149
-COMAMID option
    MVS to OS/2 with APPC, example 107
    OS/2 to OS/2 with APPC, example 108
    spawner program 137
COMAMID SCL function 202
COMAMID= system option 51, 53–54
    APPC 104–105
    APPC on CMS 97
    automatic logon script 66, 79–82
    CMS to MVS with APPC, example 106
    DECnet, starting SAS/CONNECT 116
    EHLLAPI, starting SAS/CONNECT 143
    in autoexec file 69
    local host 183–184
    manual logon script 67, 82–85
    micro-to-host link releases 322
    MVS to CMS with APPC, example 106
    NetBIOS, starting SAS/CONNECT 133
    OS/2 to MVS with APPC, example 108
    remote host 184
    requested link not found 161
    script example 73–74
    specifying via Signon window 63
    syntax 174
    table of values 174–183
    TCP/IP, starting SAS/CONNECT 125
    TTY-to-VSE connection, sample 153–155
    Windows 32s to MVS with APPC, example 106
combining data from remote sessions
    example 49–52
commands, submitting locally for host processing 193
Communication Services Break Handler window 88–89
communications directory files 95
communications mode
    APPC on OS/2 specification 100
    APPC on Windows 32s, specification 102
communications port, setting for TTY under ASYNC 150
compute services 3, 18–19
    client/server diagram 4
    combined with data transfer services, examples 52–57
    examples 34–40
    Remote SQL Pass-Through (RSPT) 5, 18, 191
    RSUBMIT command 193
condition code, SAS/CONNECT
    checking under APPC on MVS 99
CONNECT TO statement, RSPT 191
connecting SAS sessions 8
continuing after an error 88–89

controller, IBM 3274
    GRLINK device driver 163
conversations, number of simultaneous
    setting as NetBIOS environment variable
        134
copying a remote screen to LOG window
    debugging host-not-active message 160–161
creating 3270 keyboard translation tables
    micro-to-host link connection 303–306

D

-D option, TTY 150
data bits, setting for TTY under ASYNC 150
data libraries
    downloading 210
    excluding members from downloading
        216–217
    excluding members from uploading 238–239
    naming destination when downloading 211
    naming destination when uploading 233
    selecting members for downloading 217–218
    selecting members for uploading 239–240
    uploading 232
data lost under ASYNC 156
DATA= option
    See also SAS data views
    DOWNLOAD procedure 45, 209
    UPLOAD procedure 231
data sets
    attributes inherited during downloading
        214–215
    attributes inherited during uploading
        236–237
    attributes replicated during upload 7
    naming conventions for downloaded
        212–214
    naming conventions for uploaded 234–236
    naming destination when downloading 211
    naming destination when uploading 233
    naming for download 209
    naming for upload 231
    omitting index on download 210
    omitting index on upload 232
    used by multiple local hosts, example 55–56
data transfer services 3, 39–40
    combined with compute services, examples
        52–57
    combined with RLS, examples 58–60
    diagram 7
    DOWNLOAD procedure 207–227
    examples of use 42–52
    UPLOAD procedure 229–249
data translation, under RLS 32–33
data views
    See SAS data views
DATABITS script statement 257
DBMS, connecting to a remote 191–192
DBMS= option, CONNECT TO statement
    191–192
DBMSARG= option, CONNECT TO statement
    191–192
DCL symbol, DECnet OpenVMS-to-OpenVMS
    connection 116

debugging scripts 78–79
DECnet access method 11
    available connections 115
    OpenVMS requirements 115
    starting SAS/CONNECT 116
    troubleshooting 118–119
    Windows 3.x requirements 116
DELAY script statement 156, 257
device drivers
    GRLINK 163–164
    specifying with a spawner program 138
DEVICE= system option
    automatic logon script 79–82
    manual logon script 82–85
display manager, invoking remote version 184
distributing
    .EXE files to local hosts, example 45–46
    reports, example 58–60
-DMR option
    MVS to OS/2 with APPC, example 107
    OS/2 to OS/2 with APPC, example 108
DMR system option
    APPC on CMS 97
    automatic logon script 79–82
    CMS to MVS with APPC, example 106
    manual logon script 82–85
    MVS to CMS with APPC, example 107
    OS/2 to MVS with APPC, example 108
    OS/2 to TSO with APPC, example 109
    script example 73–74, 77–78
    syntax 184
    TTY-to-VSE connection, sample 153–155
    Windows 32s to MVS with APPC, example
        106
dollar sign ($)
    in userids and passwords 98
DOS environment variable
    DECnet Windows-to-OpenVMS connection
        117
double quote (")
    marking case sensitivity in scripts 71
DOWNLINK.SAS program 49
DOWNLOAD procedure 7, 9, 207
    carriage control characters missing 166
    carriage control characters not translated
        166
    defining filerefs and librefs 226
    downloading file from remote host 191
    FILENAME statement 191
    micro-to-host link releases 325
    procedure not found 164–165
    segmented files 165
    symbol not recognized 165
    syntax 208–212
    transferring graphics catalogs 163
downloading
    binary data 209
    binary data without translation 224–225
    catalog entries 7, 44, 209
    catalogs 43, 209
    data library 210
    data set attributes inherited 214–215
    data sets 43
    excluding catalog entries 216–217
    excluding data library members 216–217

downloading *(continued)*
    external file 210
    from remote systems to local 40-41
    library members 7
    member types 211
    naming data sets 209
    naming destination catalogs 212
    naming destination data libraries 211
    naming destination data sets 211
    naming destination files 212
    omitting data set indexes 210
    partitioned data sets 47-49
    selected catalog entries 217-218
    selected catalog entry types 220-223
    selected data library members 217-218
    selectively applying translation table 219
    specifying member types 219-220
    status 223-224
    text files with record length over 132 bytes 227
    variable block records 227
    with WHERE processing 7
-DRIVER option, spawner program 138
driver table network
    setting as NetBIOS environment variables 134-135
DROP= data set option 45

E

-E option, TTY 150
EBCDIC, translation to ASCII 285-288
ECHO script statement 158, 161
    debugging scripts 79
    syntax 258
echoplex
    setting for TTY under ASYNC 151
    toggle on and off 151
EHLLAPI access method 12, 141
    available connections 141
    handling host messages 89-91
    manual logoff with a script 68
    manual logon 65
    manual logon with a script 67
    OS/2 requirements 142
    starting SAS/CONNECT 143
    troubleshooting 144-145
    Windows 3.x requirements 142-143
    Windows 32s requirements 142
    with a script 72-75
ENDRSUBMIT statement 51, 53-54
    See also RSUBMIT statement
    example 199-200
    in autoexec file 70
    syntax 188
ENTRYTYPE= option
    DOWNLOAD procedure 43-44, 209
    TRANTAB statement 220-223, 242-245
    UPLOAD procedure 231
environment variables, OS/2
    APPC 99
    APPC_LUNAME 100
    APPC_LU62MODE 100

APPC_SECURE 100
APPC_SURROGATE_LUNAME 100
environment variables, Windows
    EHLLAPI 143
environment variables, Windows 32s
    APPC 101
    APPC_LUNAME 102
    APPC_LU62MODE 102
    APPC_SECURE 102
    APPC_SURROGATE_LUNAME 102
EOPCHAR script statement 258-259
errors, statements not processed following 168
ET= option
    DOWNLOAD procedure 209
    UPLOAD procedure 231
ETYPE= option
    DOWNLOAD procedure 209
    UPLOAD procedure 231
examples
    accessing remote data with WHERE statement 36
    administration tasks for remote data sets 20-21
    APPL definition on VSE 103
    BINARY option, DOWNLOAD procedure 225
    BINARY option, UPLOAD procedure 247
    combining data from remote sessions 49-52
    distributing data to local host users 45-46
    distributing reports 58-60
    downloading a partitioned data set 47-49
    downloading file from remote host 191
    ENDRSUBMIT statement 199-200
    FILENAME statement 190
    local update to a remote data set 37-39
    printing a list of reports 35
    querying a table in DB2 27
    remote applications from a local host 21-22
    remote graphics processing 22-25
    RSUBMIT command 194
    RSUBMIT statement 199-200
    saving remote results on local host 20
    SCL program with WHERE statement 37
    signing on CMS to MVS with APPC 105-106
    signing on MVS to CMS with APPC 107
    signing on MVS to OS/2 with APPC 107
    signing on OS/2 to MVS with APPC 108
    signing on OS/2 to OS/2 with APPC 108
    signing on OS/2 to TSO with APPC 109
    signing on OS/2 to VSE with APPC 109
    signing on Windows 32s to MVS with APPC 106-107
    SIGNOFF command/statement 196
    SIGNON command/statement 198-200
    submit statements to remote host 53-54
    subsetting remote data 39-40
    subsetting remote SAS data 28
    %SYSRPUT statement 200-201
    testing for successful upload/download completion 56-57
    transferring data with data set options and attributes 45

transferring data with WHERE statements 42
updating remote data 36
uploading catalog with graphics output 47
EXCLUDE statement
   DOWNLOAD procedure 42–44, 216–217
   DOWNLOAD procedure, syntax 216–217
   UPLOAD procedure 42–44
   UPLOAD procedure, syntax 238–239
EXEC file, CMS APPC session
   CMS $SERVER$ NAMES directory entry 96–97
EXECUTE statement, RSPT 191

F

-FILENAME option, spawner program 138
FILENAME statement 51, 226, 248
   in autoexec file 68
   in SAS autoexec file 190
   in UPLOAD/DOWNLOAD procedures 191
   micro-to-host link releases 325
   syntax 189
filerefs
   assigning RLINK in autoexec file 68
   associating with external file 189–191
   default in scripts 189
   defining 226, 248
   defining to an autoexec file 190
   setting in a script 68
files
   distributing across workstations 7
   downloading 210
   moving between releases 7
   naming destination when downloading 212
   naming destination when uploading 234
   transferring between hosts 7
   uploading 232
format catalog entries, uploading 44
FROM-clause component, RSPT 191

G

gateway name, CMS communications directory entry 95
GCS (Group Control System)
   See Group Control System (GCS)
GLOBALV statement, CMS
   specifying UNIX domain 125
GOPTIONS NODISPLAY option
   not supported with GRLINK driver 23
GOTO script statement 259
graphics
   adapters 163
   changing background color 164
   rotating 164
   transferring catalog entries with 25
   transferring catalogs 163
   uploading catalogs with 47
GREPLAY procedure
   remote graphics processing 25
GRLINK device driver 24–25, 163–164
   specified only on remote host 25

Group Control System (GCS)
   APPC on CMS 94
GSEG catalog 25

H

-H option, TTY 150
handshaking method
   setting for TTY under ASYNC 151
HANDSHAKING script statement 259
help
   requesting with a spawner program 138
   TTY under ASYNC 151
-HELP option, spawner program 138
hosts
   definition 9
   messages 90–91
   preserving numeric precision 167
   summary of available connections 14
hot keys 292
hyphen (-)
   dividing a TYPE statement 72
   on EXCLUDE statement 216, 238

I

ICAT (Installation and Configuration Automation Tool)
   See Installation and Configuration Automation Tool (ICAT)
IF script statement 260
INCAT= option
   DOWNLOAD procedure 43–44, 209
   downloading graphics catalogs 163
   UPLOAD procedure 43–44, 231
   uploading graphics catalogs 163
INDD= option
   DOWNLOAD procedure 210
   UPLOAD procedure 232
INDEX= option
   DOWNLOAD procedure 45, 210
   UPLOAD procedure 45, 232
indexes
   omitting on download 210
   omitting on upload 232
INFILE= option
   DOWNLOAD procedure 46, 210
   UPLOAD procedure 46, 232
initiating a connection 9
INLIB= option 42–43
   DOWNLOAD procedure 45, 210
   UPLOAD procedure 45, 232
INPUT script statement 261
INPUT statement
   automatic logon script 79–82
   script example 77–78
Installation and Configuration Automation Tool (ICAT)
   configuring TCP/IP for OS/2 124
interactive line mode 9
Internet address
   assigning to a macro variable 125

interrupting
    processing 87–88
    remote job after error 88–89

K

keyboard translation table
    setting for TTY under ASYNC 150
keyboards, non-English 226–227, 248–249
KEYS window
    assigning RSUBMIT command to a key 193
keystrokes, capturing in a script 72

L

LIBNAME statement
    DOWNLOAD procedure 226
    RLS example 34–35, 39–40
    RSPT example 28–29
    UPLOAD procedure 248
library members
    uploading or downloading 7
librefs, defining 226, 248
Line noise, ASYNC 157
LINEWAIT script statement 156
    syntax 261
links
    initiating 197
    setting active number as NetBIOS
        environment variables 134
    terminating 195
    verifying establishment 202–203
LIST catalog entries, uploading 44
Local Area Networks, OS/2 162
local connection, definition 9
local update to a remote data set, example
    37–39
log activity, TTY under ASYNC 151
LOG script statement 262
    debugging host-not-active message 160–161
    manual logon script 82–85
    script example 73–74, 76–77
logical unit (LU)
    specifying for APPC on OS/2 100
    specifying for APPC on Windows 32s 102
logmode table, for APPC on VSE 103
logon, automatic
    sample script 79–82
LOGOUT command, automatic logon script
    79–82
LU (logical unit)
    See logical unit (LU)
LU name for remote MVS session
    specifying for APPC on OS/2 100
    specifying for APPC on Windows 32s 102
LUFIRST= system option
    APPC on MVS 98
    CMS to MVS with APPC, example 106
    OS/2 to MVS with APPC, example 108
    OS/2 to TSO with APPC, example 109
    Windows 32s to MVS with APPC, example
        106

LULAST= system option
    APPC on MVS 99
    CMS to MVS with APPC, example 106
    OS/2 to MVS with APPC, example 108
    OS/2 to TSO with APPC, example 109
    Windows 32s to MVS with APPC, example
        106
LUPOOL= system option
    APPC on MVS 98
    CMS to MVS with APPC, example 106
    OS/2 to MVS with APPC, example 106
    OS/2 to TSO with APPC, example 109
    Windows 32s to MVS with APPC, example
        106
LUPREFIX= system option
    APPC on MVS 98
    CMS to MVS with APPC, example 106
    OS/2 to MVS with APPC, example 108
    OS/2 to TSO with APPC, example 109
    Windows 32s to MVS with APPC, example
        106
LU62MODE= system option
    APPC on MVS 98
    CMS to MVS with APPC, example 106
    OS/2 to MVS with APPC, example 108
    OS/2 to TSO with APPC, example 109
    Windows 32s to MVS with APPC, example
        106

M

manual logon, sample script 82–85
MAXI script statement 262
    compensating for line noise 157
    not valid for access method 157
MAXO script statement 263
    compensating for line noise 157
    not valid for access method 157
member types
    downloading 211
    uploading 233
MEMTYPE= option
    DOWNLOAD procedure 42–43, 211
    TRANTAB statement 219–220, 241–242
    UPLOAD procedure 42–43, 233
messages
    APPC 110–113
    DECnet 118–119
    displaying from remote host 79
    from host 319–321
    host 90–91
    host not active 160–161
    JOB OPTIONS...SUBMITTED 169
    missing from SAS software start-up 160
    No terminal connected to the SAS session
        168–169
    packet failure 159–160
    requested link not found 161
    snapshot after error 89
micro-to-host link
    ASYNC access scripts 296
    automated remote processing 312–315
    automatic logon scripts 296
    BREAK window 316–318

checklist 297–298
COMAMID= system option 321
creating 3270 keyboard translation tables
    303–306
display manager window 318
distributing a .EXE file to local hosts 312
DOWNLOAD procedure 325
downloading catalog entries with graphics
    output 315–316
EHLLAPI access scripts 296
FILENAME statement 325
hardware requirements 290
protocol converters 321–322
remote graphics processing 312
REMOTE= system option 323–325
software requirements 290–291
TELNET scripts 295–296
troubleshooting 331–335
TTY emulation program 298–300
UPLOAD procedure 326–331
mixed-type variables restrictions, RLS 32
MODE command, modem settings for TTY
    under ASYNC 150
mode name, SNA session
    CMS communications directory entry 95
MODEL script statement 263
modem settings for TTY under ASYNC 150
monitor remote host 79
MSG script statement 264
MT= option
    DOWNLOAD procedure 211
    UPLOAD procedure 233
MTYPE= option
    DOWNLOAD procedure 211
    UPLOAD procedure 233
multi-observation buffering 33
multi-user server
    accessing 35
    compared to single-user 283–284
    connecting to remote 191–192
    initialization 284
    password 191–192
multiple sessions
    starting from autoexec file 69
MVS
    APPC access method 97–99
    EHLLAPI access method 141
    interrupting processing 88
    JOB OPTIONS...SUBMITTED message from
        remote submission 169
    script directory 65
    signing on to CMS with APPC, example 107
    signing on to OS/2 with APPC, example
        107
    TCP/IP connections 122
MVS/ESA
    APPC on MVS 97–98

N

NAME= argument, TRANTAB statement
    218–219, 240–241

naming conventions
    downloaded data sets 212–214
    uploaded data sets 234–236
National Language Support (NLS)
    translation tables 187
NCP (Network Control Program)
    DECnet OpenVMS connection 118
NetBIOS access method 11, 131
    available connections 131
    OS/2 requirements 132
    scripts not needed 133
    starting SAS/CONNECT 133
    system requirements 132
    troubleshooting 135
    Windows NT requirements 133
    Windows requirements 132
-NETNAME option, spawner program 137
network adapter
    setting as NetBIOS environment variables
        134–135
network name, specifying with a spawner
    program 137
nickname, for DECnet ACI 116
NLS (National Language Support)
    See National Language Support (NLS)
NO$SYNTAXCHECK option 168
-NO$SYNTAXCHECK option
    MVS to OS/2 with APPC, example 107
    OS/2 to OS/2 with APPC, example 108
NO$SYNTAXCHECK system option
    CMS to MVS with APPC, example 106
    OS/2 to MVS with APPC, example 108
    OS/2 to TSO with APPC, example 109
    Windows 32s to MVS with APPC, example
        106
non-terminal bound access method
    unable to send screen images 12
noninteractive line mode 9
NOSCRIPT option
    SIGNOFF command 195
    SIGNON statement 197
-NOTERMINAL option
    MVS to OS/2 with APPC, example 107
    OS/2 to OS/2 with APPC, example 108
NOTERMINAL system option
    CMS to MVS with APPC, example 106
    OS/2 to MVS with APPC, example 108
    OS/2 to TSO with APPC, example 109
    Windows 32s to MVS with APPC, example
        106
NOTIFY script statement 264–265
numeric precision, preserving 167

O

open mode, definition 33
OpenVMS
    AXP TCP/IP connections 124
    VAX TCP/IP connections 123
OPT= option, TRANTAB statement 219, 241
options, SAS system
    COMAMID= 174–183
    DMR 184

options, SAS system *(continued)*
  REMOTE= 185-186
  TRANTAB= 186-187
OPTIONS statement
  for automatic logon script 66
  for manual logon script 67
  in autoexec file 69
OS/2
  APPC 99-100
  EHLLAPI requirements 142
  interrupting processing 87
  NetBIOS 131
  script directory 65
  setting environment variables for APPC 99
  TCP/IP connections 122-124
  TELNET 126
  to MVS with APPC, example 108
  to OS/2 with APPC, example 108
  to TSO with APPC, example 109
  to VSE with APPC, example 109
OS/2, RASYNC access method
  manual logoff with a script 68
  manual logon with a script 67
OS/2 Extended Services
  for APPC on OS/2 99
OUT= option
  DOWNLOAD procedure 45, 211
  UPLOAD procedure 45, 233
OUTCAT= option
  DOWNLOAD procedure 43-44, 212
  transferring graphics catalogs 163
  UPLOAD procedure 43-44, 234
OUTDD= option
  DOWNLOAD procedure 211
  UPLOAD procedure 233
OUTFILE= option
  DOWNLOAD procedure 46
  UPLOAD procedure 46, 234
OUTFILE= option, DOWNLOAD procedure 212
OUTLIB= option
  DOWNLOAD procedure 42-43, 45, 211
  UPLOAD procedure 42-43, 233

P

-P option, TTY 150
packets
  resending after error 89
  setting end-of-packet character 258
  setting maximum length 262-263
  setting start-of-packet character 269
parity, setting for TTY under ASYNC 150
PARITY script statement 265
partitioned data set, downloading
  example 47-49
password
  CMS communications directory entry 95
  for multi-user server 191-192
  passing to remote host 98
  signing on OS/2 to VSE with APPC, example 109
  specifying for APPC on OS/2 100
  specifying for APPC on Windows 32s 102

specifying for DECnet 116
specifying restrictions with a spawner program 139
PMENU facility
  in manual logon 67
  interface to SAS/CONNECT 62-63
pound sign (#)
  in userids and passwords 98
printing a list of reports, example 35
PROC DOWNLOAD statement 42-44, 45, 46
  building with SOURCE procedure 48
PROC OPTIONS statement, verifying environment variables
  NetBIOS 134
  OS/2 100
  Windows 32s 102
PROC SERVER statement 192
PROC statement, remote submission fails 167
PROC UPLOAD statement 42-44, 45, 46
profile, CMS
  editing for APPC 97
PROFILE EXEC file, CMS
  editing for APPC 97
PROGRAM EDITOR window
  environment variables, APPC on Windows 32s 101
  executing RSUBMIT command 193
  setting NetBIOS environment variables 134
  setting OS/2 environment variables for APPC 99
  starting and stopping SAS/CONNECT 62-63
  submitting automatic logon script 66
  submitting manual logon script 67
program generator, definition 18
program-to-program communications 11
PROMPT script statement 266
prompting from remote host
  defining in a script 79-82
prompts, issuing
  TTY under ASYNC 151
-PROTECTION option, spawner program 139
protocol converters
  micro-to-host link releases 321-322
  transparent mode 147
  troubleshooting 155-158
  with ASYNC access method 147-149
PT2DBPW= option, CONNECT TO statement 191-192
pull-down menus
  starting SAS/CONNECT 62-63
  stopping SAS/CONNECT 63

Q

queries for remote databases
  creating with RSPT 25
querying a table in DB2, example 27
question mark (?)
  prompting for DECnet username or password 116
quitting TTY under ASYNC 151

R

R command 89
RASYNC access method 150
   manual logon/logoff with a script 68
remote
   applications from a local host 21–22
   connections, definition 9
   data libraries, accessing 34
   data services 3
   graphics processing 22–25
   session, identifying 185–186
remote data services
   component diagram 4
   data transfer services 6–7
   remote library services (RLS) 6–7
REMOTE engine 8, 25
remote graphics processing
   micro-to-host link connection 312
remote library services (RLS) 3, 8
   combined with data transfer services 58–60
   combined with data transfer services, examples 58–60
   data translation 32–33
   examples 35–40
   mixed-type variables restrictions 31
   not supported by terminal-based communications 12
   processing model diagram 8
   reducing network traffic 33
   short numerics restrictions 31
   types of data accessible 31
   UPLOAD procedure 7
REMOTE= option
   specifying via Signon window 63
-REMOTE option
   MVS to OS/2 with APPC, example 107
Remote SQL Pass-Through (RSPT) 5, 18
   diagram 6
   statement syntax 191
REMOTE= system option 51, 55–56
   APPC 104–105
   APPC on CMS 97
   CMS to MVS with APPC, example 106
   debugging host-not-active message 161
   DECnet OpenVMS-to-OpenVMS connection 116
   DECnet Windows-to-OpenVMS connection 117
   for APPC on CMS 95
   for automatic logon script 66
   for manual logon script 67
   in autoexec file 69
   micro-to-host link releases 323–661
   MVS to CMS with APPC, example 107
   OS/2 to MVS with APPC, example 108
   OS/2 to OS/2 with APPC, example 108
   OS/2 to TSO with APPC, example 109
   remote submission, example 185
   SIGNON, example 185
   starting SAS/CONNECT with DECnet access method 116
   starting SAS/CONNECT with EHLLAPI 143
   starting SAS/CONNECT with NetBIOS 133
   starting SAS/CONNECT with TCP/IP 125
   syntax 185
   table of values 174–183
   Windows 32s to MVS with APPC, example 106
requestor window, suppressing 167–168
resending information after an error 89
resource destination name
   CMS $SERVER$ NAMES directory entry 96–97
   CMS communications directory entry 95
RETCODE macro variable 56–57
RETRY script statement 267
   compensating for line noise 157
return codes
   sending from host to local session 56–57
RETURN script statement 267
RLINK fileref
   assigning in autoexec file 68
RLINK SCL function 202–203
RLS (remote library services)
   See remote library services (RLS)
ROTATE= option
   remote graphics processing 25
rotating graphics 164
RSESSION SCL function 203–204
RSPT (Remote SQL Pass-Through)
   See Remote SQL Pass-Through (RSPT)
RSTITLE SCL function 204
RSUBMIT command 18
   See also ENDRSUBMIT statement
   assigning to a key 193
   different from SUBMIT command 193
   syntax 193
RSUBMIT statement 49–52, 53–54, 56–57
   example 199–200
   in autoexec file 70
   syntax 193

S

S command
   viewing remote host messages 91
-S option, TTY 150
SAPW= option, CONNECT TO statement 191–192
SAS autoexec file
   definition 190
SAS configuration file
   environment variables, APPC on Windows 32s 101
   setting NetBIOS environment variables 134
   setting OS/2 environment variables for APPC 99
SAS data views
   DATA= option, DOWNLOAD procedure 209
   DATA= option, UPLOAD procedure 231
   data types accessible to RLS 175–176
   RSPT example 172–173
SAS/GRAPH software
   remote graphics processing 22–25
   troubleshooting 162–164
SAS macro variable
   DECnet OpenVMS-to-OpenVMS connection 116

SAS Multiuser program
    signing on OS/2 to VSE with APPC,
        example 109
SAS server 25
    connecting to for RSPT 26
    connecting to remote 191–192
SAS sessions
    initiating a link 197
    terminating link 195
SAS/SHARE compared to SAS/CONNECT
    283–284
SAS system options
    COMAMID= 174–183
    DMR 184
    REMOTE= 185–186
    TRANTAB= 186–187
SAS$CONN.COM command file
    DECnet OpenVMS connection 118
SASFRSCR= system option 85–86
SASSCRIPT= system option 85–86
saving remote results on local host, example
    20
SCANFOR script statement 268
    See also WAITFOR script statement
SCL (Screen Control Language)
    See Screen Control Language (SCL)
SCOMDIR NAMES communications directory
    file 95
Screen Control Language (SCL)
    functions 201–205
    locating and storing scripts 85–86
    program with WHERE statement 37
screen size
    limiting transmission packet size 12
script statements
    ABORT 254
    BAUD 254
    BREAK 255
    CALL 255
    CHARWAIT 256
    DATABITS 257
    DELAY 257
    ECHO 258
    EOPCHAR 258–259
    GOTO 259
    HANDSHAKING 259
    IF 260
    INPUT 261
    LINEWAIT 261
    LOG 262
    MAXI 262
    MAXO 263
    MODEL 263
    MSG 264
    NOTIFY 264–265
    PARITY 265
    PROMPT 266
    RETRY 267
    RETURN 267
    SCANFOR 268
    SNAPSHOT 268
    SOPCHAR 269
    STOP 269
    STOPBITS 270
    TIMEOUT 270–271

TRACE 271
TYPE 271–275
WAITFOR 276–279
XCLOCK 279
XTIME 280
scripts 64–65
    ABORT statement 254
    alias for WAITFOR statement 268
    automatic logon, sample 79–82
    automatic, starting SAS/CONNECT 66
    baud rate 254
    BAUD statement 254
    bits per character 257
    BREAK statement 255
    CALL statement 255
    capturing keystrokes for 72
    case sensitivity 71
    CHARWAIT statement 256
    conditional processing 260
    copy remote screen to local LOG window
        268
    DATABITS statement 257
    debugging 78–79
    default fileref 68
    defining filerefs 189–191
    definition 9, 293
    DELAY statement 257
    displaying characters from remote host 258
    duration of break signal 255
    ECHO statement 258
    ECHO statements 158, 161
    EHLLAPI connections 72–75
    EHLLAPI, samples 143
    end-of-packet character 258
    EOPCHAR statement 258–259
    GOTO statement 259
    handshaking method 259
    HANDSHAKING statement 259
    IF statement 260
    INPUT statement 261
    invoking a routine 255
    jumping to another statement 259
    LINEWAIT statement 261
    locating with SCL 85–86
    location 65
    LOG statement 262
    losing data under ASYNC 156
    manual logon, sample 82–85
    manual, starting SAS/CONNECT 67
    MAXI statement 262
    maximum packet length 262–263
    MAXO statement 263
    messages, remote host 264
    MODEL statement 263
    modem settings for TTY under ASYNC 150
    MSG statement 264
    not needed for DECnet 117–118
    not needed for NetBIOS 133
    NOTIFY statement 264–265
    overriding the default prompt 266
    parity 265
    PARITY statement 265
    pause between characters 257
    PROMPT statement 266
    requesting user input 261

retry attempts 267
RETRY statement 267
RETURN statement 267
samples provided by SAS 294–295
SCANFOR statement 268
sending a message 264
sending a message to a log 262
signaling the end of a routine 267
specifying via Signon window 63
start-of-packet character 269
starting SAS/CONNECT with APPC 105
stop bits 270
stopping normally 269
stopping on error 254
storing with SCL 85–86
summary of statements 251–253
syntax 71
TCP/IP 126
TELNET 127
timeout 270–271
TRACE statement 158
tracing statement execution 271
TTY samples 153–155
type characters to remote host 271–275
wait time 256
waiting after a prompt 261
waiting after 3270 X-clock disappears 280
waiting for a condition 276–279
waiting for 3270 X-clock to appear 279
security
  password exposure 100
  proxy access for DECnet 116
  spawner program 138–139
  specifying for APPC on VSE 104
segmented files during upload/download 165–166
SELECT statement
  DOWNLOAD procedure 43–44
  DOWNLOAD procedure, syntax 217–218
  RSPT 191
  UPLOAD procedure 42–43
  UPLOAD procedure, syntax 239–240
semicolon (;)
  closing the OPTIONS statement 167
  in script syntax 71
server 8
$SERVER$ NAMES directory
  for APPC on CMS 96–97
SERVER= option, CONNECT TO statement 191–192
sessions, remote
  creating descriptive information 204
  obtaining descriptive information 203–204
SET APPC_LUNAME configuration file option
  signing on Windows 32s to MVS with APPC, example 106
SET APPC_LU62MODE configuration file option
  signing on Windows 32s to MVS with APPC, example 106
SET command
  OS/2 environment variables 99–100
SET commands, CMS
  specifying for APPC 97

SET= option
  EHLLAPI for Windows and OS/2 143–144
short numerics restrictions, RLS 32
signaling a break to the host
  TTY under ASYNC 151
SIGNOFF command 9
  example 196
  syntax 195
  with automatic logoff script 68
SIGNOFF option, PROGRAM EDITOR window 63
SIGNOFF statement 51, 53–54
  example 196
  examples 199–200
  syntax 195
  with automatic logoff script 68
SIGNON command 9
  examples 198–200
  syntax 197
  with automatic logon script 66
  with manual logon script 67
SIGNON option, PROGRAM EDITOR window 62–63
SIGNON statement 49–54, 197
  examples 198–200
  with automatic logon script 66
  with manual logon script 67
Signon window, PROGRAM EDITOR window 63
simultaneous partners
  specifying for APPC on OS/2 102
single quote (')
  marking case sensitivity in scripts 71
single-user server
  accessing 35
  compared to multi-user 283–284
  connecting to remote 191–192
  initialization 284
snapshot messages after an error 89
SNAPSHOT script statement 268
  debugging host-not-active message 160–161
  debugging scripts 79
  manual logon script 82–85
  script example 74–75
SOPCHAR script statement 269
SOURCE procedure 48
spawner program 137
SQL procedure Pass-Through Facility 25
  passing statements to remote DBMS 6
  passing statements to SAS SQL 6
square brackets ([])
  unable to submit remotely 168
starting SAS/CONNECT
  APPC 104–105
  DECnet 116
  EHLLAPI 143
  NetBIOS 133
  pull-down menus 62–63
  reference table 174–184
  scripts 66
  TCP/IP 125
starting TTY with SAS/CONNECT 152
statements
  See also entries for specific statements

statements *(continued)*
  directing to remote hosts 70
  indicating end of group 188
STATUS= option
  DOWNLOAD procedure 212
  UPLOAD procedure 234
stop bits, setting for TTY under ASYNC 150
STOP script statement 269
  example 74-78
STOPBITS script statement 270
stopping SAS/CONNECT
  from pull-down menu 63
  with a manual script 68
  with an automatic script 68
SUBMIT command
  automatic logon script 66
  manual logon script 67
SUBMIT function key
  automatic logon script 66
  manual logon script 67
SUBMIT statement
  automatic logon script 66
  manual logon script 67
submitting
  local commands to remote host 193
  statements to remote host, example 53-54
subsession of a local operating system
  initiating 12
subsetting
  remote data, example 39-40
  remote SAS data, example 28
$SYNTAXCHECK option 168
SYSINFO macro variable 56-57
SYSRC macro variable
  APPC on MVS 99
%SYSRPUT macro statement 56-57
  APPC on MVS 99
  compared to %LET macro statement 200
  examples 200-201
  syntax 200

T

TBUFSIZE= option, SIGNON command/
    statement 197
TCP access method
  MAXI and MAXO parameters not valid 157
TCP connection, handling host messages 89-91
TCP/IP access method 11
  available connections 122
  OpenVMS on AXP 124
  OS/2 requirements 124
  specifying UNIX domain under CMS 125
  starting SAS/CONNECT 125
  Windows NT requirements 125
  Windows 3.x requirements 124
  Windows 32s requirements 124
TELNET access method 12, 121
  available connections 126
  full-screen mode not supported 127
  handling host messages 89-91
  system requirements 127
  troubleshooting 127-129
Terminal I/O 12

terminal-based communications 11
  cannot support RLS 12
terminating a link 9, 51
testing for successful upload/download
    completion
  example 56-57
TIMEOUT script statement 270-271
TOBSNO= option 33
toggle echoplex on and off
  TTY under ASYNC 151
Token Ring Networks, OS/2 162
TRACE script statement 158, 161
  debugging scripts 79
  syntax 271
transaction program name
  CMS communications directory entry 95
transfer status window 223-224, 245-246
transferring
  data with WHERE statements, example 42
  files without character conversion 45
  specific catalog entry types 43-44
translation tables
  applying selectively on download 219
  applying selectively on upload 241
  specifying 186
  specifying for catalog transfer 7
transmission packet size
  limited by screen size 12
transparent mode 147
Transparent Services Access Facility (TSAF)
  APPC on CMS 94
TRANTAB statement syntax
  DOWNLOAD procedure 218-219
  UPLOAD procedure 240-241
TRANTAB= system option 186
troubleshooting
  See also messages
  APPC 110-113
  ASYNC 155-158
  DECnet 118-119
  EHLLAPI 144-145
  general 159-169
  micro-to-host link releases 331-335
  NetBIOS 135
  protocol converter 155-158
  TELNET 127-129
  TTY 155-158
TSAF (Transparent Services Access Facility)
  See Transparent Services Access Facility
    (TSAF)
TTY, quitting under ASYNC 151
TTY terminal emulation program
  ending 153
  functions 151
  micro-to-host link connection 298-300
  program options 150-151
  sample scripts 153-155
  setting communications parameters 151
  starting with SAS/CONNECT 152-153
  troubleshooting 155-158
  with ASYNC access method 147, 149
TYPE= option, TRANTAB statement 219,
    241
TYPE script statement
  automatic logon script 79-82

dividing 72
in a script 72
manual logon script 82–85
script example 73–74, 77–78
syntax 271–275
TTY-to-VSE connection, sample 153–155

U

UAPW= option, PROC SERVER statement 192
UCOMDIR NAMES communications directory file 95
UNIX
  interrupting processing 87
  script directory 65
  specifying domain under CMS 125
  TCP/IP connections 122
  TELNET 126
UPDATEM macro 56–57
updating remote data, example 36
UPLOAD procedure 7, 9, 229
  defining filerefs and librefs 226, 248
  FILENAME statement 191
  micro-to-host link releases 326–331
  procedure not found 164–165
  segmented files 165–166
  symbol not recognized 165
  syntax 230–231
  transferring graphics catalogs 163
uploading
  binary data 231
  binary data without translation 246–247
  catalog entries 7, 231
  catalogs 43, 231
  catalogs with graphics output 47
  data libraries 232
  data set attributes inherited 236–237
  data sets 43
  excluding catalog entries 238–239
  excluding data library members 238–239
  external files 232
  fixed format records 249
  format catalog entries 44
  library members 7
  LIST catalog entries 44
  member types 233
  naming data sets 231
  naming destination catalogs 234
  naming destination data libraries 233
  naming receiving data sets 233
  omitting data set indexes 232
  replicating data set attributes 7
  selected catalog entries 239–240
  selected catalog entry types 242–245
  selected data library members 239–240
  selectively applying translation table 241
  specifying member types 241–242
  status 245–246
  text files, record length over 132 bytes 249
  with WHERE processing 7
USER= system option 44
-USERCMDS option, spawner program 139

userids
  APPC on MVS, passing to remote host, 98
  CMS $SERVER$ NAMES directory entry 96–97
  CMS, configuring for APPC 95–97
  OS/2 to VSE with APPC 109
  specifying for APPC on OS/2 100
  specifying for APPC on Windows 32s 102
username
  specifying for DECnet 116
  specifying restrictions with a spawner program 139

V

variables, preserving numeric precision 167
VAX, interrupting processing 88
viewing remote host messages, S command 91
VM/ESA
  APPC on CMS 94
VM/SP Release 6
  APPC on CMS 94
VMS
  script directory 65
  TELNET 126
VQDLLNAME environment variable
  EHLLAPI for Windows and OS/2 143–144
VSE
  APPC access method 102–104
  EHLLAPI access method 141
  interrupting processing 88
  script directory 65
  TTY connection with protocol converter, sample 153–155
VTAM (Virtual Telecommunications Access Method)
  APPC on MVS 97
  for APPC on VSE 102
  specifying application ID to APPC on VSE 104

W

WAITFOR script statement
  See also SCANFOR script statement
  automatic logon script 79–82
  case sensitivity 160–161
  debugging scripts 79
  in a script 72
  manual logon script 82–85
  problems with ASYNC 157
  script example 73–74, 77–78
  syntax 276–279
WHERE processing
  uploading or downloading 7
WHERE statement
  DOWNLOAD procedure 42, 55–56
  DOWNLOAD procedure, syntax 215–216
  UPLOAD procedure 42
  UPLOAD procedure, syntax 237–238
windows
  BREAK, micro-to-host link connection 317

windows *(continued)*
  Communication Services Break Handler 88–89
  display manager, micro-to-host link connection 318
  SAS/CONNECT Attention Handler 87–88
  suppressing unwanted 167–168
  transfer status 223–224, 245–246
Windows
  EHLLAPI manual logoff with a script 68
  EHLLAPI manual logon with a script 67
  interrupting processing 87
  NetBIOS 131
  script directory 65
  TCP/IP connections 122
Windows NT
  NetBIOS 131
  TCP/IP 125
  TCP/IP connections 122
  TELNET 126
Windows 3.x
  requirements for EHLLAPI 142
  TCP/IP 124
  TELNET 126
Windows 32s
  APPC access method 101–102
  requirements for EHLLAPI 142
  signing on to MVS with APPC, example 106–107
  TCP/IP 124

X

-X option, TTY 150
X statement, restrictions 12
XCLOCK script statement 279
XTIME script statement 280

Special Characters

(double quote)
  See double quote (")
$ (dollar sign)
  See dollar sign ($)
; (semicolon)
  See semicolon (;)
- (hyphen)
  See hyphen (-)
? (question mark)
  See question mark (?)
: (colon)
  See colon (:)
(pound sign)
  See pound sign (#)
@ (at sign)
  See at sign (@)
' (single quote)
  See single quote (')
" (double quote)
  See double quote (")

[] (square brackets)
  See square brackets ([])

3

3270 access method 12, 141
  See also EHLLAPI access method
  handling host messages 90–91
  key mnemonics 274–275
  keyboard translation tables, micro-to-host link 300–303, 306–311
  specifying alternate keyboard translation table 189

Your Turn

If you have comments or suggestions about *SAS/CONNECT Software: Usage and Reference, Version 6, Second Edition*, please send them to us on a photocopy of this page or send us electronic mail.

For comments about this book, please return the photocopy to

>SAS Institute Inc.
>Publications Division
>SAS Campus Drive
>Cary, NC 27513
>**email:** yourturn@unx.sas.com

For suggestions about the software, please return the photocopy to

>SAS Institute Inc.
>Technical Support Division
>SAS Campus Drive
>Cary, NC 27513
>**email:** suggest@unx.sas.com